ENTERPRISING NONPROFITS

ENTERPRISING NONPROFITS:
A TOOLKIT FOR SOCIAL ENTREPRENEURS

**J. Gregory Dees,
Jed Emerson, and
Peter Economy**

JOHN WILEY & SONS, INC.

New York · Chichester · Weinheim · Brisbane · Singapore · Toronto

This book is printed on acid-free paper. ⊚

Library of Congress Cataloging-in-Publication Data:

Dees, J. Gregory.
    Enterprising nonprofits : a toolkit for social entrepreneurs / J. Gregory Dees, Jed Emerson, and Peter Economy.
       p. cm. — (Wiley nonprofit law, finance, and management series)
    Includes index.
    ISBN 0-471-39735-0 (alk. paper)
    1. Nonprofit organizations—Management—Handbooks, manuals, etc. 2. Social action—Handbooks, manuals, etc. I. Emerson, Jed. II. Economy, Peter. III. Title. IV. Series.

HD62.6 .D44 2001
658'.048—dc21

                                                   00-065287

Printed in the United States of America

DEDICATION

To Ewing Marion Kauffman who led his successful business and foundation based upon a simple but powerful value statement: "Treat others as you would like to be treated," and to social entrepreneurs everywhere who are actively engaged in providing social value and entrepreneurial leadership to our communities and their citizens.

ACKNOWLEDGMENTS

I want to thank my good friend Steve Roling at the Kauffman Foundation. Without his vision and drive, this project would not have gotten off the ground. It has also been a rare treat to work with both Jed Emerson and Peter Economy. Jed's unique combination of passion, intelligence, experience, and receptivity make him the very best kind of colleague. Peter has a wonderful gift for making complex concepts accessible and for keeping a major project, such as this, on track. Our authors have demonstrated not only their expertise but also their patience and flexibility, as we worked to make sure themes and concepts were integrated across the chapters.

I am deeply grateful for all the friends and colleagues who encouraged and supported my work on social entrepreneurship. It would be futile to attempt a complete list here. Many colleagues from McKinsey, Yale, Harvard, MACED, and Stanford have served as role models, coaches, mentors, cheerleaders, and intellectual partners. Numerous social entrepreneurs and philanthropists have helped me understand the power and limits of bringing business concepts into this arena. Nearly thirty of them agreed to be the subjects of case studies. Many more have provided invaluable feedback. Together, these friends, colleagues, and social entrepreneurs gave me the strength to persist when other people were telling me that working on social entreprenuership was either fundamentally misguided, unimportant, or unwise from a career point of view. This has proven to be the most satisfying work of my life.

Finally, I want to thank my wife, Betty Ann, for her patience and support throughout this process. She has been my best friend and an anchor of stability in a very hectic life.

J. Gregory Dees

Peter Economy would like to thank his co-editors Greg Dees and Jed Emerson, both for their patience, and for freely imparting their great knowledge and insights on the topic of social entrepreneurship. I would also like to thank our guest authors for being so responsive to the needs of this long-term project—it's been a real pleasure working with each one of you. A special thanks to Alison Carlson for first introducing me to the project team, to John Tyler and Suzanne Mathes at EMKF who many times dropped everything to help out, and to Martha Cooley—our original project editor at John Wiley—for helping to develop this book and bring it to fruition. And thanks most of all to Steve Roling at EMKF for inviting me to join the *Enterprising Nonprofits* team. Your ongoing leadership on this project has been inspiring, and I'll always be grateful to you for allowing me the privilege of being part of this book

Peter Economy

I would like to express my deep thanks and appreciation to George R. Roberts for his invaluable trust that allowed me to both maximize my work as a social entrepreneur and learn how best to assist other social entrepreneurs. Sincere thanks go to Melinda Tuan, without whose partnership I would not have learned as much nor had the ability to travel and spread the gospel of social entrepreneurship. I would also like to publicly thank my parents for their confidence in my work. My sincere thanks to Kelly for her support, and Pearl and Rasta for their patience. I would also like to express my thanks to my colleagues at Harvard Business School for their support and contributors to my intellectual journey.

Jed Emerson

ABOUT THE AUTHORS

J. Gregory Dees is the Miriam and Peter Haas Centennial Professor in Public Service at Stanford University and co-director of the Center for Social Innovation at Stanford's Graduate School of Business. Greg also serves as an entrepreneur-in-residence with the Kauffman Foundation's Center for Entrepreneurial Leadership. Through his research and teaching, he has been instrumental in developing the field of social entrepreneurship. Before joining Stanford, Greg taught at the Harvard Business School, where he helped launch the Initiative on Social Enterprise, including a new course on "Entrepreneurship in the Social Sector." In 1995, Greg received Harvard's Apgar Award for Innovation in Teaching. He previously taught at the Yale School of Management and worked as a management consultant with McKinsey & Company.

Peter Economy is a prolific business writer with numerous works to his credit, including *Leadership Ensemble: Lessons in Collaborative Management from the World's Only Conductors Orchestra, Managing For Dummies, At the Helm: Business Lessons for Navigating Rough Waters, The Complete MBA For Dummies, Better Business Meetings, Home-Based Business For Dummies,* and many others. He is the home-based business expert for the AllBusiness.com Website, writes a regular column for independent professionals for 1099.com, and is consulting editor for Bob Nelson's *Rewarding Employees.* He was formerly director of administration for Horizons Technology, Inc., a San Diego based software development firm, and vice president for project management and operations for a nationwide computer services firm. Peter has a Bachelor of Arts degree with majors in economics and human biology from Stanford University and is currently pursuing MBA studies at the Edinburgh Business School.

Jed Emerson has been active in community and social work since the mid-1970s, spending the past decade focusing his efforts on the areas of social entrepreneurship and venture philanthropy. Jed is co-founder of the Roberts Enterprise Development Fund and the Bloomberg Senior Research Fellow at Harvard Business School. In 1996, he co-edited and wrote numerous chapters in *New Social Entrepreneurs: The Success Challenge and Lessons of Social Purpose Enterprise,* published by The Roberts Foundation, San Francisco, California. Jed is well known for his writings and public speaking. He was selected by the *Nonprofit Times* in both 1998 and 2000 as one of the "50 Most Influential People in the Nonprofit Sector" in recognition of his advocacy and advancement of concepts such as social return on investment, social enterprise, and innovative approaches to philanthropy. Jed holds Masters degrees in both social work and business administration. Other articles and writings of his may be found at the Fund's Web-site (www.redf.org).

Steve Roling, Senior Vice President of the Ewing Marion Kauffman Foundation of Kansas City, Missouri, has spent his professional career involved in various for-profit and not-for-profit organizations. While still in graduate school, he was resident director of Butterfield Youth Services—a residential treatment facility for at-risk youth. He then joined the staff of former U.S. Senator Tom Eagleton (D-MO) as a legislative assistant in Washington, D.C. for six years. He returned to his home state of Missouri to become a banker for four years before he spent six years as Publisher of the *Kansas City Business Journal.* For the last 10 years, Roling has worked for the Ewing Marion Kauffman Foundation, and is currently responsible for the foundation's Youth Development investments. Steve and his wife Judi have two daughters in college, Stephanie and Susie. He has both an undergraduate and graduate degree from the University of Missouri, Columbia.

Bruce Hopkins is the country's leading authority on tax-exempt organizations and is a lawyer with the firm Polsinelli, White, Vardeman, and Shalton. He is also the author of thirteen books, including *The Legal Answer Book for Nonprofit Organizations; The Law of Tax-Exempt Organizations,* 7ed.; *The Law of Fund-Raising,* 2ed.; *Private Foundations: Tax Law and Compliance; A Legal Guide to Starting and Managing a Nonprofit Organization,* 2ed; and *The Tax Law of Charitable Giving,* 2ed., as well as the newsletter *The Nonprofit Counsel,* all published by Wiley.

Rob Johnston is Senior Vice President, Program, of the Peter F. Drucker Foundation for Nonprofit Management whose mission is "to lead social sector organizations toward excellence in performance." His work focuses on collaborating with 250 thought leaders to further the mission through program development. Working with the Foundation's volunteers and staff, he has led leadership and management conferences, the annual Drucker Award for Nonprofit Innovation, and publication development. He was Executive Producer of the Foundation's 1997 Nonprofit Leader of the Future, a video teleconference broadcast to 10,000 social sector leaders at sites across the United States. He has editorial responsibilities for the Foundation's Web site (drucker.org) and is a senior editor for its quarterly journal, *Leader to Leader.*

Jerry Kitzi is the president of Social Venture Partners of Greater Kansas City. SVP-GKC is an exciting model of venture philanthropy designed to grow philanthropy and strengthen the nonprofit sector. It provides investors a hands-on opportunity to combine their financial investments with their business expertise to address the day-to-day growth issues of the nonprofits they select for investment. Before helping to launch SVP—GKC, Kitzi served as the vice president, Youth Development division, with the Ewing Marion Kauffman Foundation where he was responsible for overall planning, coordination, and implementation of the Youth Development division's approved operating and grant-making strategies. Kitzi also served as the executive director of Adolescent Resources Corporation in Kansas City, a nonprofit organization dedicated to improving the quality of life for teenagers and their families.

Kristin Majeska is the Founder and Executive Director of Common Good: Investments in Nonprofit Solutions, which helps Maine nonprofits apply smart business tactics to further their social purposes and increase their financial self-sufficiency. Common Good's "investments" take the form of grants, hands-on business assistance, performance measurement tools, and leveraging both private and nonprofit resource people. Kristin founded Common Good after spending a year as a Farber Fellow running The San Francisco City Store, a Roberts Enterprise Development Fund (REDF) portfolio business that employs at-risk youth and formerly homeless adults. She contributed several chapters to the REDF publication, *Social Purpose Enterprises and Venture Philanthropy in the New Millennium: Practitioner Perspectives.* Prior to moving into the social enterprise arena, Kristin was a Principal of Mercer Management Consulting in the US and in Spain, where she focused on customer understanding.

Tom McLaughlin has over 25 years of nonprofit experience as a nonprofit manager, trade association executive, and consultant. He joined BDO Seidman, LLP in 1990 to develop and manage the firm's Division of Tax-Exempt and Governmental Services. Tom assists all types of nonprofit clients with strategic, operations, and financial projects. He is nationally recognized as an expert in nonprofit mergers and alliances, financial management, and strategic planning. He is on the management faculty at Brandeis University and Boston University where he teaches MBA and MSW graduate students. Tom is a contributing editor for the *Nonprofit Times,* for which he writes a monthly column. He is the author of three books: *Nonprofit Mergers and Alliances: A Strategic Planning Guide, Trade Secrets for Nonprofit Managers,* and *Streetsmart Financial Basics for Nonprofit Managers,* all published by Wiley.

Jeanne Rooney is the Vice President and Director of UMB Bank Nonprofit Financial & Advisory Services. The mission is to foster the financial empowerment of nonprofits by offering a wide range of business-related products, services, and education to nonprofits, philanthropists, and their advisors. For more than a decade, Rooney was an independent management consultant, assisting the nonprofit sector with adopting the best business practices, including business planning and finance management. Her major clients were the Ewing Marion Kauffman Foundation, The Francis Family Foundation, and the Metropolitan Community Colleges. She was previously employed by Sprint, ending as Director of Taxes. She received her CPA certificate while employed at Ernst & Young. She is the President of the University of Chicago Club in Kansas City and is a member of the Advisory Board for the Center for Business & Industry at Johnson County Community College. Rooney has held volunteer leadership roles with the Coterie Children's Theatre, Heart of America United Way, Kansas City Consensus and the Mid-Continent Council of Girl Scouts.

CONTENTS

PREFACE

Ewing Marion Kauffman (Mr. K) was a successful businessman and former owner of the Kansas City Royals baseball club. When he started his foundation (the Ewing Marion Kauffman Foundation), he initially planned to devote his substantial accumulated wealth to helping children and youth become productive members of society. This meant initiating a variety of programs in the Kansas City area to help young people develop moral and ethical behaviors, abstain from drug and alcohol use, be prepared to enter school ready to learn, and successfully graduate from high school, trade school, or college.

After a few years of operating these four programs within the foundation, Mr. K decided that he needed to do more to help children, youth, and their families become more self-sufficient. Because Mr. K had always been an entrepreneur—and because he had turned his own modest personal savings into a fortune through hard work and an unbounded entrepreneurial spirit—he naturally believed that, by encouraging and accelerating entrepreneurship in America, he could achieve this goal. After several months of careful study, he decided that his foundation should be a leader in teaching and promoting the concepts of entrepreneurship to children, youth, and adults—and he set about turning that idea into a reality.

Under the dedicated leadership of a dynamic Board of Directors and a determined and resourceful staff, the Kauffman Center for Entrepreneurial Leadership at the Ewing Marion Kauffman Foundation has developed and funded many innovative and groundbreaking programs to teach entrepreneurship to youth and adults. Although the early work in this area was focused entirely on for-profit enterprises, as time went on, Mr. K noticed that the same skills and attitudes seen in successful for-profit entrepreneurs were also prevalent in many successful non-profit leaders. At Mr. K's urging, the foundation soon began to devote its significant resources to developing, supporting, and encouraging entrepreneurs who practice in the non-profit sector as well.

We have met many wonderful, inspiring, dedicated, and courageous social entrepreneurs over the years—many of whom are written about in this book. Non-profit organizations have always been faced with a dilemma: how to balance the competing needs for providing necessary services to clients who could not afford to pay for them. For years, nonprofits have relied on the financial largesse of the government, corporations, foundations, and individuals to generate operating and program funds. Without these traditional sources of funds, most nonprofits would not exist today. Over the past decade, however, many of these traditional sources of funds have dried up. According to an Independent Sector study, federal government spending on programs of concern to nonprofits (not including assistance to individuals) has decreased by more than $30 *billion.*

In response to these trends, more and more non-profit organizations are beginning to consider new and different ways to generate the funds they need to operate. Indeed, for many organizations, social enterprise—the adoption of entrepreneurial behaviors and techniques by non-profit organizations—is rapidly becoming a necessity for survival rather than just another management buzzword. Instead of viewing the world of business as the enemy, many nonprofits are beginning to learn how to take business skills and frameworks and apply them within a community context to create social value.

Make no mistake about it: This is really hard work. For the most part, social entrepreneurship is not a science that can be simply copied from the for-profit world—nonprofits *are* different. That is exactly why this book exists. Not only will *Enterprising Nonprofits* help social entrepreneurs determine how and when for-profit entrepreneurial skills can help them achieve meaningful results and create social value for their clients, but it will also provide them with all the tools and resources necessary to put these important concepts into practice.

Mr. Kauffman died in 1993. His legacy lives on, however, through the work of his foundation, and through the lives of all the people he has touched over the years. Mr. Kauffman would be pleased that entrepreneurs—both for-profit and non-profit—are working together now more than ever before to create a better world. As Mr. K said: "All the money in the world cannot solve problems unless we work together. And if we work together, there is no problem in the world that can stop us as we seek to develop people to their highest and best potential."

We hope this book is a practical tool to help you fulfill *your* potential to create meaningful social value for your clients.

Steve Roling
Ewing Marion Kauffman Foundation

Editors' Introduction

You hold in your hands the first fruits of a conversation that started at the Kauffman Foundation's Center for Entrepreneurial Leadership in the spring of 1998. The conversation was about how we could help non-profit leaders draw on the lessons and tools that have come out of decades of research on business entrepreneurship. Those of us participating in the conversation had experience in both sectors and knew that the wholesale transfer of business practices would not be helpful. Social sector leaders can already find excellent books on business entrepreneurship. The bookstores are filled with them. However, much of the material in these books is foreign to someone coming from a nonprofit environment and some of it is simply inappropriate if your mission is to create social value rather than financial profit. Lessons from the business world have to be adapted to reflect the distinctive missions, operating environments, and norms found in the social sector. This kind of cross-sector translation is not easy, but we were convinced it would be worthwhile. This book contains our first efforts to make that translation.

In order for this book to be effective, we knew that it would have to meet several special requirements. It would have to:

- Be grounded in best thinking about effective business entrepreneurship,
- Modify that thinking to make it appropriate for use in the social sector,
- Integrate that thinking with the best ideas about nonprofit management,
- Take a very practical "hands-on" approach, and
- Be accessible to readers with no prior business training.

In sum, we decided to produce a down-to-earth toolkit to help social sector leaders hone their entrepreneurial skills and, thereby, serve their social missions even more effectively. We are not trying to turn nonprofits into businesses. That would be tragic. Rather, our goal is to help forward-thinking nonprofit leaders learn from business, be more enterprising, and have greater positive, long-term impact in their chosen fields. This is not a book on "social entrepreneurship appreciation" or the theory of social venturing. It is very much a "how to" book, grounded in research on and experience with entrepreneurs in both sectors.

CONTENT OF THE BOOK

When we first attempted generating a list of all the topics we thought were important, we ended up with more than twenty chapters. In the end, this proved to be too much for one book. With help from the editors at Wiley, we decided to split the content into two books, as well as developing a supporting web site. The two volumes together with the web site should give the reader plenty to work with as you begin your journey of entrepreneurship or seek out new perspectives on your current work.

This first book offers an essential toolkit that covers the core elements of effective social entrepreneurship. It should engage, challenge, and help even the most experienced readers. It provides you with a starting point for understanding and applying the core concepts of social entrepreneurship. It will take you from defining your mission to creating a business plan for a social enterprise. The various steps in between include identifying opportunities, mobilizing resources, exercising accountability, managing risks, understanding customers, being innovative, and handling your finances. Each chapter presents several tools that you can put to use.

The second book, tentatively titled *Enterprising Nonprofits II: More Tools for Social Entrepreneurs,* will add important tools to your toolkit. It will help you define your service vision, develop a strategy, manage your staff and board, measure performance, and deal with the opportunities and challenges of growth. Our plan is to have the second volume out by early 2002, about nine months after this volume is released.

In addition to the two books, we have decided to create a web site to provide you with up-to-date information about resources and support available to social entrepreneurs. You'll soon be able to find the web site directly at *www.enterprisingnonprofits.org* or through the Kauffman Foundation's EntreWorld web site (www.EntreWorld.org). The EntreWorld site serves as a resource for entrepreneurs around the country.

THE STYLE OF THIS BOOK

This book has been designed to be used, not just read. Although each author has his or her own style of writing, we required some common elements of style. We wanted to make it easy for you to locate what you need and to apply the relevant ideas to your current situation. Specifically, we have used lots of headings, bullet-points, charts, and summaries to make specific topics readily visible. We have even placed icons in the margin to highlight particularly important items. The icons we use are as follows:

core concept   **Core Concept:** An important new concept or framework.

tool of the trade   **Tool of the Trade:** A framework or technique for applying core concepts.

practical tip   **Practical Tip:** A tidbit of advice on effective and cost-conscious use of the tools.

reality check   **Reality Check:** An in-depth example illustrating the application of a tool.

gem of wisdom   **Gem of Wisdom:** A relevant quote from a person of great experience or wisdom.

red flag   **Red Flag:** A potential problem, risk, trap, or complication.

action step   **Action Step:** Specific activities allowing readers to put concepts and tools to use.

concept check   **Concept Check:** A review of concepts and tools previously introduced.

Our efforts to create a practical and "user friendly" book went well beyond formatting devices. We urged our authors to use examples and case studies in order to bring their concepts, frameworks, and tools to life. The examples were chosen for their power in illustrating particular key points. But remember: in this context, they are teaching tools, and not endorsements of specific organizations. All organizations have their strengths and weaknesses. The examples chosen for this book tend to focus on the strengths and lessons we feel may be of use to you.

Of course, the ultimate value of this book lies in your ability to apply the tools we offer to your own situation and see improved performance as a result. If that does not happen, we have failed. No amount of bullet points, icons, or examples will do this for you. You have to do it for yourself, but we can help. At key points in the text, our authors challenge you to put their ideas to the test, and they guide you through the process by offering exercises, checklists, and action steps. Of course, good entrepreneurial management cannot be reduced to formulas or cookbook-style recipes. Our frameworks can point you in the right direction, but you will definitely need to adapt what our authors suggest to your specific situation. Keep in mind that in order to make the material in this book most relevant to your own situation, you may well need to improvise on the themes of a given chapter. Improvisation is consistent with the spirit of entrepreneurship. For every practical tool in this book, our authors have endeavored to provide sufficiently detailed explanations, so that you can improvise on the details while remaining true to the underlying logic of the core ideas. In case our explanations do not go far enough, we have included additional suggested readings in Appendix B. The books and articles that you find there give you an opportunity to dig more deeply into the subject matter of each chapter.

SUMMARY

Far too many "how to" and "self-help" books are purchased with good intentions and high spirits, but end up sitting on the shelf, unused. We will be deeply disappointed if that is the fate of this book. We have worked hard to make it practical and easy to use. However, if you take what it says seriously, it may require you to change your mindset, adopt new behaviors, and develop new skills. We hope the process will be fun, and we are confident that it will be rewarding, if you see it through, but we know it will not be easy. Give this book a try and tell us, via our web site, how well it works for you. We welcome your suggestions and comments. Besides, all the royalties from the sale of this book will flow back to the Kauffman Foundation in order to support work on social entrepreneurship. Your comments could help us make sure that those royalties are well spent!

We wish you the best in your entrepreneurial endeavor . . . and remember, fortune favors the prepared mind—so use this book and build learning organizations that will help you achieve your dreams and those of your community. The best is yet to come!

J. Gregory Dees   Peter Economy   Jed Emerson

Chapter 1

SOCIAL ENTREPRENEURSHIP

J. Gregory Dees, Miriam and Peter Haas Centennial Professor in Public Service, and co-director of the Center for Social Innovation, Stanford Graduate School of Business

Peter Economy, BA, Business Author, www.petereconomy.com

IN THIS CHAPTER

What is social entrepreneurship?

What makes an enterprise a social enterprise?

Why social entrepreneurship is important to you

Factors leading to entrepreneurial success

More than ever, nonprofit leaders need to be entrepreneurs. As any leader in the nonprofit sector knows, the job of running a nonprofit organization has become increasingly complicated. The nonprofit world is changing. Nonprofit leaders face government funding cuts, rising demands for performance measures by foundations, corporations that want strategic benefits from their philanthropy, new forms of competition from the business sector, and serious questions about the effectiveness and appropriateness of traditional charitable remedies for social problems. These changes pose both opportunities and challenges. Politicians on both sides of the aisle are looking to nonprofit organizations for innovative solutions to social problems. To respond effectively, nonprofit leaders must be particularly enterprising. They have to sharpen their entrepreneurial skills and put them to use. These changes also open the door for new social entrepreneurs to enter.

The idea of entrepreneurship has been around for hundreds of years. Say the word *entrepreneur,* and anyone can likely conjure up a vision of what that word means. For some people, an entrepreneur might be a woman who starts a popular bookstore in a local mall. Others might picture someone who puts his life's savings (and perhaps a second mortgage on his home, and the outstanding balances of all his credit cards) at risk by buying a McDonald's franchise. Still others might imagine someone like Bill Gates—a man who with his partner Paul Allen founded Microsoft in 1975, and built it into the world's largest software company with annual sales of nearly $23 billion in 2000.

Although you may feel fairly certain that you know what entrepreneurship means in the world of business, you may be less clear about how the term *entrepreneurship* applies to the world of nonprofit organizations—a world where success is generally measured not by how much profit you make, but by how well you serve your social mission.

Indeed, there *is* a difference between entrepreneurship in a profit-making environment and in the world of nonprofits; however, the difference may not be as big as you thought.

This chapter defines what entrepreneurship is and how it can be an incredibly powerful and positive force in nonprofit organizations. We'll explore the reasons why social entrepreneurship should be on your radar screen and a part of your organization's strategic plans, and you'll have the opportunity to take a self-scoring quiz to assess your own social entrepreneurship skills. Finally, based on the results of your assessment, we'll determine what areas you should focus on to maximize your effectiveness as a social entrepreneur.

As the old saying goes:

Tell me . . . I forget

Show me . . . I remember

Involve me . . . I understand

Many of you already are social entrepreneurs, even if you would never have used that phrase to describe yourself. You may well see yourself in the following pages. Even if you are a social entrepreneur, you can probably get even better at it. Not only will we show you how to become a more effective social entrepreneur, but we will also involve you in the process by helping you identify areas where you should consider building your skills and then develop goals for learning the skills you'll need to be an effective social entrepreneur. Ultimately, the more you put these skills to work for you in your own organization, the better you'll get at it, and the more effective your organization will become.

WHAT IS SOCIAL ENTREPRENEURSHIP?

You've no doubt heard about entrepreneurs, those adventurous individuals who seem to enjoy nothing more than creating new businesses out of thin air. Whether they are starting some new Internet business phenomenon, building a boutique steel mill, or simply opening a new delicatessen down the street, entrepreneurs are often credited with being the force that drives innovation and growth in our economy today. But where does that leave *you?*

As a leader or follower in a nonprofit, can't you also enjoy the benefits of thinking and acting entrepreneurially? As we illustrate throughout this book, you can—and you *should*. Before we get into the details of how you can become a social entrepreneur, however, let's first define exactly what we are talking about.

ENTREPRENEURSHIP IS . . .

There is no single definition of the word *entrepreneurship*. Although French economists coined the term *entrepreneur* approximately 200 years ago, it has evolved in both meaning and significance over the years. These changes have created a strong tradition that reflects the inherent strength of the entrepreneurial spirit.

core concept
In its original French, *entrepreneur* means literally someone who undertakes—not an undertaker in the sense of a funeral director, but someone who undertakes an important task or project. The term soon came to be associated with venturesome individuals who stimulated economic progress by finding new and better ways of doing things.

The French economist Jean Bapiste Say summed it up at the turn of the 19th century when he described entrepreneurs this way: "The entrepreneur shifts economic resources out of an area of lower and into an area of higher productivity and greater yield." In other words, entrepreneurs create value.

Early in the 20th century, economist Joseph Schumpeter boldly declared that "the function of entrepreneurs is to reform or revolutionize the patterns of production." They can do this ". . . by exploiting an invention or, more generally, an untried technological possibility for producing a new commodity or producing an old one in a new way, by opening up a new source of supply of materials or a new outlet for products, by reorganizing an industry and so on." In Schumpeter's mind, entrepreneurs create value through innovation.

More recently, management guru Peter Drucker described entrepreneurs and entrepreneurship this way: "the entrepreneur always searches for change, responds to it, and exploits it as an opportunity." Entrepreneurs see the opportunities rather than the problems created by change.

It's the old question: "Is this glass half empty or half full?" Harvard psychologist Ellen Langer got right to the heart of this question in her landmark study of the attitudes of schoolchildren toward people with disabilities. In the first classroom, she posted a picture of a person in a wheelchair and asked, "Can this person drive a car?" The answer was an overwhelming "no," along with *lots* of reasons why not. In the second classroom, Langer asked, "*How* can this person drive a car?" After a brief pause, students came up with *lots* of creative ideas about how a person in a wheelchair could drive a car.

Similarly, entrepreneurs have an *opportunity orientation* that leads them to see the possibilities and to think in terms of *how* they can get something done, rather than seeing the problems and thinking of excuses why they *can't*. Howard Stevenson, a leading theorist of entrepreneurship at Harvard Business School, added an element of resourcefulness to the definition, based on research he conducted to determine what distinguishes entrepreneurial management from more common forms of "administrative" management. He suggests defining the heart of entrepreneurial management as "the pursuit of opportunity without regard to resources currently controlled." He found that entrepreneurs not only see and pursue opportunities that elude administrative managers, but entrepreneurs also do not allow their own initial resource endowments to limit their options. Entrepreneurs mobilize the resources of others to achieve their entrepreneurial objectives.

core concept   If we distill down all the thinking on what makes someone an entrepreneur, we would be left with this definition:

> **Entrepreneurs are innovative, opportunity-oriented, resourceful, value-creating change agents.**

Never satisfied with the status quo, entrepreneurs are a forceful engine of growth in our economy. Therefore, and for other reasons we will soon learn about, it's easy to see why social entrepreneurs can have such a strong and positive impact on their clients and on their communities.

WHAT MAKES SOCIAL ENTREPRENEURS DIFFERENT?

Social entrepreneurs are different from business entrepreneurs in many ways. The key difference is that social entrepreneurs set out with an explicit social mission in mind. Their main objective is to make the world a better place. This vision affects how they measure their success and how they structure their enterprises.

Another important difference is that social entrepreneurs do not receive the same kind of market feedback that business entrepreneurs get. Business enterprises that efficiently create value for their customers are rewarded in the long term—rewards that eventually find their way back to investors in the form of profits; however, creating social value does not necessarily lead to long-term rewards for the enterprise or entrepreneur creating it. In these environments, for example, lack of profitability is not a reflection on organizational performance. As a result, social entrepreneurs face different challenges in attracting resources and in justifying their existence.

core concept

The best measure of success for social entrepreneurs is not how much profit they make, but rather the extent to which they create social value. Social entrepreneurs act as change agents in the social sector by behaving in the following ways:

✔ *Adopting a mission to create and sustain social value.* For social entrepreneurs, the mission of social improvement is critical, and it takes priority over generating profits. Instead of going for the quick-fix, social entrepreneurs look for ways to create lasting improvements.

✔ *Recognizing and relentlessly pursuing new opportunities to serve that mission.* Where others see problems, entrepreneurs see opportunities! Social entrepreneurs have a vision of how to achieve their goals, and they are determined to make their vision work.

✔ *Engaging in a process of continuous innovation, adaptation, and learning.* Social entrepreneurs look for innovative ways to ensure that their ventures create social value and obtain needed resources and funding as long as they are creating value.

✔ *Acting boldly without being limited to resources currently in hand.* Social entrepreneurs are skilled at doing more with less and at attracting resources from others. They explore all resource options, from pure philanthropy to the commercial methods of the business sector, but they are not bound by norms and traditions.

✔ *Exhibiting a heightened sense of accountability to the constituencies served and for the outcomes created.* Social entrepreneurs take steps to ensure that they are creating value. They seek to provide real social improvements to their beneficiaries and their communities, as well as an attractive social and/or financial return to their investors.

Social entrepreneurs create social enterprises. They are the reformers and revolutionaries of our society today. They make fundamental changes in the way that things are done in the social sector. Their visions are bold. They seek out opportunities to improve society, and they take action. They attack the underlying causes of problems rather than simply treating symptoms. And, although they may act locally, their actions have the very real potential to stimulate global improvements in their chosen arena, whether that is education, health care, job training and development, the environment, the arts, or any other social endeavor.

THE CHARACTERISTICS OF ENTREPRENEURS

No one is born an entrepreneur. People learn to be entrepreneurs over the course of their lifetimes, some sooner than others. They develop the necessary characteristics and skills over time. If you are not now a social entrepreneur, you may yet become one, and if you are one already, you can learn or improve your skills quickly and easily by simply focusing on the areas that need work.

This is not to say that everyone is cut out to be an entrepreneur. Although research shows that no single personality profile exists for entrepreneurs, they do tend to exhibit certain behavioral characteristics that are associated with their success.

tool of the trade   According to William D. Bygrave, director of Babson College's Center for Entrepreneurial Studies, entrepreneurs exhibit the following characteristics—what Bygrave calls the "10 D's." We have modified Bygrave's explanations slightly to suit social entrepreneurs.

- ✔ *Dreamers.* Social entrepreneurs have a vision of what the future could be like for them, their organizations, and society. And, more important, they have the ability to implement their dreams.

- ✔ *Decisiveness.* They don't procrastinate. They make decisions swiftly, and their swiftness is a key factor in their success.

- ✔ *Doers.* Once they decide on a course of action, they implement it as quickly as possible, making any needed adjustments as they go.

- ✔ *Determination.* They implement their ventures with total commitment. They seldom give up, even when confronted by obstacles that seem insurmountable.

- ✔ *Dedication.* They are totally dedicated to their ventures, sometimes at considerable cost to their relationships with friends and families. They work tirelessly. Twelve-hour days and seven-day work weeks are not uncommon when a social entrepreneur strives to get a new venture off the ground.

- ✔ *Devotion.* Social entrepreneurs love what they do. This love sustains them when the going gets tough, and love of their mission makes them effective at delivering on it.

- ✔ *Details.* It is said that the devil resides in the details. That is never more true than in starting and growing a new venture. The social entrepreneur must be on top of the critical details.

- ✔ *Destiny.* They want to be in charge of their own destiny rather than dependent on an employer.

- ✔ *Dollars.* Getting rich is not the prime motivator of social entrepreneurs, but money is important to keeping their ventures alive. They understand the economics of their ventures and work tirelessly to sustain them.

- ✔ *Distribution.* Social entrepreneurs distribute responsibility and credit to key stakeholders who are critical to the success of the efforts.[1] They give others a sense of ownership in their activities.

INTERVIEW

BILL STRICKLAND,
MANCHESTER CRAFTSMEN'S GUILD

Bill Strickland is president and CEO of the Pittsburgh, Pennsylvania–based social enterprises Manchester Craftsmen's Guild and the Bidwell Training Center. Founded in 1968, the Manchester Craftsmen's Guild uses art to teach at-risk youth life skills and to break the cycle of poverty. The Bidwell Training Center, founded by Strickland in 1972, focuses on building partnerships with local companies to train displaced adults for real work in real jobs. Nearly 500 students participate in Manchester's programs free of charge. Another 4,000 students each week attend guild-sponsored workshops in Pittsburgh's 12 public high schools. Every summer, students are invited to attend arts residency programs at local universities.

Strickland was named to a six-year term on the board of the National Endowment for the Arts (NEA) by President George Bush, and he received a MacArthur Fellow Award in 1996 for his leadership and ingenuity in the arts.

Bill Strickland exhibits many of William Bygrave's characteristics of successful entrepreneurs—his 10 D's—as described in the previous section. Strickland certainly has a dream, he's determined, and he's a doer. As you read this interview, see if you think he exhibits any of the other D's, as well.

QUESTION: What makes Manchester Craftsmen's Guild and Bidwell Training Center different from other non-profit organizations?

STRICKLAND: A couple of things. One is the attitude both the staff and the organization bring by stressing a set of values that have to do with quality and excellence and performance and measurement—and not using the non-profit status as an excuse for not having a businesslike skill set. The second thing is that our staff is encouraged to be innovative and entrepreneurial in the way they pursue their careers and their professions.

QUESTION: How did you become a social entrepreneur?

STRICKLAND: Totally by accident. I'd like to say it was all analysis and foresight, but I'm not quite sure it worked out that way. But I do recall being very encouraged in my work by the Harvard Business School, when I spoke there years ago. I showed up with a slide show of my work, and I got a standing ovation. At the end of class, the professor declared that I was a social entrepreneur—it was the first time I ever heard the term. Prior to them designating me that, what I thought I was doing was creating a diversified revenue and program strategy for my organization—some of which fell into this category of special enterprise.

(continued)

QUESTION: What did you do that was so unique?

STRICKLAND: I focused on developing partnerships with the marketplace. Number one, I asked employers what they wanted in an employee before I taught them—there was a direct alignment between what we were training for educationally and what these companies expected. Number two, I insisted that we exceed the expectations of the employers in terms of the quality of the people that we trained and turned out—we stood behind our product. Number three was to actually get to know these companies in more than a single-dimensional way. For example, we train chemical technicians for the Bayer chemical company, and they have a polymer division. When we got interested in polymers, two things came out of that: a polymer injection molding training program that we are going to create next year, and Bayer's plastic went into our jazz CDs that won us a Grammy award—and that's going to spin off into a new company next year. So, the conversation with Bayer ended up with us using their plastic in our compact disc products, and could end up making us a lot of money.

QUESTION: What have you got in mind for the future?

STRICKLAND: A couple of things. One, we're going to replicate what we do here in Pittsburgh in San Francisco. Mayor Willy Brown is interested and he's backing us. We have a design, we have a board comprised of folks from Hewlett Packard, Cisco, Wells Fargo, Arthur Andersen, and Charles Schwab, we have land on San Francisco Bay, we have an architect, and we have funding. So we are going to start building a 90,000-square-foot-high-technology arts and training center modeled on the one in Pittsburgh. Two, with a friend, we hope to build a 45,000-square-foot-high-technology greenhouse here in Pittsburgh to grow orchids and hydroponic tomatoes for market. Three, we're now in a formal partnership with a public school system, and they want us to build the high school of the future using technology as the focal point. In effect, they are saying to us, "We want you to take over vocational education for the public school system."

QUESTION: What advice do you have for aspiring social entrepreneurs?

STRICKLAND: It's important to have people—in your administrative and your governing structure—who think entrepreneurially. Because it's such a new and developing field, you are going to need entrepreneurs who think this way to help encourage you day in and day out. It runs against the traditional kind of bureaucratic, do-it-the-way-it-has-always-been-done school of thought, which, unfortunately, tends to govern a lot of these organizations—particularly in the public environment. So you need to get people on your board and on your staff who can contribute to the conversation rather than just challenge it.

The next time you get a few minutes in your busy schedule, step back from your job and think about how well *you* exhibit the aforementioned characteristics. Are some of them at the heart of the way you do business, but others yet to be developed fully? Take a moment to pat yourself on the back for each characteristic that you now exhibit, and resolve to yourself to work on improving in the areas where you need to. By consciously focusing on each area of improvement, you'll find yourself doing it before you know it!

WHAT MAKES AN ENTERPRISE A SOCIAL ENTERPRISE?

The social sector in our nation is quite large, well developed, and diverse. It includes churches and synagogues, colleges, universities, private schools, hospitals, nursing homes, drug and alcohol rehabilitation programs, family counseling services, job training programs, emergency relief agencies, affordable housing developers, soup kitchens, food banks, performing arts centers, museums, environmental conservation groups, community service programs, and many, many other kinds of organizations.

Whether we realize it or not, our lives are touched by social organizations almost every day of the week. From the day we are born, until the day we die—and many days in between—our lives are enriched because of the services that social organizations provide to their clients and to their communities.

DIFFERENT KINDS OF ORGANIZATIONS
FOR DIFFERENT KINDS OF NEEDS

Social enterprises such as the Habitat for Humanity, the many local food banks affiliated with Second Harvest, Goodwill Industries, and others like them are different from traditional businesses such as Sears & Roebuck, Sony, Chevron, IBM, and that mom-and-pop diner down the street.

But what are the key characteristics that make them different from business enterprises? The following are two important aspects of social enterprises:

✔ *Social enterprises have a social objective.* The *primary* objective of a social enterprise is to maintain and improve social conditions in a way that goes beyond financial benefits created for the organization's funders, managers, employees, or customers.

✔ *Social enterprises blend social and commercial methods.* In addition to using their ability to tap into the goodwill of some of their stakeholders, they look for creative ways to generate revenue, like businesses.

Where businesses are completely commercial, social enterprises are a hybrid of commercial and philanthropic methods.

Are you still unsure what a social enterprise is? Here are some examples of successful social enterprises that have had a tremendous impact on their clients and on their communities:

Rubicon—Rubicon Programs, Inc. is a social enterprise based in Richmond, California, whose business ventures generate almost $4 million in revenues annually by way of a bakery, home care, and a buildings/grounds maintenance business. Its primary objective is social—to provide job-training opportunities for people who most businesses would not take a chance on. Its ventures are primarily staffed by program participants—area homeless and disabled residents—and revenues generated by the ventures pay about half of the funds required to operate Rubicon's programs. For the remainder of their funding, Rubicon relies on the goodwill of donors. These programs include job training, housing, mental health counseling, and employment.[2]

The Nature Conservancy—The Nature Conservancy, a global, nonprofit organization headquartered in Arlington, Virginia, operates the largest private system of nature sanctuaries in the world. With more than 9 million acres of ecologically significant land protected in the United States since its founding in 1951, and 60 million acres more outside the United States, the Nature Conservancy has had a hugely positive impact on the environment and in achieving its social mission, which is "To preserve plants, animals, and natural communities that represent the diversity of life on Earth by protecting the lands and waters they need to survive."[3] The Nature Conservancy acts entrepreneurially. For example, it established a for-profit company, the Eastern Shore Sustainable Development Corporation, to generate profits and create jobs while achieving its goal of protecting the environment.[4] It has also formed a partnership with Georgia Pacific to engage in environmentally sustainable harvesting of timber from selected conservation lands. But it also depends on the goodwill of its 1 million members and other donors.

Orpheus Chamber Orchestra—The New York City–based Orpheus Chamber Orchestra is a nonprofit organization with the goal of bringing the highest level of musical experience to its neighbors, to the City of New York as a whole, and to the world. Headquartered in the historic Riverside Church in the Morningside Heights neighborhood of upper Manhattan, Orpheus has very strong ties to its community. In addition to its regular appearances at Carnegie Hall, the orchestra inaugurated a popular community concert series at Riverside Church in 1996, has initiated a highly successful classical music appreciation program in the New York

CASE STUDY

BUILDING A HABITAT FOR HUMANITY

What would you call an organization that is among the top 20 home builders in the nation, having created more than 70,000 homes in more than 50 countries and providing safe, affordable, and decent shelter to more than 350,000 people? Or an organization that has adopted an extremely powerful social mission and that works relentlessly to serve it? We would call it Habitat for Humanity International, the Americus, Georgia–based social enterprise founded in 1976 by Millard and Linda Fuller.

Habitat for Humanity is a nonprofit, ecumenical Christian housing ministry dedicated to eliminating substandard housing and homelessness worldwide and to making adequate, affordable shelter a matter of conscience and action. Habitat builds and sells homes to partner families at no profit, and financing is provided via affordable, no-interest loans. Its growth is one of the most dramatic examples of social entrepreneurship in the past three decades.

Although the primary engine that makes Habitat work is the goodwill reflected in a growing pool of volunteer labor and tax-deductible donations of cash and building materials, the organization is unique in requiring future homeowners to invest between 300 to 500 hours of their own labor into the building of their homes—and the homes of other program participants—as sweat equity. Not only does homeowner participation reduce the cost of construction, but it also gives homeowners a very personal stake in their homes, while helping to build partnerships with others in the community. Homeowners are also required to pay a modest mortgage on the house. They buy their homes with their labor and money.

Habitat has garnered much media attention because of its affiliation with former President Jimmy Carter and his wife Roslyn. In 1984, President Carter endorsed Habitat's idea of initiating an annual Jimmy Carter Work Project, during which he and his wife—and an army of volunteers—focus their efforts for one week on a selected location. The goal is to build 100 low-cost homes for those in need. In 1999, Carter, along with 6,000 volunteers, built 100 homes in Houston, Texas, in one week's time. They did so by nailing together 500,000 linear feet of lumber, eating 70,000 meals, drinking 35,000 gallons of water, and being cooled off by 100,000 pounds of ice.

Without a doubt, Habitat for Humanity International is an organization driven by a strong social objective—providing housing to low-income people, while building self-reliance and self-esteem—but it is a social enterprise that blends commercial and social methods to generate

(continued)

much of the cash, labor, and materials needed to conduct its programs. Habitat creates partnerships, not dependencies, with its clients. Says President Carter, "We demonstrate to people through equal treatment that we are partners. It's not charity; it's not giveaway." By working closely with its clients, and by helping them to experience the pride of owning their very own piece of the American Dream—a piece that they work hard to attain by investing their own time, energy, and money—Habitat for Humanity International is creating islands of hope in a vast sea of poverty. And as more and more people are helped by Habitat, these islands of hope are growing.

City public schools—a program recently expanded in part by a $250,000 grant from the Peter J. Sharp Foundation—and created a new residency with Baruch College of the City University of New York. Orpheus Chamber Orchestra is very entrepreneurial, generating operating funds by selling concert series subscriptions, recording CDs (more than 50 to date), developing sponsorships with for-profit corporations, and much more.[5]

Why Social Entrepreneurship Is Important to You

The social sector has undergone massive change over the past several decades. Gone are the days of charitable relief—cash handouts and subsidies that do more to create dependencies in program participants than to prepare them to take on the world themselves. Gone, too, are the days of easy money from government and foundation grants, for which results and accountability were rarely required or enforced.

Current trends in the social sector

core concept

There is a new spirit in social organizations, and this spirit is social entrepreneurship at work. This spirit is characterized by several trends that have emerged and steadily gained strength over the past couple of decades, including the following:

1. Heightened concerns about the effectiveness of traditional governmental and charitable approaches to meeting social needs.
2. A search for more innovative solutions that lead to sustainable improvements.
3. An increased openness to experimentation with market-based approaches and businesslike methods in the social sector.

4. A growing shift toward the privatization of public services, leading to government contracting with both for-profit and nonprofit providers.

5. A parallel shift toward outcomes-based (rather than needs-based) approaches to funding on the part of both private philanthropies and government agencies.

6. A new, more engaged and strategic approach to corporate involvement in social and community issues.

Together, these trends are creating major changes in how societies around the world are dealing with providing public goods and services. They are leading to a blurring of sector boundaries and a call for more entrepreneurial spirit in the social sector. Specifically, they have led social entrepreneurs to search for more sustainable solutions to social problems and to more sustainable funding sources.

Although traditional charitable relief will always be part of the social sector, many proponents of new approaches argue that it does not address the underlying problems and that it can create unhealthy dependencies and be demeaning to program participants.

 core concept

As a result, social entrepreneurs are shifting the emphasis from charitable relief to new, more systemic ways of improving social conditions. In particular, they engage in the following:

- Reducing the need for charitable assistance rather than simply meeting the need (as we saw with Rubicon's employment programs).

- Engaging people in and allowing them to take some responsibility for improving their own lives (as we saw with Habitat's requirements that homeowners work on and pay something for the houses they receive).

Although good, old-fashioned charitable assistance will always be a necessary part of the lifeblood of many social organizations, it is widely acknowledged that new approaches are needed to address growing problems.

Social entrepreneurs are also shifting away from heavy reliance on philanthropy toward adopting the kinds of business methods most often seen in entrepreneurial private-sector organizations. Philanthropic sources can be fickle, faddish, and unreliable in the long term. Seeking grants can result in consuming far too much time and organizational energy. As a result, social entrepreneurs are looking for new funding sources. In doing so, they are performing the following tasks:

- Exploring commercial methods of generating funds (as we saw with Orpheus Chamber Orchestra)

- Starting mission-related businesses (as we saw in the Rubicon example)

- Forming mutually beneficial partnerships with corporations (as we saw with the Nature Conservancy)

New opportunities, new challenges

The new spirit of social entrepreneurship has created all kinds of new opportunities for nonprofit organizations. It has simultaneously created more than its share of challenges, particularly for organizations that have become dependent on charitable assistance to support operations and programs, or that simply don't have the skills or staff to implement these changes.

New Funding Opportunities

If anything, social enterprises today are learning that the universe of possible opportunities for introducing entrepreneurial activity into their organizations is limited only by their imaginations.

Here are some of the most common ways that social enterprises are applying entrepreneurial funding strategies in their organizations—and greatly improving their ability to reduce their dependencies on pure philanthropy in the process:

Fee-for-service and repayment plans.   These programs require program participants to pay at least a portion of the cost of providing the service or, in the case of loans or other obligations, to repay at least some portion of the debt over a period of months or years. Fee-for-service and repayment plans offer the following advantages:

- ✔ They provide market feedback.
- ✔ They reduce the sense of dependence and charity on the part of program participants.
- ✔ They serve as a screening and commitment device.

Commercial ventures and business partnerships.   Many social enterprises have found great success starting their own commercial ventures or entering into partnerships with for-profit businesses. Whether it's the YMCA selling exercise programs to the public, the Girl Scouts selling cookies, or the Arthritis Foundation licensing its logo to pharmaceutical manufacturers, increasingly nonprofit organizations are attempting businesslike strategies. Commercial ventures and business partnerships offer the following advantages:

- ✔ They improve efficiency or effectiveness.
- ✔ They model self-sufficiency.
- ✔ They provide an unrestricted funding stream.

The Social Enterprise Spectrum

tool of the trade   Social entrepreneurs realize that they have a wide range of options for structuring their organizations. The social enterprise spectrum

	Continuum of Options		
	Purely Philanthropic	Hybrids	Purely Commercial
General Motives, Methods, and Goals	Appeal to goodwill	Mixed motives	Appeal to self-interest
	Mission-driven	Balance of mission and market	Market-driven
	Social value creation	Social and economic value	Economic value creation
Key Stakeholders			
Beneficiaries	Pay nothing	Subsidized rates and/ or mix of full payers and those who pay nothing	Pay full market rates
Capital	Donations and grants	Below-market capital and/or mix of full payers and those who pay nothing	Market rate capital
Workforce	Volunteers	Below-market wages and/or mix of volunteers and fully paid staff	Market rate compensation
Suppliers	Make in-kind donations	Special discounts and/or mix of in-kind and full price	Charge market prices

EXHIBIT 1.1 The social enterprise spectrum.

illustrates that range (Exhibit 1.1). It is a simple way of illustrating the two extremes of social enterprises—purely philanthropic organizations on one end, and purely commercial on the other—and all the other possibilities in between.

Where does your organization fit into the social enterprise spectrum today? Where would you like it to be in the future?

New Challenges

Perhaps it's no surprise that the new opportunities that social entrepreneurship can bring into an organization also come with many potential new challenges. It's important to be aware of these challenges—and to be ready with solutions—as your social enterprise evolves. For instance, as your organization explores new options toward the commercial end of the social enterprise spectrum, you will need to anticipate the following challenges:

✔ New organizational capacities can be hard to build.

✔ Managerial resources are often in short supply.

✔ The new mode of funding can create culture clashes.

✔ Original funders may reduce their funding.

✔ Key stakeholders may find the move objectionable.

✔ Political opposition can arise outside the organization.

✔ "The tail can start wagging the dog."

FACTORS LEADING TO ENTREPRENEURIAL SUCCESS

Management guru and Harvard Business School professor Rosabeth Moss Kanter developed a list of items that can help ensure the success of a business—the "Four F's." This list has since been expanded into the Nine F's for entrepreneurial success by William D. Bygrave at Babson College's Center for Entrepreneurial Studies. As you read through *tool of the trade* this list, consider whether or not your organization exhibits the same characteristics.

1. *Founders.* Every startup company must have a first-class team of entrepreneurs. Without true entrepreneurial spirit powering the organization, the chances of success are far less than certain.

2. *Focused.* Entrepreneurial companies focus on niche markets; they specialize. Rather than attempting to be everything for everybody, entrepreneurs find out what they do best and what customers would most benefit from their products or services, and they concentrate their efforts on doing just that. Nothing more, nothing less.

3. *Fast.* They make decisions quickly and implement them swiftly. This is not to say that entrepreneurs make decisions recklessly or without thought—quite the opposite. Entrepreneurs are able to make quick decisions because they have taken the time to research everything about a decision in advance and prepare for it. When the time is right, they *act!*

4. *Flexible.* They keep an open mind. They respond to change. Instead of becoming stuck in the past, they are always looking for ways to take advantage of new opportunities and changes in the marketplace.

5. *Forever-innovating.* They are tireless innovators. They truly believe that there is always a better way to do something—whether it's providing a better product or service at lower cost to customers, or improving quality or customer responsiveness—and they are constantly on the lookout for new ways to make a good thing even better.

6. *Flat.* Entrepreneurial organizations have as few layers of management as possible. There is no time, money, or patience to afford employees who contribute little or nothing to an organization's mission.

7. *Frugal.* By keeping overhead low and productivity high, entrepreneurial organizations keep costs down. This keeps them extremely competitive versus competitors that lack the same fiscal discipline.

8. *Friendly.* Entrepreneurial companies are friendly to their customers, suppliers, and workers. Who would *you* rather deal with—an organization that seems to really care about you, or one that doesn't?

9. *Fun.* It's fun to be associated with an entrepreneurial company. There's probably nothing more exciting in the world of work than being a part of an organization that is growing fast and that has an adventurous attitude about doing business. You may work harder than you ever have before in your life, but the rewards—both mental and financial—can far exceed even your wildest dreams.[6]

Do you recognize any of these indicators of entrepreneurial success in your organization? If not, make a point of seeking out ways that you can develop them and make them a part of how your organization does business.

SUMMARY

More and more nonprofit organizations are finding out that becoming more entrepreneurial can be very rewarding—not just in a financial sense, but also in terms of the spirit and energy that can potentially be released within the organization and its staff, volunteers, patrons, and clients. This chapter defined social entrepreneurship, and we've learned exactly what makes an enterprise a *social* enterprise. We've learned why social entrepreneurship may be important to you and to your organization, and we've reviewed the characteristics of successful enterprises. As you read the rest of this book, keep in mind that you can choose how entrepreneurial your organization will be. There is no single right answer—the right answer is what is best for your organization, your clients, and your stakeholders.

Key points to remember are the following:

✔ Entrepreneurs are innovative, opportunity-oriented, resourceful, value-creating change agents.

✔ Social entrepreneurs are entrepreneurs with a social mission in mind.

✔ The best measure of the success of social entrepreneurs is not how much profit they make, but rather the extent to which they create social value.

✔ There are two key differences between business enterprises and social enterprises: (1) Social enterprises have a social objective, and (2) Social enterprises blend social and commercial methods.

✔ Reduced funding and support from traditional, philanthropic, and government funding sources is driving more nonprofits into entrepreneurial ventures.

✔ The new spirit of social entrepreneurship has created new opportunities *and* challenges for nonprofit organizations.

✔ The social enterprise spectrum extends from organizations that are purely philanthropic to those that are purely commercial; most lie somewhere in between.

Endnotes

1. William D. Bygrave, *The Portable MBA in Entrepreneurship* (New York: John Wiley & Sons, 1994), p. 5.
2. Heather McLeod, "The New Social Entrepreneurs," *Who Cares,* April 1997, p. 34.
3. www.tnc.org (The Nature Conservancy's Website).
4. J. Gregory Dees, "Enterprising Nonprofits," *Harvard Business Review,* January-February 1998, p. 66.
5. Orpheus Chamber Orchestra press kit, February 2000.
6. Bygrave, *The Portable MBA in Entrepreneurship,* p. 23.

Chapter 2

DEFINING YOUR MISSION

Rob Johnston, Senior Vice President, Program, The Drucker Foundation

IN THIS CHAPTER

Mission as the entrepreneur's most useful tool
How to define your organization's mission
Planning and leading through mission

Mission is the cornerstone of effective organizations in all sectors. Mission provides leaders, funders, customers—*all* of the people involved with the organization—with a clear understanding of its purpose, its reason for being. With this secure point of understanding, the entrepreneurial organization can be opportunity- and customer-focused, looking for openings in the marketplace, for customers seeking new services or products, for funders or investors seeking opportunities that match their interests. Used daily, the mission becomes a powerful tool for the entrepreneurial organization. It is both glue and guide. It unites people around a common purpose and provides a basis for decision making in a world of opportunities and choices.

> *"Mission is the star we steer by. Everything begins with mission, everything flows from mission."—Frances Hesselbein*[1]

> *"Mission defines a direction, not a destination. It tells the members of an organization why they are working together, how they intend to contribute to the world. Without a sense of mission, there is no foundation for establishing why some intended results are more important than others. . . . Mission instills both the passion and the patience for the long journey."—Peter M. Senge*[2]

Mission must be more than choice words to hang on the wall. Mission can provide an organization with lofty inspiration and practical guidance.

When entrepreneurial organizations employ mission as a regular part of their discipline, it can become the most useful tool available.

MISSION AS THE ENTREPRENEUR'S MOST USEFUL TOOL

For thousands of leaders and their organizations, the definition and communication of a clear purpose are priority concerns. For them, making the mission—the organization's reason for being—an open and debated issue is a practical way to build cohesion and focus that contributes to the organization's success.

MISSION IS . . .

core concept

Before employing this useful tool, it's helpful to have a clear understanding of what the mission is. In practice, conversation, and management literature, there are several variations on the definition of mission. Throughout this book, we use the following definition:

> *Mission: "why we do what we do," a reason for being, purpose.*

Peter F. Drucker wrote that an organization benefits from a mission that is short, sharply focused, and easily communicated. He noted, "It should fit on a T-shirt."[3] If you are very ambitious, you can use his first suggestion, that the mission should "fit on a bumper sticker."[4] To best employ a mission, leaders should not compete to write the world's shortest mission statement. A more appropriate target would be a widely known mission, something that is understood by customers, volunteers, staff, partners, funders, competitors, and the general public. An effective example that serves an organization representing many languages and countries is the mission for the International Federation of Red Cross and Red Crescent Societies, *to serve the most vulnerable.* These five words can generate passion and commitment, and explain clearly why those organizations "are in business."

ON CUSTOMERS . . .

The word *customer* is used throughout this exploration of mission to describe who must be satisfied in order for the organization to achieve results. The customer is one "who values your service, who wants what you offer, who feels it's important to *them.*"[5] Social sector organizations have two types of customers. The *primary customer* is the person whose life is changed through the organization's work. *Supporting customers* are volunteers, members, partners, funders, referral sources, employees, and others who must be satisfied. Combined, the *primary* and *supporting* customers form the multiple constituencies that the organization must be accountable to for performance. If an organization can maintain an open conversation with all of its customers, it can remain open to new opportunities and be prepared for new challenges. Mission can be shaped by the opinions and choices of customers and define which customers the organization will serve, and which it will not serve.

MISSION AS A LEVER

The lever is one of humanity's simple, but essential tools. Using a lever, an individual or small group of people can move many times the weight they could without it. Legend has it that Archimedes said "Give me a lever long enough and a fulcrum on which to place it, and I shall move the world." Nonprofit organizations and social entrepreneurs can use mission as their lever to move hearts and minds, and to create the bottom line that all social sector organizations hold in common— "changed lives."

In organizations in all sectors, mission can enable the leader to multiply the contributions of numerous people toward specific ends (see Exhibit 2.1). This leverage results from aligning the purposes and contributions of the people from within and outside of the organization. The result is not compliance through command and control, but rather commitment through pursuit of a common mission. The productivity of people who are contributing their own thinking and commitment to the mission of the organization is *always* more powerful than the result of those same people complying with commands. Mission-driven actions are powered by decisions of many minds, and the superior results reflect those higher-quality decisions.

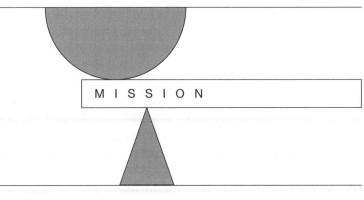

EXHIBIT 2.1 Mission as a lever.

The Annie E. Casey Foundation has as its mission, *To help build better futures for disadvantaged children in the U.S.* With a well-defined, well-understood, and well-employed mission, an organization can truly move the world, changing the lives of thousands of people.

LEADERSHIP LEVERAGE

The mission can be a means of sharing responsibility and leadership. Employing the mission as the purpose by which customer results are evaluated enables individuals throughout the organization to make the right decision for customers and the mission. In studies of the U.S. Army's National Training Centers and corporations undergoing significant transformations, Richard Pascale and colleagues have noted the critical role of understanding mission. They explain one of the disciplines in sustaining change: "An organization's members do best when they can bridge the gap between overall strategy and individual performance. An understanding of both the big picture [mission] and the particulars of their situation enables people to connect the broad strategic intentions and operational factors that are keys to execution and ultimate success."[6] (The role of mission as the origin of a circular planning process is illustrated on page 31.)

In an organization in which the mission is used to set the standards for performance, all people can share in the decision making. Mission clarity enables and supports shared responsibility throughout the organization.

MISSION AS A DISCIPLINE

Mission plays a critical role as a discipline. It provides the person or organization confronted with challenges and opportunities throughout the day and year with the information to make intelligent decisions. A mission that a person can wear on a T-shirt can be used at any time to evaluate the attractiveness of an opportunity or the seriousness of a threat. The mission is the standard against which these novel ideas are compared and ranked. The exciting opportunity with no relevance to the mission will lose out to the equally exciting possibility that furthers that mission. The mission of the American Diabetes Association is, *To prevent and cure diabetes and to improve the lives of all people affected by diabetes.* Although there are many ways to further this mission, there are also many activities that do not further it. With a purpose this clear, an organization can weigh alternatives and choose wisely those opportunities that further the mission.

The discipline of mission also extends to accountability to funders, customers, supporters, and the public. With a clear purpose defined and shared widely, the organization can develop clear measures for performance. For example, Sister Barbara Rogers, headmistress of the Newton Country Day School in Massachusetts, described how developing renewed clarity about the school's mission helped it to rebuild declining enrollment and increase endowment sixfold. She notes, "Being clear about our mission gives us the freedom to change; it also gives us the ability to make decisions quickly. We're not capricious, but we're free to be unpredictable."[7]

MISSION AS A FLEXIBLE TOOL

To employ mission most effectively, leaders and their organizations must revisit the mission at least every three years. This schedule ensures that everyone throughout the organization understands that the mission is a living guide and that its validity needs to be examined regularly. If times are stable, this three-year schedule may help to ensure that the organization does not get stuck working for yesterday's purpose. When times are more fluid, and the needs of customers and communities are changing more rapidly, the mission may need to be revisited more frequently, even if in an expedited manner. During this revisit, the Board and staff explore the current validity of the mission, the present and future needs of customers and the environment, and their personal level of commitment to the mission. Changes in these areas may require revising the mission or developing a new mission.

HOW TO DEFINE YOUR ORGANIZATION'S MISSION

Defining or refining the mission for an organization, a collaboration, or an enterprise project can be challenging. This process can be addressed in several ways, through a group activity or personal introspection. A diagnostic approach and key principles for defining the mission are described here. A more complete process, using a mission writing group and preparing for presentation to a governing board is included at the end of the chapter (see the case study, "A Group Approach to Defining Mission," page 37).

For many people working in the social sector, mission comes naturally and explains the reason they show up. We come to our jobs with a belief in the purpose of the organization. For the leader of the social sector organization, the mission is even more important. Used wisely, the mission can be the foundation of an effort joining people and money to make significant changes in the lives of people. The mission can be used to attract resources, to develop strategies, and to inspire commitment from people.

✔ *Mission can be the essential, defining idea.* The commitment and excitement that people hold can be built around the mission of the organization. That purpose can make it clear why the organization operates, and it can provide everyone involved with a sense of their progress and the significance of their work.

✔ *Mission must be shared and developed with others.* To build an effective organization from a compelling mission, the leader must be a "missionary," sharing that purpose with others. As the mission is refined, the people involved with the organization also must be involved in its evolution. If the many constituencies in the organization's world are given a voice, the relevance of that mission and the effectiveness of the organization will increase.

✔ *Mission adjusts to changes in the world: Sometimes it is achieved, other times outgrown.* Leaders must be prepared for the mission to change and must lead that process when it's needed.

✔ *Mission is meaningless without action.* Peter Drucker speaks of the entrepreneur as exploiting opportunities. A well-formed mission gives a social sector organization a powerful opportunity to create change. A mission without a plan and coordinated action is only good intentions.

✔ *Mission and action can change the world.* Social sector organizations are uniquely positioned to bring the best thinking, best hearts, and resources together to produce significant change in the lives of people and the society. When resources are limited, mission can provide the inspiration to persevere. As Hesselbein and Senge note, mission can be the "star we steer by" and provide the "passion and patience" required for meeting difficult challenges.

DO YOU NEED TO REVISIT YOUR MISSION? A SIMPLE DIAGNOSTIC APPROACH

tool of the trade   Most organizations and social entrepreneurs have a social mission that inspires and guides their work. Does your mission inspire the best from your colleagues, customers, and contributors? Does it move their hearts and minds and produce the benefit of many contributing to the same effort? Does your mission enable you and your organization "the freedom to change" and "the ability to make decisions quickly," as it does for Sister Barbara Rogers? The following diagnostic approach might help you to determine whether the organization's mission works, or whether it should be revisited to better meet the needs of your customers and the challenges of today and tomorrow.

1. Without referring to any sources, think about your current mission.

✔ Can you write it down accurately?

✔ Can you write it in 25 or fewer words?

✔ Can you say it to someone in 30 seconds?

2. Assess your mission using the checklist found in Exhibit 2.2.

Is the mission:	Yes	To some extent	No
✔ Short and sharply focused?			
✔ Clear and easily understood?			
✔ A statement of why you do what you do or why the organization exists?			
✔ About purpose, not means?			
✔ Sufficiently broad?			
✔ A direction for doing the right things?			
✔ Focused on your opportunities?			
✔ Matched to your competence?			
✔ Inspiring your commitment?			
✔ Stating what, in the end, you want to be remembered for?			

EXHIBIT 2.2 Diagnostic approach to determine if you need to revisit your mission.

Share the mission and these questions with members of the Board, a trusted colleague, an advisor, or a mentor. Ask for their rating of the mission's performance on this scale.

3. Does the mission work to attract resources, motivate action, and lead the organization toward results?

✔ Do potential donors understand and respond positively to the mission?

✔ Can three of your colleagues articulate it?

✔ Can three of your Board members?

✔ Do they all provide the same answer?

✔ Does your staff know the mission? Does it come up in conversation? In meetings? In internal memos?

Scoring

There are no hard and fast rules for evaluating your mission's perform-ance against these questions. First of all, you (perhaps in collaboration with Board members, a trusted colleague, an advisor, or a mentor) must be the judge. Second, the circumstances, age, and opportunities facing your organization can produce different conclusions. Perhaps you have led the organization with your own understanding of its mission. You may decide that you don't need to revise that mission. You may decide, how-ever, that you want to make that mission more widely understood by those *supporting customers:* Board, staff, funders, and others who can help your organization reach its goals.

Key Principles of Defining a Mission

If you want to define or revise your mission, the following principles should help.

1. *Don't do this alone.* This process is a remarkable opportunity to de-velop shared commitment with many of the constituencies on which the organization relies. Board and staff can contribute their desires, their knowledge of the field and customers, and their hopes for the future of the organization. Their new ideas can help produce a better result, and their involvement begins the process of *manag-ing for the mission* that will be your role as a leader going forward.

2. *Agree on evaluation criteria.* The criteria listed in Exhibit 2.2 pro-vide a starting point for a process of defining a mission. To build commitment and clarity about the process, it is helpful to review these criteria and agree on those that are essential for your organ-ization. Most of the criteria should be incorporated, but your or-ganization may want to place greater emphasis on some or reduce the emphasis on others. Your organization may believe it is impor-tant that the means—how the organization works—should be in-cluded. For example, the Golden Gate Community in San Francisco has as its mission: *To transform the lives of at-risk 18-30 year olds by providing them with pathways of personal growth and economic op-portunity.* Determine *your* organization's criteria at the beginning of the process, and use those criteria throughout.

3. *Draft possibilities.* Take advantage of the opportunity to explore dif-ferent ways of presenting the core ideas of the mission. Produce a draft, test it against the criteria and feedback, then repeat the process.

4. *Test possibilities against criteria and additional feedback.* With each draft, review it against the evaluation criteria and share it with Board members, colleagues, current and potential supporters, and

customers. Listen to their responses, record their questions, and record your assessment against the criteria. Use the results of this review to revise your mission and to draft new possibilities.

5. *Follow your organization's policies for approval and communication.* The definition of a mission is an important part of the board's work. If your organization or project is operating with a Board, be sure that you enlist Board leadership, employ the Board's contributions, and respect the Board's authority. Meet with the Board chairman and provide updates on progress. Include the chairman in the mission group, if that works. (See more details about the Board's role in this process in Summary: Mission in Action.)

    Next in importance to coordinating with the board is communicating with the staff and other constituencies. When you are defining a mission, their comments and contributions are critical. When the mission is defined, their understanding and commitment become even more important.

6. *Exercise Flexibility.* The aforementioned principles can be employed in many different ways, by groups of different sizes and intentions. The goal is that you apply a simple discipline to the process of defining mission. It's important to remember that this definition process can be a unique opportunity to nurture and encourage commitment to an organization and its purpose. Therefore, the decision to include more people in the process, although perhaps less efficient, could produce greater results in the long term. A more complete process is included in the case study, "A Group Approach to Defining Mission" at the end of the chapter.

Planning and Leading through Mission

Mission serves a critical role in planning for nonprofit organizations. (Exhibit 2.3 illustrates how the organization's internal planning activities occur within the environment and customer opportunities.) For all organizations, planning for results begins outside. The environmental scan provides the organization and its leadership with a picture of the world in which they operate. It defines the opportunities and threats facing the organization as it undertakes its plans. Using that big picture, the organization must talk with customers to develop an understanding of how they see the organization and what they seek from it. The information gathered from the environmental scan and careful customer research enables the organization to develop a plan to further its mission that is sensitive to the environment and customer, while also exploiting the organization's special strengths and capabilities.

ENVIRONMENTAL SCANNING

Exploiting Opportunity

gem of wisdom

Peter F. Drucker, in *Innovation and Entrepreneurship,* describes the value of seeking and responding to changes in the environment:

"The entrepreneur always searches for change, responds to it, and exploits it as an opportunity."[8]

When we conduct an environmental scan, we can see change as a challenge, a threat, or an opportunity. The change does not identify itself. Each leader must adopt an entrepreneurial attitude and say, "How can we use this change?" "How can we exploit it to further our mission?" Drucker uses the word "exploit" without its shadings of taking advantage of people. For example, in the Drucker Foundation 1999 Annual Report, he notes "And only the social sector nonprofit organization performs in the community, exploits its opportunities, mobilizes its local resources, solves its problems." All social sector leaders should strive to exploit the opportunities of change for furthering their mission.

What are the Challenges? What are the Opportunities?

Organizations exist not to continue their own survival, but to serve people, the community, and the society that surrounds them. To remain relevant to those constituencies, leaders of all organizations must be focused on the opportunities and challenges presented by the environment, its stable features, and the many changes to come. The environmental scan must answer two simple questions faced by every organization: What are the challenges? What are the opportunities? The process of conducting an environmental scan varies across organizations and settings. Some of the common data elements to collect include the following:

- ✔ Changing demographics of current and potential customer groups
- ✔ Evolving community issues and conditions the organization might address
- ✔ Relevant cultural or social trends
- ✔ Trends in the economy, availability of funding and people
- ✔ State of the organization's partnerships, collaborations, alliances, and affiliations
- ✔ Politics, legislation, or regulation that affects the organization and those it serves
- ✔ Competition
- ✔ New technologies, models, or methods

Internal data from the organization can also be included in this scanning process. These materials include the following:

✔ Current mission
✔ Historical summary
✔ Values statement
✔ Code of Ethics
✔ Customer or member demographics
✔ Services delivered
✔ Results measures
✔ Other measures of organizational performance
✔ Organization chart
✔ Financial data
✔ Publications
✔ Annual report[9]

The environmental scanning process should result in a sense of the opportunities and challenges within which the organization will operate. This environmental information is not sufficient for the organization seeking to build a plan for results; it needs also to gather information from customers—past, present, and future.

CUSTOMER RESEARCH

In planning, the purpose of customer research is to bring the voice of the customer directly into the organization's discussions and decision making. There are two schools of thought about how to conduct this research. The "objective outsider" school holds that only people not directly associated with the organization can ensure that the research is objective and free of personal bias. The "involved insider" school holds that people involved with the organization can benefit more from direct contact with customers. Given proper training and an atmosphere of open inquiry, this approach can produce valid results at lower costs.[10] One must include in the cost calculation the time an employee spends on the research as time not available for other projects. This opportunity cost could affect your decision.

This examination employs the "involved insider" approach mostly because it raises the personal commitment of the individuals involved in the study. The suggested techniques for conducting this research include using the following tools:

✔ Conversations
✔ Focus groups
✔ Surveys, other research

Employ the approaches and tools that enable you to capture a sense of what your customers seek from your organization. The goal is that the customers' needs, wants, and aspirations—what they value—are understood by you and all of the members of the organization who are seeking to plan its direction.

Unexpected Successes

Peter F. Drucker, in *Innovation and Entrepreneurship,* describes the discipline of innovation. His chapter on the unexpected opens with the following statement:

> *"No other area offers richer opportunities for successful innovation than the unexpected success. In no other area are innovative opportunities less risky and their pursuit less arduous. Yet the unexpected success is almost totally neglected; worse, managements tend actively to reject it."*[11]

Throughout the environmental scan and the customer research process, open your eyes, ears, heart, and mind to the unexpected successes. Who are the customers you didn't *intend* to serve? Where are your services making a difference you didn't plan on?

Are you paying attention and pursuing these unexpected successes? Have you considered how they can be built upon? How they can be extended? How they affect your sense of customers and mission?

DEVELOPING THE PLAN

Mission serves a critical role in planning for nonprofit organizations. Exhibit 2.3 shows the integral role mission plays in a cycle of planning for an organization. The planning cycle takes place within an environment and in response to customers. With those parameters established, the organization starts with its mission, its purpose and reason for being.

Mission—With a clear sense of its purpose, an organization can proceed with developing a plan for results.

Goals—Describe the desired future of the organization. They should be limited in number so that everyone can understand and support their achievement.

Objectives—Are developed from the goals. The objectives provide specific and measurable targets of performance.

Action steps—Describe how the objectives will be pursued.

Budget—In this process, the budget is developed after the action plan is formed. Thus, the financing of the activities is the financial reflection of the plan of work. In the entrepreneurial organization, this budget

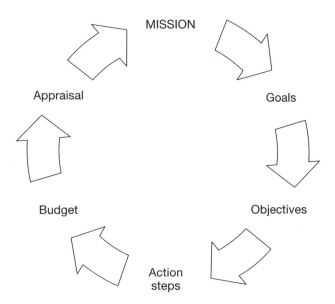

EXHIBIT 2.3 The role of mission in the planning cycle.

may call for developing resources not currently on hand. Even if the finances need to be developed, this planning process puts them in the proper position relative to the goals, objectives, and actions the organization will undertake to further its mission.

Appraisal—The effective organization builds evaluation into all of its activities and endeavors. In this process, there are ongoing measures of performance against which action steps and objectives can be evaluated. At the end of each year, an annual review is completed in which the targeted objectives and action steps are compared to results. In addition, these contributing activities are compared to the goals and the financial expectations in the budget.

Mission—The process does not end but circles around again to mission. In the spirit of ongoing improvement and evaluation, every three years the mission is revisited, before the annual planning process is initiated.

Governance and Management

In most nonprofits, mission and goals are the strategic areas that involve the Board and its governance role. The tactical plan developed by management begins with developing objectives and continues with the action steps and budget needed to carry out those tactics. The Board is again responsible for reviewing performance and for revisiting the mission every three years.

LEADING THROUGH MISSION

Building an organization and coordinating the work of many people is a true leadership challenge. The social entrepreneur is in the special position of having a commonly held purpose available for inspiration and guidance. The use of a clear mission has certain costs—the leader must be faithful to the language and spirit of that mission and must have a true dedication to making that language understood by all. The advantages are profound. In many ways, a clear, widely understood mission provides an organization with the foundation for performance-oriented focus and activities.

tool of the trade   James L. Heskett and Leonard A. Schlesinger, in *The Leader of the Future*,[12] describe the qualities that define effective leaders as "shapers and keepers of performance-oriented cultures," and present six qualities that these leaders demonstrate in their work.

- ✔ *Speaking a Different Language.* Heskett and Schlesinger note that the leaders they profile use surprising language, commenting that "the chairman of the board of ServiceMaster, the most successful support services organization in the United States, looked for a 'servant's heart' as the primary criterion in selecting his successor to serve as CEO. The former head of what many regard as the best-led and best-managed social sector organization, the Girl Scouts, described her job as ensuring that the organization remained 'mission-focused, values-based, and demographics-driven,' with the latter term directed at the need for greater diversity in the organization. The CEO of the most successful major U.S. airline, Southwest Airlines, talked to us about hiring as a 'near-religious experience.'" They comment that the language used by these leaders is not what one would expect from "tough-minded, tough-talking leaders. But tough talk by others apparently has not produced the kind of results these leaders have delivered."

- ✔ *Listening versus Telling.* In a conscious effort to acknowledge the voice of the customer and the employee, leaders emphasize the contributions of others, and seek them out. "For example, the CEO of Southwest Airlines goes to Employees (always capitalized at Southwest) if they will not come to him. It enables him to listen better."

- ✔ *Living the Values.* Organizations that embrace values that reward sensitivity to the needs of customers, employees, suppliers, and other important constituencies have special claims to success and longevity. "At ServiceMaster, senior executives work alongside employees of customers' organizations and engage in extensive outside charity work. At the Girl Scouts, the former executive director consistently used the same language to convey the mission and values of the organization, indicating to us that 'the power of language is so important in this job.'"

✔ *Ensuring Employee Capability.* The most important determinants of profit and growth are customer loyalty and satisfaction, factors that directly relate to employee satisfaction and the loyalty and productivity that go with it. Employees report that the capability to do their jobs is the most important determinant of their satisfaction. Capability is developed in many ways, including selection and assignment, training, technological support, and expert advice. "ServiceMaster spends several times more than its competitors to develop cleaning materials, equipment, and processes that ensure maximum productivity and quality in the work." "The Girl Scouts has sponsored what, by any measure, has to be one of the world's largest training programs in leadership outside of the military. With more than 750,000 volunteers, many of whom are leading for the first time, it considers leadership training the key to organizational and individual capability."

✔ *Defining, Shaping, and Using Core Values.* Although the need to define, shape, and use commonly held values of the organization is not new, the leaders Heskett and Schlesinger profile have rediscovered the usefulness of the process. They note, "It is all too rare today for values to be defined, shaped, communicated, and used, but this is always done in the organizations whose performance has caught our attention." They note that the CEO of Banc One "periodically validates the importance and communicates the elements of the Uncommon Partnership. The values underlying the Partnership are applied whenever each of Banc One's many acquisition prospects are evaluated; they must have integrity and the capability to manage themselves. At ServiceMaster, values are reviewed as part of the longer-range planning process every five years under the leadership of the CEO."

✔ *Power Through Dignity.* One source of the power of the leaders profiled is "the dignity they nurture in those around them and at all levels in their respective organizations." Their power lies in the areas of expertise outlined here: "use of language, listening skills, propagation of values, enhancement of employee capability, clarification of core values, and assurance of dignity." Finally, their power lies in "their ability to foster relationships."

Remaining Focused, Yet Fluid

A challenge for all mission-focused organizations is balancing a focus on the mission of the organization with a flexibility about the definition of that purpose. Maintaining this balance is a difficult process, and many organizations learn about it by straying too far in one direction or the other. The two extremes in this process of finding the correct attention to mission are sometimes defined as "mission rigidity," and "mission drift," or "mission creep." The chart below presents some of the characteristics of organizations at three points on this scale. In general, there is a rough relationship of the extent of entrepreneurial focus and these varying levels of mission dedication. Organizations on the left side of the chart would be less entrepreneurial, more focused on internal operations. Organizations on the right side would be more opportunity-focused, with less guidance from the mission.

Mission Rigidity	Mission Focus	Mission Drift or Creep
Mission is seen as an absolute (e.g., "eliminate hunger").	Mission is used daily as a guide.	Mission not used as daily discipline.
It is so difficult to attain that measurement and evaluation become impossible.	Leaders understand that mission can be changed, the periodic revisit of mission is an opportunity to make it more closely match customers and capabilities.	Opportunities pursued even if they do not further mission.
Focus is on maintaining and building existing efforts. New opportunities can be ignored.	Customers or others can understand the mission by observing the organization's actions.	Any attempt to understand mission from the organization's actions will yield a statement without focus.

EXHIBIT 2.4   Balancing focus with flexibility.

Entrepreneurial organizations may find themselves with "mission drift" after pursuing opportunities with funders or customers. For them, it is wise to ensure that the mission is revisited so that everyone understands the organization's reason for being. The mission *can be* changed during such a revisit. With a renewed sense of purpose, the entrepreneurial organization can free its people to explore opportunities that further the mission.

For organizations wishing to balance attention to opportunities and mission, it's best to understand that the organization's mission defines its purpose in terms of how it can change the lives of customers. The measure of changing those lives provides the guidance for leaders and organizations surrounded by opportunities. A relevant, vital mission provides the measure for what to say "no" to. At the same time, it shows when new opportunities are right, and when they will enable the organization to pursue a market or funding opportunity that furthers the mission and produces real results in the lives of customers.

THE DISCIPLINE OF REVISITING THE MISSION

The world changes. Customers find old services unnecessary and new ones more important. The technology that supports your work becomes more important, or its use by others becomes more frequent. The mission of a social sector organization is a critical part of its intentions and work. The mission does not, however, have to be written in stone, forever unchanging as the world and the organization's customers and environment change. Therefore, to keep the mission as the lever that enables leaders and organizations to change lives, the mission must be revisited with regularity. If the organization revisits its mission every three years, it can be sure that the critical decisions it makes based on its mission have a contemporary validity and are based not on tradition but on the needs and realities of today's customers and today's environment.

HOW TO REVISIT THE MISSION

When an organization decides to revisit the mission, it can use the previously described mission definition process, or it can use its own process to develop a mission that explains the purpose of the organization and guides the Board and staff as they further that purpose. The critical ingredients of this exploration are those presented in the first steps of the planning process: *environment, customers,* and *organization.* The organization must explore the changes and status of these components and determine whether its mission can be endorsed for the future or how it might be revised to more accurately meet new needs for customers and changes in the environment and the organization's capabilities.

MANAGING FOR THE MISSION

Incorporating mission into the everyday activities of everyone within the organization is one of the leader's most important challenges. The task of *managing for the mission* (to borrow Frances Hesselbein's term) can be made a regular, routine part of the organization's operations. This is when the mission truly makes a difference within the organization and, more important, with the customers. In everyday work, the mission should be a central idea. To make that possible (and practical), leaders must do the following:

- **Act consistently.** Consistency is seen in the leader's behavior and in its match against the organization's mission. Decisions and actions of the leader and the organization must be explained and understood as furthering the mission.

- **Communicate and share.** The leader's job is to share the mission and its relevance to the organization's work. Peter Drucker has noted that the only way we identify a leader is "someone with followers." Therefore, the leader must inspire and guide wise choices based on the mission. This means modeling the behavior: in conversation, weighing decisions against the mission, and asking, "does this further the mission?"

- **Establish the means to make the mission practical.** The organization must have systems for getting work done and for making clear the connection between mission and everyday decisions and tasks. One such approach is the planning process presented earlier.

Live Your Mission

Good intentions may have brought you into this world of social sector organizations. Your belief and commitment to a mission can keep you and the people and resources you need to coordinate going. Following are four action steps leaders can take to make the mission a more central part of the organization's life. Use them, modify them, expand them, and contract them. Take them as a capsule of the pervasive role of mission in the social sector organization, and *exploit* them so that your organization's mission can be furthered.

Share the mission—Make your mission available in your organization's communications. Give it a position of importance on your brochure. Make it prominent on your Website. Tell people you meet about the organization's mission. Ask them about their mission. Talk about the mission in your meetings with staff, funders, Board members, everyone.

Use the mission—Place the mission on your reports to the Board. Organize your planning documents to begin with mission. Use the mission in conversations with staff members. Make decisions with the mission as an important criterion.

Explore the mission—Keep the validity of today's mission an open topic for all of the constituencies you serve. Promote and share it, and keep your mind and ears open to others' thoughts about the mission and its relevance. Compare the mission to the opportunities presented to your organization every day. Revisit the mission regularly.

Celebrate the mission—The mission inspires those doing the critical work in your organization. Celebrate their accomplishments and the mission they are furthering. Keep yourself and everyone you work with "mission-focused" through reminders and appreciation. Acknowledge what the mission means to you.

SUMMARY: MISSION IN ACTION

For many people working in the social sector, mission comes naturally and explains the reason they show up. We come to our jobs with a belief in the purpose of the organization. For the leader of the social sector organization, the mission is even more important. Used wisely, the mission can be the foundation of an effort joining people and money to make significant changes in the lives of people. The mission can be used to attract resources, to develop strategies, and to inspire commitment from people.

A Group Approach to Defining Mission

tool of the trade   This approach is adapted from Gary J. Stern's Process Guide of *The Drucker Foundation Self-Assessment Tool.*[13] It employs a mission-writing group, has 10 steps, and uses a set of group and individual activities that conclude with presentation to the Board for approval. The 10 steps are as follows:

1. Establish a mission-writing group.
2. Adopt criteria for an effective mission statement; gather ideas and suggestions for first drafts.
3. Develop one or more draft statements.
4. Judge initial drafts against criteria and suggest revisions or new options.
5. Develop second drafts.
6. Gain feedback from outside the writing group.
7. Summarize feedback and distribute second drafts and a summary to the writing group.
8. Propose a draft mission statement or determine the next steps.
9. Gain preliminary endorsement of the proposed mission statement.
10. Present the proposed mission statement for Board approval.

This process can be followed as presented, or it can be adapted to better suit your project, organization, or opportunities. You may find that this process is too complex for your circumstances. If the full series of meetings and drafts is not required, feel free to shorten the process to the basics of *establishing criteria, drafting possibilities, gathering feedback,* and *approving a statement.* These steps help in the formation of any mission or purpose statement. Following is a detailed presentation of the 10 steps.

Step 1: Establish a mission-writing group

The task of the mission-writing group is to agree on a draft mission statement to be presented to the governing body for approval. Members of the group should include the chief executive, the Board chairman or another representative of the Board, a writer, and additional members who represent different parts of the organization and who are keen to participate. Having a facilitator is helpful and can be particularly beneficial if the facilitator is familiar with the organization, its customers, and work.

Step 2: Adopt criteria for an effective mission statement; gather ideas and suggestions for first drafts.
The "too many cooks spoil the broth" syndrome that besets so many writing groups is substantially solved by agreeing on a recipe in advance. Before a first meeting, group members should review the following criteria for an effective mission statement. (They can also review Peter Drucker's examination of mission in the *Self-Assessment Tool* Participant Workbook.[14]) At the first meeting, the writing group should post these criteria on a flip chart or chalkboard, review them, consider amendments, and adopt the criteria *they will use* to judge the effectiveness of the mission statement they are about to develop. The following criteria require the mission:

✔ Is short and sharply focused

✔ Is clear and easily understood

✔ Defines why we do what we do, why the organization exists

✔ Does not prescribe means

✔ Is sufficiently broad

✔ Provides direction for doing the right things

✔ Addresses our opportunities

✔ Matches our competence

✔ Inspires our commitment

✔ Says what, in the end, we want to be remembered for

After adopting the criteria, the group gathers ideas and suggestions for the mission statement. At this point, the group should develop the widest possible set of options without being overly critical of any ideas. An individual acting as the recorder or the facilitator notes the groups' responses. Idea-generating techniques include the following activities:

✔ Open brainstorming: any thought or idea is welcome

✔ Each group member finishes the sentence, "The mission should be . . ."

✔ Small teams "compete" in a very short time span to draft and nominate the "best" new mission statement

✔ Go around the group two or three times asking for the *one* word that *must* be in the mission statement

✔ Each person quickly draws a picture of the mission, then "shows and tells"

✔ Other techniques that suit the group

To conclude this step, the group completes the following tasks:

✔ Posts and reviews all ideas and suggestions. The facilitator draws a circle around the words or phrases that appear most often.

✔ Discusses key ideas or themes that must be captured in the new mission statement.

✔ Discusses key ideas or themes that must not be part of the new mission statement.

Step 3: Develop one or more draft statements.

After the meeting, the writer—either alone or with a small subgroup—develops drafts of at least *two* possible mission statements that are distributed to all members before the next meeting.

Step 4: Judge initial drafts against criteria and suggest revisions or new options.

The second meeting of the mission-writing group should begin with a discussion of the protocol (steps A–I as follows) that will be used to judge the drafts and make suggestions. People should also be encouraged to "listen between the lines." This step is highly structured, but often someone in a group offers a comment or phrase that turns out to be the perfect nugget on which to build the new mission statement. If the group has a "Eureka!" moment, go with it. To judge drafts and make suggestions, use the following protocol:

A. The group reviews the agreed-upon criteria for an effective mission statement.

B. The first-draft statement is posted on a flip chart or writing board at the front of the room.

C. Group members individually rate the draft (i.e., meets, meets somewhat, doesn't meet) for each criterion.

D. The facilitator polls and records the group's response for each criterion to determine the overall strengths and weaknesses of the mission draft.

E. The group first discusses the merits of the draft and then makes specific suggestions for how it might be improved.

Note: The group is not engaging in collective editing or rewriting. All suggestions—even if they contradict one another—are encouraged and recorded.

F. The second draft statement is posted, and steps C–E are repeated.

G. The group compares and contrasts its reactions to the two drafts.

H. The facilitator instructs each group member to be ready to write, then gives everyone two minutes to write his or her recommended mission statement at this point. At the end of the writing time, each member reads the statement aloud; the statements are collected and given to the writer.

I. The meeting concludes with discussion to determine:

✔ If the group believes it has developed an effective statement to put forward.

✔ Whether the writer should return a single modified draft or two options.

✔ What the writer should most keep in mind when developing the next draft(s).

✔ Who outside the group might be asked for feedback on the emerging statement or next draft(s).

✔ The scheduling of the group's next meeting.

Step 5: Develop second drafts.
After the meeting, the writer or subgroup develops a second draft of one or more new mission statements.

Step 6: Gain feedback from outside the writing group.
This step puts the emerging statement or draft(s) to the test by other members of the organization, customers, and funders. The Board chairman and chief executive decide who outside the writing group will be asked to give feedback. In some settings, organizationwide input is invited. In others, a smaller group of Board members and staff is selected. Gaining feedback from a few key individuals or groups outside the organization may also be valuable. The chief executive oversees the process of gaining feedback. If the Board chairman is not a member of the writing group, his or her feedback at this point is essential. Each individual or group being contacted for review is shown the criteria for an effective mission statement and asked for the following information:

A. A rating (i.e., meets, meets somewhat, doesn't meet) of each draft based on the criteria

B. Comments on the merits of the draft(s)

C. Ideas or recommendations for improvement

Step 7: Summarize feedback and distribute the second draft(s) and a summary to the writing group.
All members of the group receive summaries of the feedback of reviewers and the second draft(s) of the mission.

Step 8: Propose a draft mission statement or determine the next steps.
With some groups, the process of developing a mission statement flows with ease to a unanimous and enthusiastic conclusion. With most, however, the process proves to be demanding but worthwhile when a strong statement emerges. A few groups come to believe they have been given the riddle of the Sphinx.

Mission-writing groups may choose to propose more than one statement for the Board chairman or full Board to consider, may ask for a Board discussion to gain input and direction, or may simply go into another round of drafts and keep at it until the issue is resolved. If a group truly gets stuck, it may be helpful to let the task lie for awhile and come back to it or take the challenge to a specialist outside the organization and gain a completely fresh perspective. As Peter Drucker reminds us, "What counts is not the beauty of the mission statement. What counts is your performance." It may, in the end, be most preferable to suggest an interim statement and live with it for awhile before making a final decision.

At the third meeting, the writing group completes the following tasks:

A. Reviews the emerging statement or second draft(s).

B. Hears and discusses a summary of feedback from outside the writing group.

C. Again rates the draft(s) against criteria and cites merits and weaknesses.

D. Attempts group editing or rewriting if they agree that they are "close and it's worth a try."

E. Determines if they have a strong enough draft to propose for approval. If so, the group makes final suggestions for fine-tuning and approves its proposed mission statement. If not, the group sums up the status of the process and recommends the next steps.

Step 9: Gain preliminary endorsement of the proposed mission statement.
The Board chairman's preliminary endorsement is necessary before he or she presents a proposed mission statement to the full Board for approval. If the chairman was not a member of the writing group, this endorsement must be obtained.

Step 10: Present the proposed mission statement for Board approval.
The Board chairman presents the proposed mission statement as part of the organization's plan or as a separate item of business.

Endnotes

1. Frances Hesselbein, *Excellence in Nonprofit Leadership,* video program (San Francisco: Jossey-Bass, 1998).
2. Peter M. Senge, "The Practice of Innovation," in *Leader to Leader* (San Francisco: Jossey-Bass, 1999), p. 61–62.
3. Peter F. Drucker, *The Drucker Foundation Self-Assessment Tool: Participant Workbook* (San Francisco: Jossey-Bass, 1998), p. 15.
4. Peter F. Drucker, conversation with Frances Hesselbein, John Jacob, Richard F. Schubert, and author, 1992.
5. Peter F. Drucker, *The Drucker Foundation Self-Assessment Tool: Participant Workbook,* p. 22.
6. Richard Pascale and Anne Miller, "Acting Your Way into a New Way of Thinking," *Leader to Leader,* No. 9, Summer 1998, p. 43.
7. Jill Rosenfeld, "She's on a (Turnaround) Mission from God," *Fast Company,* May 2000, p. 34.
8. Peter F. Drucker, *Innovation and Entrepreneurship* (New York: HarperBusiness, 1985), p. 28.
9. Information list and data sources adapted from Gary J. Stern, *The Drucker Foundation Self-Assessment Tool: Process Guide* (San Francisco: Jossey-Bass, 1998), p. 34–35.
10. The customer research outline and two schools of thought taken from Gary J. Stern, *The Drucker Foundation Self-Assessment Tool: Process Guide,* p. 67–68.
11. Peter F. Drucker, *Innovation and Entrepreneurship,* p. 37.
12. James L. Heskett and Leonard A. Schlesinger, "Leaders who Shape and Keep Performance-oriented Culture," *The Leader of the Future.* (San Francisco: Jossey-Bass, 1995), p. 111–119.
13. Gary J. Stern, *The Drucker Foundation Self-Assessment Tool: Process Guide,* p. 133–139.
14. Peter F. Drucker, *The Drucker Foundation Self-Assessment Tool: Participant Workbook,* p. 14–16, 20.

Chapter 3

RECOGNIZING AND ASSESSING NEW OPPORTUNITIES

Jerry Kitzi, President, Social Venture Partners of Greater Kansas City

IN THIS CHAPTER

Opportunity recognition is a skill, not a character trait

Always on the lookout!

The value of a strategic plan

Assessing opportunities

Window of opportunity

One of the most important aspects of entrepreneurship is opportunity recognition. In its purest form, opportunity recognition for social entrepreneurs is about new or different ways to create or sustain social value.

Clarity of direction is fundamental for weighing opportunities that have the potential to contribute to organizational success. Without it, "mission drift" becomes a significant reality for organizations pursuing opportunities that represent potential revenue but that lead the organization down a different path than intended.

Ideas are always plentiful. Yet, it's unlikely that every exciting idea can be developed into an opportunity to create or sustain social value. Good opportunities are subject to timing issues. A window of opportunity is subject to changing environments and or human conditions just as it is in the for-profit sector. There is also the reality of running a social enterprise in this day and age, which requires an application of sound business skills and principles to sustain new and innovative programming.

Social entrepreneurs relentlessly pursue opportunities by applying both science and art to create or sustain social value. This chapter suggests different means for identifying opportunities and provides you with instruments to help assess their potential.

Opportunity Recognition Is a Skill, Not a Character Trait

The ability to recognize opportunity does not depend on personality type. Many people mistakenly believe that only the optimist can be a successful social entrepreneur, but that is not true!

Are character traits important? Absolutely. Numerous studies indicate common characteristics of successful entrepreneurs; however, just because you are a passionate, driven, hard-working, eternal optimist doesn't mean you have good opportunity-recognition skills. In fact, the opposite may be true.

Consider the advice of Jerr Boschee offered in *Merging Mission and Money: A Board Member's Guide to Social Entrepreneurship:*

> *"The first raw material for social entrepreneurs is candor, and it is probably the toughest challenge for any entrepreneur. Starting a new venture, or even an earned income strategy, is difficult enough without being honest about your product or service, your market, your competition, your resources, and numerous other factors that help determine success or failure. The mantra here is very simple: Beware of yourself."*[1]

With any new venture, there are difficult times, uncertainty, and disappointment. Optimism is very helpful. *"The relentless pursuit of opportunity"* necessitates a "can do" attitude against all odds, but optimism is not enough. Taking advantage of opportunities that contribute to organizational success is a skillful process that requires careful analysis, entrepreneurial instinct, and follow-through.

Always On The Lookout!

How many times have you thought of something that would make you rich? How many times have you thought of something that would change the world? How many times have you heard, "If I had a nickel for every idea I ever had, I'd be a rich man?" The point is that ideas are a dime a dozen, and an idea may or may not represent an opportunity. It all depends on what you see, when you see it, and how it relates to other conditions.

gem of wisdom

Several factors must be present to make an idea a true opportunity. Consider the advice of Jeffry Timmons in his book, *New Venture Creation: Entrepreneurship for the 21st Century:*

"While at the center of an opportunity is always an idea, not all ideas are opportunities. In understanding the difference between an opportunity and just another idea, you must understand that entrepreneurship is a market-driven process. An opportunity is attractive, durable and timely, and is anchored in a product or service that creates or adds value for its buyer or end-user."[2]

Certain conditions must exist to turn an idea into reality, and often the end result looks a lot different than the original idea. An idea for innovation in the way a service is delivered or a different location of a service might seem plausible at first glance. But it usually takes several trial-and-error applications of the basic assumptions that the new idea is based on in order to determine if the innovation is viable. The opportunity mindset for social entrepreneurs usually opts for refining an idea unless overwhelming negative factors suggest dumping the idea. Therefore, it is common for adjustments and assumptions that don't meet the challenge to be dismissed, further tested, and so on.

Brilliant ideas are just raw material that you have to work on to build your opportunity. Many ideas fall by the wayside, but some, on the other hand—combined with timing, demand, and other factors—have the potential to be life-changing opportunities.

INNOVATION

action step So where do you look and how do you train your mind? The common place to start looking is the work site—innovations in existing services and products. Try the following activities:

✔ *Look through a different lens.* Have you looked at the service from the eyes of the user? Are decisions about a service or product made by management or by the people closest to the service? Is a mechanism in place for regularly obtaining feedback from staff or volunteers?

✔ *Change the basic assumptions.* Are the basic assumptions, which were originally used to design the product or service, still practical in light of changing conditions? Does the current literature still support your assumptions about your customer or service?

✔ *Brainstorm with colleagues/competition.* What do providers offer in other communities locally and nationally? What do other organizations that are targeting your customers offer that is better and/or more effective? Could a partnership with another provider improve your service and increase your chances of achieving desired results?

✔ *Brainstorm with the customer.* Do you seek feedback from your customers? Are you asking the right questions? Are you listening to what they are saying, or are you hearing what you want to hear? Do you evaluate programs/services to determine if there is any change in behavior, condition, or level of satisfaction by the customer?

These techniques are not easy. If the only tool you have had to build a house is a hammer, then it's hard to imagine a different way of joining two boards. We get so deep into the routine task that we actually develop blinders to innovation. After all, we are creatures of habit. It's easy to stay the course behind the mantra, "If it ain't broke don't fix it." But it might be getting old, and it might have become less effective. It often takes an outside challenge or threat for us to think *innovation*.

NEW PATTERNS

Another approach is to use our experience to our advantage through what Herbert A. Simon, a professor at Carnegie-Mellon University, calls "pattern recognition"[3] in his working paper, "What We Know About the Creative Process." Simon believes that our own experiences over time allow us to see potential relationships or cross-associations. These "50,000 chunks" of experience, as Simon puts it, provide the entrepreneurial mind a way of seeing patterns or connections where others do not.

Have you or your staff recognized any unique patterns of use? Cyclical times of greater need? Age-dependent variables that prohibit participation? A simple Behaviorist rule of thumb is that past behavior is the best indicator of future behavior. Do your customers exhibit a pattern of behavior that you have not previously identified but that is now observable?

Have the demographics of your community changed? Is the community aging? Are young families of different races or ethnicities immigrating into your area? Are the typical indicators of economic conditions within the neighborhood changing—employers closing up business or moving out or into the community?

A community development corporation would want to track various housing trends in order to apply the most relevant strategies for changing conditions. Certain strategies are applicable when housing stock is declining and property values are falling—middle class flight—as compared to different strategies needed when property values are rising in poor neighborhoods through gentrification—poor people displacement.

NETWORKING

Martin Luther King, Jr. often said that his position of leadership in the civil rights movement was a matter of being in the right place at the right time. Many other successful social entrepreneurs and Fortune 500 CEOs refer to being in the right place at the right time as key to taking advantage of an opportunity that led to success. We all probably believe that to some degree, but are you satisfied with waiting for opportunity to knock on your door?

Being in the right place at the right time has more to do with the connections people make than their geographic position under the stars! The larger your network of colleagues, the greater your chances of hearing about new ideas or stumbling across an opportunity that presents itself during brainstorming sessions. Relationships do matter!

action step Join a coalition, a council, or another form of an alliance of people who are focused on an issue or issues that are relevant to your organization's mission. Coalitions, councils, networks, and so forth are the research and development area of the not-for-profit sector. This is especially true for communities that have learned the value of collaboration versus highly competitive, turf-conscious strategies where scarcity of resources is the norm.

Join membership organizations that have direct or indirect connections. Attend the trade shows of your industry, and develop relationships with your competitors. The more connections you make and the more people who know and understand your mission, the greater your chances of finding new opportunities.

UNINTENDED EVENTS

We all make assumptions about how future events will turn out, based on some current or past action—on our part, or on the part of others. If the action was intentional, then the reaction was probably anticipated—typically called a "plan." We try to predict what the result of the action will be based on some basic assumption.

This assumption often occurs in the idea-testing stage. And, as you can imagine, there are often unplanned reactions to a strategy. Some result that wasn't planned may actually have benefit or it may have consequence. It may have no relation to the original idea whatsoever, but it may actually represent potential. The *best* chance to identify opportunities with time for you to take advantage of the opportunity is in this area—*unplanned* benefits or consequences to some action.

This area is so exciting because entrepreneurs see these opportunities first. The social entrepreneur has developed a mindset that is constantly looking for opportunity in the middle of chaos or the innovation with real potential rising out of a catastrophe.

For example, the Internet was intended to bring about enormous changes in the exchange of information at home, in the office, or anywhere someone could get on the "information highway." It has presented enormous unintended benefits for entrepreneurs. In 1998, Internet sales totaled approximately $10.4 billion, and the number is expected to climb to $100 billion by 2003. Amazon.com, for example, generated $150 million in sales in three years with a Website and a warehouse. It took Sam Walton and Wal-Mart 12 years and 78 stores to reach $150 million in annual sales. (However, amazon.com has yet to turn a profit.)

The Internet also had numerous unintended consequences—viruses, for example, and jammers who saw an opportunity to cause havoc for millions of customers. When the Internet was designed, no one anticipated this phenomenon, but once it occurred, the market was wide open for antivirus software development companies.

CASE STUDY

CyberAngels—An Internet Case Study of Social Entrepreneurship

Chat rooms were designed to increase communication opportunities for everyone who had access. One unintended consequence was the emergence of predators who roamed chat rooms looking for vulnerable and naïve youth. A recent Time/CNN survey projected approximately 14 million youth logging onto the Internet by the beginning of the 21st century. Another consequence of the Internet was the proliferation of pornography. It is now suggested that pornography-related Websites are popping up at the rate of approximately 1,000 per month—serious unintended social consequences!

However, several social entrepreneurs have formed social enterprises or reinvented themselves to address these concerns. CyberAngels is an organization with an army of volunteers patrolling Websites and chat rooms, looking for predators and other abuses of the Internet, such as illegal child pornography. This group has also developed curriculum for schools, provides consulting services, and is now developing a Cyber-911 number to help quickly identify predators and other Internet violators.

The social entrepreneurs who reinvented themselves in light of this opportunity are the Guardian Angels. The same group that had a mission of making the streets safer is now making cyberspace safer. According to Curtis Sliwa, the founder of Guardian Angels and founder of CyberAngels, the group simply responded to a terrible social challenge that fell within their view of their mission. A caller to Sliwa's radio show in New York actually made him aware that there was another street out there he could make safe—the information highway!

Referrals from CyberAngels, working in cooperation with the U.S. Customs' Cyber-smuggling Unit and the FBI Innocent Images Unit, have led to an increasing number of arrests and convictions.

Opportunities are ever present and there for the taking. It's simply a matter of seeing them and seizing them. Innovation in existing services or products represents the most common and practical place to look, but it does require looking and listening. Looking for new trends or new patterns of behavior that emerge from changes in public policy, economic conditions, or technology is another fruitful place to pick up on new opportunities for social benefit. Likewise, imagine what's possible when reviewing the unintended results of new changes in public policy, economic conditions, or technology. Lastly, get out there and network—relationships matter!

THE VALUE OF A STRATEGIC PLAN

Clarity of direction in the not-for-profit sector is just as critical for success as it is in the for-profit sector. Without it, focus and a clear sense of purpose for those connected to the organization will slowly wither, along with any chances for success. Therefore, a strategic plan can be the unifying document—the compass or roadmap for the organization. A compelling vision, well-articulated mission, and clearly stated desired results and strategies to achieve them are fundamental components of a good strategic plan.

The following three issues are related to the value of a strategic plan as a general resource for screening opportunities:

1. The plan can help you screen out opportunities that may seem exciting but that can lead to "mission drift"—getting unfocused.
2. It can refocus you on where to spend your time and energy if you were adrift.
3. It helps you keep your eyes on the horizon in order to anticipate tomorrow's opportunities.

Not all businesses should do strategic planning because it is usually a function of established, growing concerns. Startups are engaged in startup-related functions and operations issues. That's not to say the future can wait, but the immediate future and making payroll at the end of the month is usually more pressing. The initial work that involved the creation of a vision statement and mission statement for the incorporation usually carries the day during the startup phase.

On the other hand, growing concerns have mastered the day-to-day operations and need to consistently look outward—examining their environment—and inward—examining their ability to deliver a quality service or product. Strategic planning creates the opportunity for the social entrepreneur and Board to get "outside the box" of day-to-day operation. Unfortunately, many organizations balk at the notion of a five- or ten-year plan because they are afraid of being tied down in a changing world. Or others use strategic planning to stay inside the box—a process to stay the course despite changing conditions.

We live in a rapidly changing world. But with the exception of environmental disasters, war, or market plunges (all three represent fertile fields for social entrepreneurs), most changes that occur in the lives of everyday citizens are discussed in public debate for an extended time. Significant public policy changes at the federal, state, or local level get scrutinized in the media in time for you and your Board to incorporate them into your planning processes. It is important to note that all kinds of recommendations come from all kinds of sources about how to plan and how often you engage in a planning process. It's not so much choosing the perfect tools as it is committing to a planning process and doing it well.

 Consider the advice of Peter C. Brinckerhoff, President and CEO of Corporate Alternatives and author of *Mission-Based Management—Leading Your Not-for-Profit into the 21st Century*:

"Good Plans actually help you remain flexible . . . they keep you and your organization focused on what is important, and assist you in not wasting resources, not getting tied down in fruitless or out-of-date services, and keeping your staff and board up-to-date on the realities of the world that you are working in."[4]

TRENDS IN STRATEGIC PLANNING

John Deadwyler, President of Benard Consulting Group and adjunct professor in the Henry Bloch School of Business and Public Administration at the University of Missouri Kansas City, provides strategic planning services to both for-profit and not-for-profit businesses. John has seen a tremendous shift over the last five years within the not-for-profit sector in relation to strategic planning. "The days of pokin' and hopin' are over," says John. Nearly 40% of Benard Consulting Group's clients receiving strategic planning support are not-for-profits. John cites the following four changes that have brought about this shift.

1. *The influence of business practices.* Executives and their Boards are thinking and behaving more entrepreneurially. In the past, suggesting the terms *entrepreneur* and *not-for-profit* in the same sentence was creating an oxymoron. Today, more social entrepreneurs realize that sound business practices are essential in a competitive environment to sustain the social value created by the business. Therefore, the bar has been raised. Board members and executive leadership of organizations from large health care corporations to

grassroots community development corporations are using strategic planning to set direction and position their organizations to take advantage of opportunities created in the marketplace.

2. *Changes in funder expectations.* Traditional funding sources like government and philanthropy have placed greater emphasis on strategic plans. Beginning in the Reagan era of government cutbacks, through the growth of foundations headed by successful entrepreneurs, to today's emphasis on "Outcomes" by United Way agencies across the country, planning is now a necessity. Quite simply, the funding community for the not-for-profit sector has increased the pressure for clear statements of vision and mission, the evidence of a plan to get there, and ways to show results.

3. *Competitive advantage.* Many not-for-profits believe that the existence of a strategic plan creates a competitive advantage. The presence of a plan creates an opportunity for the organization to market itself, not just the services or products provided, but also the businesslike nature of the organization.

4. *Organization decline.* Finally, many not-for-profits try to engage in strategic planning exercises out of a sense of futility because their organization is in a state of decline or flux and they believe they need a plan to right themselves. "These organizations are not in need of a new plan, but instead are often times in some deep OD doo doo—low trust, negative culture, split board, etc. Strategic planning in these circumstances is doomed to failure and a total waste of time and resources," according to Deadwyler.[5]

Strategic planning creates a broad directional framework for the organization. It provides the first general screen for considering opportunities or new direction for the organization. It is fundamental to good business practice and may also provide advantages to fund development in a highly competitive market.

ASSESSING OPPORTUNITIES

Assessing opportunities is a blended process of data collection and gut instinct. It is both a science and an art. Too much dependence on one or the other can lead to failure. Going on gut instinct without collecting enough information about market potential, achievable results, or sustainability can be hazardous to organizational health. Likewise, spending too much time collecting data can lead to "analysis paralysis." Or it can become cost prohibitive and/or cause delays in startup that reduce or eliminate potential competitive advantage. Be clear about how much

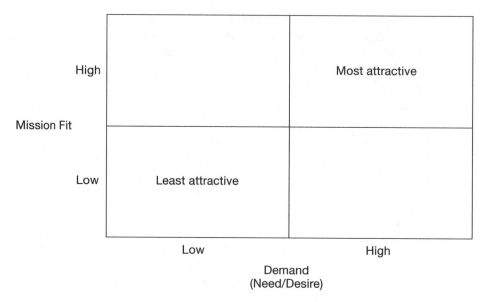

EXHIBIT 3.1   Opportunity assessment: quick guide.

information you and/or the Board may need to move forward. That may vary depending on the scale and scope of the opportunity you are assessing (see Exhibit 3.1).

Demand

A simple assessment can be used when first considering a new opportunity. Is there demand? Does this opportunity address a social need, and is there some evidence of desire on the part of the target population to use the service? For example, a youth-serving organization is considering adding a stop-smoking program to its afterschool services. Cigarette smoking by youth is on the increase and is well documented; however, according to numerous prevention studies, youth are not inclined to participate in smoking-cessation programs. The smoking-cessation program does address a serious social need, but it may not represent a good opportunity because the target population has little desire to use the service; therefore, it gets a *low* score on the scale.

Mission fit

Does it fit with the mission? An adolescent pregnancy organization is also concerned about the increase in cigarette smoking, especially among pregnant teens. Cigarette smoking during pregnancy is a high risk factor for poor pregnancy outcomes. Would the smoking-cessation program be a fit? It would rate a *low* score if the mission and primary purpose were to prevent pregnancy, but the program may rate a *high* score if the mission and purpose included positive pregnancy outcomes.

Once determined to be an idea worth pursuing, a more formal assessment model should be used. Keep in mind that new ventures are filled with unknowns, and any idea in its current state may appear to have less potential than it might otherwise have after testing, refinement, and alteration, or adequate information may not be available when first considering the potential.

OPPORTUNITY ASSESSMENT MODEL

William D. Bygrave, in his book *The Portable MBA in Entrepreneurship,*[6] provides a wonderful tool for evaluating opportunities for new businesses. He analyzes certain criteria within a context of varying degrees of potential for success. The same kind of model can be used in the nonprofit sector, although the criteria are much more specific to the social value and sustainability issues and conditions inherent in this work.

tool of the trade   Analyze the opportunity you are considering using the framework provided as follows:

SOCIAL VALUE POTENTIAL

Value Added	High		Low
Strategic Alignment	Service/product creates social value that is aligned with the mission	⟺	Service/product creates social value but is loosely or indirectly aligned with the mission
Achievable Outcomes	Service/product will create a significant change in user behavior, condition, or level of satisfaction	⟺	Service/product will create minimal change in user behavior, condition, or level of satisfaction or indirectly linked to changes
Partnership and/or Alliance	Additional partnership(s) would have a synergistic effect and improve or increase chances for desired results—social value	⟺	Service/product has minimal change potential and would not benefit by a partnership or alliance strategy
Organizational Benefit	Successful service/product will increase or create positive community perception of and/or political support for the organization	⟺	Unsuccessful service/product will have negative effect on community perception and/or political support for the organization

MARKET POTENTIAL

Demand	High		Low
User Need	Evidence of social need and an open window of opportunity	⟺	No data or other evidence of social need or a closing window of opportunity
User Desire	Evidence of user interest or evidence of success of similar services in other communities	⟺	No data or other evidence of user interest available, declining participation in services in other communities
Funder Interest	Evidence of interest, or noticeable trends in grant making or government contracts for similar service	⟺	No data or other evidence or findings of interest for similar services
Market Share	Evidence of an open market with little competition	⟺	Evidence of highly competitive market or no data or other evidence of competition's interest or involvement in the market

SUSTAINABILITY POTENTIAL

Capital Needs	High		Low
Idea Development	Research and development resources are available or easily accessible	⟺	No funding or staff time available or readily accessible
Startup	Low cost of startup and/or easily accessible funding for startup	⟺	High cost of startup and/or scarcity of available resources or interest
Cost-to-Benefit Ratio	Low total program costs compared against high public benefit	⟺	High total costs compared against low to marginal public benefit
Organizational Capability	Board, staff, or volunteer capability is present and aligned with potential service or project	⟺	Absence of capability among existing Board, staff, or volunteers
Income Potential	Target population with discretionary income potential and/or evidence of ability/ desire to pay fees	⟺	Target population has little discretionary income or evidence of ability/desire to pay minimal fees
Organizational Capacity	Internal structures, space, technology, etc. are in order or easily adjusted for new services or expansion of services	⟺	Internal structures are limited or in need of substantial upgrade to support presenting opportunity
Funder Interest	Trends or other evidence of funder interest for three- to five-year horizon	⟺	Funder interest unknown or evidence of declining interest over the last three to five years

Social Value Potential

The for-profit market does an extremely good job of weeding out services or products that do not produce value for the customer. There is no such comparable market test or comparable return ratios for benevolence or social benefit in the not-for-profit sector. Preventing the spread of AIDS, preventing water pollution, providing care to the indigent and elderly, or providing quality Head Start experiences for children living in poverty all may have significant social value; however, one enterprise may have extremely high social value to one investor and yet may be considered a total waste of money by another.

Successful social entrepreneurs are good at assessing the value of an opportunity in their area of expertise. They know their customers, both in terms of those who consume the service or product—those who benefit—and those who purchase or invest in the service or product to create a benefit for those in need. As you consider this tool, also place the perceived social value along a continuum from extremely high social value to low or minimal social value.

- ✔ *Strategic alignment.* Does the presenting opportunity fit with the current mission statement? Using the previous CyberAngels example, the mission of the Alliance of Guardian Angels focused on keeping streets safe for children, youth, and families. Did it represent an opportunity to create or sustain social value? Was the information highway really a fit with keeping streets safe? Determine where your idea fits along the continuum of strategic alignment.

- ✔ *Achievable outcomes or desired results.* Does the service or product have the potential to produce the desired change in behavior, condition, or level of satisfaction of the user? If the intended outcome of the smoking-cessation program mentioned previously is to have stopped smoking and the service is geared strictly to an education strategy for youth, then, according to prevention studies, it is less likely to achieve desired results. (low potential)

- ✔ *Value-added partnerships/alliance.* Would a partner(s) or strategic alliance have a synergistic effect on the service or product and improve or increase chances for achieving desired results? For example, the smoking-cessation education program forms a partnership with a pharmaceutical company for product donation— nicotine patches. The education strategy alone would have low to marginal results, according to recent findings; however, the partnership with the pharmaceutical company and inclusion of product donation with education increases the chances for achieving desired results. (high potential). This category can also be considered when assessing the sustainability potential.

Would a partnership create desired results and actually lower costs and/or increase the likelihood of sustainability?

✔ *Organizational benefit.* Does the service or product contribute to community acceptance and/or political support of the organization? A new service that provides positive results in the community actually improves the acceptance level among users, funders, or other political (small "p") supporters, which, in turn, improves or increases acceptance or participation in other programmatic efforts, thereby increasing the social value of the organization. As mentioned earlier, the increased perception of value for the organization increases the sustainability potential!

Market Potential

Despite the positive indicators of a healthy and growing economy that defined the human condition at the close of the 20th century in the United States, social need still far exceeded supply. The independent sector grew from approximately 276,000 not-for-profits in 1976 to more than 650,000 by the end of the century. These not-for-profits have an estimated $500 billion in revenue and represent about 6 percent of the nation's economic output. Since 1970, the sector has grown four times as fast as the national economy. Yet, need still far exceeds supply, and competition for resources and customers is fierce.

This section of the instrument is designed to help you assess the position of the opportunity in terms of meeting market demand for both customers (the user of services) and funders (the purchaser of services).

✔ *User need.* Is there evidence of need and/or an open(ing) window of opportunity in relation to the recognized need? In the CyberAngels example, the projected numbers of youth logging onto the Internet was enormous. When combined with the huge increase in the number of new porn sites starting each month and increasing numbers of reports of adult predators in chat rooms, real need with an opening window was the resulting assessment. (high potential)

✔ *User desire.* Is there evidence of user interest in the service or product or evidence of user interest shown by rates of participation in similar services in other communities that have reasonably close demographics/conditions? There may be a real social need but little desire to access services by the user. Homelessness is a serious social issue. Yet, there is less desire for shelter assistance by young homeless males. (low potential) However, shelter assistance for homeless women with children has been on the rise, especially for victims of domestic violence. (high potential)

✔ *Funder interest.* Is there evidence of interest within philanthropic circles (e.g., foundations, corporate giving programs, United Way)?

Is there an increase in contract services offered by local, state, or federal government agencies? Reproductive services for low-income women are a well-documented need with user desire for services. Yet many potential funders shy away from participating in such an emotionally charged social issue. The government refused to intervene, and foundations were unaware of the social need in the case of CyberAngels. It took great personal sacrifice by the executive Parry Afrat and her volunteers to launch the project. (low potential—but they did it anyway!)

✔ *Market share.* Assuming such things as evidence of need, desire, and funder interest, is there evidence of potential market share? Is the market crowded with competitors? Is there enough room for entry at a level that can justify capital expense? For example, is there room for another provider of leadership development services for youth in a community that has well-established scouting, campfire, 4H, and YMCA services? The answer could be "yes" depending on levels of use and target population numbers. Or your innovation could lure away customers if your marketing plan and services demand. Determine what your niche is and its potential compared to others already in the field.

Sustainability Potential

Unless capitalized by a substantial endowment, most not-for-profits face the issue of sustainability on a day-to-day basis. The soft money that typifies the sector is subject to constantly changing conditions such as shifts in political winds, fluctuations in quarterly earnings for corporate donors, or economic downturns that tighten up discretionary funds that customers might be spending in full or in part for your service or product.

An opportunity might have high social value potential but very low sustainability potential at point of assessment; however, it could gain feasibility over time as conditions change or resources become accessible from different investors or your own budget shifts.

Tension will always exist between pursuing opportunities that provide resources to sustain the enterprise and pursuing opportunities that create social value but don't come with substantial sources of revenue to cover costs. Not-for-profits rarely have a research and development budget!

✔ *Idea development.* Do you have the resources to invest in the first phase of service/product development? Do you have staff time you can carve away from existing work to develop the idea? Do you have the resources, or will you need to bring in technical assistance/consultation; travel to observe similar services in other communities; obtain staff training, curriculum development, focus group testing, and so on? Do you have potential funding sources that will let you include these costs for idea development in a proposal for service or program implementation?

✔ *Startup.* Are the capital needs for startup cost prohibitive? Can existing staff, technology, facilities, equipment, and so forth be used for startup? Can other partners' facilities be used? Can contract staff be used or are full-time FTEs needed? Will potential funders raise concern about proposed costs?

✔ *Cost-to-benefit ratio.* What is the ratio between the cost to deliver the service to one client and the value of the desired outcome? Youth Build USA is a youth development program that has a per-client cost of about $20,000. Scouting has an average per-client cost of less than $1,000 with most of that expense covered by fees. Both have excellent outcomes in terms of value to the participant and community perception of the public benefit. Who doesn't stop and take notice of an Eagle Scout? It would seem obvious that the more efficient program according to the ratio— $1,000 for high social value versus $20,000 for high social value— would be scouting. Yet, the target population for Youth Build USA is very high-risk youth, typically school dropouts who have had brushes with the juvenile justice system. Predictable outcomes for this population are a life of unemployment and periodic incarceration. The typical prison cost of one inmate per year can range from $25,000 to $40,000, depending on the type of detention facility and location. Not to mention the loss of productivity and taxable income. Is a $20,000 investment that produces educated, well-trained, determined young people prepared for a productive life worth the program cost when compared to the loss of meaningful life expectancy and high public costs for incarnation? (high potential)

✔ *Organizational capability.* Does your organization have the existing human resources to pursue this opportunity? Will the new opportunity require new staff/volunteers with different expertise or extensive training for existing staff/volunteers in a new content area? Does the new opportunity create a significant lag time before human resources are ready to provide the services or product? Could a partnership(s) with other organizations with existing capability reduce your costs while providing desired results?

✔ *Organizational capacity.* Does your organization have the capacity to launch the new program or service? Does it require additional technology, space, a financial accounting system (patient billing, for example), transportation needs, and the like? Will funds be easily accessible if these needs are significant? Would a partnership(s) resolve capacity needs?

✔ *Income potential.* Does the program or service have the potential to generate revenue from the client/customer? Is there sufficient need and desire combined with some degree of discretionary income that could generate some fees based on a sliding fee structure? The not-for-profit sector is usually the delivery system of last resort; however more foundations and corporate giving programs are pressuring for service- or program-related income, even minimal amounts, before a grant will be considered. Keeping in mind that the greater the existence of income potential, the greater the involvement of for-profit enterprises competing for the same client. The client may have zero income and no means whatsoever to pay a service fee. In that case, the potential for this factor would be low. Keep in mind that the assessment rating for this factor does not mean that the opportunity should be disregarded!

✔ *Funder interest.* Is there evidence of funder interest—existing grants or contracts for similar services? Ultimately, foundations, United Ways, government, corporate giving programs, and others will ask the sustainability question, "How will this program/service be sustained beyond our three-year grant?" Many executives consider this question to be unanswerable and—based on the realities of soft money in the sector—irrelevant. Yet, it is always asked. In the absence of program or service endowments, or government contracts, there are few options for addressing long-term sustainability potential.

Does your research indicate movement by foundations making grants in areas related to this opportunity? In the CyberAngels example, the social need was growing rapidly but there was little, if any, recognition by foundations or other charitable funding sources. Again, a low potential rating in the absence of funder interest.

This tool could be helpful as long as you recognize that assessment is an imprecise, ongoing process that includes judgment calls and refinement along the way. Assessment isn't a simple "either/or" decision. Using an assessment tool will provide you a picture of how the opportunity lines up in terms of low to high potential, but it will not provide you with a scientific formula for success. Says Jerr Boschee:

> *"It takes a genuine entrepreneur to act despite the absence of certainty. Wanna-be entrepreneurs want to wait until they have the perfect plan. But a pretty good plan executed with passion today will always defeat a perfect plan tomorrow. (Primarily because there is no such thing as a perfect plan.)"*[7]

The assessment instrument can also be used to analyze existing services or programs to gauge whether or not it is time to discontinue a service or program in light of other presenting opportunities. An assessment can help you identify low hanging fruit as well as recognize the time to harvest existing fruit before it dies on the vine.

WINDOW OF OPPORTUNITY

Opportunities have a shelf life. The key is to determine the position of the window related to the opportunity that presents itself. The highest potential is when the window is first opening. An established market that appears to have longevity is good as well. Estimating how long the window stays open is more of an art form because it is subject to any combination of changing factors, such as economic conditions, political change, customer desire, and so forth.

Therefore, a critical issue becomes your speed of response to the position of the window. The market has no interest in waiting for special people. The most mission-minded, passionate people with great ideas will be left in the lurch if they can't plan quickly, marshal resources, or train staff before the factors that influence the window changes.

In his book *New Venture Creation: Entrepreneurship for the 21st Century*, Jeffry Timmons discusses the importance of seizing an opportunity while the window of opportunity in the marketplace is opening. He offers the following analogy:

gem of wisdom

> *"Another way to think of the process of creating and seizing an opportunity in real time is to think of it as a process of selecting objects (opportunities) from a conveyor belt moving through an open window (window of opportunity). The speed of the conveyor belt changes, and the window through which it moves is constantly opening and closing. That the window is continually opening and closing and that the speed of the conveyor belt is constantly changing represent the volatile nature of the marketplace and the importance of timing. For an opportunity to be created and seized, it needs to be selected from the conveyor belt before the window closes."*[8]

Numerous conditions affect the window of opportunity. Demand may be high and market conditions wide open, but the window may still be closed if there is absolutely no chance for launch or sustainability. Some windows may be engineered, as in the case of a substantial request for proposal (RFP) by a large philanthropy or government agency. And despite the abundance of knowledge and resources available in this country, the human condition is still fragile, and a window of opportunity for services or products that create public benefit may stay open for many years. Get a clear picture of where the opportunity presents itself in the broader terms of the window. Timing is a critical criterion for success.

SUMMARY

Opportunities give organizations direction, and they help to create or sustain social value. Good opportunities, however, are subject to all sorts of issues, including timing, changing environments, and human conditions. The ability to recognize and then pursue opportunities is a critical skill for success in the world of nonprofit organizations. In this chapter, we considered the ability to recognize opportunities and how to keep your eyes open to all possibilities. We considered the value of developing a strategic plan and the best ways to assess opportunities. Finally, we examined recognizing windows of opportunity and how to take advantage of them before they go away.

Key points to remember are the following:

✔ Optimism is not enough.

✔ Think innovation in existing services or products.

✔ Recognize trends and new patterns of behavior.

✔ Know that there is opportunity in chaos or catastrophe.

✔ Relationships matter—make others aware of who you are and what you are trying to accomplish—Network!

✔ A great idea may or may not represent a good opportunity.

✔ Assessment is an imprecise, ongoing process that includes judgment calls and creative refinement of the idea along the way.

✔ A budget is just a planning document; pursue opportunities without being limited by resources currently in hand.

✔ Opportunity recognition is both a science and an art. Collect the right amount of information relevant to the size, scope, and time available. But ultimately, gut instincts must weigh heavily in any decision-making process.

✔ The amount of human and financial resources that go into answering assessment questions should depend on the level of commitment required to move forward.

✔ A clear understanding of the position of the window of opportunity is necessary before taking action because timing is everything!

Endnotes

1. Jerr Boschee, "Merging Mission and Money: A Board member's Guide to Social Entrepreneurship," (Washington, DC: National Center for Nonprofit Boards, 1998), p. 9.
2. Jeffry A. Timmons, *New Venture Creation: Entrepreneurship for the 21st Century,* (New York: Irwin McGraw-Hill, 1994), p. 20.
3. Herbert A. Simon, "What We Know About the Creative Process," (Carnegie-Mellon, PA: Carnegie-Mellon University, 1984).

4. Peter C. Brinckerhoff, *Mission-Based Management: Leading Your Not-For-Profit into the 21st Century,* (New York: John Wiley & Sons, 1994), p. 132.

5. Interview with John Deadwyler, President, Bernard Consulting Group (1999).

6. William D. Bygrave, *The Portable MBA in Entrepreneurship* (John Wiley & Sons, 1994), p. 34.

7. Jerr Boschee, "Merging Mission and Money: A Board Member's Guide to Social Entrepreneurship," (Washington, DC: *National Center for Nonprofit Boards,* 1998), p. 16.

8. Jeffry A. Timmons, *New Venture Creation: Entrepreneurship for the 21st Century,* (New York: McGraw-Hill, 1994), p. 90.

Chapter 4

MOBILIZING RESOURCES

J. Gregory Dees, Miriam and Peter Haas Centennial Professor in Public Service, and co-director of the Center for Social Innovation, Stanford University, Graduate School of Business

IN THIS CHAPTER

It's not just about the money

Assess your resource needs—entrepreneurially

Ten tips for reducing your initial cash needs

Develop your resource mobilization strategy

Entrepreneurs, by our definition, boldly pursue opportunities without being limited by the resources currently in hand. To succeed in doing this, they must be resourceful, meaning that they find ways to do more with less, and persuade others to provide resources on favorable terms. This chapter introduces you to the entrepreneurial art of resourcefulness and gives you the tools needed to improve your resource- mobilization skills on both of these dimensions.

IT'S NOT JUST ABOUT THE MONEY

When you think about resources, fundraising may be the first thing that comes to mind. If so, think again! Raising money is important, but if you start by focusing on money, you will miss key factors that are even more important for long-term success. Money is only a means to an end. It lies in the middle of a process that begins with your idea, as well as the intangible resources you bring to your venture, and ends with the capabilities you need to deliver your social results.

✔ *It's not what you own that counts, but what you can do or get done.* At its heart, entrepreneurship is about getting things done or changing the way things are done. It's *not* about amassing assets. Cash is simply a tool for helping you develop the *capabilities* you need in order to create the social value that lies at the heart of your mission.

✔ *Value-producing capabilities are a function of many factors.* Money is not the only tool necessary to create social value. Skills, relationships, knowledge, integrity, and reputation are but a few of the intangible factors that are also needed for success. Money can help you attract people with skills, knowledge, relationships, and reputations, but it is not sufficient to ensure that they will employ their human capital effectively and creatively in pursuit of your mission. A shared commitment to your mission can be much more important than money in motivating your team to do what it takes to produce results.

✔ *It's easier to turn intangible resources into money than money into intangible resources.* Every social entrepreneur starts with a stock of intangible resources, including an idea, relevant knowledge, experience, relationships, reputation, passion, and commitment. These resources are used to attract the money and the other resources needed to get the venture off the ground. Savvy social entrepreneurs know how to convert their intangible resources into results, using as little money as necessary.

Assess Your Resource Needs—Entrepreneurially

This section walks you through a four-phase decision-making process for assessing your resource needs. This process forces you to think carefully and creatively about just how you intend to pursue the opportunity that you see. To be *entrepreneurial* about this, you need to adopt the following approach:

✔ Start with the result you want to produce, not the limited resources you have in hand.

✔ Consider less resource-intensive ways of achieving these results.

✔ Take into account the uncertainty that surrounds your venture.

This process is a useful preliminary exercise for developing your full-fledged enterprise plan. The four phases are driven by the result you want to create (see Exhibit 4.1).

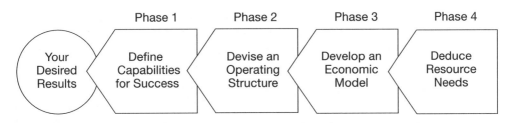

EXHIBIT 4.1   Four phases of an entrepreneurial resource assessment.

Phase 1: Define the capabilities required for success

This first phase involves visualizing your desired results and defining the capabilities needed to produce them. Based on your mission (Chapter 2) and the way you've defined your opportunity (Chapter 3), you should have a specific idea of the way in which your venture will create its social value. This idea can be used to determine the things you'll need to do (or get others to do). Visualize your desired outcomes—the creation of value to your target audience—and then list all of the steps required to create this value, until you come to inputs that can be easily purchased on the open market. For each step, describe the capabilities required to complete it successfully. Because most social ventures are service organizations, key steps are likely to include program or service development, marketing, service delivery, and follow-up or assessment. Each may involve different components. Once you've identified the key steps in your social value creation process, add the administrative capabilities that support this process.

action step   Create the list of required capabilities for your new venture. Then challenge a knowledgeable friend, advisor, or teammate to find anything that is missing from your list.

Phase 2: Devise a resource-smart operating structure

Now you can start to get creative. Building on your list of required capabilities, you need to devise a resource-smart operating structure, which is determined by your answers to the following questions:

1. Which capabilities will you develop in your own organization?
2. Which capabilities will you get from suppliers or contractors?
3. Which capabilities will be delivered by partners?

CASE STUDY

STEVE MARIOTTI AND NFTE

Steve Mariotti founded the National Foundation for Teaching Entrepreneurship (NFTE) in 1987.[1] Mariotti was an entrepreneur-turned-teacher in the New York City public school system, where he found that teaching at-risk students how to start their own businesses got them interested in learning and gave them hope. Mariotti saw an opportunity to promote entrepreneurial literacy among at-risk youth by teaching courses on this topic using a curriculum similar to the one he developed in the public schools. Armed with this idea, Mariotti could identify all of the capabilities needed for his new venture to be a success. At a general level, for NFTE to be successful, someone would have to perform the following steps:

- ✔ Recruit at-risk youth for the program
- ✔ Provide a suitable teaching environment
- ✔ Teach the course
- ✔ Select and train teachers
- ✔ Develop an effective curriculum
- ✔ Supply the materials for delivering the curriculum effectively
- ✔ Provide funds or in-kind support to help participants start their businesses
- ✔ Assess program performance and revise as needed
- ✔ Provide administrative support (accounting, purchasing, fundraising, etc.)

A resource-smart structure allows you to create and sustain social value while making efficient use of scarce resources. This does not mean always looking for the cheapest way to do things because the cheapest way could undermine the quality of your programs. You want to balance results with efficiency. The key is finding a structure that creates the value you desire, that fits with your strengths and market realities, and that makes wise use of scarce resources. Keep in mind that "Many roads lead to Rome."

Imagine Different Operating Structures

The first step is to imagine the range of possibilities. This can be done by going through the list of required capabilities and asking yourself: Could this capability be delivered by someone else? If so, who would that be and how would it work? Not all possible combinations are worth exploring, but it is helpful to consider seriously a few combinations that you didn't have in mind when you started. Many social entrepreneurs begin

Consider the range of NFTE's options. At one extreme, NFTE could do it all in-house—set up its own learning centers in inner cities, market to potential students or their parents, develop the curriculum, and hire and train teachers. This approach would be resource-intensive. At the other extreme, NFTE could focus on only one element, for example, curriculum development—just writing and packaging lesson plans for teachers. NFTE could find a sales representative or publisher to market the curriculum. This approach would require far fewer resources, but would it be effective in serving NFTE's mission? In addition to these extremes, NFTE had several other options. As a thought experiment, identify at least three other possible operating structures for NFTE.

with a preconceived idea of how their organizations will work. This exercise may make you aware of new options.

Pick a Structure That Is Both Promising and Efficient

Now that you see the different roads, how do you decide which one to take? In advance of doing it, you may not know which structure would be optimal, but you can make a judgment call. The following four questions should help you select a structure that is resource-smart:

1. *Which capabilities are you particularly well suited to provide—your strengths?* Most social entrepreneurs bring distinctive capabilities to their ventures, things that they do particularly well. What capabilities do *you* bring to this venture? Can you really do these things better than or more efficiently than others who are already out there? How do you know this? It makes sense for you to do the things you do best relative to other potential providers. If you are starting this venture with a partner, you can ask the same question of the partner.

2. *Which capabilities are most crucial to the value-creation process?* Some capabilities are likely to be more crucial than others, in that they have the potential for a disproportionate effect on the value created. To identify potential core capabilities, ask yourself: Is this an area in which errors are likely to be made without close attention to quality? If errors are made, how much damage will they do? You should be highly cautious about contracting out any functions for which you are vulnerable to costly errors. What if you find that some functions are core to the venture, but you're not particularly good at them? You have two choices: (1) you can do what it takes to build the capability in-house, or (2) you can find a highly motivated and skilled partner to provide the needed capabilities. The

latter option is likely to require fewer resources, but finding the right partner can be difficult.

3. *Which activities motivate and provide meaning for you and your team?* If you or your initial team members particularly enjoy certain activities and do them reasonably well, you probably shouldn't outsource them—even if others could do them slightly more efficiently. Your venture isn't going to work for you unless you do at least some of the things you most enjoy doing.

4. *Which capabilities can be bought cheaper and easier than they can be built?* Cost becomes important for capabilities that are not strengths, not crucial, and not passions of yours. Some capabilities can be built only through a major investment of time and money. Others are needed only on a temporary or part-time basis. In either case, it may be prudent to contract for the provision of these capabilities by others who have already made the investment. How easily could you build the needed capability? Do you know of outside providers who would provide it much cheaper than you could build it? If you cannot find outside providers at all, you may have no choice but to build the capability in-house.

CASE STUDY

NFTE's key operating decisions. Mariotti brought two important strengths to NFTE. He had developed a curriculum for teaching entrepreneurship to at-risk youth, and he was a gifted teacher. Based on this background, he believed he could recruit and train teachers. Teaching was also the activity he felt most passionate about, which was fortunate because the most crucial capability for NFTE's success was high-quality teaching. A good teacher can improve on a weak lesson plan and compensate for deficiencies in the venue, materials, and other support systems. An ineffective teacher can easily ruin a program no matter how good everything else is. Getting the right students in the classroom was also crucial, but Mariotti had no particular strength at doing this, and he had no desire to build his own learning centers. He turned to highly motivated and trustworthy partners who already had access to the students and the facilities. NFTE's first partner was the Boys & Girls Clubs of Newark. NFTE's initial operating structure kept the teaching and some of the curriculum development, along with basic administrative functions, in-house. Key partners provided the students and the venues for teaching, at no expense to NFTE. Contractors provided help with accounting, fundraising, and some of the curriculum and materials design. Other necessary supplies were acquired on the open market.

Using these four questions, you can decide on an operating structure that builds on your strengths, protects core capabilities, keeps you motivated, and is cost effective. This should be a resource-smart structure. Of course, picking a structure is an art, not a science. You must make judgment calls based on limited information. As your venture unfolds and you learn more, your operating structure is likely to change. This process of considering other options should prepare you for change. For now, you simply need to define a starting point.

action step   **Explore alternative operating structures.** Describe three different plausible operating structures for your new venture and rate the resource-smartness of each one using the four questions.

PHASE 3: DEVELOP A RESOURCE-SMART
ECONOMIC MODEL

With this operating structure in mind, you must develop an economic model for your venture that is also resource-smart. An economic model describes where funds will come from and where they will go in your venture. It addresses two key questions: (1) Will you generate operating revenues to reduce your need for outside resources? and (2) on what terms will you acquire the various inputs for your venture?

tool of the trade   Your economic model is likely to change over time as you get a better sense of what's feasible. For now, make judgment calls and be creative. The Social Enterprise Spectrum (Exhibit 4.2) can help. You should think of this spectrum as describing a continuous range of choices with purely philanthropic and purely commercial options as the extreme endpoints. Your venture is likely to be somewhere in the middle, but where? Consider each stakeholder dimension—beneficiaries, capital providers, workforce, and suppliers.

Beneficiaries: Capturing Some of the Value You Create
You can reduce your need for outside resources by finding a viable revenue stream that does not hamper your ability to serve your mission. You need to ask the following questions:

1. Who benefits (or could benefit) from your venture?
2. Is it appropriate and practical to charge them a fee for this benefit?
3. How much could you charge while still achieving your social objectives?

You should consider three possible sources: your primary intended beneficiaries, third parties with a vested interest, and parties who benefit indirectly from your activities.[2]

	Continuum of Options		
	Purely Philanthropic	Hybrids	Purely Commercial
General Motives, Methods, and Goals	Appeal to goodwill	Mixed motives	Appeal to self-interest
	Mission driven	Balance of mission and market	Market driven
	Social value creation	Social and economic value	Economic value creation
Key Stakeholders			
Beneficiaries	Pay nothing	Subsidized rates and/or mix of full payers and those who pay nothing	Pay full market rates
Capital	Donations and grants	Below-market capital and/or mix of full payers and those who pay nothing	Market rate capital
Workforce	Volunteers	Below-market wages and/or mix of volunteers and fully paid staff	Market rate compensation
Suppliers	Make in-kind donations	Special discounts and/or mix of in-kind and full price	Charge market prices

EXHIBIT 4.2 The social enterprise spectrum.[3]

Should you charge your intended beneficiaries? Many social entrepreneurs are reluctant to charge their primary beneficiaries, especially when the beneficiaries are poor or are seen as deserving the benefit. This reluctance is morally appropriate in some cases, but it can also be patronizing and paternalistic. In Chapter 1, we noted that one of the trends in social entrepreneurship is encouraging people to take responsibility for addressing their own problems. Sometimes charging a fee, even a small one, can add to people's sense of empowerment and responsibility. Charging fees screens out those who aren't serious. Those who choose to pay a fee tend to have a greater commitment. Finally, charging a fee opens you to a market discipline that can be helpful. If no one will pay, you may not be delivering the value you think you are. Paying also gives beneficiaries more right to complain than if they receive free services. Creative structures can be developed to address affordability issues. These structures include sliding scales (with lower fees for poorer people), scholarships, and deferred payment options.

HOW USER FEES CAN IMPROVE IMPACT.

As part of its program to promote family planning in Bangladesh, Population Services International (PSI) sold condoms. The price didn't cover the full costs of the condoms, but it did offset some of PSI's costs. The benefits went much further. Pricing condoms helped ensure that the men who got them used them. Charging a price also opened up a new distribution channel—the small village stores where the men would hang out. Because of the limited space in these stores, owners were unlikely to stock unprofitable items. Pricing the condom allowed the store owners to make a profit and gave them an incentive to keep condoms in stock. Free distribution would have probably happened through government or nonprofit clinics, which are less convenient and more awkward for the men.

Could you get contracts with third parties who have a vested interest in your success?   Third parties sometimes have a vested interest in your work. Two likely candidates are the government and business owners. Government agencies may save money by contracting with you for service delivery to those receiving government benefits. Employers may provide access to social services to improve employee productivity. In either case, you may be able to contract for service provision. Of course, third-party payment doesn't have all the advantages of user fees because the party most directly benefiting isn't making the payment decision. This can be dealt with by using a hybrid system, with intended beneficiaries making small co-payments.

MIXING THIRD-PARTY AND USER FEES.

GuateSalud provides health care and preventive medicine to rural workers in Guatemala. With the permission of farm (finca) owners, the founders set up health services on the finca, with a worker trained as a physician's assistant available full-time and a doctor making periodic visits. The finca owner pays startup costs and a monthly fee, and workers who visit the clinic make a modest co-payment per visit and pay small amounts for medicine. The finca owners get healthier workers, and the workers get access to low-cost health care and free health education.

Could you find ways to charge people who benefit indirectly from your success?   Many social entrepreneurs are finding ways to create enterprises that serve their mission and generate revenue from customers who are not the primary beneficiary. Think of a restaurant that serves as a job training program for homeless youth, or an ecotourism venture that educates participants about environmental issues and uses profits to support conservation activities. By producing private benefits for paying customers, you may also be able to serve your social mission. It is worth considering ways to align the interests of paying customers with programs that create social value.

Capital Providers: Raising Cash from the Right Sources

Even if you can charge fees, you are likely to need startup capital, working capital, and expansion capital. Social ventures that don't generate sufficient earned income to cover all operating costs also need to raise ongoing operating subsidies. You need to ask the following questions:

1. From whom could you raise capital for your venture?
2. What are all the costs associated with these capital sources?
3. Which are likely to be the most cost-effective sources for serving your mission?

At this point, you do not need a full fundraising plan. For your economic model, you just need a rough idea of your capital sources and their costs.

What are your options?   If you are planning to set up a nonprofit venture, you could get capital in the form of (1) grants and donations, (2) recoverable grants (similar to zero-interest loans in that you have to repay all or part of the grant), (3) below-market-rate loans, (4) tax-exempt market-rate loans or bonds, (5) full-market-rate loans, and (6) above-market-rate loans (made by loan sharks). These options are arranged according to repayment costs. If you create a true for-profit business to serve your mission, you can also tap into equity funding.[4] Equity investment has very different characteristics from debt. Equity holders take more risk in that they get paid last, after all debt obligations are covered. Equity has no fixed repayment schedule but has an unlimited upside. Debt holders get no more than the interest they were promised. Equity holders make their money from profit distributions and by selling their interest, either back to the organization or to someone else. If you plan to use equity capital, consider what kind of return your equity holders will expect and when. It's important to have an exit plan for them.

THE SPECIAL CASE OF PROGRAM-RELATED INVESTMENTS.

Program-related investments (PRIs) are loans or equity investments made by foundations at below-market rates relative to the risk involved. Most PRIs take the form of loans to nonprofits, but they can include equity investments in for-profits when this clearly fits the foundation's mission and does not unduly benefit private parties.

The MacArthur Foundation, for instance, is a major equity investor in Shorebank Corporation, the leading community development bank holding company in the United States. Several major foundations have PRI programs.

Could you repay capital providers? If you do not plan to have any sources of earned income, it will be hard to attract providers who are looking for a return. In theory, you could repay investors out of future grants and donations, but few investors will bet on your will and ability to do that. Your future donors may object to their money being used to pay off earlier investors. Your best bet for capital may be grants and donations. Even so, you will want to look for those that are least costly, all things considered.

GRANTS ARE NOT FREE.

Even though you do not have to repay them, grants impose costs. Different providers impose different costs. In evaluating your options, you should consider all of the acquisition costs (including the time it takes to get approval), the costs of managing and maintaining the relationship (including meeting restrictions and special reporting requirements), as well as the costs of depending on a funding source that may not be easily renewable.

Why not just use grants and donations for everything? Grants and donations seem like the resource-smart way to raise capital, even if you expect to have strong earned-income streams. In many cases, they are the best source for startup and early-stage capital, but not always. As just mentioned, grants and donations are not free. Other sources may prove to be more cost-effective, more responsive to the timing of your needs, less restrictive, and more renewable. Reducing your dependency on philanthropic funds can also be symbolically important for organizations that want to signal their commitment to self-sufficiency. Finally, if you can repay capital providers, it frees up those funds for investment in other projects, including your future projects. It is a form of recycling cash, which is resource-smart in a global sense. By not tying resources up in a venture that can repay them, they are freed for use in ventures that truly need them.

When should you consider repaying capital providers? Even for new social ventures with earned-income potential, it can be hard to raise capital that must be repaid. Without a track record of producing income, most lenders or investors will not be sufficiently confident in your will and ability to repay. Even social-purpose, for-profit businesses are often perceived as risky investments. You will either need to find investors looking primarily for a social return or demonstrate a strong potential upside for them. Later in this chapter, we discuss strategies for attracting resource providers and managing risks. For now, you need to decide when it might be resource-smart to pursue capital that you have to repay. Consider repayable capital when you have the following needs:

- **Major capital expenditures with predictable future revenues.**
  With predictable future revenues, it may be easier to raise large amounts of capital via a loan or equity investment rather than a grant. For instance, Pioneer Human Services, an entrepreneurial nonprofit in Seattle that operates businesses that train and employ disadvantaged people, received a multimillion-dollar PRI loan from the Ford Foundation to start a new venture by purchasing a for-profit printing business.

- **Working capital cash flow needs.**
  Sometimes you have to pay expenses well before you receive revenues. As long as the revenues are reliable, you may be eligible for a working capital loan to bridge the gap. For instance, Success for All sells its curriculum to schools and provides implementation assistance. Its costs are incurred early in the year, but it gets paid by the schools much later. In order to grow, Success for All needed funding to pay the bills while it waited for schools to pay. To meet this need, Success for All accepted a loan from the New Schools Venture Fund.

- **Risk capital needs for starting a potentially profitable business.**
  If you need capital to start a for-profit business that will serve your mission, it may be wise to look for equity. Loans make sense only when you are relatively certain of your ability to repay them on time. Equity capital does not require you to pay out any cash unless and until you have excess cash on hand. In addition to the MacArthur Foundation, many other social investors made equity investments in the Shorebank Corporation to help it get started and to help with key expansions.

Work Force: Balancing Compensation and Performance

The single most important factor in your success is your team. Their skills, attitudes, and other intangible assets can make all the difference when it comes to your success. Your economic model has to make some assumptions about whether and how much you will pay for the human capital behind your organization's capabilities. You need to ask the following questions:

1. What skills are needed to support your in-house capabilities?
2. Which, if any, of these skills could be effectively supplied by volunteers?
3. Should a commitment to volunteerism be part of your mission?

4. How many and what kinds of paid staff will you need? How well will you pay them?

The wide range of workforce strategies in the social sector is stunning. Some organizations rely heavily and successfully on part-time volunteers, including in major leadership positions. Other organizations put a premium on professionals and use volunteers only in limited roles—as Board members, fundraisers, and advisors. How will your venture be staffed? It is worth thinking through different possibilities.

What should be the role of volunteers?   The answer to this question should be driven by practical considerations and values. On the practical side, you have to ask which functions could be legitimately, effectively, and reliably provided by volunteers. This will vary widely from venture to venture. Using volunteers is clearly the low-cost way to deliver your services, where it is feasible. Even so, it may not be the resource-smart approach if it does not produce desired results. For some organizations, the use of volunteers is considered a deeply held core value and part of the mission. It allows you to create an additional kind of social value—the value that arises from private citizens joining together voluntarily to provide for the common good. If this is part of your mission, then it should be included in the outcomes you intend to produce and given appropriate weight in your staffing decisions. It may compensate for some inefficiencies.

How well should you pay your staff?   Few organizations can function effectively without at least some paid staff. Where you don't use volunteers, you must decide on compensation levels. How easy is it to get this skill at below-market wages? Is a low wage sustainable? Although low wages are common in the social sector, this practice may not be resource-smart if it makes recruiting difficult, increases turnover, or contributes to low morale. People in the social sector often accept lower wages because they care about the cause. In effect, they're donating their foregone

CASE STUDY

Breaking the low-wage tradition.
Mariotti decided early on that teachers were NFTE's most important asset and that school teachers were typically underpaid. He made a commitment to pay his teachers well. He said that he wanted to treat them like Harvard professors, in stark contrast to the way many public school teachers are treated. This move signaled NFTE's commitment to reward those who provide its most crucial capability. Mariotti used other devices to screen teachers for commitment to the mission.

wages to the venture for a "social return." Low wages help ensure that you are getting people who care about your mission and not just the money; however, even with this kind of commitment, it can be demoralizing when your staff members have peers in the business world are making orders of magnitude more. You want to find a wage level that is optimal for producing results by attracting and retaining productive and committed team members in key positions.

Suppliers: Finding Efficient Deals and Sustainable Relationships

In finalizing your economic model, consider your suppliers, including any contractors or partners needed to deliver required capabilities. To define your economic model, you need to ask the following questions:

1. Of the capabilities others will provide or support, which are most crucial?
2. What is the best way to ensure that crucial capabilities will be provided reliably?
3. What is the most cost-effective way of ensuring that noncrucial capabilities are supplied with adequate quality and reliability?

As with other stakeholder relationships, a wide range of arrangements are available, including in-kind donations, discounts, and market-rate contracts.

How do you build strong relationships with crucial suppliers, contractors, and partners? In selecting an operating structure, you have already identified crucial capabilities. You should revisit that list with particular attention to those crucial capabilities that you plan to leave to others. These are your most crucial suppliers, contractors, or partners. It is particularly important that you structure these relationships to ensure high-quality, reliable performance. These suppliers, contractors, or partners should highly value their relationship with your organization for business reasons, social reasons, or, ideally, both.

- **Business reasons can be direct or indirect.**
  The most direct business reason is when you are a major paying customer that this supplier would not want to lose. This kind of power will be out of reach for many new social ventures in their early stages. Indirect business reasons include the close relationships you may have with important customers. Perhaps your Board chairperson provides a great deal of business to this supplier. Indirect business reasons are more common and can lead to in-kind donations, pro bono services, or significant discounts.

- **Social reasons should reflect a deep ongoing commitment.**
  The main social reason to value a relationship with you is a shared commitment to your social mission or at least to an integral part of

MIXING DIFFERENT MODELS: HELP THE WORLD SEE

In 1997, 10 years after its founding, Help the World See (HTWS) was providing for eye care in developing countries in three very different ways: (1) It sent volunteer missions of doctors and technicians to perform eye examinations and provide glasses for free; (2) it distributed recycled eyeglasses free of charge through other channels; and (3) it partnered with local organizations to create permanent, revenue-generating eyeglass clinics that sold glasses at prices well below the going rate but in excess of the direct costs of producing the glasses. In its first nine years (1987–1996), HTWS sent 52 missions to serve 100,000 patients, distributed nearly 800,000 pairs of recycled glasses, and started revenue-generating clinics in three countries. Each of its approaches was highly cash efficient. Its annual expenses in 1996 were barely $90,000. How was this possible? HTWS received approximately $300,000 of in-kind donations that year. That's more than a 3:1 ratio of in-kind donations to cash expenses. HTWS also made heavy use of skilled volunteers for its missions, while maintaining a small paid staff. The local clinics were staffed by paid employees but were housed in donated space, received discounts on supplies, and charged fees for glasses that were designed to cover operating expenses. The partners helped support the clinics locally.[5]

it. Social reasons can also lead to favorable terms; however, if this is the primary source of strength in your relationship, you need to make sure the supplier's commitment is enduring and deeply held.

What kinds of financial terms are appropriate for partners? If the capability is crucial and the supplier is deeply committed to the same values as you, it might be resource-smart to create a partnership. You could co-sponsor programs, with both of you putting your reputations at stake. The economic implications of a partnership vary depending on its terms. The flow of funds is a strategic choice determined by the relative strengths and weaknesses of you and your partner. Which of you is best positioned to provide funding and which one has the strongest bargaining position? Consider NFTE's relationship with Boys & Girls Clubs of Newark, its first partner. The funding flowed through the Club to NFTE, almost as if NFTE were a contractor. By contrast, Working Capital, one of the leading microenterprise programs in the United States, started off by providing funds to help community-based organizations implement its programs. After it became more established, Working Capital began exploring a different model, one in which the community organizations paid Working Capital for its programs and technical assistance. In making assumptions about the economic terms you can expect with partners, think about your relative bargaining positions.

 Consider different economic models: Based on your preferred operating structure, define two or three distinct, but plausible economic models for implementing that structure. These models should differ significantly on at least two dimensions of the Social Enterprise Spectrum. Which one do you think will better serve your mission while making effective and efficient use of scarce resources?

PHASE 4: DEDUCE YOUR RESOURCE REQUIREMENTS

Armed with a preferred operating structure and economic model, you are now in a position to estimate your resource requirements. This is a detailed, intense process. Many entrepreneurs shy away from it, knowing that any plan is likely to change as the work progresses, but this is a mistake. Working through this process deepens your understanding of your new venture and prepares you to deal with change. The approach recommended here is broken into nine bite-sized steps. Take them one at a time. The process is inspired by McGrath and MacMillan's concept of "discovery-driven planning."[6] This kind of planning starts with what you want to accomplish and works backward to determine what it will take to get there, and it requires you to track your assumptions, test them, and refine your plan as you go.

Step 1: Define Your Performance Targets for the First Three Years.

What do you expect to accomplish in each of your first three years of operation—in terms of social outcomes and financial goals? Drawing on your mission and the magnitude of the opportunity you're pursuing, set realistic social performance goals. As much as possible, state these goals in concrete terms that will allow you to determine the resources needed for reaching them. NFTE's goals might include the number of students who successfully complete its programs. If you have explicit financial operating objectives, such as covering some or all of your costs with earned income, these should be defined. For instance, you might plan to cover 10 percent of your costs in year one, 25 percent in year two, and 50 percent in year three.

Step 2: Create a Calendar of Activities Necessary for Achieving Your Goals.

Your capabilities list and operating structure should help you draw up your activities list. This is more concrete and specific than your list of capabilities. This is a month-by-month "to do" list. Again, it's helpful to start with your goals and work backward. For example, if NFTE wants 200 youth to complete its programs in the first year and class sizes are typically 20 students, then it will have to conduct 10 programs. If Mariotti thinks he can handle only five programs per year, he will need to hire another teacher. Be sure to include important administrative activities, filing for your tax status, setting up an accounting system, and so on. Decide what needs to be done in each month to reach your goals. Do this for the first three years, and it should be an eye-opening experience. If possible, have someone with experience review the calendar to see if it is realistic.

Step 3: Estimate Your Cash Needs Using a Hypothetical Checking Account.

Now it is time to have some fun with numbers! Forget about projecting fancy income statements and balance sheets. You do not need them for this. All you have to do is envision a checking account with complete overdraft protection. Negative balances are to be expected. Out of the account, you will pay all of your startup and operating expenses. Into the account, you will deposit cash generated by your operations (earned income). Capital does not come into the picture at this point because we are trying to determine your capital needs. Using your activities calendar, estimate what it will cost to ensure that each of these activities takes place on time. You can allow for volunteer help or in-kind donations, but only if you are confident about them. Record these expenses in your imaginary checking account each month on a cash basis—when you would expect to write the check. This can be different from when the activity occurs. If you don't have to pay for your legal fees for 30 days, record the cost in the month after the legal services are rendered. Now record all incoming cash from operations (earned income) as deposits. Again, record the deposit only when you expect to have the cash in hand.

Next, subtract the checks from the deposits for each month separately to create your net monthly cash flows. This net of your outflows and inflows helps you see the patterns over time. Finally, using the monthly results, create a running balance for the account, starting from the first month. The running balance reflects your total cash needs to that point in time. The month with the largest negative running balance reflects the total amount of cash you must raise to get through this three-year period, if things go as planned! In case they don't, you may want to build in a cash reserve. It would be prudent to add 10 or 20 percent to your operating cash needs to create this reserve. If you are stunned by the total needed, you may want to reconsider your operating structure, economic model, or your performance targets.

Step 4: Write Down Your Assumptions and Identify the Most Crucial Ones.

All along, you've been making assumptions. New ventures are fraught with uncertainty, but assumptions are necessary to do any planning. Make a list of your assumptions. For instance, Mariotti might have assumed that

20 students is an optimal class size, that a good teacher should be paid $40,000 per year plus benefits, and that students who start ventures need on average $150 in startup capital and can pay this back in three months. Include only assumptions that might make a difference in your expected cash flows or other resource needs. For each crucial assumption, you should ask the following questions:

1. To what extent could a mistake about this assumption affect your resource needs or your chances for success?
2. How confident are you about this assumption?
3. What evidence do you have in support of it?

Those assumptions with potentially great effects about which you are least confident are the most crucial ones.

Step 5: Design Your Venture with Explicit Milestones that Reflect the Points at which You Will Have Tested Your Most Crucial Assumptions.

Crucial assumptions need to be tested and refined along the way. Some can be tested with further research, but others are best tested by action. Your venture is a living experiment testing your ideas and assumptions. Establish milestones in your calendar for revisiting crucial assumptions in light of your experience. It is wise to find early, low-cost ways to test crucial assumptions. Think about ways to do that. This may require you to change your activities calendar and your cash-flow estimates, but it will be worth it. If you are wrong about a key assumption, you and your resource providers will benefit from knowing it sooner rather than later. Using your projected operating checkbook, you can determine how much money you need to reach each major milestone.

Step 6: Plan for Contingencies by Envisioning Different Scenarios that Might Arise.

Chances are, things will not work out exactly as you've planned. Some of your assumptions will prove to be wrong. This is the nature of new ventures. If you are lucky, you will be wrong only about a relatively small matter, and the adjustment will be easy. Now that you have identified your crucial assumptions and established milestones, you might want to think about "Plan B"—what you will do if your assumptions are way off the mark. For each milestone, you should envision plausible scenarios in which you learn something new that brings into question your approach and/or raises your resource requirements. What those scenarios might be depends on the nature of your most crucial assumptions. Thinking in advance about potential "rainy day" scenarios that would increase your cash needs can help you see the value of building a cash reserve. This exercise can even help you estimate the amount you would want to have in reserve. To take this a step further, you could identify your venture's "Achilles heel," its greatest potential weak spot when it comes to assumptions. What would be the best response if this assumption is seriously flawed? Could you adjust by changing your operating structure or economic model? How would it change your resource needs? Would your venture still be worth pursuing?

Step 7: List Your Significant Noncash Resources Needs.

The checkbook exercise focuses on your cash needs, but you have other resource needs to accomplish the activities on your calendar. Some of these activities, such as meeting with the mayor, will require noncash resources, such as someone who knows the mayor or the mayor's staff well enough to get you the time you need. Using your activities calendar, make a list of all significant noncash resources you will need.

Step 8: Compare What You Need with What You Already Have To Determine Your Resource Gap.

You no doubt are starting with some resources. Mariotti started with a proven curriculum and a strong teacher (himself). If you're starting from the base of an existing organization, you might be able to tap into resources from that organization to get started. By subtracting what you have from what you need, you can identify your resource gaps—things you need to acquire or develop.

Step 9: Create Fundraising Targets, a Shopping List, and a Cultivation List.

These are the three concrete end products of your resource assessment. The first is a set of *fundraising targets.* These targets state how much you need to raise by different points in time. Using your earlier assessment of capital providers, you can match your capital needs with the kinds of capital providers that are appropriate for your venture. The second product is a *shopping list,* which includes the resources you will use cash to acquire. Be as specific as possible about the characteristics you are looking for; it will help you shop. Finally, make a *cultivation list* of the resources you need to develop, but can't buy, or at least not easily.

TEN TIPS FOR REDUCING YOUR INITIAL CASH NEEDS

Here are 10 tips that could help reduce your cash needs in the early startup stage. This isn't about thinking small or handicapping yourself by starting with too few resources. It's about doing more with less cash. You have to assess whether any of these tips are useful to you based on their effect on your ability to serve your mission. If a specific tip would jeopardize your mission, *don't do it!*

Tip 1: Stage your venture, funding only one or two stages at a time. Staging investments is a powerful tool for resource management. The idea is to raise just enough cash to reach your next major milestone, or just beyond it. Once you reach the first milestone, you should have more information to use in raising additional funds. Although this technique is common in the venture capital world, it is not so common with foundations. If you wait until you've demonstrated results from the first stage of your venture to write a proposal for the second stage, it could be months before you get your next grant. The delay could be deadly. You may need to educate your foundation partners in order to get them to see the value of proceeding in stages, putting more funds in as you both learn more.

Tip 2: Convert fixed costs into variable costs. Fixed costs are the costs you incur no matter how many people you serve or projects you complete—such as rent, utilities, compensation for full-time salaried employees, and so on. Variable costs go up or down based on your level of activity. You can convert fixed costs into variable costs by changing the way you pay. Royalties, commissions, piece-rates, and the like make the costs variable. If NFTE paid all of its teachers a salary, teaching would be a relatively fixed cost. This could be converted to a variable cost, by paying teachers on a per-student basis. Payments often have both fixed and variable components. The idea here is to incur costs only when you are delivering your service. This is particularly helpful for earned-income ventures because their revenues are tied to service delivery as well—costs go up only when revenues go up—but it can be useful in other ventures as well. Lower fixed costs usually mean lower startup costs and lower operating costs in the first few months of operation, as you build up your volume of activity. Your cash needs go up only if you are successful. In which case, you should be in a stronger position to raise more money.

Tip 3: Look for excess capacity and underutilized resources. Identify potential suppliers that have recently expanded their facilities or lost a big customer. For example, businesses that move into new offices often have more space than they need right away, leaving room for growth. If you're willing to start off with temporary office space, they might be willing to give you a deal. In terms of human resources, people who are currently unemployed are more motivated than people with jobs. Recently retired accountants may welcome the chance to put their skills to work for you.

Tip 4: Help new suppliers establish themselves. Businesses, law firms, and accounting firms that are new to your area will be aggressively looking for business. They may be willing to strike a good deal to get the work and build their reputation. On a personal level, newcomers to a community may be looking for ways to get involved. Newly promoted executives or professionals may be looking for ways to gain experience and visibility in community leadership. Of course, you take more risks with new players, but you'll generally get a better deal. You have to make a judgment about how much risk you can take in a particular area.

Tip 5: Make yourself a low-cost customer. Make an effort to understand your resource suppliers' economics. You may see ways to reduce their costs of serving you. Many businesses experience times when they are busy (peak) and times when things are slack (off-peak) during a day, a week, or even a year. If what you need could be provided during off-peak times, the supplier should be motivated to give you a better deal.

Tip 6: Make yourself a value-added customer. You may be able to find ways to provide additional value to your suppliers beyond what you might pay. Your status as a social entrepreneur gives you special leverage with potential for-profit resource providers. Helping you may enhance their reputation, if you give them public recognition. You may have other supporters who would be inclined to give their business to this supplier, if the supplier offers you a favorable deal. This could be formalized as a "cause marketing" campaign in which your relationship is used to generate business for the supplier.

Tip 7: Explore the possibilities of sharing assets with others, preferably assets they own. Many of the resources you need could be shared with others. Think of copiers, fax machines, conference rooms, even someone to answer the phones. Of course, you have to deal with the logistics and structure a fair arrangement, but if you can make this work, it can lower your cash needs significantly. This is one of the benefits of business incubators, where young businesses share all kinds of resources. Nonprofit incubators are not as common, but they do exist. Often the incubator offers technical assistance, as well as sharing of facility costs with other new ventures. Incubators aren't intended to be permanent homes. You need a plan for weaning yourself from the incubator's assistance that fits with the incubator's policies regarding when you should exit.

Tip 8: Manage the cash you do have carefully, by collecting early, paying only when it's due, and earning interest on your balances.[7] Make sure the cash you have on hand is working for you. Any excess above your immediate needs should be earning interest. You don't want to tie it up for long periods, but it should be invested in a way that will make it available when you need it. This is particularly important for managing large grants that come in at the beginning of the grant period. You can maximize the cash invested by managing your cash flow wisely. This means collecting cash as early as possible. You should politely make sure you are paid in a timely fashion. Conversely, don't pay your bills any earlier than necessary. This keeps your cash in the bank. Of course, there are two exceptions to this rule. Some suppliers will offer you a discount to pay early. If you're earning only low interest rates on your cash, it may be worth it. The second exception is more strategic. If this is a particularly important supplier with which you want to build a strong and long-term relationship, you may want to pay earlier. If you have the cash, the forgone interest may be worth giving up to strengthen the relationship.

Tip 9: Take advantage of special deals and shop for bargains. If you shop around, you can often find resources that will serve your purposes adequately, but that aren't first rate or are offered under special terms and conditions. The Internet is making the search for deals even easier. Consider buying used furniture and equipment. It's often easy to get used furniture and equipment donated as an in-kind gift. Find the relevant colleges or universities in your area and see if they have courses that require students to complete research or community service projects, or if they run supervised internship programs. Look for group rates. Insurance and employee benefits are two areas in which associations often get better deals than individual organizations could get on their own. You may have to join an association to get the deals, but it could be worth the cost. Finally, take full advantage of your nonprofit status to get access to free goods, special prices, pro bono services, and volunteers.

Tip 10: Negotiate on price, but only with those who have the authority to cut a deal. Everything is negotiable, but front-line customer service representatives rarely have the authority to go beyond standard discounts. Few of them would reap any benefits from cutting a special deal. If you want to press further, go up the chain of command until you reach someone who would reap the benefits and has the authority. If it's a small business, go to the owner. If it's a chain or larger business, find someone with "profit-and-loss" responsibility. For example, in a law firm or accounting firm, this would be a partner.

DEVELOP YOUR RESOURCE MOBILIZATION STRATEGY

Now that you know which resources you need, how do you get them? Resource mobilization can be a difficult process for new ventures with little or no track record. You need to raise money, build a team, form partnerships, and attract clients. It can be a delicate balancing act to get the commitments you need. Team members may be reluctant to commit until you raise the money. Capital providers may be reluctant to provide funding until you have a team in place or agreements with partners. You can meet these challenges with a four-pronged strategy of (1) capitalizing on the intangible resources you bring to the venture; (2) managing and allocating risks strategically; (3) matching your providers with your needs; and (4) cultivating the intangibles that you cannot buy.[8]

The rest of this chapter is designed to help you build your skills in each of these areas.

PRONG 1: CAPITALIZE ON YOUR KEY INTANGIBLE RESOURCES

It all starts with three key intangible resources. These are your *social capital,* your *credibility* in launching this venture, and the degree to which potential resource providers have a *shared commitment* to your mission and methods. These three intangibles allow you to attract the resources you need and do it on favorable terms.

Take Stock of the Social Capital You May Use for This Venture

Your *social capital* is the reservoir of goodwill and trust that you've built through your relationships with other people.[9] It's not just who you know, it's who knows you, who likes you, who owes you a favor, who trusts you, and who's interested in your success. In this regard, social capital has both breadth and depth. The *breadth* of your social capital is determined by the number of people who know you. Think of your family, friends, current and former co-workers, schoolmates, fellow members of clubs or religious groups, people you've met at meetings or conventions, and informal acquaintances. A broad network extends your reach. The *depth* of your social capital is determined by the strength of your ties—the extent to which people in your network would go out of their way to help you. Depth, of course, is a matter of degree and can be hard to judge. You may not know much about the depth of your social capital until you test it.

Social capital is especially important in the early stages of a new venture when you have little track record.[10] As a social entrepreneur, you need to be aware of the social capital that you bring to the venture and think strategically about how to use it. People in your social network may provide resources on favorable terms, lend you their own social capital, or provide information about other possible resource providers.

action step **Identify friendly potential resource providers.** With your fundraising targets, shopping list, and cultivation list in front of you, go through your social networks and look for potential matches. Who in your *broad* network might be able to provide or give you access to resources you need? Once you have compiled a working list, rate each of these parties with regard to the *depth* of their ties with you on a scale of 1 to 5. A score of 1 means they barely know you; 3 means they would do you a modest favor, such as taking an hour out of a busy day to advise you; and 5 means they would do just about anything for you—either because they owe you or because they have a very strong bond with you.

Honestly Evaluate Your Credibility in Launching This Venture

Your *credibility* is the confidence you can create in relative strangers that you will be able to make your venture a success, based on what you bring to it. It is about what you have done, your trustworthiness, the skills and knowledge you have developed, and your ability to demonstrate these characteristics to others. Credibility requires more than just having the requisite human capital. It requires confirmation and communication. It helps to have an easily verifiable track record and the right credentials. If you do not, you may face an uphill battle. This is why you can find immigrant engineers driving taxis in the United States. They may have the human capital to be an engineer, but their track record and credentials cannot be easily verified.

The power of credibility is that it helps you move beyond your immediate social network and makes it easier for you to attract resources even within your network. If the people to whom you are pitching your venture don't have confidence that you can succeed, even good friends may try to steer you in another direction, rather than helping you get in over your head.

action step **Assess your credibility.** Ask a friend or advisor to take the role of a potential major capital provider who does not know you. Give this person your résumé, background information, and anything else you would use to demonstrate your credibility for launching this new venture, and ask for a critique. Does your past experience, as conveyed in these documents, show that you have the kinds of skills needed to launch a new venture or dramatically change an old one? Their assessment should include general characteristics associated with successful entrepreneurs, such as persistence, ambition, integrity, creativity, negotiating skills, and management skills, as well as the specific skills, characteristics, credentials, or knowledge needed in this venture. If their answer is "no," you need to decide if it is because you do lack the necessary human capital or because you have not effectively conveyed your human capital. In the former case, you may need a partner or other team members to provide what you lack. Finding this additional human capital should become a priority. Otherwise, you may need better documentation of what you bring to this effort.

Gauge the Level of Shared Commitment to Your Mission and Methods

Shared commitment is the degree to which potential resource providers embrace the values embedded in your social mission and believe in your approach to serving that mission. As with social capital, shared commitment has both breadth and depth. *Breadth* is determined by the number of potential resource providers who care about your venture's mission, values, and methods. Breadth can extend your reach in finding resources. *Depth* is determined by how much support these kindred spirits would be willing to provide and on what terms.

Shared commitment is typically the magnet that attracts many resource providers and the glue that keeps them committed to a social venture. The financial terms are rarely sufficient alone. The values that underlie shared commitment relate to method as well as mission. People and institutions sometimes have strong, value-driven views about appropriate methods. Two people concerned with high rates of teen pregnancy might passionately disagree over the right means for dealing with it—one favoring an emphasis on abstinence and adoption, the other favoring education about birth control and accessible abortion. The challenge for you is to find resource providers who share a commitment to your mission and believe your methods are appropriate and likely to be effective.

action step **Identify potential resource providers with strong shared commitments.** Again, using the end products from your resource assessment, begin to make a list of potential resource providers who share a commitment to your mission and methods. To complete this list, you may need to do research, but you can start it now, on your own or brainstorming with others who are knowledgeable about the field. For major capital providers, such as foundations, you may be able to name specific institutions that have made their values known publicly. Directories and annual reports can help you refine and extend this list. For individual resource providers, your descriptions may have to be more generic. You might think in terms of members of interest groups that have missions and values that are close to yours, or people whose lives have been touched by the issue you're addressing. How could you reach individuals who share your values and have the resources you need? You might consider conventions, newsletters, e-mail lists, and Websites sponsored by like-minded groups. For instance, the Mountain Association for Community Economic Development in eastern Kentucky found a Website developer who was committed to rural economic development and knowledgeable about small business through a posting in an electronic newsletter put out through the Aspen Institute's program on rural development. The person was working in eastern Oregon at the time. The key is to identify channels for reaching potential resource providers with strong shared commitments.

Develop an Approach That Builds on All Three Intangibles

These intangible resources help you identify resource providers who are most likely to help you. It's usually easier to start your search close to home and with people who'll be favorably inclined toward your venture. Once you've started, it becomes easier to approach strangers. You have more of a story to tell and more of a track record to share. To start, you should do the following:

Spread the word broadly among your friends and acquaintances about what you're planning to do. Social networks can be very effective at spreading information and drawing interested parties to you. You may not know in advance all of those in your network who have the ability and interest to help you with this venture.

Identify high-potential targets—It helps to start where you have an advantage. You need to identify potential resource providers with whom you have a strong relationship or who have a deep commitment to the values behind this venture. If you completed the action steps in the social capital and shared commitment sections, you are already on your way to identifying the most likely providers. Providers who appear on both lists should be given high priority. Among those who appear on either list, you should also give priority to those with whom you already have credibility or could demonstrate it easily. Credibility becomes even more crucial as you move down these lists to those with weaker ties and commitments.

Develop your pitch that describes your mission and the values behind it, establishes your credibility in launching this venture, and touches on the kinds of help you need to get it off the ground. Brevity is important. Prepare an "elevator speech"—a statement that could be delivered on a brief elevator ride to capture someone's attention. You

CASE STUDY

Hypothetical elevator speech for NFTE: "Have you seen what's happening to kids in our inner cities? Too many talented youngsters are becoming demoralized at an early age and turning to violence and drugs. Better education could turn this around, but the public schools aren't reaching many of these kids. For the past four years, I've worked with the toughest kids in some of the toughest schools in New York, and I found a way to get through to them. By showing them how to start and run their own businesses, I've been able to get them interested in learning again. But the public school system isn't ready to teach entrepreneurship. We have to find a way around the public bureaucracy to help these kids save themselves. So I'm leaving my teaching job to launch the National Foundation for Teaching Entrepreneurship, using the same techniques that I used in the schools. But if I'm going to pull this off, I'll need some help." Mariotti might then get more specific about the kind of help needed, depending on what the person has to offer and the nature of their relationship.

should also develop *backup materials* for those who want to know more about your venture after the pitch.

Then ask for what you need, but be strategic about when and how you do it. Some people are hesitant to close the deal. Successful entrepreneurs need to be willing to sell and close a deal, even with friends and acquaintances. Asking friends for help is not "taking advantage of them," unless you are insincere or unreasonable. Using your social capital isn't manipulating people. It's about giving them opportunities to do what friends like to do—namely, help out. You are giving them a chance to be part of something exciting and important. Just be honest and respectful. The following suggestions may help, if you are uncomfortable asking:

✔ Start by letting people know the kind of help you need in general and give them an opportunity to offer on their own. They may save you the trouble.

✔ Listen to them, gauge their interest in your venture, and think about what they might get out of being involved with your venture, before asking for something specific.

✔ If they don't offer on their own, but seem interested, help them see how they could support your venture and enjoy doing it. Propose ideas that fit their interests and abilities.

✔ Don't be shy about asking, but ask only for things that you believe they could provide without undue hardship. Be realistic and open to their counteroffers.

✔ If they do help or get someone else to help, express your gratitude formally and be willing to reciprocate should the occasion arise.

✔ If they want to "think about it," be persistent, but not annoying. Frame your requests so that it's easy for them to decline gracefully without losing your friendship, but do not lose sight of your need to move ahead.

✔ If they remain hesitant, offer them a low-risk, low-commitment way to get involved, such as serving as a reference, reviewing a section of your enterprise plan, or introducing you to one of their friends. Once the seed is planted, their commitment may grow.

✔ If the person you're approaching has relevant expertise, engage them by asking for their advice. They may give you advice that's even more valuable than the resources you were seeking from them.

✔ Set a goal of coming away from every meeting with something useful, such as a referral to someone else. Even critical feedback about why your targets are not interested can be valuable.

PRONG 2: MANAGE AND ALLOCATE RISK STRATEGICALLY

Fundraising expert Kay Sprinkel Grace says that nonprofit leaders should think of donors as "investors." This is a powerful point that should be extended to all resource providers who accept below-market-rate financial compensation. As Grace puts it, "Investors in nonprofits look for two bottom lines (financial and values) but one principal return: the knowledge that their investment will have the intended results and make an impact on the organization and the community."[11] But return isn't the only thing investors are concerned about. Different investors have different levels of risk tolerance, and they typically want greater returns for taking greater risks. Because they have no track record and often operate on a tight budget, new social ventures are inherently risky. Smart social entrepreneurs manage the risks and uncertainties in ways that make "investing" more attractive for potential resource providers.

Reduce Resource Provider Risk

Although you can't eliminate uncertainty and risk in your new venture, you can take steps to reduce the risks taken by your resource providers. The idea is to reduce the harm that could be created if your venture fails and/or the probability that it will fail. These are the two main components of investor risk. Some of the methods are similar to those used to lower your initial cash needs. Others address risk in different ways. To reduce risk, you could consider the following:

✔ *Allow investors to stage their investments.* If you stage your venture around assumption-testing milestones, resource providers can make their commitments incrementally, one stage at a time. They have less to lose and preserve their options to exit, reduce support, or increase their investment, according to your success. The first stage generally poses the greatest risk and, thus, appeals to resource providers with greater risk tolerance. If all goes well, at each successive stage, more uncertainties are resolved and risk is reduced for the investors.

✔ *Lower your fixed costs.* Higher fixed costs means higher risk exposure in the sense that you stand to lose more if no one or too few clients use your program. You can pass the risk reduction on to resource providers by allowing them to make variable commitments that increase if you are successful. A team member may agree to start on a volunteer or part-time basis, while holding onto another job, increasing to full time with you only when your success justifies it.

✔ *Offer immediate benefits that do not depend on later success.* With some creativity, you might think of something that offers the resource provider a benefit immediately. Public recognition can give investors favorable exposure in front of a group that matters to them. Their good intentions are appreciated regardless of your later success.

✔ *Offer anonymity to investors who desire it.* Ironically, you also may be able to reduce a resource provider's reputation-related risk by keeping that provider's support anonymous until your success is clear. Requests for anonymity are usually based on moral or religious beliefs, but they can also reduce the risk of any negative impressions that might come from being associated with a failed effort.

✔ *Form a partnership with a larger, more stable organization.* By absorbing some of the risk, your partner reduces the risk that others may take. Of course, this requires your partner to be risk tolerant. The partner's reputation is at stake, and it may be called upon to provide support in tough times.

Find Providers with High Risk Tolerance

No matter what you do to reduce resource provider risk, your new venture is likely to present some irreducible risk, especially early on. Therefore, you must find at least some intrepid souls who are willing to live with the risk and uncertainty. You could use the following methods:

✔ *Consider providers with the size to take the risk.* Risk is relative to your resource provider's circumstances. To a large resource provider, the investment you are looking for may be relatively small—not a big concern. Large resource providers can usually diversify away some of the risk associated with your new venture.

✔ *Look for providers who enjoy being part of risky new ventures.* Some people just like being part of new ventures, even though they know the risks. You can see it in their track record. They may intrinsically enjoy taking risks, or the excitement of being part of something new compensates for the risks. Be prepared for these providers to leave when your venture is no longer new and exciting.

✔ *Focus on providers with the motivation to take the risk.* Providers with few other viable options should be less concerned about the risk of your venture. A foundation that needs to make grants quickly to meet its IRS minimum pay-out requirements for the year will be less worried about risk. Someone who has taken early retirement will be less concerned about the risk of working for you because he or she already has a base income to fall back on.

✔ *Conduct a broad search.* Because risk preferences are often hard to determine, it can pay to conduct a broad search for resource providers. For instance, Steve Mariotti of NFTE wrote letters to 160 of the wealthiest people listed in *Forbes* magazine. Only one responded. That person, who preferred to remain anonymous, provided initial support for NFTE and helped secure NFTE's first contract with the Boys & Girls Clubs of Newark. This shotgun-style approach can be costly, but in some cases, it may be the only way to find what you need.

Reduce Perceptions of Risk

Finally, you can work to reduce the perceptions of risk among your potential resource providers by providing information or by managing appearances.

✔ *Provide information to reduce uncertainties.* Sometimes potential resource providers perceive more risk than there is. Prevent this from happening by providing—in a credible and digestible fashion—the relevant information for making a judgment about risk. A well-developed plan for your new venture can help by addressing perceived risks directly. It can show that you've done your homework. Short of that, you need to determine where resource providers see risks and develop a response that addresses their concerns directly.

✔ *Manage impressions, applying a positive spin.* Entrepreneurs sometimes try to hide or downplay the inherent risk in their ventures. This is a questionable, but common tactic. Often, this isn't done with conscious duplicity, but out of a firm belief that they will make their venture work no matter what. Occasionally, entrepreneurs explicitly devise schemes to make their ventures appear more solid than they are.[12] Vague references can create the illusion that other resource providers have already committed. Misdirection can also work by focusing attention on the future, the desperate need, or the values inherent in what you are doing. If you engage in impression management, you need to be clear about where you draw the moral line between benign spin and unethical deception. The publicity test might be helpful. How would you feel if your actions were featured on the front page of your hometown newspaper?

Preserve Some Shared Risk with Key Providers

Shared risk is a powerful motivation for key strategic resource providers to do all they can to make the venture work. Be careful not to undermine this incentive. The value of shared risk is clear with important strategic partners and with key team members. You need their active involvement. Having something significant to lose provides a powerful motivation for them. The value of shared risk extends to key capital providers as well. This is one of the ideas behind the rise of "venture philanthropy." Venture philanthropists, like venture capitalists, make a few select, large "investments," and they get actively involved, providing strategic guidance. By making this high level of commitment to a few organizations, they are taking more risk than if they spread their money over a larger group and did not get involved beyond that. Each individual investment becomes important. The strategic management of risk includes knowing when it is helpful to maintain a certain level of shared risk with crucial resource providers.

PRONG 3: MATCH YOUR RESOURCE PROVIDERS WITH YOUR NEEDS

In business, it is common to talk about matching the sources and uses of funds. For instance, funds from investors looking for a short-term profit should not be invested in projects that require long-term, patient capital. This matching principle is also appropriate in the social sector, and it can be extended to all kinds of resources, not just money. You should consider the nature of each resource need and develop a provider strategy that fits with the nature of your needs.[13]

Analyze Your Needs and Target Appropriate Providers for Each

Your resource needs vary widely, as do the interests and capabilities of potential resource providers. Skillful entrepreneurs understand the character of each need and try to match it with an appropriate provider. The following questions should help you find the best matches:

✔ What is the duration of the need? Short-term, temporary needs can be met by providers who are not willing or able to make a long-term commitment. Think of specialized legal services for a one-time event, such as buying a building. Ongoing needs are best served by providers who are willing to provide steady support over time. Loyal individual donors or paying customers fall into this category. Unlike many foundation grants, their support is renewable, as long as you meet their needs. Still other needs are short-term, but recurring. Think of special events or periodic audits. For these, you must ask how often the need will recur and how important it is to have the same provider for each recurrence? For instance, it might be good to have the same auditor each year.

✔ How crucial is this need? Every venture has a core set of activities that must be supported in order for the organization to function at a minimal level, including a base level of service delivery and certain required administrative functions, such as accounting, fundraising, and marketing. Many organizations also have commitments that can't be easily reversed, such as servicing a long-term contract. Ideally, to meet these needs, you want resource providers who are willing to make firm commitments and reliable in keeping those commitments.

✔ How big is the need relative to the capacity of potential providers? Some needs require relatively little time, expertise, or money relative to what potential resource providers have to offer. Others would strain any but the largest resource providers. Large needs can sometimes be broken into smaller packages, but this process can be costly and cumbersome. Ideally, you should match your large needs with resource providers who have the capacity to handle them without too much strain.

✔ Is the need expected to grow, decline, or remain at the same level? It is important to look ahead at how the need will change over time. For instance, if you expect earned income to cover an increasing percentage of your operating costs in the future, your needs for philanthropic subsidies will decline. In such a case, foundation grants that are time limited could be appropriate. If the need is going to grow, you will want to tap into sources and providers that could grow with it.

Anticipate Transitions and Plan for Sustainability

No matter how well you try to match your needs and providers, the results won't be perfect. Many of your needs will be ongoing, even growing, but not all resource providers will stick around long-term. Early-stage resource providers (staff and capital providers) who enjoy helping new social ventures get off the ground may be ready to move on when your venture becomes more mature—even though your needs are likely to continue. You should anticipate the departure of some of your resource providers and have replacement sources ready. It is prudent for you to perform the following activities:

✔ Identify your areas of greatest potential vulnerability. List your most strategically important and continuing resource needs. These are areas in which you would experience serious damage if you failed to mobilize the resources needed to support them.

✔ Assess the risk associated with your resource providers in these areas. Make a list of the resource providers you're counting on in these areas and rank them with regard to the risk they pose to you. How crucial is their particular resource commitment? What is the probability that they might stop providing these resources? Could they be easily replaced? Using these questions, you can create a rough ranking of these providers from the most risky to the least.

✔ Reduce the vulnerability of depending on risky providers. You have essentially three options: (1) reduce the probability of the provider leaving, (2) develop potential replacements, or (3) reduce the harm that would result if the provider leaves. You may be able to reduce the risk of the provider leaving by strengthening that provider's identification with your venture or by finding ways to make staying more attractive. If that approach is not promising, you could identify and start building relationships with potential providers who might be willing to step in and who have more staying power. You may want to shift to a different kind of provider— for instance, from foundation funding to corporate sponsorship. Keep the matching principle in mind. Finally, you could look for ways to reduce the potential harm. This can be difficult, but it can be done by developing new ways to exercise the capability in question with fewer outside resources, or by changing your operating structure so that the capability is no longer crucial.

✔ Consider diversification of providers, but be sensitive to costs. Having many resource providers can reduce the risk associated with any one of them leaving, but diversification has its costs. First, you incur the transaction costs of dealing with many providers. Small resource providers can place disproportionate burdens on an organization. Second, resource providers aren't completely interchangeable. One of the key points of this chapter is that money isn't the only, or even the most important, resource. Finally, if diversification means that each of your providers on average make smaller commitments, it can give them less of a stake in your success. Remember that diversification is a means of risk reduction, not an end in itself. It's a costly means, especially while your venture is small, so use it with care.

✔ Consider raising endowment funds to replace risky capital sources. Endowment income, if the funds are prudently managed, provides the most sustainable source of cash an organization can have. If your most crucial cash needs are covered by endowment, your worries about risky capital providers are over; however, raising an endowment is not easy, especially for a new venture. Few people are willing to endow something that is unproven. You may need to wait several years. You also have to be prepared to raise a lot of money. It takes about $20 of endowment to generate $1 in spending money annually. Think about raising 20 times the cash you need for core operating expenses. The downside of an endowment is that it buffers you from market discipline. You no longer have to justify your venture to resource providers. No one would dream of endowing a business to run forever, regardless of how it is doing in the marketplace. Too much endowment can lead to ineffective practices, unless other mechanisms are put in place to compensate for it, such as a strong Board and independent performance assessments.

PRONG 4: CULTIVATE AND BORROW WHAT YOU CAN'T BUY

You made a list of your noncash needs earlier in this chapter. You might be surprised to see that most (if not all) of them are closely related to the three intangible resources that we discussed earlier. They are typically about building new relationships (social capital), developing expertise and a reputation (credibility), or motivating action (shared commitment). You have already explored how to use these three intangibles in your resource-mobilization strategy. This section explains how you can build or augment your intangible resources.

Enrich Your Social Capital

You can build social capital by expanding the number of people in your network and deepening your bonds with key members of your network. How you direct your efforts depends on your specific needs and priorities.

✔ *Broaden your network.* You can extend the breadth of your social capital by taking the time to meet and engage with new people. This can be done by going to meetings and conferences, joining in civic and recreational activities, and just starting up a conversation with the person next to you on an airplane. This can all seem like a waste of time for a busy entrepreneur, but even relatively weak ties can have great value. The key is to make the most of the opportunities you have and to keep track of the contacts you make. If you have more specific targeted needs, be strategic in going to events, joining clubs, and participating in activities that put you in contact with the particular people you need to know.

✔ *Borrow social capital from others.* In addition to developing your social capital, you can acquire it from others. The simplest way is to ask people you know for referrals and introductions. This tactic can be very useful, even if you are trying to get to a specific person. It works best when the person making the introduction has a strong bond with you and with the person to whom they're introducing you. You should look for the "connectors" in your network.[14] These are people with extensive social networks who enjoy putting people together when they see a common interest. Beyond your personal network, you can borrow some of the social capital of the early stakeholders in your venture, team members, Board members, advisory board members, strategic partners, and consultants. As you select key participants in your new venture, you should consider the social capital they can contribute.

✔ *Deepen key relationships.* Be thoughtful about which relationships you want to deepen because you won't be able to do this with every relationship. The depth of your social capital is typically developed one person at a time. How do you strengthen a social bond?[15] More frequent communication and information sharing can help a great deal. You don't need to be intrusive, just stay in touch with people. Another way to deepen bonds is to help others when they ask, or, even better, to volunteer help before they ask. People tend to be grateful and look for opportunities to return favors. Surprisingly, asking people to help you can strengthen their ties to you. It's not unusual for someone to develop a vested interest in your future success if they helped you in the past. Finally, giving people opportunities to demonstrate their skills or their good character in front of others can help deepen your relationship with them. People commonly like to be recognized for their abilities and contributions.

 There's a fine line between building a mutually beneficial network of contacts and engaging in blatantly self-serving networking. Be sincere and respectful. If you add someone to your social network, be prepared to be part of theirs. They may call you before you call them. You shouldn't see that as a problem but as an opportunity to deepen that relationship.

Strengthen Your Credibility

Even though you cannot (morally or legally) change your track record, you can build your credibility in several ways.

✔ *Document your track record and share it.* Document your relevant experiences and make it easy for interested parties to verify your track record and see its relevance to your current venture. Ask yourself: Why should people bet on me in launching this new venture? What have I done that prepares me for this undertaking? How can I use my past experience to demonstrate my ability and character to others? Keep in mind that even past ventures that failed can help build your credibility if they were useful learning experiences and you handled the failure well. People may not take your word for it, so be prepared to document your past performance with information that can be verified. You may want to openly seek publicity, although this is potentially risky because the press isn't always accurate or fair. But it can get your personal story out to a wide audience. NFTE and Steve Mariotti came to the attention of ABC News and were featured twice in human-interest pieces that were broadcast nationwide. The videos of those segments helped Steve's and NFTE's credibility tremendously. If you're uncomfortable "blowing your own horn," find others who will do it for you and who can speak about you with authority.

✔ *Demonstrate self-confidence through your actions.* You can build credibility indirectly by your willingness to "bet" on yourself, for instance, by quitting a good job to start your venture or by using some of your own funds to cover early expenses. As your venture grows, you can continue to build credibility by taking bold steps that symbolize success and exhibit confidence. Remember Bill Strickland of Manchester Craftsmen's Guild (MCG) from Chapter 1? One of the factors that helped MCG attract major corporate partners in Pittsburgh was the high-quality building located in a tough section of town. Among other things, this stunning facility made a statement about Strickland's and the board's confidence in MCG's ability to grow and succeed.

✔ *Extend your positive track record with "early wins."* You can build credibility by having visible successes in the early stages of your venture. You need to document and celebrate these initial successes, even if they are relatively small wins. To have early wins, set clear benchmarks that can be used to demonstrate your capabilities and the venture's viability. These may be linked to the milestones in your plan, or they can be steps taken before you even reach the first milestones. Early wins help build everyone's confidence in you and the venture. Successful recovery from an early setback can also help instill confidence in your ability to handle the uncertainties associated with a new venture.

✔ *Borrow credibility from others, particularly the "bell cows."*[16] As with social capital, you can build credibility by borrowing it from the core team members you recruit, Board members, and major investors or donors. When they stake their reputations on your venture, their track records are added to yours. "Bell cows" can be particularly helpful. Bell cows are individuals with such strong reputations that they give instant credibility when they make a commitment. The herd follows them in! Who are the bell cows in your community or your field of endeavor? How could you get them on board? Many social entrepreneurs use advisory boards to capture some of the credibility of others who aren't prepared to make a major commitment to their ventures. This can work well; however, smart resource providers do understand the difference between an advisory board role and a more substantial commitment. They may discount the bell cow's endorsement accordingly. In addition to their reputations, your key stakeholders can lend you their credibility in concrete ways. For instance, they can guarantee a line of credit for you. This gives you a reserve to draw on and allows you to build your own credit rating by using and repaying the credit line. Soon you won't need their guarantee.

Don't oversell yourself or create a misleadingly positive spin. Exaggerations and hype can lead to unrealistic expectations. Failure to meet these expectations can seriously damage your credibility. Too big a halo can attract investigative reporters who want to get at the "true story" and tarnish the halo if they can. You need to build people's confidence in you and your venture while creating realistic expectations about what you will accomplish.

Enhance Shared Commitment

Of the three intangibles, shared commitment is the hardest to build on your own. Unlike social capital and credibility, the breadth and depth of shared commitment among potential resource providers is largely a function of social conditions that aren't in your control. Nonetheless, you can take steps to create commitment in specific individuals or in larger groups through advocacy. In order to advocate your cause to potential future resource providers, you need to perform the following tasks:

✔ *Identify the values that support your mission and methods.* People are motivated by values, particularly when it comes to investing their time and resources in a social venture. What are the values that could lead someone to support your mission and your methods? Start with the values that make it attractive to you, but don't stop there. Different people might support your mission for different reasons. For instance, the NFTE pitch earlier in this chapter draws on concerns for the welfare of children, economic empowerment of disadvantaged people, social and racial justice, and the role of entrepreneurship in creating economic prosperity. Anyone who cares deeply about one or more of these values is a candidate to embrace the NFTE concept. Developing your ability to articulate these value connections is the first step in building shared commitment to your mission.

✔ *Develop factual support for your efforts.* Values get you started, but you must make the case that your approach will effectively serve the values that potential resource providers hold dear. They may not see the connection as clearly as you do. Be prepared to document both the need for and the promise of your approach. For instance, people who are committed to education might not see the connection to a childhood nutrition program until they are shown how poor nutrition causes poor school performance. A combination of statistics and stories is usually needed. The statistics help document the magnitude, intensity, and growth rate of the need. Stories bring the message closer to home; they make it human and real.

✔ *Make your case to the right audiences.* Think of who you want to reach with your advocacy message. How do you get it out to the right resource providers—on an individual or a group basis? Once they're identified, create a presentation that builds on your "elevator pitch." The key is to tailor your message to your audience and connect with their deepest values. Pictures, slides, and videos can bring rhetoric and statistics to life. You also need access to the right venues to put you in front of the people you need to convince. Do they go to conferences? Could you speak at one of these conferences? What periodicals do they read? Could you publish an article in that periodical or be interviewed in it?

SUMMARY

This chapter has provided tools and frameworks to help you assess your needs and mobilize resources for your new venture. The approach proposed here is different from that found in most nonprofit management books. Instead of focusing primarily on fundraising, this chapter urges you to take a broader view, which should help make you a more effective and efficient fundraiser, and more important, a more effective social entrepreneur. If you are relatively new to this sector and need more specific guidance on fundraising, you'll have no trouble finding that information elsewhere.[17] You should take away from this chapter new perspectives and tools. Key points to remember are the following:

✔ Mobilizing resources isn't about amassing cash or assets; it's about building capabilities to deliver on your mission.

✔ Money is only one resource that you'll need and not the most important one.

✔ Consider alternative operating structures and economic models before settling on one approach; you may find a more resource-smart way of serving your mission.

✔ In assessing your resource needs, start with the social value you want to create, then work backward to determine your resource needs, keeping track of your assumptions.

✔ The success of your resource-mobilization efforts rests heavily on three intangibles: social capital, credibility, and shared commitments. Cultivate and manage these carefully.

✔ Be sensitive to the risks that resource providers are taking, and develop strategies for managing and allocating these risks.

✔ As best as you can, find resource providers whose capacities and interests match the character of your ongoing resource needs.

This chapter has provided some guidance on the resource-mobilization process; however, entrepreneurship is very much a trial-and-error process. Resource mobilization is no different. No simple formula or set of principles will guarantee success. Success will be determined partly by your willingness to hustle and to be opportunistic. Whatever plan you devise, be flexible and open to change. Things rarely go according to plan. Have fun![18]

Endnotes

1. Facts for this example are drawn from "Steve Mariotti and NFTE," Harvard Business School case #391–169, prepared by Alice Oberfield under the supervision of J. Gregory Dees, revised December 7, 1994.

2. See my article "Enterprising Nonprofits," *Harvard Business Review,* Jan.–Feb. 1998, for a more thorough discussion of the options and the pros and cons of earned income strategies.

3. Versions of this spectrum have appeared in the author's "Enterprising Nonprofits," *Harvard Business Review,* Jan.–Feb. 1998, and in two earlier Harvard Business School notes, "Social Enterprise: Private Initiatives for the Common Good," with Elaine Backman (#395–116) and "The Social Enterprise Spectrum: Philanthropy to Commerce" (#396–343).

4. How you raise it depends on the legal structure of your for-profit, whether it is a proprietorship, partnership, limited partnership, regular corporation, limited-liability corporation, or subchapter-S corporation. For an explanation of these choices, see, for instance, Barbara S. Shea, esq., with Jennifer Haupt, *Entrepreneur Magazine Small Business Legal Guide* (New York: John Wiley & Sons, 1995), especially chapters 2–4.

5. Jeffrey Orenstein, under the supervision of Professor J. Gregory Dees, "Help The World See: Self-Sustaining Eye Care in Belize," Harvard Business School case #897–142.

6. Rita Gunther McGrath and Ian C. MacMillan, "Discovery-Driven Planning," *Harvard Business Review,* July–August 1995.

7. This point is inspired by Dick Levin's *Buy Low, Sell High, Collect Early & Pay Late* (Englewood Cliffs, NJ: Prentice-Hall, 1983).

8. This section of the chapter draws particularly on four publications that are highly recommended to the interested reader. Amar Bhide, *The Origin and Evolution of New Businesses* (New York: Oxford University Press, 2000); Amar Bhide and Howard Stevenson, "Attracting Stakeholders," Harvard Business School note #389–139; Bob Reiss, *Low Risk, High Reward* (New York: Free Press, 2000), and Jennifer A. Starr and Ian C. MacMillan, "Resource Cooptation via Social Contracting: Resource Acquisition Strategies for New Ventures," *Strategic Management Journal,* vol. 11, 1990.

9. This concept is applied to both individuals and to collectives. Although he did not coin the term, Robert D. Putnam is primarily responsible for its current popularity. See, for instance, his *Bowling Alone: The Collapse and Revival of American Community* (New York: Simon & Schuster, 2000).

10. See, for instance, the analysis by Jennifer A. Starr and Ian C. MacMillan, "Resource Cooptation via Social Contracting: Resource Acquisition Strategies for New Ventures," *Strategic Management Journal,* vol. 11, 1990.

11. Kay Sprinkel Grace, *Beyond Fund Raising: New Strategies for Nonprofit Innovation and Investment* (New York: John Wiley & Sons, 1997), p. 88.

12. For examples, see Bhide, *The Origin and Evolution of New Businesses* (Oxford: Oxford University Press, 2000), pp. 80–82.

13. These points are inspired by Regina Herzlinger, "Effective Oversight: A Guide for Nonprofit Directors," *Harvard Business Review,* July–August 1994.

14. See Chapter 2 in Malcolm Gladwell, *The Tipping Point* (Boston: Little Brown & Company, 2000).
15. These suggestions are based on categories suggested by Starr and MacMillan, pp. 86–87.
16. See note 8 on "Attracting Stakeholders" by Bhide and Stevenson.
17. A useful place to start is Kay Sprinkel Grace's *Beyond Fund Raising: New Strategies for Nonprofit Innovation and Investment* (New York: John Wiley & Sons, 1997).
18. The author wants to thank Melissa Taylor for invaluable assistance in editing this chapter down to a reasonable size.

Chapter 5

THE ACCOUNTABLE SOCIAL ENTREPRENEUR

*Jed Emerson, Co-founder, Roberts Enterprise Development Fund and Bloomberg
Senior Research Fellow in Philanthropy, Harvard Business School*

IN THIS CHAPTER

Defining accountability and understanding its dimensions

The rationale for being an accountable social entrepreneur: why bother?

*The accountability trap: feeling accountable to all, being accountable
to none*

Making accountability work for you: moving from concept to action

On stubbing your toe: possible implications of being accountable

The six steps to meaningful accountability

Social entrepreneurs are swash-buckling, independent thinkers striking
out to create social change! They stand on the bow of the ship, crashing
through the sea of injustice, setting sail for a new land of effective programs and thrilling social innovation! They are accountable to no one,
blazing a trail through needy communities, leading the people to a
brighter tomorrow! Uh . . . actually . . .

Although there are those who, in their more daydreamy moments,
would submit to this vision, the fact of the matter is that real social entrepreneurs are not "loners" but work as a part of an extended network
of individuals and groups, all of whom are concerned with the common
goal of addressing a critical social issue or community need. Therefore,
all social entrepreneurs must work hard to communicate with and be accountable to various stakeholders. In fact, social entrepreneurs are probably more concerned about issues of accountability than many people
given their commitment to the fundamental values of social change and
effectiveness. This chapter is about accountability: what it is, why it's an
important issue for social entrepreneurs, and much more.

DEFINING ACCOUNTABILITY AND UNDERSTANDING ITS DIMENSIONS

core concept Webster's defines *accountable* as being "subject to giving an account: answerable." Giving an account means more than describing what you have done. It also means addressing the question of what you have actually accomplished and explaining your performance. But being accountable isn't limited to what one has done in the past. Responsible social entrepreneurs make an effort to inform various stakeholders where they are headed and how they intend to get there. Responsible entrepreneurs are committed to continual improvement and growth as they are to whatever more general social or other policy agenda they are attempting to pursue; however, we are not simply social sector news racks on the street, dispensing information in a "one-way" direction. If one is answerable to someone and responsible for providing them with information, then it only follows that one must also allow one's "audience" to influence the course of actions being described and undertaken. The person to whom you are responsible has some influence or power based on how they like your account of your actions and efforts to improve on them. After all, it would be ineffective to simply say, "We are accountable to the community, so we publish our information, but the community should have no say as to what our organization does on their behalf!" Accountability for social entrepreneurs entails a trust we are given and one that we must fulfill by both communicating our experience to those outside our organization and responding to feedback provided by others.

THE RATIONALE FOR BEING AN ACCOUNTABLE SOCIAL ENTREPRENEUR: WHY BOTHER?

Social entrepreneurs are more than simply people with interesting ideas. Social entrepreneurs are people with vision, insight, and enthusiasm, but they are also first and foremost people who ask others to *trust* their vision, insight, and enthusiasm. From a legal standpoint, this trust is expressed by virtue of the fact that you are given a special tax status (tax exempt) that says, "We think what you are doing is so important for society that we are going to free you from one of the two most certain things in life: Taxes!"[1] In exchange for this special status, you must promise to pursue your social goal with integrity and honesty—in a very real sense, you are given a public trust to have and protect. Being publicly accountable is how social entrepreneurs demonstrate fulfillment of that trust.

Sometimes in the course of saving the world, social entrepreneurs can easily forget that this trust is central to their effectiveness. In the midst of battle (whether fundraising, developing new programs, or managing a thriving enterprise), it can be easy to forget about the need for accountability because, after all, ". . . we're here doing things that are good for society—of course we're doing the right thing!" Indeed, it is easy to view accountability as a burden—something you *have to do,* but a time- and process-intensive task that gets in the way of actually *doing* the work itself.

BUILDING AN EFFECTIVE NONPROFIT ORGANIZATION

The truth is, however, that accountability is an important component of building an effective nonprofit organization. In the for-profit sector, organizations are held accountable to a variety of constituents: customers, investors, and lenders, among others. Each of these groups plays a role in ensuring that the corporation does as it says it will. They act as checks and balances to management and employees of the corporation. And, depending on how management responds, they can help make the organization highly profitable. Regina Herzlinger has presented the following "three basic accountability mechanisms" that nonprofits lack but businesses have:

1. "The self-interest that comes with ownership."
2. "The competition that would force efficiency."
3. "The ultimate barometer of business success, the profit measure."[2]

By contrast, in the nonprofit sector, there are really no comparable checks and balances. With the exception of the legal responsibility of the nonprofit Board of Directors to oversee the activities of staff, nonprofit customers must often accept services on a "take-it-or-leave-it" basis. Advocates can convene press conferences and issue papers "in the name of the community" without really being required to be accountable to that same community. Funding decisions may be made by individuals who are often far removed from the ultimate target of those decisions. The nonprofit sector really operates in a much different environment when it comes to accountability.

ACHIEVING MISSION AND VISION

Without such direct "feedback loops," however, social entrepreneurs are also often at a loss to know whether they are truly fulfilling their own mission and vision. Critical questions to be answered include the following:

✔ Are all of our core players committed to our central mission?
✔ Are we truly effective in our work?

✔ Are we efficient in our application of resources?

✔ Do we have a responsible funding strategy that is consistent with our stage of organizational development?

✔ Do we have a management information system (for both core program and our finances) in place that is appropriate for our organization's future?

✔ Does our work have an appropriate impact?

✔ Do our words reflect the reality of our actions?

Each of these issue areas should be the focus of discussion and inquiry for the nonprofit engaged in creating a long-term commitment to accountability. For effective social entrepreneurs, the pursuit of accountability becomes a mechanism to help ensure that they *are* achieving their goals and being responsive to their social cause and mission. Accountability is an opportunity to document the added value that social entrepreneurs bring to the community marketplace. In the best-case scenario, accountability becomes a central part of any social entrepreneur's agenda.

Finally, managers who pursue the creation of a culture of accountability within their organization must be convinced that, as Epstein and Birchard state, the benefits of doing so include the following improvements:

✔ Improved decision making

✔ Accelerated learning

✔ Better strategy execution

✔ More empowered workforce

✔ Better ability to communicate your story

✔ Enhanced loyalty[3]

Accountability can be used as a tool to create a more effective, higher-performing organization. As Epstein and Birchard state:

gem of wisdom

"The concept [of accountability] evokes the image of a higher authority, stern-faced, banging on the table for an explanation . . . However, this menacing, autocratic form of accountability contrasts with an appealing, empowering variety. Rather than act as a stick to keep people in line, the principles of accountability can act as a carrot to keep them climbing to higher levels of performance. The greatest beneficiary of accountability need not be some higher authority, an outsider or special interest group. It can be the organization itself . . ."[4]

Part of the leadership responsibility of the social entrepreneur is to create an operating environment that enables all those involved—both staff and volunteer—to realize their full potential contribution to achieving the organization's mission. Building an organizational structure that enables people to understand performance expectations and show the world how those expectations are being pursued and exceeded is one important aspect of being an effective social entrepreneur.

THE ACCOUNTABILITY TRAP: FEELING ACCOUNTABLE TO ALL, BEING ACCOUNTABLE TO NONE

Let's face a truth: When many nonprofit managers hear the word "accountability," they immediately see a wave of reports and forms drowning them in a sea of multiple demands from countless sources, such as the following:

- ✔ Board and staff members who want to know what is going on and how the organization is doing.
- ✔ The new client advocacy group that formed last year and wants a say in how you design your program.
- ✔ Public sector funders with their monthly reports and public hearings.
- ✔ The small merchant up the street who came and testified against allowing "yet one more nonprofit" to open a new program in the neighborhood.
- ✔ Ten different private foundations and four major national foundations, each of which gave you a grant and each of which has a different evaluation form they expect you to complete.
- ✔ The group of key individual investors, each of whom put up "new money" and each of whom thinks they should tell you what to do with it.
- ✔ The general public: people calling for annual reports, copies of your 990, and information on how well you are meeting your goals, so they may decide whether or not to send in their $50 check.

All of these demands are enough to turn today's idealistic social entrepreneur into tomorrow's burnt-out manager! So, before we explore who is out there and what you owe them, let's all take a deep breath and repeat, in a slow, calm voice:

We are not all things to all people.

We are accountable first to ourselves and then to others.

We can give everyone what they need, if not what they want!

THE THREE KEYS TO PRIORITIZING STAKEHOLDERS

If we attempt to respond to all demands for information and account-ability in the same way, we will be overwhelmed. With a little thought and reflection, however, we can prioritize the various stakeholders to whom we feel accountable and provide them with information opportunities that give them what they need to know, while keeping you sane. In addition to giving out information, we can create several mechanisms to allow us to gather information we may then use to make sure we are pursuing the right analysis and strategies. So, how do we begin building such a system within our organization?

action step   First, accountability begins with entrepreneurs making sure that their organizations have an openly stated mission, one that is clear and unambiguous. The mission statement is the social entrepreneur's primary contract with society, funders, clients, members (if the organization has them), and employees. Performance against mission is the most important thing a social entrepreneur owes anyone.

Second, within this mission, one must recognize and accept the fact that different constituencies have different interests and understandings of your organization and how it should be applying its resources. Balancing competing demands can be tough, but one must first accept the fact that upon being provided with the information you do have available, some folks will ask for or demand more than you may have the capacity to give. Simply recognizing and making peace with that fact at the outset will help make your journey to accountability much easier.

Third, there are three basic criteria to keep in mind when attempting to assign various stakeholders with a level of priority in your accountability strategy:

1. *What is the extent of their **prior contribution** to your organization?* People and organizations that have helped make your non-profit what it is today should have greater priority for your attention than those who have made no contribution of resources to assist in your success. This contribution is certainly not strictly a financial proposition. Those who served on committees, provided you with the intellectual capital you needed to understand a particular issue or strategy, or took other steps to provide you with what you needed to get going deserve an accounting of how you applied their contribution and what results you have leveraged from it, unless you simply paid them for a service or contribution of some type.

2. *What is the extent to which they may be **vulnerable to poor performance** or **mismanagement** on your part?* Who is most at risk if you perform badly? How well positioned are these groups or indi-

viduals to "protect" themselves from this risk? The most vulnerable groups are often those that, by choice or circumstance, place the greatest trust in your vision and stated ability to fulfill your mission. These individuals may be clients or program participants, but they could also be area residents, your staff, or others. If your actions will affect others, you are accountable to them.

3. *What is the importance to you of their **future support?*** This criteria is clearly a pragmatic one and may not have the same standing as the previous two; however, it is an important consideration when assessing the relative priority of stakeholders and others. If you do not respond to groups whose participation or investment is crucial for your future survival and success, you will not survive or succeed for long. You may not "owe" them an account of your progress, unless they also fall into the other groups, but it would be wise to give them one.

ON BEING ACCOUNTABLE

In addition to the three criteria for prioritization discussed in the previous section, two more things are worth reflecting upon:

First, what do you owe the tax-paying public in general and, more specifically, within your field of practice? The American public has extended to you the right to avoid taxation in exchange for your commitment to create real social value. You owe it to the public to make a real effort to track your performance and report to them on how you are doing in your work. Although "society" can seem generalized and far away, your field of practice is not. Very few social entrepreneurs operate in a vacuum. Others helped you along as you came through your learning curve, and others are still behind you, who have a right to expect that you will work, at least in part, to build the field of knowledge in order to continually innovate and improve on the strategies and efforts being executed by your organization.

This doesn't mean that all entrepreneurs have to work evenings and weekends to write thick books analyzing their work, or spend hours of their time helping last year's "organizational development" consultants to become this year's "social entrepreneur consultants." It does mean that building the intellectual capital and practitioner networks of the field is important. Social entrepreneurs make a genuine effort to create and leave documentation of their work and impact. We should all promote our various learnings that came out of our experience and be proud to discuss the difference between what we initially understood and what we came to understand through experience. We should attend conferences and participate in online listserv discussions. We should write about and discuss ideas with our peers. It is easy to get swamped with requests for information and knowledge, yet we should share openly with our nonprofit partners and the general public through strategic use of Websites, paper dissemination, and discussions. This effort is all a part of pursuing accountability.

Second, it is important to understand that our sense of priority may be situational and change or evolve over time as relationships shift, new resources are committed, and new partnerships are forged. As you consider relative groupings of stakeholders, think about the variation in value brought by each member of a group and how they relate together. For example, one stakeholder category may be "foundations." The amount of priority given to each funder will differ based on your relationship with them, the funding history, the amount of funds already committed, and the amount of funds you hope to secure in a future investment. Being aware and comfortable with the situational nature of prioritizing stakeholders can help you feel less stress and less torn by multiple demands from those in the same general group.

MAKING ACCOUNTABILITY WORK FOR YOU: MOVING FROM CONCEPT TO ACTION

As we think about how to approach making our commitment to accountability a reality, it may be helpful to create a "punch list" for accountability, a framework we can use to organize our work. Let's begin by stating that when you pursue an accountability agenda for your organization, you should complete the following tasks:

1. Identify those constituencies to whom you are accountable and for what.
2. Measure your performance in meaningful ways (in a way that helps you answer the *why* questions, as well as the *what* questions).
3. Communicate to your key constituencies an understandable, timely, and accurate account of your performance.
4. Create processes to ensure that those to whom you are accountable can voice their reactions and exercise appropriate influence on your future actions.
5. Build management systems that respond to both the internal performance information and the external feedback from the constituencies to whom you are accountable.[5]

In the following sections, we take a close look at each of the framework's elements in turn.

IDENTIFY THOSE CONSTITUENCIES TO WHOM YOU ARE ACCOUNTABLE AND FOR WHAT

Obviously, if one is interested in being more accountable, it is important to know to whom we are supposed to be directing this effort at greater accountability! Figuring out "who's in and who's out" can be quite a task, so Exhibit 5.1 might help by presenting a jumping-off point for your mapping process. The main point here is for you to brainstorm with your Board and staff to identify as many of the relevant key players as possible.

The left side of the chart lists some general categories to get you started. Fill in as many specific names and organizations as possible. And, of course, add additional categories and types of players in the blank spots as appropriate. The main point is to begin to think about and answer the questions along the top axis of the chart. These central questions are as follows:

✔ Who are they?

✔ What role do they play?

✔ How are you connected with them?

✔ What is the most effective way for you to communicate your work to them?

✔ On a scale of 1 to 3, with 3 being least important, what priority ranking would you assign to them?

✔ How can you develop a stronger connection to them?

Understanding and Identifying *"Complementors"*

Before we prioritize your list, look at it carefully and think about which organizations are existing or likely "complementors." Adam Brandenberger and Barry Nalebuff coined the term *complementors* to describe players whose products or services complement yours. As Brandenberger and Nalebuff put it: "A player is a complementor if customers value your product more when they have the other player's product than when they have your product alone."[6] Thus, the day care center is a complementor to the job-training program for young mothers, even if the two have no formal relationship.

Some complementors are organizations with whom you have already developed a natural relationship and others are ones with whom you may share a potential competitive advantage, but with whom you have not yet "inked a deal." Understanding the potential for creating new strategic alliances is a large part of understanding how to frame issues of accountability in the social sector. Go back through your list and place a

EXTERNAL ENVIRONMENT

KEY PLAYERS

Governmental Contracting Authorities

Government, Planning, and Regulatory Officials

Business

  Small Business Leaders

  Large Business Leaders

Local Community Residents

Civic Groups (Chamber of Commerce, Lions, Junior League, etc.)

Bankers

Faith-Based Organizations

Local Business Schools and other Academic Institutions

Legal Services Groups

Professional Organizations

Suppliers

Competitors

Media Outlets

Media Contacts

(continues)

EXHIBIT 5.1   Who's in and who's out.

Regulatory Agencies

National Associations

Special-Interest Groups

Political Adversaries

EXTERNAL STAKEHOLDERS

Area Residents

Community Associations

Direct Allies

Direct Competitors

Communities of Interest

Joint-Venture Partners

EXTERNAL INVESTORS

Foundations

Government

Individual Donors

INTERNAL ENVIRONMENT

INTERNAL STAKEHOLDERS

Board

Staff

Program Participants

EXHIBIT 5.1   Who's in and who's out (continued).

small "c" next to each organization you think does or may act as a "complementor" to your organization and assess how they "stack up" in your priority ranking of other players in your grouping.

Prioritizing and Organizing . . .

Now that you have your list of players in your marketplace, you are ready to prioritize your groups. To help organize all of this information, it may be best to "clump" your various accountability groups and then prioritize within each group. In their book *Counting What Counts,* Epstein and Birchard focus on four core groups: shareholders, employees, customers, and communities. And in her forthcoming book *The Four By Four Report,* Professor Regina Herzlinger identifies the four key constituencies for the nonprofit sector as clients, staff, donors, and society. In light of our focus on social entrepreneurs, we would build on this idea of four key groups as defined by Dr. Herzlinger, but further refine them as the following entities:

- ✔ Program participants, clients, and the "beneficiaries" of public policy initiatives supported by the non-governmental organization (NGO)
- ✔ Staff: both salaried and nonsalaried
- ✔ The general tax-paying public
- ✔ Investors

Now, take your mapping list and further divide them into these four groups, while ranking them as to whether they should receive a 1, 2, or 3 in your priority ranking within each of these constituent areas (with 1 being most important). With this listing now in place, you are set to move to the next area of focus—namely, figuring out what information you will track and how you will share it with your target groups.

MEASURE YOUR PERFORMANCE IN MEANINGFUL WAYS (TO HELP ANSWER THE WHY QUESTIONS, AS WELL AS THE WHAT QUESTIONS)

Having completed the previous exercise to identify each player and understand how you might best relate to them, you are more than halfway to building an effective accountability strategy. In fact, having a process in place to ensure accountability can help you actually *be* accountable. To paraphrase a common saying, *The destination of accountability is the journey toward being accountable!*

As you engage groups in discussion concerning your interest in providing them with the type of information they think would help them understand more about what it is you do and what challenges you confront, you are being more accountable to them and responding to their stated needs. Achieving accountability is not simply a question of stopping at any one point in time and saying, "We are an accountable organization." It is a matter of engaging in a series of steps that communicate your work and process to those outside and inside your organization who have a vested interest in contributing to your evolving success.

Therefore, the first step in communicating information to others is having information that is available and of interest to players inside and outside your organization. Countless books and articles discuss the issue of evaluation. These will no doubt be of interest to you; however, keep in mind that what is at issue here isn't necessarily a question of whether you are evaluating what you do as much as a question of whether you have built adequate management information systems to track what you do, providing you and others with valid information regarding your work. It is important to have the appropriate measurement and performance systems in place, but without the appropriate management information systems present to assist you in organizing and processing that information, the information is useless to yourself and those with an interest in your work.

In addition to having the appropriate systems functioning inside your organization, the effective social entrepreneur also maintains a way to gather information and measure performance in the external environment. The flamboyant former mayor of New York, Ed Koch used to pride himself on being out in the community and on the street. When he greeted his constituency, he didn't ask them, *"How are you doing?"* Instead, he hollered out, "Hey! How am *I* doing?" He was always looking for feedback and gathering information on his performance.

Who is your Ed Koch? What is your mechanism to ensure that you are listening not only internally but also externally? Examine your organization and its operations to see how you can reach outside your traditional operating environment to ask, *"Hey! How are we doing?"*

You will be amazed at the type of information you will receive— information that may make a critical difference in not only the degree to which you are accountable to your communities of interest, but also the degree to which you are successful in continually improving how your organization meets its goals and fulfills its mission.

COMMUNICATE TO YOUR KEY CONSTITUENCIES AN UNDERSTANDABLE, TIMELY, AND ACCURATE ACCOUNT OF YOUR PERFORMANCE

Many organizations publish year-end annual reports to send out to donors and others from whom they would like to solicit support. We are all familiar with the standard government and foundation reports we complete in order to fulfill the terms of our funding. But, when we use the word "communicate," we are talking about a lot more than simply a reporting relationship wherein we have finished the task once we have published our annual numbers and written about all the great things we did the prior year. By communication, we mean that the organization should engage in an effort to really connect with its various audiences and stakeholders in a way that is tailored to the needs of the group with which we are attempting to interact.

The Role of the Policy Statement

Oddly enough, the first step to truly communicating as an organization is often creating a policy that really affirms our intent and specifically tells internal and external players how we intend to fulfill that commitment. Perhaps the first step for any organization concerned about fulfilling its commitment to being accountable is to draft a policy stating its commitment and outlining what the public and other stakeholders may expect to see from the organization.

Such a policy statement would include the following elements:

✔ Dates by which time financial statements will be publicly available

✔ Schedules of committee and other meetings that are open to public input and participation

✔ Other "nontraditional" ways by which the organization intends to engage in communication with those important to it

✔ Identification of documents (e.g., annual reports, financial analyses, social audits) to which individuals may be directed that provide access to information of interest to those who seek a deeper understanding of the program and its activities

Such a policy of documenting and regularly communicating with others provides more than direction to those who want to have information about the organization—it supports creating an organizational culture that views itself as open to public accountability responsiveness and learning.

CREATE PROCESSES TO ENSURE THAT THOSE TO WHOM YOU ARE ACCOUNTABLE CAN VOICE THEIR REACTIONS AND EXERCISE INFLUENCE

In a classic sense, the nonprofit Board of Directors is supposed to be the vehicle by which a community holds its nonprofit sector to accountability. A Board of Directors is supposed to represent the interests of society and community. At a minimum, the nonprofit Board of Directors is the primary, formal, and legal oversight mechanism for nonprofit organiza-

CASE STUDY

THE JOHNSON & JOHNSON CREDO

A great example of a sound corporate policy statement that affirms the organization's intent and interests in communicating and developing a sound relationship with its key players is the "J&J Credo," which reads, in part, as follows:

"We believe our first responsibility is to the doctors, nurses, and patients, to the mothers and fathers and all others who use our products and services." It then articulates the responsibilities to these customers (i.e., quality products, reasonable prices, prompt and accurate service).[7]

The company credits its credo, which places the customers first among the big four, with guiding senior management through the Tylenol poisoning crises at Johnson & Johnson.

Of course, a policy statement on its own is of little use—it must be made real by a set of systems that allow the organization to share its performance with those outside the organization, internalize that feedback, and make whatever adjustments are deemed necessary to improve on its performance. It must create a process by which those outside of the organization can have their voices heard and responded to.

tions. Aside from the IRS and state attorneys general, however, which usually get involved only in cases of extreme malfeasance, the Board is often the only ongoing "accountability mechanism" available—and all too often its functioning is often weak, behind the curve, and not directly connected to the many communities of interest that might have a stake in the organization's mission.

Boards of Directors and Accountability

For-profit Boards of Directors are not always without problems; however, in that case, shareholders have the legal right to remove Board members and redirect corporate affairs—not an easy task, to be sure, but a legal right nevertheless. In fact, in recent years shareholder activism has been a significant way many community and advocacy groups have worked to raise community and social concerns at the highest level of corporate America. Indeed, even mainstream investors such as CalPERS, TIAA-CREF, and other large institutional investors have forced many for-profit boards to shape up by appointing more independent directors, provide more complete disclosure of corporate affairs, be more forthright regarding executive compensation, and so forth.

Unfortunately, many nonprofit organizations stand behind the curtain of the Wizard of Oz, removed from their communities and seemingly unaccountable for their actions. This state of affairs has even led to legislative initiatives in cities such as San Francisco where "sunshine" legislation for nonprofit organizations receiving city funding is being considered to open the books of nonprofit agencies serving the city's citizens.

A Community Committee Structure

In addition to creating a policy statement affirming the organization's accountability and interest in being open to public input, social entrepreneurs should also consider creating formal opportunities for stakeholders to hear what is happening and (if appropriate) be recruited to participate in support of the organization's work.

Creating an appropriate committee structure can provide stakeholders with a formal way to learn what is happening and what challenges the organization is addressing. Such an approach might include the more traditional community advisory and/or management support committee or the convening of an annual Community Congress, at which a "Community Accounting" is presented to the public and others interested in the affairs of the nonprofit and at which the operating agenda is set for the coming year. Every nonprofit organization should seek to recruit community members for Board service on its various standing committees.

But a community committee structure could also promote more operationally or project-focused committees. For example, a Venture Committee structure has been helpful for those engaged in social-purpose enterprise development. Such committees also provide a vehicle for both financial and other investors to be briefed on and engaged in strategy development. Such a committee might address accounting issues, marketing, e-commerce, product development, new program development, and other issues specific to the organization itself.

BUILD MANAGEMENT SYSTEMS TO RESPOND TO BOTH THE PERFORMANCE INFORMATION AND THE FEEDBACK FROM THE CONSTITUENCIES TO WHOM YOU ARE ACCOUNTABLE

Finally, the central purpose of life for social entrepreneurs is to create positive social and other changes in society. Knowing whether or not you are actually *doing* so can be a major challenge for many groups, regardless of the specific area being addressed. Historically, such efforts have fallen under the general catchall of "evaluation" and have not been widely embraced by many entrepreneurs. For many, evaluations have tended to be externally imposed and not very helpful in contributing to creating a better approach to what are often challenging issues.

More recently, social entrepreneurs have come to view this issue not in terms of evaluation, but rather as an opportunity to build management information systems that can assist both entrepreneurs and staffs in understanding more about what effects their particular approach is having and how to maximize organizational effectiveness. To successfully pursue this approach, entrepreneurs must proactively enunciate what goals are sought and how the proposed strategies achieve those goals. Furthermore, those investing in the organization must support investing in strategies to build information systems to effectively track program performance.

Once these systems are in place, the practitioners and their supporters must use that data to educate the organization's stakeholders and the general public regarding both the issue itself and the challenges of addressing it. This means more than simply reporting that "X" number of people were served or "Y" number of events held, but rather can be an opportunity to get behind the numbers to explain factors relating to causation and efforts to effectively intervene in a given community or social challenge.

At this level, being "accountable" is more than simply publishing financial information or describing general program goals, but rather provides an opportunity to use the *process* of being accountable to further communicate your message and purpose. The long-term effect of this strategy is that you become successful at engaging a broader potential audience in becoming your collaborators, working toward your future success!

ON STUBBING YOUR TOE: POSSIBLE IMPLICATIONS OF BEING ACCOUNTABLE

So, you've taken the leap and decided to become fully accountable to your various constituencies—you are the "responsible social entrepreneur" marching toward the creation of the "best of breed" in social enterprise, charting new directions in communicating, documenting, and distributing your knowledge, when—BAM!—you stub your toe on the reality of execution. Being accountable can be tough!

Accountability may also require the social entrepreneur to consider other factors as well—factors that may actually have a downside and that if you don't anticipate can become rocks in your road to success—rocks on which you can stub your toe! In this final section of the chapter, let's address some of those rocks and discuss ways you can see them in advance and step right over them!

A good way to approach this topic is to stop right where you are (stop walking *right in the middle* of the road you are currently on) and turn around for a second to look back at where you have come. Pause for just one minute to reflect on the following three questions:

1. What rocks have we already seen in our path on this road?
2. What were the issues we confronted and who were the key players involved?
3. How did we mobilize ourselves to step over (or move around) that rock?

Having done that, turn back around to face your new and emerging direction and ask the same questions:

1. What rocks can I see from here?
2. What are the issues we are likely to confront and who may be key players involved?
3. How could we mobilize ourselves to step over (or move around!) that rock?

How did you do? If you're having problems imagining what challenges you might face on your road to accountability, maybe some of the following examples will help:

✔ *"Nothing is constant but change."* Some people love and thrive within change, but most people hate it! Change can be scary, awkward, and numbing. It can make you feel nervous, ill prepared, and vulnerable. Creating a culture of accountability will, for many folks, be perceived not as an opportunity, but rather as a threat. So, accept that reality right up front. Change—and, more specifically, the resistance to change—will be one of the most obvious rocks in the road. Therefore, you should anticipate it, plan for it, and not be shocked when you're confronted with it.

✔ *"Do what I say, not what I do."* If accountability is to be meaningful, it needs to be integrated into the organization. This means creating a culture that values accountability. It should be obvious that organizational culture is heavily influenced by the *behavior* of leaders in the organization—by deed and not word. A very real rock in the road is that the leaders of the organization will convene a big meeting, make a huge presentation on the need for more accountability, and then days pass, months go by, the leaders move on to the next crisis or priority, and the need to pursue a culture of accountability is never heard of again. As the social entrepreneur in charge, it is your job to do as you say and model a behavior of accountability. Ask for people's input, value their contributions, and act on their suggestions. Open yourself up to the "accountability opportunity" in the same way you are asking your staff and Board to be at risk.

You will be amazed at not only the great benefits that will come to you, but also the great weight that can be lifted from your shoulders. When you open the doors and engage a broader set of stakeholders in your work, you will find that many others are willing to share the burden of moving your organization toward the attainment of its goals. "Modeling" accountability as a leader can be a liberating experience for *you* as well as your organization!

✔ *"Do you think I can get last month's report by sometime next year?"* The integration of accountability into an organization goes far beyond simply modeling behavior and affirming a culture of accountability. Accountability has to be made part of the management systems that are developed or that evolve within an organization or new venture. Opportunities for accountability must be integrated into the operating systems of the organization and become a part of a connected web flowing from policy making to strategy to reward/compensations and budgeting.

✔ *"We don't have any time, money, or resources. How can I help you?"* Although efforts to be more fully accountable can lead to the creation of organizations that are more effective and successful in the long-term, in the short-run being accountable can also require an investment of additional time and resources on the part of the organization. Therefore, it makes the most sense for organizations in early development to build a commitment to accountability into the culture of the organization from the beginning. Why make this effort to engage stakeholders at an early stage of organizational development? Because over time the benefits far outweigh any possible downside of additional resource requirement. Perhaps more important, the young organization that builds a commitment to accountability is better positioned in the long run to build honest partnerships and take on advocacy and other positions with greater integrity.

✔ *"When I asked what you thought, I didn't really think you'd tell me!"* By stating an organization's perspective and strategies openly and publicly, almost by definition one is leaving the organization open to being challenged by those with differing views. Furthermore, by publicly discussing your shortcomings, you may be open to those who would challenge both your approach and your ability to manage it. We may all be concerned about education, for example, but there is clearly an array of possible routes one might take to address that concern. In addition, although we all may share a given concern, others may raise questions regarding how an organization's funding is allocated, programs are developed, and directions are taken. Being accountable, however, does not mean one must be buffeted by the winds of public discourse on an issue. It simply means using the opportunity of being challenged by others to take in a different perspective, weigh its merits relative to your initial strategy, readjust your own approach to integrate what is valuable from this differing view, and in so doing continue to advance your own cause—that of yourself and your former "adversary."

THE SIX STEPS TO MEANINGFUL ACCOUNTABILITY

tool of the trade At the end of the day, what does this all mean? What final points should be held in mind? What are the Six Steps to Meaningful Accountability? Let's take them as follows:

1. *Embrace a Vision of Accountability.* Social entrepreneurs must come together with their key stakeholders and forge a stated commitment to the task and vision of the type of open, empowered organization they seek to create. You can't get to the next town without walking on the road, so figure out what town (Accountaborough?) you are heading to and make a commitment to get there.

2. *Make an Accountability Map.* Take yourself and your key players through the process outlined earlier and actually map out the organizations and individuals to whom you are accountable. Know them—and if you don't know them now, get to know them soon! Figure out which players fall where on the priority list and know why they have what rankings on your list.

3. *Develop an Accountability Strategy.* What steps stand between you and your goal? What rocks might be on your road? How will you get to where you want to go and what mechanisms will you need to have in place to get there?

4. *Act, Analyze, and Respond.* Get out there, engage your targets, hear what they have to say, think about what they said, and figure out an appropriate response. It's not enough to have a policy and a few committees organized; you must be fully connected and engaged in a process of reaching out, hearing, and responding to your targets.

5. *Do It Again.* As we move along in life, old habits die hard. You may have a sincere and genuine commitment to maintaining a posture of accountability, but things come up, new demands are placed on you, and you often have to place your focus elsewhere. If you fall away onto a side path for a few feet, don't worry. Just get back on the road to accountability and keep moving forward.

6. *Celebrate the Journey.* Sometimes being accountable can be a real pain in the ass. You have tons of meetings; if you ask some-

one what they think, that means you have to respond somehow to what they say; sometimes the whole thing is just more than you think it is worth. Don't worry! Be happy! You're building a better, stronger, more effective organization (even if you can't quite see around the next bend in the road to know you are headed in the right direction and getting closer). And that's what it is all about. Celebrate the process of becoming a truly great social entrepreneur!

SUMMARY

Although people working in the private sector are accountable primarily to their supervisors, social entrepreneurs are also accountable to the many stakeholders who are concerned with the common goals of addressing a critical social issue or community need. In this chapter, we defined accountability, and we considered the question of *why* social entrepreneurs should be accountable. We considered the implications of the accountability trap, learned how to move from concept to action, and discovered the possible implications of being accountable. Finally, we discussed the six steps to meaningful accountability.

Key points to remember are as follows:

✔ Real social entrepreneurs are not loners but work as part of a network of like-minded individuals.

✔ Responsible social entrepreneurs make an effort to inform stakeholders where they are headed and how they intend to get there.

✔ Accountability helps social entrepreneurs ensure that they are achieving their goals and being responsive to their social cause and mission.

✔ Consider creating a "punch list" for accountability, a framework that you can use to organize your work.

✔ The destination of accountability is the journey toward being accountable!

✔ Communicate your performance to your key constituencies in an understandable, timely, and accurate manner.

✔ Watch out for the roadblocks to accountability.

Endnotes

1. The other, of course, being death, which is beyond even our control!
2. Regina E. Herzlinger, "Can Public Trust in Nonprofits and Government Be Restored?" *Harvard Business Review,* March–April 1996, p. 99.

3. Marc Epstein and Bill Birchard, *Counting What Counts: Turning Corporate Account-ability to Competitive Advantage* (Reading, MA: Perseus, 1999), pp. 12-16.
4. Ibid p. 4.
5. This outline is inspired by a similar one presented by Marc Epstein and Bill Birchard in *Counting What Counts: Turning Corporate Accountability to Competitive Advantage* (Reading, MA: Perseus, 1999).
6. Adam Brandenberger and Barry Nalebuff, *Co-opetition* (New York: Doubleday, 1996), p. 18.
7. Laura Nash, *Good Intentions Aside* (Cambridge, MA: HBS Press, 1990), p. 41.

Chapter 6

Understanding Risk, The Social Entrepreneur, and Risk Management

Jed Emerson, Co-founder, Roberts Enterprise Development Fund and Bloomberg Senior Research Fellow in Philanthropy, Harvard Business School

IN THIS CHAPTER

What does "risk" really mean?

The art of calculated risk taking

Understanding risk, reward, and the reason we're playing the game!

Understanding your options: strategies for managing risk

The potential costs of risk-reduction strategies . . . A word of caution

Learning from your mistakes

Traditional nonprofit managers usually think about risk in broad terms: "If we don't get that grant, there's a good chance we'll have to close that program." Or perhaps, "If we launch that program, we'll have to assume we'll be able to raise the funds to keep it going into the future."

These are both risk statements; however, there is a difference between how many nonprofit managers view the many and complex ways of understanding risk and the approach taken by many businesspeople or seasoned social entrepreneurs. This difference can be seen in the fact that a traditional grant proposal doesn't include a section on "risk factors" or "risk analysis," whereas every good business plan includes such a discussion.

What Does "Risk" Really Mean?

core concept

Although the for-profit sector has a large body of literature regarding risk, its various forms, and how to approach a quantitative analysis of risk exposure, the nonprofit sector really has no parallel understanding to guide our discussion. For the purposes of our approach to nonprofit risk, we may simply say that risk is the "possibility of an undesirable outcome." We can further define risk by saying that it can be understood as having two basic components that allow us to determine the potential severity of risk: (1) the potential *magnitude* of undesirable outcomes if they do occur—the "downside"—and (2) the *possibility* that these undesirable outcomes *will* actually occur.

It helps to understand that the overall level of risk is determined by "multiplying" these two factors together. In the most basic terms, *the product of magnitude and possibility* is the risk inherent in any given opportunity.

THE DIFFERENCE BETWEEN RISK EXPOSURE, A WILLINGNESS TO TAKE RISKS, AND GAMBLING

Some people think that to be an entrepreneur is to be a risk taker and a gambler. In many ways, risk is a central element of being an entrepreneur, and a social entrepreneur must be especially comfortable with that fact. For a traditional, for-profit entrepreneur, risk is most often tied to the performance of the business opportunity under consideration. As early as the 18th century, economist Richard Cantillon stated that entrepreneurs were risk takers who "buy at a certain price and sell at an uncertain price, therefore operating at a risk."[1] For those social entrepreneurs who operate social-purpose enterprises, such as a bakery employing untrained residents of a low-income neighborhood or a bike shop employing homeless youth, the business venture and specific risk it represents are important considerations.

Although there is some debate regarding the actual percentage of small business failure in the United States, it must be recognized that the challenges confronting any startup venture are often significant and should not be taken lightly.[2] Regardless of the type of enterprise under consideration, several risks must be taken into account—ranging from lack of operating capital, to a highly competitive market, to difficulty in penetrating one's sales targets—many of which are discussed later in this chapter. The reality, however, is that regardless of the type of social enterprise or program managed by the social entrepreneur, risk must be factored in, risk of a type and character with which the traditional entrepreneur may not be familiar.

Furthermore, on top of this different type of enterprise risk, social entrepreneurs deal with an array of *additional* risk factors not present in a traditional business venture. Namely, all social entrepreneurs are pursuing social goals and objectives that can often mean additional layers of both risk and reward. Yet, while the businessperson often has debt/

equity ratios and other metrics by which to understand risk,[3] how can the social entrepreneur best think about risk?

DEALING WITH RISK AND UNCERTAINTY

The good news is that by understanding risk and how best to manage risk exposure, social entrepreneurs can move ahead with some degree of confidence that they have "done their homework" and understand what may lie ahead. They may then turn their attention away from worrying needlessly about risk and toward the effective management of the enterprise. By being strategic, you can control an element of risk and work to create situations where, even if the "breaks" don't go your way, you are positioned to manage them effectively. This section explores how we understand the potential magnitude of what is at stake, think of the possibility of failure, and move to manage risk exposure as we proceed.

The Magnitude of Our Potential Loss

Kris Kristofferson said it best: "Freedom is just another word for nothing left to lose." If one has nothing at stake in a given proposition, one is completely free to walk away from the table without a care or concern for the outcome of the bet being wagered. Entrepreneurs, however, almost always have something at stake and must always carry the weight of their risk. That "weight" may best be understood as the magnitude of our potential loss—what undesirable outcomes may come from the outcomes not going our way? If we "bet the farm," it is not simply the fact that we stand to *lose* our farm if the deal goes bad, but the reality of all the related outcomes that might come from that single event—the total magnitude of the potential loss. We will have to move. We will lose a piece of land our family has worked for 100 years. We will have to shift our place in the community. When considering risk exposure, we must first pause to answer the most basic question: What is truly at stake? For the social entrepreneur, we want to avoid the following outcomes:

✔ Financial loss
✔ Damaged external reputation
✔ Damaged internal morale
✔ Loss of political leverage
✔ Missed opportunities
✔ Mission drift
✔ Negative (or severely disappointing) social returns

The amount of investment an organization is considering in a venture also influences the amount of planning one should engage in before

CASE STUDY

LEADERS OF SOCIETY—TOMORROW

Consider the following scenario and see how many of these risks you can identify:

Leaders of Society—Tomorrow (LOST) is a youth services organization located in Enterprise, Oklahoma. LOST is considering opening a food cart in downtown Enterprise to train youth in customer service. The financial investment they are considering is $10,000. Their planning group is also looking at opening a neighborhood restaurant to achieve the same purpose of training youth, but the build-out of the restaurant space will require an investment of $150,000. They have received a planning grant from the Mayor's Office of Community and Social Development for Enterprise and Affiliated Unincorporated Areas of $20,000. The grant was presented to them at a high-profile press conference hosted by the mayor of Enterprise and at which their district representative spoke glowingly of LOST's wonderful program track record and innovation in creating leadership training opportunities for young people of all races, creeds, and genders.

LOST's planning team is made up of the organization's executive director (an individual with more than 20 years of experience running nonprofit organizations), three Board members who sit on LOST's program development committee, and a youth representative from an outlying area of Enterprise. The idea for undertaking the venture came in part as a result of LOST's primary public funder having shifted its grant-making focus from the general category of "Youth in Crisis" (under which LOST had received support for the past seven years) to "Enterprise Opportunity Grants," a new grant-making category created after the victory of the mayor, who ran on a "Teach Each to Hunt, Don't Teach Each to Beg" platform. Although the executive director has long been interested in the idea of social enterprise, he is clear that LOST must reinvent itself to meet the challenges of a changing time.

What is the magnitude and types of financial *and* nonfinancial risk to which LOST is exposed?

Now, think about why you are reading this book and the type of venture you either presently manage or are considering. In thinking about your own situation, using the chart provided in Exhibit 6.1 may help you organize your definitions of risk. It may help to think of the possibilities of what is at stake for your own organization as falling into the general categories presented as follows. Next, rate each one in terms of the rank you would assign it. The purpose of this exercise is to help you consider one critical element of risk, the undesirable consequences and possible downsides of the proposition you are considering.

Risk Category	Specific Exposure	Risk Ranking
	(List what is specifically at risk; either in terms of the amount of funds for planning expense, capital expense, or other category of expenditure)	(Rank each specific risk exposure from A to D, with A being the most significant risk exposure)
Financial Risk	1.	1.
	2.	2.
	3.	3.
	4.	4.
Social Return Risk	1.	1.
	2.	2.
	3.	3.
	4.	4.
Political/Public Relations Risk	1.	1.
	2.	2.
	3.	3.
	4.	4.
Internal Organizational Risk	1.	1.
	2.	2.
	3.	3.
	4.	4.

EXHIBIT 6.1 Risk magnitude measurement: defining what is at stake and how much is at risk.

launching the enterprise. To continue our LOST example, if a food cart is being considered, the amount of resources invested in planning will no doubt be less than for a full-size restaurant. Unless an organization is viewing the launch of a small venture as the first step in the complete redesign of the sponsoring organization and its reinvention as a social-purpose enterprise for the new century, it is probably not necessary to bring in big-name industry consultants to work as part of a six-month planning committee that travels the country examining other food cart sites! Again, the risk exposure represented by a food cart is different from that of a restaurant and does not necessarily require the investment or the same amount of planning resources, thus fewer resources are at risk.

There is another wrinkle in understanding risk, magnitude of risk, and what is at stake: Many entrepreneurs focus on what has been invested without fully appreciating that *it is not simply a question of what is invested, but rather what you stand to lose!* Furthermore, a high level of investment does not necessarily mean a high level of overall risk. High investment (financial or nonfinancial) usually makes the potential loss high (provided that the investment is irreversible and salvage value is low); however, it may make the other element, the *probability* of the losses coming about, low. For example, undercapitalization of both nonprofit and for-profit enterprises may reduce the amount at risk, but it also increases the chances of failure, thereby making the total risk higher in the presence of a lower level of investment.

Finally, before leaving our discussion of the magnitude of what is at risk, it is worth specifically identifying an aspect of social risk that is important, namely that of client or human impact risk. When many social and economic innovations are vetted, we tend to focus on the perceived added value of a given proposal—new jobs, more people served, or greater efficiencies achieved—while overlooking or not giving equal consideration to the client or human impact risk involved. Whether a small, community-based nonprofit or a large human services organization, intended or unintentional impacts on the lives of people in our community or targeted group must be acknowledged and addressed.

When a neighborhood shelter moves from crisis intervention to long-term residential services with job training, the intent and shift of mission may be laudable, yet this shift may also have an adverse impact on people's lives. Indeed, if one considers the impact of welfare reform, one must take into account that although the number of individuals receiving support from welfare has decreased, the "weight" of the experiment in welfare reform does not rest on the policy makers or program managers, but on those very low-income individuals attempting to feed their families and change their lives. The magnitude of what is at stake as we pursue innovation in the social sector is not simply a question of organizational investment and risk but also individual life and prospects. This element of risk can never be taken too lightly or understated in our analysis. We may still opt to experiment with new approaches or explore new connections among programs, services, and social impact, but we must never lose sight of those whose interests are what is really on the table when we sit down to assess an opportunity or new idea.

The Possibility of Failure

The first thing we have to understand is that every opportunity under consideration contains various possibilities for a negative outcome—there are degrees of risk. Running across a busy freeway represents one level of risk, driving a car on that freeway represents another, and flying over the freeway in a commercial jet represents a third. Although risk is a central part of our lives, various degrees of risk are involved in every action we take. In thinking about their social enterprises, social entrepreneurs need to reflect on the degree of risk involved by asking the following questions:

- ✔ What is the real possibility that they will fail?
- ✔ What factors were present in the failure of others undertaking similar enterprises that did fail?
- ✔ In retrospect, could or should steps have been taken to increase the likelihood of success?
- ✔ What is the degree of risk they are considering in the venture?

THE ART OF CALCULATED RISK TAKING

The first step toward understanding the art of calculated risk taking is to know that there are two levels at which risk itself is experienced: individual and organizational. The way we experience risk (whether we are comfortable with it or we feel our heart beating rapidly high in our throats!) is known as "risk tolerance." Therefore, in order to accurately assess risk, we must first understand our own risk tolerance. What is extremely high risk for one person or organization may not be viewed as risky at all by another. On an objective or statistical level, some activities and undertakings are themselves more "risky" than others; however, our level of risk tolerance determines our ability to calculate what type of risk is actually represented *for us* by that given activity. And that is where some of the art of calculating risk takes place!

INDIVIDUAL RISK TOLERANCE

If you are reading this book, you probably have some sense of your own comfort level with risk at this point in your life. Individual risk tolerance is simply a matter of individual preference, taste, experience, and personality. Recognizing this, it must also be acknowledged that one's risk tolerance changes over time and in different circumstances. It is often said that young people are more comfortable with risk than older folks because they have "less to lose" and are less "conservative"; however, we all know young people who are extremely conservative when it comes to risk and older people who seem to have lost all sense of perspective as they climb mountains and race mountain bikes! Personal risk tolerance, then, is not a function of age, but rather a function of individuality and life.

Each of us must reflect on the degree to which we are comfortable assuming what levels of risk. There are various tools one may use in this process. Although it might seem odd, many retirement planning software packages include "risk tolerance tests" that assess whether one is a conservative, moderate, or higher-risk investor. By surfing the Web, you can find these tests and use them as part of your self-assessment process.

The following "Individual Checklist for Willingness to Take Risks" may also give you a good, thumbnail sketch of your ability to support different levels of risk exposure. Take a minute now and go through these simple questions to consider them with reference to how you might rate as a risk taker.

INDIVIDUAL CHECKLIST FOR WILLINGNESS TO TAKE RISKS[4]

- Can you take risks with money; that is, invest and not know the outcome?
- Do you take an umbrella with you every time you travel? A hot water bottle? A thermometer?
- If you're frightened of something, do you try to conquer the fear?
- Do you like trying new food, new places, and totally new experiences?
- Do you need to know the answer before you ask the question?
- Have you taken a significant risk in the last six months? A modest risk? Have you simply stayed home and phoned in sick?
- Can you walk up to a total stranger and strike up a conversation?
- Have you ever intentionally traveled an unfamiliar route?
- Do you need to know that it's been done already before you're willing to try it?
- Have you ever gone on a blind date?

Keep in mind that there is really no single test to take or a "best score." You should use this list as a discussion tool with your Board, planning committee, or management team as you go about your process of assessing each team member's perspective on risk and the role risk may play in making decisions with regard to starting new programs and social enterprises. From personal experience and knowing your own self, you are really the only one who can determine your degree of risk tolerance. The important thing is to be sure to reflect on this question before you and your team get too far down the path of social entrepreneurism!

If you discover that you are not a big risk taker, that does *not* mean you should give up on your dream of being a successful social entrepreneur. It does, however, mean that you will need to take that trait into consideration as you build your management team and begin pursuing your goals.[5] You *will* want to explore how you best deal with risk and how you can most effectively share that risk with others.

ORGANIZATIONAL RISK TOLERANCE

Different nonprofit organizations also have different degrees of risk tolerance. To some extent, this difference in risk tolerance is driven by organizational culture, as seen in the two following examples:

One nonprofit serving youth decided they wanted to open a store. They spent more than a year involved in their planning process, interviewing area residents, engaging in traffic counts, and learning everything they could about the type of store they wanted to open, and finally, opened a successful retail outlet.

Another nonprofit serving youth also decided they wanted to open a store. They spent 60 days looking for what they "felt" would be a good location, spent time discussing how their store would be "different" from others in the neighborhood, and launched the venture within 90 days of first deciding they wanted to do it.

In this case, both ventures turned out to be successful, but make no mistake about it—the second organization assumed a much higher degree of risk than the first. This was a function of the social entrepreneurs managing each venture and the culture of the nonprofits involved: one slow, deliberate, and concerned with attempting to minimize risk to the greatest degree possible; the other fast and focused, and willing to assume a greater degree of risk exposure. Which one was right? Both! Each organization understood its level of risk tolerance and ability to manage a process that worked for them.

In addition to the question of culture, one important element of organizational risk exposure is capacity. Organizational capacity is defined as the amount and type of infrastructure an organization brings to its work—staffing, operating systems, networks—essentially everything a nonprofit can put toward its effort and everything that may mean the difference between success and failure.

Assessing organizational capacity as it relates to risk can, however, be deceptive. Many practitioners assume that large, established organizations that have been active for many years represent less overall risk exposure because they have more resources, greater perceived stability, and what is felt to be an increased ability to successfully launch a new venture—whether a social-purpose enterprise or an innovative program. It should be recognized, however, that established organizations also bring more "cultural baggage" to the process of innovation. Those managing such organizations have, to one degree or another, a vested stake in current practice, goals, and programs. They are used to "doing things our way" and may not, in fact, be as entrepreneurial and innovative as those operating smaller, more agile organizations with less of an established track record that can respond more rapidly to shifts in the market and emerging challenges.

Regardless of the age and size of the organization, social entrepreneurs should assess their organization's level of risk tolerance and prospects for how that tolerance might affect the execution of their development strategies. What factors should you consider when assessing your organization's tolerance for risk? Some of the following areas would be important to explore:

Organizational Checklist for Willingness to Take Risks

- How does your organization make decisions? Is it a "process-intensive" culture or one where managers are encouraged to pursue their ideas and "apologize later"?
- What management systems are in place related to accounting, social reporting, and organizational evaluation? Are these systems closely controlled by either a department or an individual who is open to change?
- What has been your organizational history in this area? Has your nonprofit attempted to undertake any type of social enterprise in the past?
- When confronted with challenges, does the organization mobilize primarily political, intellectual, or human capital to overcome the challenge?
- Do you have a diversity of talent and skill sets, either on your staff or Board, that may be employed on challenges you are confronting or does it tend to be the "head of X" who gets charged with addressing a particular issue on their own?

Gambling versus risk taking

Finally, many people confuse risk taking with gambling, but the two are not the same. Understanding the difference can help a social entrepreneur manage when moving forward in uncertain times. In a phrase, *gambling* is when the house controls the cards and you are playing their game, whereas risk taking is when you define the game and seek to minimize all known risk factors in order to maximize the chances you will win.

True entrepreneurs demonstrate an ability to live with uncertainty *and* analyze risk. They are *informed* risk takers, not "seat of the pants" gamblers. Successful entrepreneurs are not simply the people with better ideas, but rather the people who know how to execute better ideas most effectively by applying appropriate resources and minimizing possible

risks that might take them out of contention.

Remember: *Take risks, but never gamble!*

Understanding Risk, Reward, and the Reason We're Playing the Game!

Of course, risk itself would be no real fun if not for the rewards that taking a risk may bring. In some cases, the reward is a fundamental one: If a tiger is chasing you and you take the risk of jumping off a cliff to dive into the water below and get away, that is a great risk—yet you get to keep living, which is a pretty good upside! In other cases, the rewards are more incremental, variable, and difficult to assess. For example, going out for dinner with your parents may give you the great reward of a wonderful evening out, sharing stories from your youth, and bonding with those who gave you life, but it also carries the risk that, when actually confronted by the sight of your folks, you will regress into a 14-year-old jerk, arguing as your parents punch every one of your emotional buttons and you run screaming from the restaurant.

What types of "upside" do entrepreneurs consider? A central one is obviously the financial upside to any business proposition. But of perhaps greater importance for both the traditional and social entrepreneur is that some of the upsides may have significant implications for the following areas:

- ✔ Diversifying your revenue or capital base
- ✔ Discovering new ways to pursue one's mission
- ✔ Redefining yourself in your "social market" as being a profoundly innovative nonprofit in your community—just to name a few!

For the social entrepreneur, there is often a major *social return* as a part of your upside—providing untrained youth with a "real-world" training opportunity, integrating environmental sustainability into a market that was engaged in wasteful production techniques, or promoting the cause you support through brand affiliation are only some of the benefits that might come to you. Therefore, it may help to understand that when thinking about the upside of risk, the following three factors are important to include:

1. Your "regret"
2. Your "upside"
3. Your "risk tolerance"[6]

We have already discussed risk tolerance, but what is "regret?" Regret is what you stand to lose if the breaks do not go your way and is another way to view the magnitude of your potential losses. How much will it hurt you if you burn through $200,000 attempting to launch a new retail store offering your organization's artwork for sale? How much do you stand to win? And how comfortable are you with hanging out between those two places until you know for sure which way it's going to go?

It must be acknowledged that developing a precise measure of risk and the likelihood that risk will continue into the future are both issues that further contribute to, uh, risk. Often with new ventures (whether new to the marketplace or simply to the organization itself), it may be extremely difficult to definitively state what the actual risk factors are and how they may be weighed against each other and the chance of their actually oc-curring. Sometimes this may simply be a function of how much or how little the entrepreneur can discover about a given proposition. A decision will need to be made with regard to how much time, energy, and other re-sources should be put into the "exploration" process. As a basic rule of thumb, never spend more on planning than you intend to spend on cap-italizing the new venture yourself. For example, if the start-up costs of a community garden are $50,000 and you project to be able to earn an an-nual revenue stream of $20,000 per year, you probably shouldn't spend $200,000 and three years on exploring what your relative risks are in launching the garden!

concept check   In addition to understanding that risk can be decreased at least in part through effective due diligence, it should also be re-membered that risk assessment is not a single, one-time propo-sition, but rather an *ongoing part of enterprise management*. The entre-preneur's understanding of products, markets, capital, and other factors will change with time (ideally increasing and thus *decreasing* risk), yet the external environment will also shift—perhaps decreasing risk exposure, but more often making the existing enterprise suscepti-ble to new and varied threats from any number of emerging or evolving areas. Entrepreneurs must be continually attuned to their environment and position within it to constantly be on the alert for the need to de-velop a new appreciation of their relative strengths, weaknesses, and risk exposure.

UNDERSTANDING FACTORS AFFECTING THE PROBABILITY OF RISK

In assessing risk exposure, a central process is to understand what fac-tors are at play that may affect the probability of a risk becoming reality; that is, the likelihood of a risk scenario actually playing out. Risk factors include the following:

- ✔ Quality of management
- ✔ Quality of the workforce
- ✔ Culture of the organization
- ✔ Strength of organizational infrastructure
- ✔ Basic enterprise concept
- ✔ Level of capitalization
- ✔ Prospects of long-term funding
- ✔ Changes in the marketplace
- ✔ Changes in technology

✔ Stakeholder backlash

✔ Competitor reaction

Let's examine each of these risk factors in turn:

Quality of Management

Perhaps the most significant risk to be considered is that of managerial risk. It has often been said that a good manager can succeed with a bad enterprise, but a bad manager will kill a good enterprise. Having the right players and working to ensure that they are an asset and not a risk is a central first step to minimizing managerial risk exposure. Questions to ask include whether the skill set of the management team is appropriate for the task at hand, how well the team works together, the degree to which the team is "rested and ready" to take on the new challenge, and other factors specific to the particular organization under consideration.

Quality of the Workforce

Although not every social entrepreneur is involved in operating business ventures, social-purpose enterprises that *do* seek to employ a given target population also represent a unique type of risk. Think about it: many social entrepreneurs attempt to run a business enterprise and make a profit with the same employees that everyone else in the marketplace has fired! The fundamental premise of the venture is extremely high risk. In a mainstream business, if workers underperform or have significant problems, one would terminate them from employment. In a social-purpose venture, however, a central element of your mission is to employ such individuals. The social entrepreneur minimizes the risk of employing low-skill individuals by ensuring that they have access to a variety of support programs (such as mental health counseling, subsidized housing, or other services) necessary for them to move toward greater personal success.

Culture of the Organization

The issue of organizational culture is woven throughout this book. Having an organizational culture that affirms entrepreneurial approaches to managing the challenge confronting the nonprofit is a crucial success factor to consider. For example, a central premise of pursuing entrepreneurial goals is the idea that if you don't have the right people for the job, you should replace the folks who can't manage the charge with those who can. This doesn't necessarily mean you terminate people with extreme prejudice, but simply that you recognize the fact that the organization will not achieve its goals or manage its risk exposure well with the wrong folks in the right slots. It is an issue of recognizing that you are doing folks a favor by helping them move into positions where they may have success and out of positions where they are having a lot of "learning experiences." Many nonprofit cultures, however, do not directly confront this reality and tolerate low or moderate performers much longer than appropriate. Having a culture appropriate to social enterprise means having an organization that supports all aspects of the pursuit of social value—for both communities and individuals. The lack of such a culture may represent a significant risk factor for the organization relative to its survival in the marketplace and should be recognized as such.

Strength of Organizational Infrastructure

The strength of organizational infrastructure is an organization's ability to take on a particular enterprise; that is, whether it has the capacity to manage a dynamic, market-based business venture. Questions to explore in this regard are as follows:

- ✔ Are all of your personnel already overextended and unable to cope?
- ✔ Does it take you six months to get last month's financial statements from accounting?
- ✔ Is the organization clear and focused on its mission, or are there competing factions driving conflicting agendas?

As discussed earlier, all organizations bring various strengths and weaknesses to the social enterprise process. Regardless of whether the initiative under consideration is a social-purpose enterprise or a new programmatic approach to a social problem, the organization sponsoring the venture brings its own element of risk to the venture's potential for success or failure. As described elsewhere in this chapter, prepared social entrepreneurs step back and assess not only their own strengths and weaknesses, but those of their organization as well.

Basic Enterprise Concept

In contrast to organizational risk, enterprise risk concerns that risk inherent in a specific program initiative or social-purpose enterprise. Questions to ask in this regard include the following:

- ✔ Is the enterprise strategy tested and reliable?
- ✔ Is it new and uncertain?
- ✔ Does the enterprise have a degree of risk greater than that of other, similar enterprises?
- ✔ What elements/factors make this particular enterprise risky?

All of these questions must be considered when assessing the relative risk of a given enterprise; however, the most important consideration of enterprise risk is that of the concept itself. You may be familiar with Gary

Larson's Far Side cartoon of two cave men attempting to sell "Porcupine-On-A-Stick." Although it makes a great cartoon, the product itself would open one up to not only significant product liability claims, but the reality of limited consumer interest as well. On a less humorous note, attempting to provide employment to those with violent-crime felony records by operating a child care center is obviously not a good idea because most parents would hesitate to become customers once they found out the history of the staff. On the other hand, Delancey St. Movers, which employs many ex-convicts and has an excellent track record of customer satisfaction, is a successful example of a much more viable business concept.

Level of Capitalization

The level and structure of capital is the amount of funds an organization will need to have on hand in order to launch a venture. Capitalization may include basic startup funds as described later, but it should also focus on costs such as equipment and plant acquisition, supplies and inventory adequate for startup, and other factors. Risk in this regard is usually tied to the ability of the organization to secure such capital and service any debt that might be a part of the capital structure.

The timing of capital infusion is also critical. It is understood that an evolving social enterprise requires various types of financing at various stages of development, but it must be recognized that the practitioner's inability to secure capital at the right time could be a significant element of risk. Many social entrepreneurs focus primarily on securing funds to plan or launch a venture and never consider (until it is too late!) the question of where *future* funds will come from. Indeed, the risk represented by undercapitalizing enterprises is not limited to social entrepreneurs but is one of the central causes of small business failure as well. Social entrepreneurs, however, should focus on this risk element and how to minimize its possible impact given the common nonprofit practice of launching social programs "on a wing, a prayer, and a seed grant." Again, it is the difference between taking a gamble and undertaking an informed amount of risk exposure.

Prospects of Long-term Funding

Funding risk includes such factors as the following:

✔ The amount of funds necessary to support the enterprise

✔ Whether or not those funds are readily available

✔ The amount of cash flow necessary to support the operation during its period of startup and expansion

Funding risk assessment should also consider the *cost* of accessing needed financial resources. If the organization must be represented at numerous meetings, complete multiple reports, and so forth, the process of securing the funds might cost more than the funds themselves are worth! This would include interest payments as well as an analysis of whether securing funds for the new venture might decrease available resources for either existing or competing programs/enterprises.

Changes in the Marketplace

Market risk is that inherent risk present in the marketplace itself—and, at a minimum, will include any of the following:

✔ The presence and actions of competitors

✔ The impact of capital market resource shifts

✔ The dynamics of the regional or national markets within which the social enterprise operates

✔ Changes in the tastes or traffic patterns of consumers

✔ Shifts in the charitable interests of donors

Market risk might also include an assessment of shifts in the public policies affecting a social enterprise. An educational initiative requiring local approval of charter schools will be at risk if the state department of education rules against supporting such efforts. A recycling venture that relies on a certain volume of recycled contributions in order to meet its margins will be negatively impacted by both the entry of a large, multinational processor of recycled items or a drop in the commodities price for recycled goods. Social entrepreneurs must remember that any given market has various segments, forces, and players, all of which must be considered when assessing components of market risk.

Changes in Technology

There are two key aspects to changes in technology: (1) internal operating technologies and (2) the role played by an organization in a given industry where technological change impacts or may even eliminate an industry sector (buggy carriage manufacturers at the turn of the last century, for example). Shifts in technology can affect how nonprofits engage in their work (PCs to facilitate processing paperwork, etc.) and can potentially lead to layoffs and effects on the economy as a whole—swelling the ranks of program clients.

Stakeholder Backlash

The concept of social enterprise may engender significant opposition from those who believe that charity is charity and business is business. Those who have assisted the organization in the past and may play a significant role in its future may not support the notion of moving toward either a social enterprise mindset for the overall management of a non-profit, or the specific operation of a social venture doing business in the for-profit market. Managing how the idea of social enterprise is introduced and acted upon is an important area of possible risk exposure and challenge for management.

Competitor Reaction

As alluded to previously, the risk represented by competitors is an important component of market risk but is also one worth addressing on its own. In the for-profit arena, competition among players is a given—people talk about it, plan for it, and, in many cases, thrive on it. In the tax-exempt sector, however, we have mixed feelings about competition. On the one hand, nonprofits are some of the most aggressive competitors around. They engage in heated competition for everything from individual donors to media coverage to volunteers; indeed, social service groups often compete for the very clients they have vowed to serve. On the other hand, many in the sector do not like to acknowledge how fierce the competition can be.

Regardless of whether one is competing in for-profit markets or the nonprofit sector, the issue isn't whether we compete (because we know there may always be a new entry coming into an area that we have always served), but rather *how* we compete.

Competitive risk is not simply an issue of someone engaging in an effort to take a piece of our pie, but rather it is a question of how we respond to that competition and the risk that we will compromise our own integrity in the pursuit of organizational or personal goals that we have become convinced are more "righteous" than those of our adversary.

Many people have built significant wealth while maintaining a reputation for integrity and honesty in their work. As more organizations engage in sharp competition with both other nonprofits and with for-profit corporations entering what have historically been nonprofit areas of activity, the nonprofit sector must reaffirm its commitment to the ideal of fairness and integrity—not simply mirror the worst aspects of for-profit marketplace competition.

It may be accepted practice in the for-profit marketplace that one brand of soap promotes its product over another by claiming greater cleaning effectiveness—when in truth, both products contain the same ingredients and are essentially identical. Such a practice is viewed as "simply an ad," and everyone understands that the claims may be inflated at best. In the nonprofit sector, however, fairness in advertising and the pursuit of fair competition should be the rule. In their enthusiasm to promote their own work, a nonprofit organization must be careful not to step over the line of fairness. They should communicate their basic cost of doing business (and the possible "profit penalty" incurred by virtue of their social mission) to any for-profit that asks for this information as well as to the general public. They must be careful not to claim that "no one else is providing services to this segment of the population," when they know that several organizations are involved in that community. As they engage in efforts to educate the public about an issue or cause, they must take special care to accurately present not simply the issue under analysis, but also to provide fair presentation to those organizations working to address that particular problem or issue.

Competition in the nonprofit sector is healthy and certainly not to be avoided, but as social entrepreneurs find themselves in situations where competitors may engage in dubious practices, they must pause and re-engage their core values. It is not "acceptable" to employ a target population at a wage that does not allow them to provide for their most basic needs, simply because they have limited employment options. It is not acceptable for nonprofit employees to lack adequate benefits packages simply to allow the organization to stretch a dollar and be more "competitive" in the social capital market. And it is not acceptable for an organization to misrepresent or minimize the work of others simply to advance their own efforts at promotion and to develop a "brand name." The first component of competitive risk is to know your particular market segment and its players. The second is to understand what each player's competitive advantages are and how they might be leveraged for both individual benefit and achievement of a broader, commonly embraced social good. And the third component is to engage in competition from a place of real integrity and consistency with your core values.

USING THE RISK FACTORS TO ASSESS YOUR RISK RATIO

The following is another exercise to assist your planning committee.[7] Individual perceptions and "weighting" of risk can be skewed by a variety of personal and other issues; however, if five of six members of your planning committee believe that the issue of capital strategy is a primary risk area for the enterprise, maybe the group needs to be focusing more attention in that area!

tool of the trade   Examine the risk factors associated with each general area of activity: your parent organization, the enterprise itself, and the operating environment. Each member of the committee should complete this form and use it to discuss your enterprise's risk exposure in any given area of interest and possible concern. Fill in your specific risk areas under each category and assign a percentage to each area you identify. For purposes of exploration with your planning committee, this fig-

	Specific Issues	Assigned Risk Ratio
Organizational	1.	
✔ management		
✔ workforce	2.	
✔ culture		
✔ infrastructure funding	3.	
	4.	
	5.	
	6.	
	7.	
		Subtotal: ___%
Enterprise	1.	
	2.	
✔ concept		
✔ capitalization	3.	
✔ infrastructure		
	4.	
	5.	
	6.	
	7.	
		Subtotal: ___%
External Environment	1.	
	2.	
✔ marketplace	3.	
✔ technology		
✔ stakeholder backlash	4.	
✔ competition		
	5.	
	6.	
	7.	Subtotal: ___%
		Grand Total: 100%

EXHIBIT 6.2   A risk ratio analysis.

ure is your "risk ratio." This thumbnail analysis will help your committee identify areas of possible risk exposure that should be further pursued. Does everyone cite managerial risk as a key issue? Maybe a conversation needs to be held with senior staff regarding staff training, development, and personnel hire issues. A strategy may then be developed to address each area of concern and minimize the real and perceived risk involved.

THE RISK OF MISSION DRIFT

All organizations, whether for-profit or nonprofit, may be victims of mission drift. For nonprofit organizations pursuing innovative strategies for dealing with some of the world's most challenging social issues, mission drift and the ability to respond to the risks represented by it, should be a central consideration. The possibility that a new program or activity may take an organization in new directions is not in and of itself threatening enough for managers to avoid a proposed course of action. Mission drift occurs as a result of at least one of two events: success or failure—or, sometimes some fuzzy thing in between!

Successful social enterprises are demanding masters. They require more money, more staff, and, perhaps above all, more attention. Failing enterprises can pull the focus of senior managers away from running the "whole" organization and force them to invest precious hours in "turn-around" meetings. In either case, the organization soon realizes that the social enterprise is demanding more time and focus than originally planned, ultimately shifting the "center" of the organization off its main course.

Therefore, as a nonprofit evolves its efforts and encounters either looming success or free-falling failure, it is especially key that its stakeholders have adequate opportunities to return to and reaffirm its core mission and purpose. In the same way that one should never allow funding opportunities to dictate organizational development (i.e., "We're a tutoring program, but the Request for Proposal asks for groups engaged in health education, so let's just tweak this here and . . ."), the social entrepreneur must ensure that a new idea or social enterprise opportunity does not redirect the organization away from its central calling.

With this in mind, many options are available to organizations that are interested in affirming their core mission while acting on emerging opportunities. Collaborations, subsidiaries, and joint ventures all allow organizations to pursue a new future while remaining true to historical purpose and experience. At the same time, needs change and capacities evolve. If those involved in a nonprofit sense a mission drift, they should take the time to step back from their activities, assess the core mission of the organization as a whole, and reinvent the organization as appropriate.

UNDERSTANDING YOUR OPTIONS: STRATEGIES FOR MANAGING RISKS

As we approach our discussion of risk-management strategies, it is important that we first understand how the social entrepreneur may take a strategic approach to risk management. To begin with, the best way to minimize risk is simply not to take any. Although some level of risk exists in all that we do, the entrepreneur intentionally assumes a higher degree of risk than others in order to attain greater future rewards. So, it is important to acknowledge at the start that you are making a choice to open yourself up to potentially greater risk exposure—and you must assume responsibility for that choice. But if you believed that assuming little or no risk was an effective strategy for you to achieve your goals, you wouldn't be reading this book!

Our approach should not be to think that we would be able to truly minimize or eliminate risk entirely, but rather simply to anticipate and manage risk effectively in the course of our work. Furthermore, it must be recognized that even with ongoing reassessment, new ventures are often fraught with uncertainty that cannot be fully (or cost-effectively) resolved until the venture is launched and tested in the marketplace. It is important for us to acknowledge this because true uncertainty is harder to manage than known risks, and the presence of uncertainty makes any effort on our part to manage risk so difficult.

In his *Harvard Business Review* article, "Strategy Under Uncertainty," Hugh Courtney and his co-authors identify the following four levels of uncertainty:

1. A reasonably clear linear future
2. Alternative futures that can be clearly described in discrete scenarios
3. A range of futures that form more of a continuum
4. True ambiguity in which even a continuum cannot be defined[8]

Analytic risk-assessment techniques work best in the first two conditions. In the latter two situations, flexibility becomes our central response to effectively manage risk—flexibility informed by the analysis we have done beforehand. Courtney talks about the importance of finding the right mix of (1) no-regret actions, (2) options, and (3) big bets for the level of uncertainty faced. In his chapter on managing in uncertainty, Hammond says that the effective manager should have (1) all-weather plans, (2) short-cycle plans, (3) option wideners, and (4) "be prepared" plans.[9] However you choose to think of it, both approaches are what could be viewed as uncertainty and complexity management tools you can apply in assisting you to plan for the inevitable risks you will confront in launching and operating your venture.

Given the long list of risk factors previously discussed and to which the social entrepreneur is susceptible, one may wonder: Why even bother! Why leave yourself open to the risks of entrepreneurism? Well, the benefits are great, and one can take several steps to guard against the potentially negative impacts of whatever level of risk exposure you decide to carry. And there are ways for us to organize and prepare for risk in order to maximize our chances of success. Before moving to address the specific steps you can take to begin managing your risk exposure, we should start by chanting a concise management mantra:

"Flexibility in execution will be the key to my success."

Repeating this mantra on a daily basis might help prevent you from getting locked into your routine habits of understanding both your organization and the environment in which it operates. Successful social entrepreneurs are, perhaps first and foremost, aware of their changing environment and nimble on their toes! We live in a time of increasingly rapid transformation. New organizations are formed and old ones dissolve. New technology comes online and eliminates old ways of communicating. New ideas are broached and old constructs fall away. All along, we must each be open to change and able to rapidly assimilate new information, understand its implications, and innovate a revised approach to our newly defined world.

In the "old" days (before 1980!), program rules and regulations guided organizational offerings and initiatives. Today, the only rule is relevance—namely, if it is not relevant to the needs of your organization, consumers, and community, get rid of it! The best prevention to ensure that you don't run the risk of irrelevance is to stay on your toes, stay wired, and stay fit. Those who are stuck in the mud will be drowned by the incoming tide. Those who seek to create positive social change must be able to read the shifting winds in order to position our various communities of concern to best negotiate the changing environment in which we will all find ourselves.

Successful social entrepreneurs are best able to be flexible in pursuing their goals and executing their strategies and thereby minimizing the risk of being left behind or, even worse, wiped out completely.

RISK MANAGEMENT CATEGORIES AND THE RISK FACTORS THEY ADDRESS

 Know what your potential risks are upfront. This category of risk management focuses on the following information-gathering techniques:

1. *Talk to experts.* Regardless of how innovative or cutting edge your business concept is, someone out there somewhere has undertaken a related approach. Find them and learn what they know. Do you have a great idea for a new service or program offering? Find a major player in the same industry and learn why they aren't doing the same thing. If they aren't, perhaps there's a reason why. You

may either have an excellent new idea or you could have simply found an obvious pit that those familiar with the industry know to avoid.

2. *Use focus groups.* Focus groups may be used in several ways. First, if you are targeting a given customer base, convene representatives of that market segment and present your ideas to them, gauge their response, and make appropriate adjustments. Second, join an industry association and attend a lunch of individuals managing similar ventures; facilitate a conversation wherein people can tell war stories to each other—and educate you in the process. Third, if you are operating a social venture that carries some element of social risk, convene a session with the folks who are most likely to have concerns or issues about your proposed venture. For example, if you intend to hire people formerly on welfare, you should know what employment barriers they encounter and have plans for addressing them. If you are launching an ecotourism business, you need to be connected with local residents or interests to understand their concerns for bringing tour groups into their area and how those concerns might be best addressed.

3. *Engage in probability estimating exercises.* Take your Board or planning group through your risk ratio analysis chart (developed earlier in this chapter) and assess what the probabilities are of a given risk actually occurring.

4. *Use a SWOT analysis—and act on your findings.* Assess your strengths and understand what you need to do to augment your weaknesses. Most people are familiar with the idea of a SWOT analysis (Strengths, Weaknesses, Opportunities, Threats). You should go through a detailed assessment of your organization with regard to each of those elements and develop strategies for how you will address and overcome any deficiencies in your organization. Allowing you time to assess what your true strengths and weaknesses are is an important step in risk management. Along these same lines, many organizations spend a significant amount of time attempting to correct weaknesses in their organization, often redirecting resources from "strong" areas of organizational competence in the misguided belief that such a reallocation of support will compensate for bad performance. Indeed, many nonprofits have a difficult time confronting the reality that a given program area or staff group is underperforming and needs to be eliminated. Peter Drucker, the author and lecturer who was a management guru *before* there were management gurus, has said that if you are not either number one or number two in a given activity, you should cease that activity and direct your resources to better use. This is a tough route to take for many groups; however, the fact of

the matter is that 80 percent of your time is probably taken up by 20 percent of your problems, and if you simply eliminated more problem areas (as opposed to working to improve them), you would be better off and decrease your risk exposure. So, again, know your weaknesses and support your strengths.

5. *Work to build networks, partnerships, and alliances* that can help feed you information in all of the aforementioned areas of activity. The nonprofit sector is long experienced at building networks to advocate for passage of key legislation or to share information of importance to network members. Increasingly, social entrepreneurs are building their own networks to connect, support each other's efforts, and learn how to be more effective at their work. Being part of a network of organizations involved in similar work or confronting similar challenges can help you see what may be around the corner and hear how others have dealt with the same risks. Few organizations are in the position of doing it all themselves and, increasingly, as resources get tighter and competition gets stronger, groups will find themselves forced to develop strategic partnerships and alliances. Instead of feeling "boxed in" by this prospect, the creative social entrepreneur embraces the possibility of creating new partnerships to collaborate and share risk. Although all partnerships require the investment of time and resources in order to effectively maintain them, they can be a critical strategy for decreasing risk exposure, sharing responsibilities, and increasing overall rewards. Partnerships can help you share the burden of the risk involved and, in the cases of corporate partnerships, can allow you to leverage resources beyond your own organization that may prove critical to your ability to anticipate, negotiate, and manage a variety of potential risk factors. Short of a formal partnership or alliance, being part of a larger network is also an important tactic for decreasing risk exposure.

6. *Compile your information into a single document or project area in order to make sure you are seeing the whole picture.* The flow of conversations and perspectives can move over you in different ways every day; some days financial considerations are front and center, whereas other days program or politics take the stage. Gathering your information together into a single binder or document and then moving through each area of potential risk exposure, considering your strategies for response, is the key to the development of a coherent, well-coordinated risk-reduction plan and response outline.

Take steps to reduce potential losses (i.e., minimize the potential *magnitude* of your risk exposure) through the following strategies:

1. *Get others to share the loss,* such as taking on partners or investors who can better afford to take the financial or nonfinancial risk (e.g., those with excess capacity). Explore the possibility of partnering equally with other players to spread the risk and liability. Consider leasing equipment with a high level of technological-change risk in order to protect yourself from rapid obsolescence in your operating systems. Explore the possibility of buying insurance coverage, especially for things that have a low probability but a high potential cost.

2. *Stage your commitments.* Staging your commitments—that is, keeping multiple options in play before making a final investment in any given strategy—allows you to keep your options open as long as you possibly can, as well as allowing you to make smaller, incremental investments over a longer time frame. In developing your effort, assess what options are available to you and how you might "stack" your investment of resources and personnel depending on how each component plays out. For example, one nonprofit organization that operates several social-purpose enterprises was planning on launching additional ones but couldn't tell at what point in time which venture would be most appropriate. The different ventures under consideration each depended on several additional variables, none of which were directly controlled by the nonprofit. Rather than simply rushing the process and making a commitment to the one course of action that appeared most likely at the time, the organization engaged in a parallel staging of its strategy. This strategy allowed it to keep its options open further along the timeline than would have been possible had they committed to a single course of action. This approach then allowed four different planning processes to move forward concurrently. As it turned out, during this period *two* of the options "broke," and the organization was then positioned to go with those two as opposed to having made commitments in areas in which it ultimately did not want to pursue.

3. *Have clearly enunciated exit options.* As a part of your business strategy, lay out multiple points in time at which you will step back, assess changed conditions, and either modify your approach or get out. Exit options allow you to reassess risk exposure and cut your losses before you have committed all the necessary resources or exposed yourself fully to possibly devastating losses.

4. *Reduce the actual loss potential.* Other strategies include efforts to use inputs and materials that conform to industry standards and,

therefore, may be sold to others in the event that the venture itself is unsuccessful. Furthermore, by pursuing a strategy of keeping fixed costs and commitments low (leasing rather than buying or contracting out elements that may carry high fixed costs), the startup organization can further minimize its exposure. Finally, in the case of concerns about risk related to the reputation of the organization (whether internal or external), steps to buffer the parent organization from the risk exposure represented by the new venture may also be taken by giving the organization a distinctly different name or establishing it as a separate legal entity. Considering what other types of "firewalls" might be effective is an important part of the effort to minimize the actual loss potential of the venture.

Take steps to reduce the chances of undesirable outcomes actually occurring (i.e., minimize the potential magnitude of your risk exposure) through the following risk-reduction techniques:

1. *Execute strategies to shore up or overcome your organizational weaknesses.* Based on your SWOT and other analyses, you should have a fairly good handle on where your organizational capacities lie and what areas of your operation may be a present or future liability. These areas may fall into such categories as managerial, workforce, infrastructure, and so forth. Strategies should be developed to specifically address the needs of each area of risk exposure but might include such actions as the following:

   ✔ Providing staff training/development
   ✔ Hiring new staff
   ✔ Creating new policies
   ✔ Implementing a concerted strategy to learn from others in a network
   ✔ Partnering with an organization that has the specific expertise you lack

2. *Implement efforts to hedge marketplace risk.* Marketplace risk can operate at several levels, but a key one is that of contracting relationships with outside organizations. To the degree possible, one should make an effort to secure fixed-price contracts for items that might fluctuate in price, which creates options for you in case the market moves in an unexpected direction (e.g., offering a range of products or services until you see what works, then focusing). On the other hand, one should also attempt to secure short-term contracts in areas of the market where you believe you may be able to increase your own fees at some future point in time.

3. *Establish ongoing assessment processes and action teams.* Every organization should have a small group of individuals that is focused on overseeing the operating reports and process of a given program or enterprise. This working group should have individuals representing various areas of the corporation and possessing various skill sets. Whether they are called the venture committee, program oversight, or action groups, such committees can help to identify and correct the controllable risk factors along the way. Furthermore, every venture—whether social-purpose enterprise or nonprofit program—should be guided by a business plan that outlines strategies, tactics, and required resources. And the execution of the business plan should be overseen not by the entire Board (unless the organization is extremely small or a startup), but rather by a working committee as described previously. This committee may consist of the organization's executive director, business manager, and appointed Board members, but should also include engaged investors and specific individuals with direct expertise (either paid consultants or volunteers). This working group gives operations managers a place to bring problems, provides a larger arena to discuss strategies, and can give access to a wider network of players to support execution of the business plan. As is true of the old adage that "two heads are better than one," a venture committee structure helps decrease risk by bringing more minds to work on the challenge of executing any given strategy.

4. *Develop and continually update a viable competitive strategy* that analyzes potential competitor actions and develops a set of responses to establish and protect your position with customers, funders, and other stakeholders. As previously stated, competitive considerations should focus not simply on what your competitor in the marketplace may do, but also on how you will respond. Although you cannot control the actions of others, you do control your posture in the market after they act. An intimate understanding of not only your assets and strategic alternatives, but also your values and mission, is critical because it assists you in responding to competition, in whatever form it may take, in a manner that is appropriate for the situation with which you are confronted and consistent with your own commitment to integrity.

5. *Diversify your portfolio.* If the venture is one of several being operated by a parent organization, pursuing a strategy to diversify your risk by creating a portfolio of programs/investments should also be considered. Portfolio risk is that risk exposure represented by your investments. Many social entrepreneurs may begin with a single program or venture, but many find that it is not long before they

are operating multiple programs at various sites in different markets. Portfolio risk is best assessed by understanding that a high-risk activity, when combined with a low-risk activity, equals a medium-risk activity. Indeed, an organization may reduce its overall risk exposure by bringing in more conservative programs and ventures to "balance off" other, more aggressive activities.

For example, a nonprofit operating a restaurant (which relies on people having enough money to go out to eat) might consider a thrift shop as a second venture because thrift shops do well in "down" markets, whereas restaurants do worse. A nonprofit involved in adult education might diversify its program offerings by adding adult recreation. A nonprofit offering programs for out-of-school youth might lower its risk exposure by developing offerings for adults reentering the labor market, and so forth. Again, assuming that mission drift and other risks are taken well into account, efforts to diversify the activities of an organization can help decrease the overall risk to which that organization is exposed.

 Although diversification of risk is a time-tested strategy, keep in mind that an organization has to have adequate resources and staffing in order to succeed in "diversifying away risk." If not properly executed, diversification can stretch core organizational resources too thinly and across too many competing areas of activity. In addition, diversifying an organization's activities may also pull away from its core competencies, into areas where the organization may actually have greater risk exposure! And this strategy is not one of balancing high risk with low risk; it is about diversifying away *idiosyncratic* risk with projects that are exposed to different, uncorrelated risks. The idea is that they will still be exposed to risk, but ideally they won't go bad all at once!

Understand that you will probably confront times when various risk elements are shifting rapidly or it is unclear what the future will bring. Understand what options you have for managing residual uncertainty and complexity in an unpredictable environment, including the following:

1. *Think through "no-regret," "all-weather" options when considering any enterprise strategy.* Look to identify courses of action with small downside risks no matter what, that do not depend on conditions that might change their success. Recognize, however, that all entrepreneurs probably have to assume some degree of risk in order to pursue the vision or reward sought.

2. *Commit to (and execute) frequent and honest reassessment.* As these reassessments are undertaken, entrepreneurs should also keep the exit or revision doors open and be willing to use them. When you reassess your position, remember that sunk costs don't count! If you have invested $75,000 in a startup effort that is now operating

at three times its predicted cash burn-rate, your initial investment is already toast. Be prepared to walk away and, when assessing your situation, focus on your future prospects—not your past investment. (Folks in the nonprofit sector are stunned when they hear of corporations closing initiatives in which they have already invested millions of dollars. They can do this—although they certainly don't like to!—because they are focused on how much the venture is likely to cost them in the future, not on how much they have put in to date).

3. *Avoid "big bets" and irreversible commitments, unless you are extremely savvy and have the money to lose.* Keep your investments focused or make sure that they can be recouped (salvage value) if and when you exit. As already stated, work to keep fixed costs low and attempt to secure contracts wherein you may link future payments to future success (e.g., piece rates, rent as a percentage of sales, etc.).

4. *Structure the deal in order to increase your options further down the line.* In addition to the multiple services or products, cultivate multiple suppliers, lease rather than buy equipment, secure space that is flexible, and be sure to put buy-out options in the lease in case you hit the jackpot.

5. *Create contingency plans, and at appropriate stopping points, have your Board run through various scenarios for steps you might take if disaster strikes or risks end up being realized.* Plan your responses to unexpected disaster and be prepared for them. Smart people who live in earthquake zones bolt their houses to their foundations, try to keep a half-tank of gas in the car, and have three days of canned food in the basement—along with a bottle of red wine! What is your "earthquake plan"?

Go one step further and take your Board or staff through various scenarios. It is surprising how many organizational strategies are developed by nonprofit managers who do not include "problem scenarios" or any type of planning for error. Yet, the fact of the matter is that nothing ever works out exactly as one had projected. Markets change, people shift, and opportunities evolve. Although it is not possible for managers to anticipate every shift from projections, the social entrepreneur should anticipate during the planning stages what possible problems may emerge and how they might best be addressed.

The point is not whether you guess what the "right" scenario is going to be, but rather that you give yourself and your team the opportunity to develop the "skills of flexibility" needed to pursue success. Remember, planning for problems does not have to take the enthusiasm out of the development process but can give greater confidence to those executing what are often very challenging strategies through the knowledge that "what if . . ." scenarios have been discussed and possible options assessed.

Special risk-reduction strategies
available to social entrepreneurs

Several risk-reduction strategies are open to social entrepreneurs that are not available to for-profit entrepreneurs. Having full knowledge of these strategies can help give you the edge you need for success—but remember, we are not talking about how to gain an unfair advantage over others in the marketplace. *Real* social entrepreneurs always operate with integrity and fairness when it comes to competition because they know that to do otherwise would undermine their core mission, which is to create greater social value and community good. The reality, however, is that because social entrepreneurs pursue social good, they may carry a significantly greater burden than their for-profit counterparts.

The lack of a profit incentive, a commitment to hire those with significant employment barriers who have been unable to find employment in mainstream for-profit companies, and any number of other social costs must be carried by the social entrepreneur. In exchange for carrying these costs, social entrepreneurs are given some tools to help manage and decrease their risk of failure. Such tools are as follows:

✔ The organization's tax-exempt status
✔ The ability to solicit and receive in-kind and other donation support
✔ Access to low, below, or zero-market-rate capital (in the form of grants, program-related investments, or other investment/capital vehicles)
✔ Access to volunteer labor

The Potential Costs of Risk-reduction Strategies . . . A Word of Caution

This chapter has focused on a discussion of the variety of approaches one may take to risk-reduction strategies, but it must be pointed out that many risk-reduction strategies have some level of cost associated with them—whether financial or otherwise. These costs may actually carry the danger of then increasing exposure to other risk factors. In assessing what risk-reduction steps are appropriate, social entrepreneurs must also examine the value added by each risk-reduction strategy to make sure that the added cost of any given strategy improves the risk/reward relationship, or at least made it no worse while reducing the risk.

INSURANCE COVERAGE AND PLANNING

With the organization's business risk strategies in place, all social entrepreneurs should consider what type of actual insurance coverage they should have in place to help protect from more traditional forms of risk: fire, theft, liability, and so forth. An insurance program is simply a formal assessment of what operational risk exposure the organization carries and which specific insurance policies are available to cover that exposure, thereby minimizing the likelihood of an event that could ultimately put the nonprofit out of business. The process for securing appropriate coverage is a basic one, outlined as follows:

1. Determine how insurable losses may occur and what type of insurance would be most appropriate:
   - ✔ Fire
   - ✔ Liability
   - ✔ Automobile
   - ✔ Worker's Compensation
   - ✔ Business Interruption
   - ✔ "Key Man" (i.e., to guard against the loss of key personnel)
   - ✔ Directors and Officers Liability (to guard against the possibility that individuals involved in governing your organization will be the subject of lawsuits)
   - ✔ Errors and Omissions Policy (to guard against liabilities arising from your giving clients and others bad advice)
   - ✔ Bonding
     — Performance Bonds (to insure that if you enter into a contract, your client will be covered in the event you are unable to fulfill the performance terms of the contract)
     — Employee Bonds (to insure *you* in the event that an employee handling large amounts of cash or other securities decides to prematurely leave your employment!)
   - ✔ Crime/Burglary
   - ✔ Rent
   - ✔ Group Life, Health, Disability, Retirement

2. Seek professional advice/consultants. Evaluating and selecting the appropriate types of insurance can be both complicated and boring—both of which can lead to mistakes! Make sure you have

adequate professional guidance as you go about assessing your needs and developing an insurance program that is right for you.

3. Shop around for the best buy. Many companies offer similar or related coverage, and if you decide to place all of your coverage with a single company, you should also be able to negotiate better rates. Shop around to make sure you are getting your money's worth!

CREATING EXIT STRATEGIES

For many nonprofit organizations used to living "hand to mouth" and making do with less, the idea of exiting—of shutting down programs or ventures that don't achieve their performance goals within a reasonable timeframe—is anathema and is, therefore, worth addressing on its own. By not having predefined exit points along the way, you increase the likelihood that you will end up in a bad situation with little room to move. Seasoned managers know that when things begin to go bad, they can go bad quickly. Social entrepreneurs must be ahead of the curve and anticipate options. Exit strategies is one part of the social entrepreneur's "flexibility tool kit." Effectiveness of exit options revolve around three main points, each of which move sequentially from one to another:

✔ Planned "time-outs"
✔ Execution of turnaround strategies
✔ Dropping the hammer (also referred to as "knowing when to play and when to fold!")

1. *Planned time-outs:* Having an effective exit option depends on having enunciated "time-outs," during which progress is assessed, the return on resources invested to date is evaluated, and a renewed decision is made to move forward. These can be qualitative benchmarks tied to certain events, or they may be clearly stated financial goals:

   ✔ We will raise all of our operating capital by June 10th.
   ✔ We will have secured five program grants of $50,000 a piece by July 15th.
   ✔ We will have found a program manager we all support by December 10th.

   With each of these points in time being clearly stated and included in the business plan, all stakeholders can be afforded the opportunity to "call the question" and exit the field.

2. *Execution of turnaround strategies:* Based on the findings of the "time-out," the organization may decide to revise both its strategy and its expectations of performance. This turnaround strategy should directly address the specific factors that led to the organization missing its benchmarks and propose a new set of short-term performance goals to be met and financial targets to be achieved. A turnaround strategy usually does not attempt to restate or examine the entire business plan, but identifies what the specific problem areas are thought to be and what immediate steps will be taken to address them. This strategy is monitored on a weekly, if not daily, basis and becomes the focus of all players' efforts.

3. *Dropping the hammer:* It may sound extreme, but the following actions are taken as a last-resort measure:

   ✔ If you have not secured your operating capital by the 10th and the organization knows it does not want to go into operating reserves to cover the expense, you shut it down.

   ✔ If you have only four grants by the date you set and you truly needed all five to adequately operate your program, you shut it down and return the funds rather than attempting to run a mediocre program.

   ✔ If you have the funds and cannot find a manager you feel can take the effort to scale, you shut it down.

These are not points of failure, but rather opportunities for responsibly exiting a nonperforming situation. Remember that giving funds back or terminating a program will not be viewed as a failure by informed investors or stakeholders, but rather as a setback. Having to close down a venture *after* the fact as a result of an inappropriate hire or undercapitalization *is* a failure in management and one you will be able to avoid if you are honest, smart, and plan ahead.

LEARNING FROM YOUR MISTAKES

Social entrepreneurs who execute good risk management today are those who have learned from their mistakes of yesterday.

In the for-profit sector, good entrepreneurs (who secure numerous backers for their next venture) have a few failures under their belts. They know their strengths and limits; have demonstrated a willingness to learn and the resilience to come back to play the game again. In the nonprofit sector, on the other hand, we are used to having to have the answer. When you draft a grant proposal for a foundation, you don't write, "Well, this is really experimental and we are not at all sure this will work, but it is our best guess at this point in time." Instead, you write, "The XYZ Group has demonstrated its ability to effectively manage this type of program and will continue to have success as we help our nation turn the corner on poverty."

This approach can often create an unhealthy dynamic that undermines the ability of our sector to learn, grow, and develop more effective strategies to advance our cause. Instead of following Shakespeare's advice to kill all the lawyers, the *first* thing we must do is develop the capacity as a field to learn from our mistakes!

A COMMITMENT TO LEARNING

As a part of this commitment to learning, effective social entrepreneurs document the process. They take the time to step back from the experience and reflect; they make an investment in writing about their experience; and they work with investors to produce cases, books, and articles documenting what was tried, what revisions were made, and what was learned. All of these steps, when taken in concert with other practitioners or even as executed by a single organization, are part of proactive risk management. By creating a paper trail of our experience, we allow others to learn from our work and go on to engage in even better, "higher-order" mistakes, pushing the envelope even more.

In order for this process to take place, however, social entrepreneurs must also work to cultivate the presence of informed investors in their process. If practitioners "sell" a certain outcome to philanthropic investors, but do not seek to engage them in a learning process about the true realities of the work, then investors will never understand the nature of the risks they are being asked to undertake.

On the other hand, the investors must seek out truth in the process of supporting social entrepreneurs and, to be honest, many supporters of nonprofit ventures are not open to assuming that responsibility. In some ways, it is more comforting to "know" that our funds helped address a critical cause or supported a wonderful event than to have to deal with the reality of the shortcomings in much of traditional philanthropy today.

Together, investors and investees must change the terms of the philanthropic relationship, engage in true innovation, and jointly assume the risk inherent in any sincere effort to effect meaningful, sustainable change for individuals, society, and our world.

Remember that without a formal understanding of how to learn from the process as you move along, you run the *added risk* of paying for an education you never get. As the saying goes, "Fool me once, shame on you; fool me twice, shame on me!" All social entrepreneurs must understand that their experiences need to be documented and widely circulated in order to ensure that mistakes made by an organization at one point in time are not repeated at another point in time—by the same organization or not!

NEVER RISK SO MUCH THAT YOU WILL NOT BE ABLE TO RETURN TO PLAY ANOTHER DAY

Although there is great romance and excitement to be had in the act of "betting the house" on a high-risk venture, and we could all do well to live by the motto "Nothing ventured, nothing gained," social entrepreneurs who bet it *all* bet foolishly. If you are simply concerned with your own personal education and experience and make that clear to all, fine—go ahead and bet the house. But the reality for most *social* entrepreneurs is that you are playing for greater stakes than your own self-interest; you are betting the lives of your clients on a "new" intervention strategy, and you are investing precious *charitable* dollars in your vision and skills. And you owe it less to yourself than to those who invest in you not to throw it all up in the air on a hope and a dream.

- Take informed risks.
- Pursue dreams grounded in reality.
- But never risk so much that you will be taken out of the game entirely because we need each and every one of the talented, passionate leaders we can muster if we are to achieve our goals!

SUMMARY

Every organization has some amount of exposure to risk, or the possibility of an undesirable outcome. The key to risk is understanding it and then determining how best to manage it. In this chapter, we defined risk and then examined the art of calculated risk taking. We considered how to balance risk and reward and took a look at the best ways to assess different risk-management strategies. We considered the inherent costs in different risk-reduction strategies and how to learn from our mistakes. Key points to remember are as follows:

- ✔ Risk is the possibility of an undesirable outcome.
- ✔ Risk is measured in two main ways: the potential magnitude of the risk and the possibility of its occurrence.
- ✔ Personal risk tolerance is not a function of age, but a function of individuality and life.
- ✔ Take risks, but never gamble.

✔ Don't expect to eliminate risk entirely, but to manage it effectively.

✔ Carefully weigh the costs of reducing risk against the potential impact of the risk itself.

Endnotes

1. Robert Herbert and Albert Link, *The Entrepreneur: Mainstream Views and Radical Critiques* (New York: Praeger Publishers, 1982), p. 17.
2. While doing research for this chapter, we found quotes such as, "A third of new businesses fail in the first six months. Three-quarters within five years. Nine out of ten companies in existence today will eventually cease to exist." Richard Snowden, *The Complete Guide to Buying a Business* (New York: Amacom Publishing, 1994). However, we are also aware that, in other studies, ownership changes and voluntary closings (e.g., when the owner retires with no successor in place or gets a great job and decides it is better than running a business) were counted as "failures." In fact, Bruce Kirchoff, formerly chief economist of the Small Business Administration (SBA) has argued that careful analysis of the data shown an eight-year survival rate of 54 percent, 28 percent with their original owners and 26 percent under new ownership. Some of those that closed (the 46 percent) apparently did so for personal reasons that had nothing to do with actual failure of the business economically. See Bruce Kirchoff, Entrepreneurial Economics, in William Bygrave, *Portable MBA in Entrepreneurship* (New York, John Wiley & Sons, 1997), pp. 458–460.
3. It should be noted, however, that there is growing interest in creating such metrics for use in the social sector as well. Writings on issues related to Social Return on Investment frameworks, the use of social betas to reflect the market risk of various target populations and quantitative approaches to understanding social risk, are gaining increasing play. For publication references, please see the articles and publications page at www.redf.org.
4. Taken from Robert Hisrich and Michael Peters, *Entrepreneurship: Starting, Developing, and Managing a New Enterprise* (Chicago: Irwin Publishers, 1995). This checklist was originally printed in Robert Hisrich and Candida Brush, *The Woman Entrepreneur* (Lanham, MD: Lexington Books, 1985).
5. In fact, the studies on risk tolerance among entrepreneurs have generated conflicting results. Entrepreneurs do not always have a high level of risk tolerance compared to the general populations, as you know from Hisrich and Peters, pp. 54–55.
6. Ron S. Dembo and Andrew Freeman, *Seeing Tomorrow: Rewriting the Rules of Risk* (New York: John Wiley & Sons). These three factors are taken from Dembo and Freeman, but have been revised for our use here.
7. You do have a planning committee, right? Under the banner of "Five heads are better than one," an important strategy for managing risk is to have others involved in your planning process.
8. Hugh Courtney, Jane Kirkland, and Patrick Viguerie, "Strategy Under Uncertainty," *Harvard Business Review,* Nov–Dec 1997, pp. 68–71.
9. Hammond et al., Keep Your Options Open with Flexible Plans, in John S. Hammond, Ralph L. Keeney, and Howard Raiffa, *Smart Choices: A Practical Guide to Making Better Decisions,* (Boston: Harvard Business School Press, 1999), pp. 173–174.

Chapter 7

MASTERING THE ART OF INNOVATION

J. Gregory Dees, Miriam and Peter Haas Centennial Professor in Public Service, and co-director of the Center for Social Innovation, Stanford University Graduate School of Business

IN THIS CHAPTER

What is innovation?

Where to look for innovative opportunities

Balancing tensions in the innovation process

Managing the resistance to innovation

Creating an innovative, adaptive enterprise

In Chapter 1, we said that social entrepreneurs engage in continuous innovation, adaptation, and learning. This sounds great, but what does it mean? And more to the point, what does it mean for *you?*

You might get the impression that social entrepreneurs must constantly come up with radical new ideas, jumping from one to the next, never seeing anything through. Or, you might have images of crazy inventors who spend all their time working on new ideas, never bringing any of them to fruition. A few social entrepreneurs are compulsive radical innovators, but this kind of obsessive creativity is not common and often is not very effective.

As you will see in this chapter, these images are built on some widespread assumptions about innovation that are just not true. Innovation is much more common than people think. It can take many forms, and does not depend on having a creative personality. Rather, it rests on a combination of being attentive to your operating environment, committed to your mission, and open to new ways of doing things. Successful innovation is as much a matter of execution as it is of having new ideas. Innovation is a real art that successful entrepreneurs, social or otherwise, learn to practice well. The most successful entrepreneurs also create a climate to support innovation by others in their organizations.

WHAT IS INNOVATION?

When people hear the word *innovation,* they tend to think of some major breakthrough idea or invention—the light bulb, the television, the personal computer. They think innovative ideas have to be totally new, created out of whole cloth. When we look at them closely, however, few innovations pass this test. Most "new" ideas are built on old ideas that have been recombined or incrementally changed in some creative way. When you study their histories, you see that many of the most powerful innovations were the result of a slow process of continuous development and improvement. People sometimes have great breakthrough ideas, but this is rare.

core concept   Put simply, innovation involves *establishing new and better ways for accomplishing a worthwhile objective.* For social entrepreneurs, this means new and better ways of serving your social mission. It is useful to say more about each of the key words of this definition.

- ✔ *Establishing* . . . Innovation is about effective action, not simply having an idea. It can be contrasted with invention, which is about generating new ideas.

- ✔ *New* . . . Innovation involves change. To be *new* in this sense is a matter of degree. Although most of us think of radical changes as innovative, even incremental changes count. A new combination of old, familiar ideas can be innovative.

- ✔ *and Better* . . . Innovation must be seen as improvements in the eyes of at least some of the people affected. Otherwise, as one author puts it, it would just be called "a mistake."

- ✔ *Ways of* . . . Innovation can take many forms, including changes in what you are doing, how you are doing it, where you are doing it, or with whom.

- ✔ *Accomplishing* . . . Innovation is about getting results, not just about being different. It is outcomes oriented.

- ✔ *a Worthwhile Objective* . . . Innovation is always understood relative to an objective that is deemed worthwhile by those involved. People may disagree on which objectives are worthwhile. When they do, they also disagree on what counts as a real innovation.

WHERE TO LOOK FOR INNOVATIVE OPPORTUNITIES

Innovation can occur in any sphere of life, from cooking to car repair. Here we are concerned with the innovations of social entrepreneurs—individuals creating enterprises to serve the common good. They tend to be involved with creating and delivering products, services, or programs. For simplicity, we will talk in these terms.

Opportunities for innovation can occur in many different places. Economist Joseph Schumpeter used five categories to classify the different ways in which business entrepreneurs can be innovative.[1] His categories can be paraphrased for our purposes as follows:

1. *Creating a new or improved product, service, or program*—one with which the users are not yet familiar or one with aspects that are new to consumers. Most of the examples people think of as innovations (the first automobiles, computers, etc.) fall into this category.

2. *Introducing a new or improved strategy or method of operating*—one that has not been used by the organization adopting it. The new method or strategy can affect one or many of the elements of an enterprise, including how the product, service, or program is designed, tested, produced, marketed, distributed, and assessed. Ford's creation of the assembly line to produce cars is a dramatic example of this type of innovation.

3. *Reaching a new market, serving an unmet need*—making a product, service, or program available to a group that did not otherwise have access to it. The Local Initiatives Support Center's effort to bring supermarkets back into inner-city neighborhoods would be an example of this type of innovation.

4. *Tapping into a new source of supply or labor*—finding a labor pool that was not previously used by this organization, which lowers costs, improves quality, and/or creates additional benefits for some new group. Pioneer Human Services, by deciding to create manufacturing businesses using ex-convicts and substance abusers as the workforce, tapped into a new labor source in a way that was mutually beneficial.

5. *Establishing a new industrial or organizational structure*—changing the relationships among existing organizations to improve performance, including mergers, spinoffs, alliances, and other contractual arrangements. The merger of America Online, Inc., the leading online service provider, with Time Warner, Inc., a company that owns lots of content as well as cable lines, is an example of this type of innovation.

Based on recent developments in the field of social entrepreneurship, we could add a sixth and seventh category as follows:

6. *Framing new terms of engagement*—changing the terms on which you relate to clients, consumers, suppliers, funders, or employees. For instance, when L. L. Bean first offered an unconditional satisfaction guarantee, they changed the terms of engagement with their mail order customers.

7. *Developing new funding structures*—exploring different options for reducing or covering the costs of producing or delivering your product or service. On the for-profit side, the development of franchising, where a local owner purchases the rights to operate a local business using a national brand name, such as McDonald's, was an innovative financing structure for growing a business.

Reminder: When we talk about "new," we do not mean completely "new to the world," we mean "new to those most directly affected" and we mean "new as a reality." Even if the idea has been around or has been tried elsewhere, it is an innovation if it is being implemented in a context in which it represents a change, radical or incremental, in the way things have been done.

concept check

Use the list of categories to generate examples of innovations that have occurred in your chosen field of interest, or more broadly in the social sector. Some things are not so easy to classify because they cross the boundaries between categories. That's fine. The purpose of the categories and the exercise is to expose the multiple dimensions of innovation. These examples can be historical or contemporary. Examples from different fields are listed to stimulate your thinking.

1. New product, service, or program: When the National Foundation for Teaching Entrepreneurship (NFTE) started offering youth entrepreneurship courses at the Newark Boys & Girls Clubs, it introduced a new product.

    Your example: _____

2. New strategy or method: When rural health clinics in developing countries started using satellite hookups to connect rural patients with specialists in urban medical centers, they used a new method of operations.

    Your example: _____

3. New market: When the City Year youth service corps program moved into a city that did not have a youth service corps, it tapped into a new market.

    Your example: _____

4. New source of supply or labor: When Habitat for Humanity decided to mobilize volunteer labor and in-kind supplies to build houses for the poor, it drew on a new kind of labor source for this purpose.

    Your example: _____

5. New industry or organizational structure: When Second Harvest was created to serve as an umbrella group for food banks, it created a new kind of structure for the food banking business.

    Your example: _____

6. New terms of engagement: When Oak St. House in San Francisco dropped its overnight shelter program in favor of a program requiring employable residents to participate in a training and job placement program, it created new terms of engagement for its residents.

    Your example: _____

7. New source of funding: When Share Our Strength created an annual "Charge Against Hunger" with American Express, it created a new funding source for its hunger-fighting activities.

    Your example: _____

BALANCING TENSIONS IN THE INNOVATION PROCESS

The innovation process can be thought of in terms of three stages (see Exhibit 7.1). The first stage is *conception.* Innovators must be able to see new possibilities and evaluate their potential. The second stage is *persuasion.* Successful innovation requires the cooperation of others. The innovator must persuade others that it is worth their while to cooperate. The third stage is *implementation.* Even with others on board, the innovative process continues. Implementation is not just a matter of following a plan. It is an ongoing creative process of learning and adjustment. Most innovations are modified at this stage.

Each stage has an inherent tension. Successful innovators are able to master the following three tensions:

✔ *Using both beginner's mind and expert's mind to* conceive *of viable innovative ideas.* "In the beginner's mind there are many possibilities, in the expert's there are few." This is a famous quote from a Zen master who helped bring Zen to the United States. Beginners bring a fresh perspective to any situation and can often see innovative possibilities better than experts in the field, who are set in their ways. A true innovator must maintain a healthy tension between beginner's mind and expert's mind. Innovators need to see the possibilities that experts miss because of their ingrained

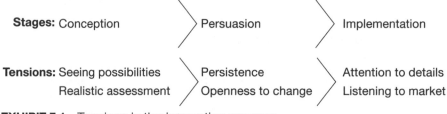

EXHIBIT 7.1   Tensions in the innovation process.

habits of thought. Of course, not all of the ideas beginners have are of equal merit. Some "beginner's" ideas may not be cost effective or they may even defy the laws of physics. In addition to seeing the myriad possibilities, innovators need to identify those with the most promise. They need to be able to evaluate ideas. Beginners cannot do this; in this stage and in this way, the "expert's mind" must kick in. Innovators must have enough expertise to identify genuinely promising innovations and to answer the detailed "how can" questions, such as: How can this idea become a viable reality?

✔ *Being persistent in the face of rejection, but also being open to changing course while* persuading *others of the merits of your idea.* If the history of innovation and entrepreneurship has any lessons to convey, it clearly shows that the original conception that someone has in mind, no matter how innovative it is, changes over time. It must adapt to the challenges of making a vision into a reality. An innovator who is locked into a particular way of doing things is more likely to fail; however, the history of entrepreneurship also shows that innovators must be persistent, especially those posing more radical innovations. Innovators have many barriers to overcome. Persistence in the face of rejection is essential. People often do not understand or they are made uncomfortable by the innovation. You must walk a fine line between persistence and its problematic cousin, stubbornness. Thus, the most effective innovators display what entrepreneurship professor Amar Bhide calls "flexible perseverance."[2] When they run into resistance, they ask themselves whether the resistance indicates a flaw in their idea and an opportunity to improve it, or simply a lack of understanding by the other party.

✔ *Keeping your ear to the ground while keeping your nose to the grindstone as you* implement *the idea.* Okay, this is a terrible mixed metaphor, but this brutal image captures a major tension facing innovators during the implementation stage. Entrepreneurs typically feel driven to focus exclusively on keeping their fledging enterprises and projects afloat; however, keeping your nose to the grindstone in this way can buffer you from important information that you need to carry on the process of innovation successfully. Innovation is not a smooth process. New ideas often have to be modified in practice. Successful innovation requires broad awareness, and this is not easy to cultivate, especially once a new venture is underway. You need to keep your ear to the ground to get the information you need to make adjustments in your innovative ideas. This is not a passive listening process but an active learning and questioning process. It means (1) listening to the people you are currently serving and, if possible, those you want to serve but don't yet serve; (2) watching the developments in your field and related fields; (3) looking for lessons in unlikely places; and (4) constantly asking whether you are learning anything that might help.

CASE STUDY

MUHAMMAD YUNUS AND GRAMEEN BANK

In the 1980s, Muhammad Yunus confounded many people in nonprofit agencies, economic development programs, government, and banking with the success of a new approach to economic development, based on the idea of making loans to the poor that allow them to start small businesses. Experts in these areas in his home country of Bangladesh and in the international aid community initially thought Yunus' concept was not feasible.

Yunus is a native of Bangladesh who was educated in classical economics. After studying as a Fulbright scholar in the United States, he returned to Chittagong University. He was immediately overwhelmed by the poverty in the villages surrounding the university. Yunus sent his students into the villages, carefully studying not only the systems within which the villagers lived and worked, but also trying to "understand the life of one single poor person."[3] He identified the obstacles encountered by the poorest of the poor in securing a minimal amount of capital with which to start and maintain very small businesses.

Yunus started asking seemingly simple questions, but his answers challenged the status quo. For example: Why are the poor not worthy of credit? Bankers responded that the poor lack collateral and they are often illiterate. Furthermore, a bank cannot afford to handle loans so small. It is too much work for loan officers. In response, Yunus came up with the idea of social collateral—the intense moral, managerial, and financial support that can be created by a small group of borrowers working together. This concept formed the core of his "peer lending" model. Small groups of borrowers in the same village would share responsibility for repayment of loans made to anyone in the group. Based

(continued)

on this concept, Yunus developed products and services that previously did not exist and used them to bring capital to people who did not previously have access to it. He innovated on multiple dimensions.

With the founding of Grameen Bank, Yunus changed the face of aid to the poor in Bangladesh and inspired similar efforts around the world. "It is the basic economic premise of the Grameen Bank that a supply of capital at a reasonable cost can help transform the surplus labor of the poor into goods and services which can then bring them new entitlements."[4] Since then, Grameen Bank has served millions of microentrepreneurs in Bangladesh. The Grameen Bank model has been studied and assessed by the international community and replicated and adapted throughout the world. Each time, innovation continues, in order to fit the model into the economic environment and cultural settings of each program.

Grameen Bank is continuing to innovate in new directions. It became apparent that lack of capital was not the only factor contributing to poverty. Poverty is exacerbated by lack of information, organization, and infrastructure. Thus, Grameen has expanded its services to give the poor access to modern technology, experiment with solar and wind energy, and build both a health insurance program and a retirement plan. For example, Grameen Phone, an international consortium, is building a nationwide cellular network throughout urban Bangladesh.

Yunus has managed the three tensions well. As a beginner in banking, telecommunications, and social work, Yunus saw possibilities that were not evident to the experts, but he also brought rigor and his own expertise to the process of assessing and refining his ideas. He researched them and tested them. He was persistent in the face of rejection, and yet he learned in the process. Bankers told him that collateral is important and that it is costly to administer small loans. So he developed the "peer lending" concept that relies on "social collateral" and lowers the costs of loan administration. He struggled to build a huge banking operation in Bangladesh, while still listening to the poor and coming up with new ideas to address their needs beyond capital.

For additional information about Muhammad Yunus and Grameen Bank, see the references for this chapter in Appendix B.

Key questions to stimulate the innovative process: The innovative process usually starts with some kind of stimulating piece of information that indicates either a problem or an opportunity. Innovators usually see problems as opportunities in disguise. The following questions are meant to stimulate your thinking. In each case, you need to ask whether your answer to the question indicates an opportunity for establishing a new and better way of accomplishing your organizational objective.

1. How well are you serving your clients, customers, etc.? Could you be doing a better job? Could you be doing other things for them? How well are your competitors serving their clients?

2. Are you reaching all of the people you would like to reach? If not, why not? Do these unserved potential clients know about your services? If so, what keeps them away? Is someone else doing a better job for them? If not, how can you get the word to them?

3. Have the demographics (e.g., age, ethnicity, preferred language, education levels, incomes, wealth) changed in the community you serve or want to serve? Should you adapt your product, service, or program to reflect these changes?

4. Have social values, moods, perceptions, or politics changed in a way that hampers your effectiveness or creates new opportunities? Are there things you couldn't do before that you can do now because of this social climate change?

5. Are your staff unhappy or frustrated in their work? Is morale low or high? What kind of attrition rate do you have? How could productivity and staff satisfaction be improved?

6. What kinds of innovations are working in other fields that might be adapted in your field? What would it take to migrate these innovations into your field?

7. Do we have any new scientific knowledge or new technology that could improve the way you operate? How could it be put to use?

To the extent that you are running a social enterprise and cannot answer these questions with confidence, you may not be keeping your ear to the ground sufficiently. Even people who think they can answer the questions confidently may have the wrong answers. How do you know that your clients and staff are satisfied? They may not tell you honestly what they feel. They may just leave. Look for credible independent indicators to answer these questions.

MANAGING THE RESISTANCE TO INNOVATION

By definition, innovation involves change. Change can be welcome when the people affected are greatly dissatisfied with the status quo, the change being proposed is not threatening to them, and change is relatively easy; however, this is rarely the case. Innovation can be threatening to people and, even when it is not threatening, people tend to resist change out of inertia. To understand resistance to innovation and to respond to it, you need to consider the level of threat implicit in the innovation and the level of inertia you are likely to encounter.

INNOVATION CAN BE THREATENING

Borrowing Schumpeter's famous phrase, innovation is typically a "creative-destructive process."[5] The new, if successful, drives out the old. Those with a vested interest in the status quo may find this threatening. Understanding and managing the potentially "destructive" aspects of innovation is essential to success.

Of course, not all innovation is threatening. Innovation, by our definition, is a matter of degree. Some changes are more dramatic and threatening than others. How a social entrepreneur approaches a particular innovation opportunity should depend largely on the character of the innovation envisioned.

Specialists on innovation distinguish *incremental* innovations from *radical* innovations. Radical innovations are typically more threatening, but we need to understand why. The threats that can be posed by innovation fall into three categories. These categories can be described in terms of Three C's.

core concept

✔ *Competence.* Does the innovation require substantially different knowledge and skills than the old approach?

✔ *Competition.* Does the innovation compete with the old approach, replacing it or significantly reducing demand for it?

✔ *Core Values.* Does the innovation require a shift in values or culture?

Let's explore each of these categories.

Competence—We use the terms *competence-enhancing* and *competence-shifting* to explain the first potential threat from innovation. *Competence-enhancing innovation* builds on existing knowledge and skills in the field in which the innovation is occurring. It extends that knowledge in a natural way. *Competence-shifting innovation* requires knowledge and expertise that is fundamentally different from the current knowledge and skill base in the field.

Of course, the difference between these two types of innovation is a matter of degree without a sharp dividing line. Most innovations build on old knowledge but also require some new knowledge and skills. We can ask of any innovation: How much of the existing knowledge and skill base is still relevant and useful? For example, the movement from two- and four-cylinder car engines to six- and eight-cylinder engines was a competence-enhancing innovation. The introduction of computer chips into automobiles is an example of a competence-shifting innovation because it relies on computer science as opposed to mechanical engineering. The creation of a totally electronic vehicle requires an even greater shift in competence, but neither of these changes is as radical as the shift from horse-drawn buggies to automobiles in the first place. Even then, some of the knowledge that buggy makers had developed was still relevant—basic knowledge about wheels, axles, springs, seats, and so on. Few innovations change knowledge requirements completely, but some innovations change the knowledge requirements enough to be a threat to those who have invested time and effort to develop the old competencies.

Competition—We use the terms *complementary* and *competitive* to explain the second potential source of threat. *Complementary innovation* augments existing methods by serving a different group of users or by serving a specific subgroup of users better. *Competitive innovation* is meant to replace existing methods. It threatens the existing approach with extinction, or at least reduces it to a much smaller role.

Again, the competitive threat may be a matter of degree, and the perception of that threat may change over time, as the new approach evolves and improves. What starts out looking like a complementary innovation can become a competitive one. The competitive nature of an innovation depends on your point of comparison. Take the example of personal computers. They were largely a complementary innovation from the point of view of large-scale mainframe computer makers, such as IBM. They brought different customers into the market. As personal computers evolved, however, they definitely became a competitive innovation from the point of view of minicomputer makers. Minicomputers were positioned between mainframes and personal computers. The companies that made them (Digital Equipment, Prime, Data General, Wang, and others) were all hurt badly as personal computers grew in sophistication.

Core values—Finally, we use the terms *core-value-consistent* and *core-value-changing* to explain the third potential source of threat. *Core-value-consistent innovation* poses no threat to and even supports the values and the culture implicit in the old approach. *Core-value-changing innovation* is grounded in a new set of values and requires changes in culture to successfully implement it.

As with the previous two distinctions, changes in values can be a matter of degree. Some values are more strongly held than others and are more resistant to change. That's why we focus on core values, those deeply held values that resist change. An example might help explain the difference. When wooden furniture was largely handcrafted, the introduction of a new woodworking tool that allowed more precise, finely detailed wood inlay was a core-value-consistent innovation. The introduction of automated mass-production methods, however, was a core-value-changing innovation. It signaled an emphasis on lower costs rather than craftsmanship. Thus, it was a difficult change for furniture makers who were most committed to handcrafted excellence. Organizational innovations can also be value-changing. Consider the shift from a top-down hierarchical management philosophy to a more team-based approach. The change in values required can be a difficult one for old-line managers to accept. This may explain why General Motors created the Saturn division as a completely separate operating unit. It would be driven by a different set of values and culture, from the manufacturing floor to the showroom floor. A new organization could do this much easier than an older, entrenched organization.

Relations among the three threats—It is important to note that innovations that are competence-shifting, are not necessarily competitive or core-value-changing. These things may often go hand-in-hand, but not always. The microwave oven was competence-shifting, requiring new knowledge; however, it was not competitive because most people want both a microwave and a conventional oven; and it was not value-changing. Even though some critics worried about its safety and effectiveness, firms making conventional ovens did not have to make a shift in values to produce microwaves. They just had to make a shift in competence. The refrigerator was a competence-changing innovation over the old ice box; it was also competitive, eventually driving ice box production to more of a novelty item, built by furniture manufacturers for decorative rather than functional purposes; but it was not value-changing.

A social enterprise example—A homeless shelter that currently provides meals for its residents might decide to extend its food services to a new market, people who are hungry but not homeless, by opening a food pantry. If there is an unmet need for this service, then this would count as a competence-enhancing, complementary, value-consistent innovation. It does not require significantly new knowledge or skills, and it does not threaten the core services of the shelter or the core values. If the same shelter decided it wanted to start a restaurant as a job-training ground for its residents, this would be a more challenging innovation. Cooking may be the same, but job-training and restaurant management skills are different from the skills of running a shelter or a kitchen. These skill needs would have to be addressed; however, this would still be complementary to the core service of offering shelter and consistent with the core values. Given the magnitude and nature of the problem of homelessness, the job-training program is not likely to make the shelter obsolete in the way refrigerators made ice boxes obsolete. It may add some new values related to empowering people to take care of themselves, but it is not likely to threaten the values of the shelter staff.

concept check Looking at the list you created in Exercise #1 in this chapter, can you determine whether the innovations you identified were competence-enhancing or competence-shifting? Which were complementary or competitive to prior practices? Which were core-value-consistent and which were core-value changing for the enterprises involved?

STRATEGIES FOR RESPONDING TO THREAT-BASED RESISTANCE

action step

Developing a strategy to deal with the threats of innovation requires three steps. The first step is assessing the nature and magnitude of the threat. The second step is using this analysis to develop an approach for addressing the threat.

Step 1: Assess the Threat Using the Innovation Threat Profile

When you come up with innovative ideas, determine whether the innovation is likely to be competence-shifting, competitive, or core-value-changing. You can complete a threat profile to determine the magnitude of the threat. For each of the threat dimensions, rate your innovation along a continuum from 1 to 10, with 10 representing the highest degree of threat.

Competence-Shifting Threat:

1	2	3	4	5	6	7	8	9	10

1=No new competence required   10=Requires completely new skills

Competitive Threat:

1	2	3	4	5	6	7	8	9	10

1=Totally complementary   10=Directly competitive with old ways

Core Value Threat:

1	2	3	4	5	6	7	8	9	10

1=Consistent with old values   10=Requires a drastic change in core values

Develop your strategies based on the risk profile.
A relatively high level of threat is at a score of 5 or above on a given scale.

Step 2: Developing an Approach for Addressing the Threat

How you manage the threat depends on the magnitude and the specific nature of the threat. If the magnitude of a given threat is low, then it can usually be handled with clear communications and reassurance to the threatened parties. If the threat is high on any of the three dimensions, then you need to develop a strategy for meeting, reducing, or avoiding the resistance the threat will cause. Consider each of the dimensions. A high rating is anything above five on the scale.

When the competence threat is high . . . The pursuit of competence-shifting innovation requires either (1) a significant investment in training the people threatened so that they develop the new competencies, or

(2) finding and working with people who already have the needed expertise. It is also possible to mix the two options, for instance by hiring people with the new skill, while training others.

The first option reduces the threat to the individuals with the old skills. It is generally preferred, provided that the people affected are willing and able to develop the new skills, the cost of the training is not particularly high, and it can be delivered in a timely fashion. If the competitive threat is high and the core-value threat is low, people should be eager to learn the new skills; however, they may not be so eager if the innovation requires a change in core values. If the switch in skills is particularly radical, the training may be an expensive and slow process that hampers the innovation effort.

The second option has its own challenges. Attracting people who already have the new competence may be difficult and costly. It depends on the supply of people with this skill and their alternatives in the labor market. Paying for these new skills can cause problems. Consider a social entrepreneur who wants to create an online matchmaking service that brings together potential volunteers with appropriate nonprofits in their community. The competence needed to build an effective Website and a sophisticated database is different from traditional volunteer-matching skills. Computer programming skills have to be acquired. These tend to be costly, especially by traditional nonprofit standards. Bringing in new, highly paid professionals can even lead to perceptions of pay inequity between the old guard and the new hires. Beyond the pay issues, you may be asking people to bring their skills into a field of endeavor that is new to them. If a mixture of old and new knowledge is required, they may have to develop their understanding of the field they are moving into.

In many cases, a combination of training the old guard while bringing in the new guard is the most sensible option. If done right, they can mentor and teach each other; however, this is only viable if both groups are motivated to do it, both groups are capable of learning from the other in a reasonable amount of time, and the mixture is not likely to result in a clash of core values.

When the competitive threat is high . . . Because competitive innovations pose a direct threat to the status quo, they are likely to be resisted by people and organizations invested in the old approach; however, this is just the kind of innovation that cannot be ignored without paying a price. Existing organizations must honestly assess and explore potentially competitive innovations. The problem is that pursuing a competitive innovation within an existing organization will be viewed as a form of "cannibalization" because it will reduce the demand for the old approach and will place a strain on organizational resources. The alternative may be worse. Someone else may pursue this competitive innovation at your expense. Online book selling is a good example in which Barnes & Noble felt pressed to create an online site, even if it cannibalized store sales, because if it did not, Amazon.com would be taking those sales away.

The process of pursuing a competitive innovation in an existing organization that is threatened by that innovation is difficult to manage because of the internal tensions it creates. The tensions are heightened when the innovation is both competence-shifting and competitive. Such innovations are sometimes referred to as "competence destroying" because they make preexisting competencies less and less relevant, as the new ways catch on. It means that old staff cannot easily be shifted to the new approach. Your options range from communications campaigns with smooth, drawn-out transition plans with retraining and incentives to more dramatic actions, such as shutting down or phasing out the old operation and laying off the associated employees. It is even worse when the innovation threatens core values as well. The special case of high levels of threat on all dimensions is discussed as follows.

When the core value threat is high . . . Core-value-changing innovations are the most difficult to pursue within an existing organizational structure. Value change, if feasible at all, is a long and difficult process. If you have a limited time to act on the innovation, then changing the values of an existing organization may not be feasible. Even if time is not a pressing consideration, value change will not be easy. What can you do? You have essentially two choices: You can create a totally new organization with new values, or you can create a separate unit, with a firewall around it, that operates within or in affiliation with the existing, old-style parent organization. The latter option leaves open the possibility that the new values will eventually seep into the old organization. This would be helpful if the innovation is also seriously competitive.

The Saturn division of General Motors was cited earlier as an example of the separate unit option. Saturn's values are different from traditional car manufacturers in many ways. For example, Saturns are sold differently from most new cars—no haggling, no commissioned salespeople, no pressure, just informed customer representatives. At the time of Saturn's creation, this approach was unheard of. General Motors and other car makers have experimented with bringing some of this approach to auto sales into more traditional showrooms, but it has not been easy. It cuts against the culture and values of traditional auto sales. Skilled salespeople tend to look down their noses at no-haggle customer representatives, seeing them as mere "order takers." Where is the skill, excitement, or challenge in that? The seeping of values from Saturn into the rest of GM is taking place, but it is a slow process.

When all three dimensions of threat are high . . . The need for a new organization is even greater in the special case when an innovation is highly competence-shifting, competitive, and value-changing. In such cases, it is highly unlikely that organizations committed to the old methods will be able to convert in a timely fashion. Resistance will be great and passions will be high. This combination makes a strong case for a new startup dedicated to the new way of operating.

INERTIA AS A SOURCE OF RESISTANCE TO INNOVATION

Innovation may be resisted even when it is not threatening. Some innovations, such as process innovations, are not visible to outside constituencies. They show up externally only in lower costs or better quality. In these cases, the inertial resistance is likely to be internal. In many cases, however, the inertia is with clients, customers, and funders. It is important to understand the sources of inertia in the marketplace, as well as in the organization.

The Liabilities of Newness

In the entrepreneurship literature, writers talk about the "*better mousetrap fallacy.*" This fallacy comes from a quote attributed to Ralph Waldo Emerson, a famous American philosopher. According to the story, Emerson said in a lecture that if a person were to build a better mousetrap, "tho' he build his house in the woods, the world will make a beaten path to his door."[6] Emerson was brilliant, but in this matter, his advice is dangerous. It is only correct in special circumstances—namely, when people need mousetraps badly, they are seriously dissatisfied with the mousetraps they have, using your new mousetrap is relatively easy, the costs of the new trap are relatively low, your house in the woods is relatively easy to find, you tell the right person about your new mousetrap, and word spreads easily to others who use mousetraps. In most situations, people are used to their old "mousetraps," which do an adequate job. Changing may require them to learn something new or to do something different. Old habits die hard. Few of them will know that you have a new mousetrap to offer unless you advertise. Those that hear about it may not be convinced that it is really better. Your word will not be enough; after all, you have a bias because you want to sell mousetraps. Until they try it or others try it, they won't know for sure how well it works. It has to be priced right and easy for them to get. Designing a better product is only the first step in the marketing process. Getting people to change their behavior usually requires a more proactive effort.

 core concept

Information gaps. People often do not rush to embrace a new approach. For one thing, they may not know that the new approach is available to them. Finding out is not always easy. Economists have a term for this—"search costs." Searching for information about alternatives and their attractiveness is costly. Think about laser eye surgery to correct nearsightedness. Many nearsighted people are unaware of this alternative to glasses. Imagine how little they would know without advertising.

Risk and uncertainty.   Even if people are aware of the new option, they may hesitate. New approaches, by definition, are unfamiliar, and the unfamiliar is risky. This risk might be reduced if they had more information, but information is not free, nor is it freely available. They can do some research and find out that a new approach exists, but to get reliable information on how well it might work for them requires lots of additional time and expense. In the case of laser eye surgery, it requires getting a doctor's opinion and finding an unbiased source of data on the procedure's success from other people with similar visual impairments who have tried it. In some cases, even with an extensive search, the information is not sufficient to clearly resolve the question of whether the new approach is really superior. Risk and uncertainty remain, and that can be a significant deterrent to many people.

Switching costs.   Even if they get reliable information that helps reduce the risk and uncertainty, people get used to doing things a certain way. Changing it imposes a "cost" on them. The cost may not be in dollar terms; it may just be a matter of inconvenience, but most people need a reason or incentive to change. This is a serious problem when "switching costs," as economists call them, are high. These are the costs, financial or otherwise, that are involved when someone shifts from one thing to another. There are high switching costs, for instance, when a company shifts from Apple to IBM computers for its employees after years of using Apples. Not only are the new machines costly, but the costs of training people on the new IBM machines and the lost productivity as people learn the new systems are high as well. Switching to a different brand of pencils has relatively low switching costs by comparison. To return to our eye surgery example, the cost of switching from glasses to laser-corrected eyes is relatively high. Unless wearing glasses is a major nuisance for you, it may not be worth it to switch.

Special Sources of Inertia in the Social Sector
The process can be even more difficult in the social sector because of the social mission of the organizations and the reliance, in many cases, on philanthropic funding or third-party payments.

Benefits to society versus benefits to the individuals involved.   Many social-purpose organizations are trying to create benefits for society, not just for the individuals who use their products, services, or programs.

Consider Population Services International, which sells birth control devices in developing countries that have serious population problems. Individual households in need of the cheap labor that children can provide in agrarian societies may not benefit directly or immediately from using birth control. Society reaps most of the benefits. Any innovation that benefits society while providing little benefit to the individuals whose cooperation is needed is likely to meet resistance. Of course, if the innovation has net benefits for the individual as well as for society, it would be an easier sell, but not all innovations work that way. Even in this case, it can be difficult if the individual benefits are intangible or they will not be evident for a long time.[7]

Convincing the third-party payers. Businesses have paying customers who can be the judge of whether a given innovation is an improvement for them; however, when social benefits are involved, it is not uncommon to have third parties pay at least part of the bill. These payers might be philanthropists, government agencies, or other interested parties, such as employers. Social entrepreneurs not only have to convince their staffs and their clients to adopt an innovative approach, but they must also convince funders. This adds another constituency and one that may not see the benefits of the innovation so clearly or quickly. In the case of some third-party payers, such as foundations and government agencies, the decision-making process can be slow and bureaucratic. This can be especially problematic when the window of opportunity is short lived. The other problem with third-party payers is that they may not be good judges of the value of a particular innovation. They may be willing to support something that is not really an improvement just because it is an innovation, and they may not see the value in true innovation. It depends on what drives their decision processes and how well they can assess the potential innovation.

Innovation Acceptance Curve

Writers in the high-tech arena use a graph to illustrate the stages of adoption for new technologies. It is called the technology adoption life cycle.[8] This idea can be helpfully generalized to the acceptance of any innovation. Exhibit 7.2 depicts a given population of clients, customers, staff, or funders facing the prospect of embracing an innovative way of doing things.

tool of the trade This curve captures the idea that some people are faster to accept a given innovation than are others. Of course, the exact shape of the innovation acceptance curve and the relative sizes of the different segments varies widely from one innovation to another. The size of each segment and the speed with which one can move from the innovators to the majority segments depends on the character of the innova-

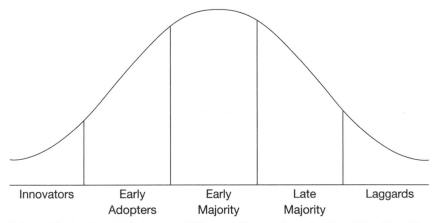

| Innovators | Early Adopters | Early Majority | Late Majority | Laggards |

Adapted from Everett M. Rogers, *Diffusion of Innovations,* fourth edition (New York: The Free Press, 1995), p. 262.

EXHIBIT 7.2 Innovation adoption curve.

tion, general satisfaction with the status quo, the culture or climate in which the innovation is being pursued, and the personalities of individuals in the target audience. Even so, it is helpful to think in terms of these kinds of segments when dealing with resistance to innovation. Let me explain each category. As an exercise, think about the adoption of recycling by U.S. households as we move along.

Innovators—In general, this is a small group of folks attracted primarily by the novelty of the innovation. They are curious and are actively searching for new things. They tolerate uncertainty. In the social sector, this is the vanguard. These people want to be on the cutting edge of social issues. Leadership is important to them and intrinsically rewarding. These are the people who lobby for a recycling center for their town, do their own composting already, and so on.

Early Adopters—This is a slightly larger group that is ready for something new. They are unhappy with the status quo and see the innovation as possibly of significant benefit to them. They are usually in circumstances in which they face little risk or cost in adopting the innovation. Unlike innovators, they are not attracted to novelty per se, but to the potential benefits. They intrinsically value societal benefits and appreciate the intangible benefits to themselves of adopting a social innovation. They are progressive and active individuals, but not the leaders of a new movement. These folks will drive to a recycling center and sort their paper, glass, and metal. They probably already engage in some conservation efforts.

Early Majority—This is a much larger group that is willing to switch to a new approach, but wants to make sure the new approach works before they shift. They may be dissatisfied with the status quo and ready for change, but they are more skeptical than the early adopters about whether new is necessarily better. They may see more cost and inconvenience to themselves in accepting the innovation. They have to be shown results but are receptive to the message. With social innovation, they are a bit more skeptical of the social benefits and the intangible benefits to themselves than are the early adopters. They require a relatively low-cost way to get started. They wait for curbside pickup for their recyclable items. They collect only what is relatively easy to collect and do only the sorting necessary.

Late Majority—This group is also sizable but is relatively content with the status quo or faces significant obstacles to adopting the new approach. They are not comfortable with their own ability to adopt and benefit from the new approach. Switching to a new approach is seen to be a headache that has to be justified with clear benefits and the comfort that lots of others have adopted the new approach. In some cases, the late majority just have slow decision-making processes. These folks respond to peer pressure to do the socially beneficial thing. They may recycle if it becomes relatively easy, if they are urged to do so by their friends and neighbors, and if they feel shamed or embarrassed if they don't.

Laggards—Finally, this group brings up the rear. Laggards are highly skeptical of anything new, relatively satisfied with the status quo, and willing not to conform even though the majority has bought into the new approach. They are wed to old ways of doing things and have to be brought along kicking and screaming. These people may never accept a particular innovation until they have to. With social innovation, these are the skeptics who want to know what is in it for them and who suspect the motives of the people pushing the innovation. They will recycle only when their trash collector (or the city dump) refuses to take mixed trash and insists on the recyclables being separate.

Each group presents its own challenges and requires different methods of persuasion. Geoffrey Moore[9] argues that the gaps between each group are larger than typically understood, and specifically that a large "chasm" exists between the early adopters and the early majority, as illustrated in Exhibit 7.2. With innovators and early adopters, the challenge is just finding them and getting the word out to them. Make it easy for them to try the new approach. Reaching the early and then the late majority requires a more proactive marketing effort, credible performance data, and methods of reducing the risks of adoption. Naturally, the chasm is wider for more radical innovations. Crossing it is far from easy.

How does this model apply in the social sector? Consider an organization that develops a radically new curriculum for using the arts to teach science and math. Persuading schools to adopt this curriculum will very likely follow the technology adoption curve. Independent schools that pride themselves on offering innovative curricula and that do not mind switching are likely to be the most willing adopters. Following that are likely to be the independent schools that are highly dissatisfied with the current methods and are open to new approaches. This might include some relatively new charter schools looking for a differentiating characteristic or an individual public school in a system with school-based management, progressive leadership, and lots of local flexibility. The chasm will be between these early adopters and larger school systems with more elaborate decision-making processes. Even those public systems that are open to change, systems in which educational outcomes have been poor, will be slower to adopt a new curriculum because of the costs of retraining teachers and the inherent conservatism in a system with many constituents. They have to see results and be able to demonstrate them to key political constituencies from the school board to the teachers' union. Late majority adopters are school districts that are doing fine and have less reason to change, but will if the new approach shows very promising results in other large school systems.

The Special Challenge of Disruptive Innovation[10]

Harvard professor Clayton Christensen has identified a form of innovation that often goes unrecognized to the detriment of firms. Most people view innovations as either lowering the cost, improving the quality, or enhancing the effectiveness of some product or service for existing, mainstream customers. Christensen calls these "sustaining innovations." Even competence-shifting, competitive, and core-value-changing innovations are commonly *sustaining.* As he puts it, "sustaining innovations improve the performance of established products, along the dimensions of performance that mainstream customers in major markets have historically valued."

Christensen contrasts sustaining innovations with what he calls *disruptive* innovations. Disruptive innovations "result in worse product performance, at least in the near term" and "bring to a market a very different value proposition than had previously been available." Disruptive innovations initially appeal to a "few fringe customers," usually looking for a low-cost alternative to the mainline product; however, these innovations evolve into attractive alternatives for mainstream customers. That is how they earn their name as disruptive. Interestingly, disruptive innovations need not threaten existing competencies or core values, and initially they are perceived as not being competitive because they serve a fringe market. They become competitive, but by the time this is recognized, the damage may be done.

The problem with disruptive innovations is that they go unnoticed by mainstream organizations until it is too late. One example of this was discount retailing, pioneered by Kresge with Kmart and by Dayton-Hudson with its Target stores. Discounter stores eventually put a real dent in department store sales, especially Sears, Montgomery Ward, and JCPenney, who targeted a mass-market audience. More recently, Wal-Mart has pushed this concept further with superstores, now competing with grocery store chains as well as department stores. Internet shopping for items such as books and groceries may prove to be a major disruptive innovation for booksellers and grocery stores. Other examples include health maintenance organizations (HMOs) as a disruptive innovation in the health insurance market and steel "mini-mills" that have come to compete with large steel plants.

The significance of this new distinction is that it is not enough to pay attention to the needs of your mainstream customers in deciding which innovations to explore. If you are operating from the base of an existing organization, you have to *watch for disruptive innovations*—new approaches that now appeal to a fringe group but that could become directly competitive with you as they evolve. If you are trying to promote a disruptive innovation in an existing organization, the kind of resistance you are likely to meet will take a different form than resistance to clearly threatening innovations. Even though disruptive innovations are threatening, they are not immediately recognized. The resistance will be a form of inertia based on the perception that your proposed innovation is not important because it serves only a fringe market and does not compare favorably on performance measures.

For more information on this topic, be sure to check out Clayton Christensen's book, *The Innovator's Dilemma* (Harvard Business School Press, 1997).

OVERCOMING INERTIA-BASED RESISTANCE

Inertia-based resistance can show up in lots of stakeholder groups, even when an innovation is not threatening. Using the Innovation Acceptance Curve and your knowledge of the specific sources of resistance, you can develop a strategy to deal with it. To minimize inertia-based resistance and move ahead, you should follow these five steps:

1. *Identify the likely innovators and early adopters within the resistant constituency.* This is, of course, easier said than done. Within any constituency, you will find a range of views regarding the openness to innovation. Get close to the constituency, and find those who:

   • Are most restless and dissatisfied with the status quo

   • Have a history of experimentation and innovation of their own

   • Will benefit most significantly from the particular innovation you have developed.

2. *Get the word out to these likely adopters and make it easy for them to adopt your innovation.* Reduce the search and information costs for these high-potential adopters by going to them. Actively get the

word out. Promise to work with these innovators and early adopters to get the bugs out of the innovation. Offer them special attention and make them part of the team. If feasible, you can try to cultivate a sense of ownership among this group. They can be an active part of the innovation process.

3. *Use the initial users to demonstrate the benefits of your innovation over the status quo.* Track the experience of the innovators and early adopters. Refine your innovation accordingly. Document the successes, and build a case that will appeal to a larger group of users and funders.

4. *Gain an understanding of the needs and concerns of other potential users, especially those who might be in the early majority.* Why are these constituents resistant? To the extent possible, get a handle on their specific concerns and be prepared to address them. Are the benefits to them unclear? Are the switching costs high? Also, in the case of organizations, make sure you understand the decision-making process and who has influence. Then determine what motivates the key sources of influence and the key decision makers. What would it take to get them to try the innovation?

5. *Make it easy for them to get the information they need, make sure that information is credible, and find ways to reduce the risks and costs of trying your innovation.* Facilitate communications among the early users and supporters and these later adopters. Let the early users tell the story. Offer demonstrations or simulations to show how your innovation works, without requiring any commitment from the potential adopters. If feasible, offer a low-cost way to try your innovation. Reduce the switching costs to your innovation and reduce the costs for switching back if they are unhappy. Offer these new users a way out if the innovation does not meet their needs.

Specific Suggestions for Dealing with Internal Resistance

Innovators often work within organizations to implement their innovations. Rarely is it wise to force an innovation on an organization because resistant staff can find many ways to sabotage it. The forced innovation approach should be used only when time or financial pressures prevent building support within the organization, and even then it is questionable. Usually, internal resistance should be met with a campaign of persuasion. The following six steps should help.

1. *Identify a champion for the innovation and help that person recruit the right team.* Every innovation in an existing organization needs a champion with the power and authority to take the innovation

forward. If the champion is not a senior staff member, the innovation may also need a senior management protector and a team that is committed to finding a way to make the innovation work.

2. *Provide a place for the most likely resisters on the team.* The composition of the team can be designed to co-opt the most likely resisters by giving them a voice in the process. At least one respected and intellectually honest resister should be put on the team. As the team works on the innovation, this resister can provide a healthy critical perspective. The resister will help you figure out how to deal with other resisters.

3. *Find a way for clients, funders, or other key external partners to have a voice in the process.* The external perspective is important with regard to any innovation that affects these external constituencies. Even businesses engage in this kind of outreach. In a ground-breaking study of midsized growth companies, Clifford and Cavanagh found that the successful innovators "regarded their customers and distributors as welcome partners in the innovation process."[11]

4. *Track the experience of the team and the results it has with the innovation.* To help persuade others of the value of the innovation, you need to build a case for its benefits relative to the organization's social mission. Start tracking this experience from early on, but give the team time to work out the kinks and refine the innovation. This information can be used by senior management to decide where and how aggressively to move forward with the innovation.

5. *Determine the source of resistance among the staff.* The resistance could just be normal resistance to any kind of change or anything unfamiliar; however, in the case of radical innovation, the resistance may come from one or more of the following sources:
   - Perceived difficulty in learning the new skills required by the innovation
   - Fear that the innovation is a competitive threat to the old way of doing things and possibly to their jobs
   - A clash in core values between staff associated with the old way and those working on the new

6. *Tailor your response strategy to the type of resistance.* If the resistance is normal aversion to change, you can use the usual management tools of persuasion: communication, training, carrots (rewards), or sticks (punishments). If the problem is related to the new skill requirements, invest in appropriate training programs. If the innovation is a competitive threat to the status quo, you need to have a strategy for shifting staff and possibly laying off staff who cannot be shifted, as the new approach takes over. If the resistance lies in a clash of values, you may have to create a separate operating unit to pursue the innovation. This should be the occasion for discussing

core values of the organization as a whole. Some innovations require fairly traumatic organizational change. This is not the place to talk about organizational restructuring, but leaders committed to innovation must be prepared to make difficult decisions.

CREATING AN INNOVATIVE, ADAPTIVE ENTERPRISE

It is not enough for you, the social entrepreneur, to be innovative. As your organization grows, you have to make sure it provides an environment that supports innovation within the ranks. Because the world is changing rapidly, effective organizations have to change with it. Any organization that is seriously committed to a social mission should constantly be striving for better results. It is not just a requirement for survival, but a moral imperative. But how do you create an innovative, adaptive organization?

TWO MIXED BLESSINGS: SUCCESS AND STRONG LEADERS

Ironically, two of the biggest potential stumbling blocks to creating an innovative organization are past success and a strong visionary leader.

The Price of Success

Most organizations go through an evolutionary process as they grow, resulting in increased bureaucracy and rigidity. Interestingly, initial success contributes to this ossification. In a landmark study of fast-growing midsized American companies, Dick Cavanagh and Don Clifford concluded: "The message is clear. The more successful a company becomes, the more difficulty it encounters in maintaining its innovativeness."[12] Success can breed complacency, the sense that "We have this figured out. Why tinker with it?"

Unfortunately, the old saying, "If it ain't broke, don't fix it," turns out to be bad management advice. Organizations that hope to survive and thrive should constantly look for better ways of serving their missions. Yet, why bother if things are going well? The answer is that if you wait until things start failing on their own, it may well be too late. In the 1980s, Digital Equipment Corporation was riding the crest of success in the mini-computer business that it pioneered. This success may have blinded it to the importance of personal computers—a potentially disruptive innovation. Digital entered the personal computer market very late and was never able to establish a strong competitive position. After serious financial problems in the early 1990s, resulting in billions of dollars in losses, Digital went through major restructuring efforts. In 1997, Digital was acquired by Compaq Computer Corporation, a leading personal computer maker.

Of course, any organization should recognize and build on its successes, but it should not rest on them. It is important to keep rocking the boat, even when things seem fine. This means that the leadership of a successful organization has to send a strong signal that success is for building on, not for resting on. *It is a platform, not a couch.*

The Downside of Strong Visionary Leadership

Many successful ventures are driven by a strong, visionary leader, the person who saw the initial opportunity and rallied the resources and troops to pursue it. The energy, power, and confidence of that person can be critical to the success of a young, innovative venture, or to revitalizing an older organization. This person can become the central innovative force in the organization. When that happens, people in the organization tend to look to this individual for new ideas. This situation can lead to an unhealthy dependency on one person, who may not be in the best position to drive the next levels of innovation. No one person in an organization has a monopoly on good ideas.

The visionary leader may even suffer from a common ailment: *founder's syndrome*. This happens when the leader/founder is reluctant to relinquish control. Sometimes the founder is so closely identified with the original vision that it discourages the kind of questioning attitude that leads to further innovation. Many entrepreneurs report that it is hard to "let go of my baby." This attitude is natural. They have poured so much of themselves into the venture they created that it is hard for them to see it as having a life of its own. But just as parents must let their kids grow up and make their own decisions, so visionary founders must let others in their organization take some initiative and enjoy some autonomy.

 Does your organization suffer from either of these problems? Answer the following three questions to assess your organization's complacency and its dependency on a central leader (possibly you):

1. How many innovations has your organization implemented or seriously tested in the last two years?

2. How many new ideas have even been suggested by staff other than the leader (you)? If an outsider asked people in your organization who had the ideas for these innovations, how many would be attributed to anyone other than the leader (you)?

3. When new ideas are presented in a meeting, do all eyes turn to the leader (you) to gauge his or her (your) reaction?

If the answer to the first question is "few, if any," then you may have a complacency problem. If the answer to the second question is "not many," and the answer to the third question is "yes," then your organization scores high on "leader-dependency." This is true even if your answer to the first question indicated a high level of innovative activity. If it is mostly coming from the leader, then the organization is not really an innovative organization.

WHEN "LEADER-DEPENDENCY" IS NOT A PROBLEM

Being leader-dependent may not be a problem if your organization falls into one of three categories. Management writer Jim Collins suggests two conditions under which an organization "should not be built to last."[13] In these cases, some level of leader-dependency may be acceptable. To his two conditions, we add a third.

Rare Genius—The clearest situation is when the organization "serves as a platform for a genius," as Collins puts it. He mentions the examples of Thomas Edison's research and development lab, Edwin Land's Polaroid, Ken Olsen's Digital Equipment Corporation, and even Bill Gates' Microsoft. Investors might debate his assertion that "there is no moral or business-logic reason why Microsoft must outlast the guiding presence of Bill Gates"; however, the point is that some organizations are really expressions of one rare genius. It would be tragic for that genius to step out of the center ring prematurely, in the name of creating a more innovative, adaptive organization. It is only natural for such organizations to depend on their leaders for innovation. It might be even better if the leader's skills at innovation could be institutionalized to allow the organization to be productive past the point at which the leader's skills begin to fade, but this may be hard to achieve given the dominant role these leaders play.

Limited Purpose—Another condition that Collins discusses is when an organization functions as a "disposable injection device." In this case, the organization is simply a catalyst for "injecting a new product or an innovative technology into the world." He is thinking of new technology businesses, but this concept can be applied to the social sector as well. Think of organizations that have a relatively short-term mission to solve a specific problem, such as cleaning up the remnants of an old environmental problem in a specific community. Once the cleanup is complete, the organization can claim victory and dissolve. Being leader-dependent during this period may not be a serious problem, if the leader is strong.

Startup—One more condition under which leader-dependency may not be a serious problem is during the early stages of starting an organization, when a clear leading founder plays the role of chief innovator, while the rest of the team focuses on execution. This natural division of labor can serve the organization effectively for a while, but as the team grows and the organization passes the initial startup, fight-for-survival stage, it is time to consider making the organization as a whole more innovative. This condition is clearly temporary.

CHARACTERISTICS OF INNOVATIVE ORGANIZATIONS

When they move beyond the startup period, few organizations have the limited purpose or rare genius that makes leader-dependency a smart strategy. Usually, leader-dependency is a serious problem that should be addressed. If the leader is not comfortable with taking the steps to reduce this dependency, the best solution may be for the original founder to leave or to take on a different role in the organization. In business, this is a common solution.

To create an innovative, adaptive organization that is not leader-dependent requires working on three dimensions to support innovation: establishing cultural norms, building organizational capabilities, and instituting reinforcement mechanisms.

Establishing Cultural Norms

Beyond the formal policies and organization charts that designate lines of authority, every organization has a culture. An organization's culture is the set of values and norms that describes "how we do things around here." Cultures can be strong or weak, rigid or flexible, open or closed. Successful organizations usually have strong-but-adaptive cultures. Building such a culture is more about what you do than about what you say. Specifically, the culture of an innovative organization is usually characterized by the following Five R's.

core concept

1. **Restless** *drive for continuous improvement.* The organization and its leaders must exhibit a strong desire for improving everything they do. Innovation must be a core value in the sense that it is expected. People at all levels should be expected to look for new ways to do things. This desire is signaled in several ways. Top management certainly has a key role in setting the tone, through performance evaluations and policy.

2. **Receptivity** *to new ideas from all levels and sources.* Most senior managers think they are receptive to new ideas, but ask the troops or watch the flow of discussion in a meeting. Often, new ideas are never expressed by anyone other than the leader, or the ideas are dismissed as soon as they are proposed. Even managers who want to encourage creative thinking can unconsciously stop it in its

tracks by the way they react to it. Stifling behavior can take many forms, including, but not limited to, senior executives being too quickly judgmental and negative, encouraging others to find flaws, simply ignoring the idea, failing to provide time or resources to explore or test the idea, changing the idea so that it becomes theirs, claiming that they thought of the same thing long ago, or structuring meetings so it is hard for people to get new ideas on the table.

3. ***Rigorous*** *screening and testing of new ideas.* This may seem to contradict the norm of receptivity, but it doesn't. *Rigor does not mean being quick to judge with limited facts.* People should be given a fair opportunity to make the case for their new idea, but they should be held to appropriately high standards. The key to combining receptivity and rigor is providing the time and resources for staff who believe in their ideas to develop them, build their case, and, if warranted, test them. Everyone involved in the process should adopt the "how can" mindset discussed previously. How can we make this new idea work so that we can better serve our mission? This does not mean that ideas should be studied to death. In many cases, the only way to know how and how well an innovation can work is to try it. Tom Peters and Bob Waterman, in their management classic, *In Search of Excellence,* talked about a bias for action in excellent companies, expressed as "do it, fix it, try it."[14] If an idea appears sufficiently promising and has a champion who is willing to take responsibility, it can be tested. The key is to start small, if possible, and to manage the downside risk, in case the idea fails. (See Chapter 5 on managing risk.)

4. ***Respect*** *for honest mistakes and calculated risk taking.* Innovations always involve risk and uncertainty. Innovative organizations experience higher project failure rates than their less innovative cousins; however, they have higher success rates as well and greater organizational vitality. An innovative culture must not only tolerate honest mistakes, but it must also respect them. This does not mean accepting shoddy work or poor individual performance. It means recognizing when the failure, the mistake, was the result of the natural uncertainty surrounding innovation, rather than poor execution on the part of the team responsible for it.

In practice, this distinction can be hard to make because in hindsight it may be easy to see how the failure could have been avoided. And it is natural to look for a scapegoat, but this tendency must be consciously resisted. Leaders must ask themselves: Was the mistake the result of an honest judgment call? Did the person responsible take appropriate action once it became apparent that this was not working (e.g., no attempt at cover up)? Do I still trust this person's judgment and ability? Do I believe they have learned from this experience and will not make the same mistake again? If the answers are "yes," then the innovator should be respected for the effort and not punished in any way.

James Burke tells the story of a failed line of new children's products he launched when he was head of a New Products Division at Johnson & Johnson. After the failure, he was called in to see the head of the firm, Robert Wood Johnson II, also known as the General. The General was a tough boss, and Burke thought he was in trouble, but the General congratulated Burke on his effort, reportedly saying, "What business is all about is making decisions, and you don't make decisions without making mistakes. Now, don't ever make that mistake again, but please make sure you make other mistakes." Burke went on to a very successful career, eventually running all of Johnson & Johnson. The story helped send a signal that even a tough boss can respect honest mistakes.[15]

5. ***Responsibility and authority*** *for innovation at lower levels.* The notion of innovation and improvement should be part of every formal or informal job description. People throughout the organization should feel a sense of responsibility for improving the way the organization works. They must also have the authority to act. This does not mean that everyone should be free to do what they like without going through an approval process, but it means that a fair amount of authority must be delegated. Approval processes for ideas that exceed authority should not be multilayered and cumbersome. They should be rigorous, as mentioned earlier, but not bureaucratic. Responses to requests should be timely, and experimentation should be supported.

Building Organizational Capabilities

Culture alone is not enough to ensure that an organization is innovative and adaptive. Innovation requires certain individual and organizational capabilities that have to be consciously developed and cultivated, including the following:

1. *Information gathering and processing.* The organization must be able to "keep its ear to the ground," as mentioned when we discussed the process of innovation. This requires that time and resources be devoted to getting reliable information on how you are doing and how you might do better. It also requires that your staff be good at listening to others inside and outside the organization, networking with other people who might have access to helpful information, analyzing and assessing the information they come across, and communicating important information internally.

2. *Working across functional lines and organizational boundaries.* People need to be able to communicate and work across functional lines because few innovations are restricted to one function. This means learning to speak one another's languages and understanding how different parts of the organization work together to produce results.

3. *Thinking creatively, critically, and constructively.* Some people are naturally creative, but most people are not. They need to learn how to think "outside the box," to view things from unfamiliar angles, to play with ideas in a constructive way, on their own or in a group, and to identify those ideas that appear to have real promise. Individual and group problem–definition and problem-solving skills are important.

4. *Thinking into the future.* More radical and path-breaking innovations require people to think beyond the information of today to envision what the world might be like five or ten years from now. Some changes can be anticipated with relative confidence, such as demographic changes, whereas others are much more speculative and require the innovators to think in terms of multiple scenarios. This viewpoint is also crucial in defending against potentially disruptive innovations that may make your work irrelevant.

5. *Managing risk, uncertainty, and timing.* As mentioned earlier, innovations always involve an element of risk and uncertainty. They often have to be tried before anyone knows whether and how they will work. If it is not managed properly, the failure of an experimental innovation can be costly. Managers need to know how to test ideas without placing significant resources at risk. They also need to know when they have time to do this and when they must act more quickly and dramatically because the window of opportunity is closing soon. (See Chapter 5 on managing risk.)

Instituting Reinforcement Mechanisms

In addition to informal norms and organizational capabilities, innovative organizations need mechanisms that support and reinforce innovative behavior. Innovation is inherently difficult. Any change in how things are done is disruptive and discomforting for people. Although a few people might enjoy change, most people do not like it. They may not want to rock the boat or cause themselves additional work. As a result, organizations that want to encourage innovative behavior need to actively stimulate it and reward it. The kinds of mechanisms that are important for this purpose include the following:

1. *Clear and compelling shared mission.* The most powerful motivation for continuous innovation is a commitment to the mission of the organization. (See Chapter 2 on the mission.) If possible, the

mission should be framed in terms of aspirations that provide a rationale for continuous improvement. It should be clear that the mission is not being served by sitting still while there is room for improvement. The mission should also be flexible on how the organization serves its mission, so that it can explore new ways of operating if these prove to be more effective or efficient. Of course, some constraints on alternative methods may make sense for moral or strategic reasons.

2. *Systems for reliably measuring organizational performance.* A system for timely and reliable measurement of performance, one that is logically tied to the mission of the organization, is essential for demonstrating the value of particular innovations. Even if people in the organization have a clear shared mission, in the absence of such a system, they can disagree on the value of taking new approaches to their work. An accepted system for measuring mission-related performance is crucial in resolving concerns and sorting among innovations to find those most worthy of pursuit. In some cases (see the following example of John Sawhill and The Nature Conservancy), a better measurement system can unleash a wave of innovation in an organization. It can help people see new ways to do their work, and it can make clear the limits of the old approaches.

3. *Strong signals sent by senior management.* The most powerful signals are sent by behavior, not just words. The leaders of the organization need to set an example in two ways: They need to pursue innovative improvements in an active and visible way, and they need to respond to innovative ideas in constructive ways. In both ways, they become role models for other staff members. Their behavior is often the subject of stories that indicate the values of the organization. You can bet that the story about how the General responded to James Burke's failed product line spread at Johnson & Johnson and affected many more people than James Burke. It sent a message.

4. *Rewards in the form of recognition and resources.* Most writers on innovation agree that purely financial rewards rarely motivate people to be innovative. Nonetheless, it is important to signal the value that someone has created through their innovative activities. The most welcome and appropriate kinds of rewards for innovation are recognition in a way that is visible to the individual's peers and team mates, and easier access to resources for pursuing more innovative ideas in the future.

5. *Funding to support experimentation.* Experimentation with new ideas usually requires resources. If your staff has to go outside for these resources on every occasion, innovation will be inhibited.

The fundraising challenge acts as a deterrent. Although it is hard to do, given the nature of funding in the social sector, it is helpful to fund experimentation and initial assessment internally. In the ideal case, you would have a pool of unrestricted "venture" funds that are available to support testing innovative ideas.

6. *Incorporation of innovation into individual performance evaluation.* The expectation that people will look for new and better ways of serving the organization's mission should be built into their job descriptions and the performance evaluation system. It may not make sense to set an objective of "three new innovations" this year, but it is appropriate to ask how the person has improved, or at least tried to improve, activities in their sphere of influence and the organization as a whole. If the evaluations also include input from subordinates or peers, it is fair to ask how receptive the person in question has been to exploring new ways of doing things.

7. *Accountability for innovation all the way up to the Board level.* Job descriptions and performance evaluations can go only so far if the responsibility is not also felt at the Board level. The Board must look at the issue of innovation when it evaluates senior management, and it must look at the same issue in any self-assessment. The Board must hold itself accountable for innovation. Board members can be a useful source of innovative ideas. The Board can also be a deterrent to innovation if it is not supportive of new ventures or experimentation.

8. *Willingness to create new units when new ventures are based on potentially threatening innovations.* As we saw earlier in this chapter, sometimes an innovation is so different that it cannot effectively be pursued within an existing organization. In these cases, it can be useful to create a separate organization to pursue the more radical innovation. We saw this approach in the Saturn example earlier. Failure to do this can either drive the radical innovators to create their own separate (unaffiliated) organization or lead to serious internal conflict that is harmful to both the innovators and the "old guard."

action step If you are building a social enterprise, you should track your progress using the guidelines in this section. To get a truly independent assessment, you should allow your staff members to provide their confidential assessments on each of these dimensions to see if their views agree with yours.

Step 1: Using the guidelines suggested earlier, create your own Innovative Organization Checklist. The checklist should allow your staff or knowledgeable observers to assess your organization on each of the

JOHN SAWHILL AND THE NATURE CONSERVANCY

Since its startup in 1951, The Nature Conservancy has had a clear mission: To preserve plants and animals and special habitats that represent the diversity of life. For decades, all traditional measurements indicated that the Conservancy was one of the most successful nonprofits. It saw dramatic increases in the number of acres under its protection, memberships, and donations. "We thought we could buy a piece of land, fence it off, and thereby protect whatever was in that preserve."[16]

In 1990, John Sawhill became the CEO of The Nature Conservancy. He initiated a planning process that included all stakeholders. Discussions quickly centered on growing concerns that the long-range effectiveness of the conservation strategy was not achieving the mission. The commercial, residential, and recreational activities outside the preserves have a significant impact on the quality of the land, water, and air inside the preserves. In some cases, the counts of species in the preserves had actually decreased. "How do you protect a species when the chief threat to that species comes from 100 miles away?"

Sawhill clearly saw that the old performance measurements simply weren't valid indicators of effectiveness. He led the development of new definitions of success that would more directly lead the Conservancy to realizing its mission over time. He then focused on measuring the activities that result in each success. "Ultimately, we have to measure our success by the species we save. But in the short term . . . we have to learn what we should be monitoring." This shift in measurement led to an innovation in strategy. For example, each conservation project had to have a "5-S" plan: "Define the ecological *system* we are trying to protect, the *stresses* to that system, the *source* of the stresses, the *strategy* for dealing with those stresses, and how we would measure our *success*." Thinking moved to the level of entire ecosystems and watersheds.

The Conservancy's new strategy led it to focus more on land use in large areas surrounding its preserves. These larger landscapes are owned and used by interests that often seem to compete with environmental objectives. The Conservancy had to address how to align economic growth with environmental protection. Staff of the Conservancy started thinking about promoting environmentally compatible development. This led to new relationships with businesses to find common ground, align agendas, and jointly and carefully protect the "Last Great Places."

Thus, the innovation in strategic thinking, driven by a clear mission and an improved measurement system, led to program innovations.

(continued)

For instance, the Conservancy created the Virginia Eastern Shore Sustainable Development Corporation, a for-profit that has three goals: profitability, job creation, and environmental protection. Its businesses include nature-tourism, specialty foods, and organic produce. In addition, the Conservancy entered into a partnership with Georgia-Pacific, one of the world's largest forest product companies, to jointly manage conservation land along the Roanoke River in North Carolina and the Altamaha River in Georgia. The objective was to allow environmentally sustainable harvesting of lumber from these regions, allowing protected lands to be economically productive.

Through an inclusive planning process and a new performance measurement system, John Sawhill helped make The Nature Conservancy into a more innovative organization.

For additional information about John Sawhill and The Nature Conservancy, refer to further readings in Appendix B.

items mentioned previously under the headings of Cultural Norms, Organizational Capabilities, and Reinforcement Mechanisms. Respondents should be able to specify how close your organization comes to operating with the norms, capabilities, or mechanisms that support innovation. For each item, ask: "How well does our organization fit with the following descriptions?" Then offer a scale for responding from 1 to 5, with 1 being "not at all," 3 being "sometimes," and 5 being "perfectly."

Step 2: After completing the checklist, respondents should be asked the open-ended question: "Based on your checklist responses and your experience with this organization, what should our priorities be if we are to become a more innovative organization?"

Step 3: Tally the responses, and based on the results, develop a plan of action for improving.

Step 4: Take your innovative pulse from time to time. Keep track of innovations that have been implemented in your organization and their source. Repeat the survey if the pace of innovation seems too slow or if the innovations are all coming from one individual or group.

CAN AN ORGANIZATION BE TOO INNOVATIVE?

Innovation can create a certain amount of turmoil in an organization. It can be disruptive and costly. So is it possible to be too innovative? Yes, it is. An organization's capacity for innovation is inherently limited by its various resources, financial and human. Innovation puts a strain on those resources. Too much can overwhelm an organization and exhaust its resources. The more radical the innovation, the more exhausting.

In any case, the benefits of an innovation usually come after it is no longer an innovation. Most innovations follow a natural learning curve. In the early stages of the curve, while the organization is just learning how to do this new approach right, the innovation is rarely efficient or effective. The true benefits come after the innovation matures and the organization develops proficiency at it. To shift to yet another new approach before the benefits of the last innovation can be reaped can lead to an ineffective organization that is always struggling with something new.

Social entrepreneurs do have to be continuously innovating, adapting, and learning, according to the definition in Chapter 1; however, this does not mean constantly being engaged in new, radical innovations. The process should follow a natural course, with most of the innovations after startup being incremental in nature. Radical innovations punctuate this ongoing learning and adapting process only occasionally, as necessary.

SUMMARY

Innovation is truly an art. It takes hard work, some natural talent, and perseverance. In this chapter, we have defined innovation in a manner that should help you see the various ways you can go about it. We have discussed the inherent tensions of the innovation process. We have also explored the natural sources of resistance to innovation and how to manage them. Finally, we explained what it takes to build an innovative organization. In the course of all this, we hope you have picked up some concepts and tools for improving your own innovation process.

Key points to remember are as follows:

- ✔ Innovation is about establishing new and better ways of accomplishing your social mission.
- ✔ It is about action as much as ideas.
- ✔ It comes in many varieties and from many sources.
- ✔ The process is fraught with tensions that need to be balanced.
- ✔ Innovation can be threatening in different ways, each requiring a different strategy.
- ✔ Inertia is a natural enemy of innovation, but it can be conquered.
- ✔ Success and strong leadership can hamper innovation, if you are not careful.
- ✔ Innovation is organizational as much as individual.
- ✔ Don't overdo it; you can get too much of a good thing.

Endnotes

1. Joseph A. Schumpeter, *The Theory of Economic Development* (Cambridge: Harvard University Press, 1934) reprinted in (New Brunswick: Transaction Publishers, 1983), p. 66.
2. Amar Bhide, "Developing Start-Up Strategies," Harvard Business School note #394-067.
3. Muhammad Yunus, *Banker to the Poor: Micro-Lending and the Battle against World Poverty* (New York: Public Affairs, a member of the Perseus Books Group, 1999), p. ix.
4. Atiur Rahman, "Rural Development From Below: Lessons Learned From Grameen Bank Experience in Bangladesh," *The Journal of Socio-Economics,* Summer 1996, v. 25, n. 2, p. 189.
5. Joseph A. Schumpeter, *Capitalism, Socialism, and Democracy,* ed. 3 (New York: Harper & Row, 1950), p. 81.
6. According to *The Oxford Dictionary of Quotations* (Oxford: Oxford University Press, 1979) this quote is attributed to Ralph Waldo Emerson by Sarah S. B. Yule in her book *Borrowings,* 1889. It reportedly came from a lecture she attended.
7. This distinction and example are drawn from V. Kasturi Rangan, Sohel Karim, Sherly K. Sandberg, "Do Better At Doing Good," *Harvard Business Review,* May–June 1996.
8. Geoffrey Moore, *Crossing the Chasm* (New York: Harper, 1991), see p. 12 for a generic version of this curve.
9. Geoffrey Moore, *Crossing the Chasm,* pp. 17–25.
10. Clayton M. Christensen, *The Innovator's Dilemma,* (Boston: Harvard Business School Press), 1998.
11. Donald K. Clifford and Richard E. Cavanagh, *The Winning Performance* (New York: Bantam Books, 1985), p. 223.
12. Donald K. Clifford and Richard E. Cavanagh, *The Winning Performance,* p. 51.
13. Jim Collins, "Built to Flip," *Fast Company,* March 2000, p. 136.
14. Thomas J. Peters and Robert H. Waterman, *In Search of Excellence* (New York: Harper & Row, 1982), p. 134.
15. Richard S. Tedlow, "James Burke: A Career in American Business," Harvard Business School case #389-177.
16. Alice Howard and Joan Magretta, "Surviving Success: An Interview with The Nature Conservancy's John Sawhill," *Harvard Business Review,* Sep.–Oct. 1995. All quotes in this example are from this article, except as noted. Additional facts came from an unpublished draft by John C. Sawhill, "Mission Impossible? Measuring Success in Nonprofit Organizations," 1999.

Chapter 8

UNDERSTANDING AND ATTRACTING YOUR "CUSTOMERS"

Kristin Majeska, Executive Director, Common Good: Investments in Nonprofit Solutions

IN THIS CHAPTER

Identifying your customers
Understanding your customers' needs and wants
Creating a winning value proposition
Pricing to maximize social impact
Promoting your product, service, and mission

The customer has moved to center stage. Company slogans, product brochures, even television commercials surround us with "customer-focused" approaches. At the same time, nonprofits are placing more and more emphasis on clients'/consumers'/customers' needs and desires as they figure out how to best accomplish their mission.

For-profit entrepreneurs are painfully aware that customers can choose whether to use their service or buy their product. Similarly, social entrepreneurs recognize that the individuals they hope to serve must make a conscious choice to participate in whatever their organization offers. Even the nonpaying clients of a homeless shelter or children attending a free art program are *voluntary* participants. In fact, accomplishing a nonprofit mission often requires convincing a range of voluntary participants—beneficiaries, volunteers, donors, Board members, etc.—to take specific actions.

Social entrepreneurs don't always use the word *customer*, but the most successful ones focus as intently on their participants as smart businesses focus on their customers. Why? Because entrepreneurs look for opportunities to achieve their goals. Customer focus is an approach from the business world that can help any nonprofit organization succeed by creating real benefits for its customers.[1] Entrepreneurs know that the only way to create big changes with limited resources is to leverage these "win/win" situations—the sweet spots where what benefits the organization's participants *also* directly advances the organization's mission. Customer understanding informs how social entrepreneurs accomplish their mission.

In the business world, customers communicate what they value by making a purchase—or not. Nonprofits rarely have such ready feedback, yet their success still depends on whether their participants make the desired choices. True customer understanding helps nonprofits ensure that they expend their efforts and resources on something of value to their participants. This value might take the form of a hot meal, increased self-confidence, a safe place to create art, an evening of superb classical music, or the skills to become an advocate for the community. In fact, because nonprofits lack the clear financial bottom-line that keeps businesses on track, focusing intently on understanding their voluntary participants might be the *only* way nonprofits can be sure they actually accomplish their mission.

core concept   Throughout this chapter, we describe practices adapted from the for-profit world. Accordingly, we'll use the term *customer* as a short-hand to refer to anyone who voluntarily participates in a mission-driven enterprise. This "customer" participation might take the form of using a service, participating in an activity, volunteering time, giving money or goods to a nonprofit organization, or even buying a service or product. A social entrepreneur's "customers" might include the following groups:

Direct Beneficiaries (the reason the nonprofit exists) who:

Use a service:	Food-bank grocery recipients
Participate in an activity:	Local library book group participants
Volunteer their time:	Low-income families who help build their own homes on donated land
Donate money or goods:	Members of a local art cinema
Buy a service or product:	Paying clients of a low-cost medical clinic

Indirect Beneficiaries (those who benefit in a secondary way from helping the nonprofit accomplish its mission, including the satisfaction of simply enjoying making a contribution) who:

Use a service:	Teens who drop off soda cans at a nonprofit recycling center
Participate in an activity:	Parents who attend meetings to "reinvent" the neighborhood school

Volunteer their time:	Local residents who track otters for conservation programs
Donate money or goods:	Corporate sponsors of a job-training program
Buy a service or product:	Purchasers of goods manufactured by trainees with multiple barriers to employment

Social entrepreneurs almost always have more than one set of customers, and it's very hard to keep all of these customers happy all of the time. Nonetheless, a few principles of customer understanding can help you convince many different kinds of customers to make the decisions that help support your mission.

IDENTIFYING YOUR CUSTOMERS

CUSTOMER GROUPS: THE SUM IS GREATER THAN THE WHOLE

Since it was founded to manage a renovated skid row hotel, the Weingart Center Association (WCA) has grown to be a large multipurpose complex of health and human services for the homeless and poor in Los Angeles, California. WCA's path to success began when it first asked itself "Who is our customer?" If it hoped to be successful, the WCA realized it had to move beyond the myths that all homeless people were disheveled men and women huddling in doorways with shopping carts. The WCA recognized that its customers formed a diverse market. The WCA focused on the circumstances that led people to homelessness and on to the type of barriers they needed to overcome to leave the streets. The organization's first president recalls helping develop different game plans for serving three distinct customer groups or "segments" of homeless individuals with very different needs. The WCA segmented its market into individuals who were on the street primarily because of:

✔ A temporary setback, often financial
✔ Substance abuse or other physical health issues
✔ Mental illness[2]

Social entrepreneurs often intuitively understand that all of their customers are not the same, yet most do not have the luxury of tailoring their services to please each individual customer. As the WCA demonstrated, however, this doesn't have to mean a "one-size-fits-all" approach to your service offerings or your marketing.

core
concept
Customer segmentation is the identification of groups of customers with common needs, behaviors, and demographic characteristics that can help you target specific groups and tailor your offerings to them.

Airlines provide one of the most familiar (and often frustrating!) examples of customer segmentation. By identifying distinct customer types, airlines can sell the same basic product—say, transportation from New York to San Francisco—in a way that both maximizes their price per seat and fills the plane. Airlines consciously target different customer segments with offers ranging from wider business class seats to frequent-flier perks, plan-in-advance promotions, last-minute specials, and Starbucks coffee. They are successful when they reach the right groups of customers with the right combinations of enticements at the right price.

Within the nonprofit world, direct mail fundraisers use segmentation constantly. They are likely to create five, ten, or more versions of a letter soliciting funds during the same campaign, tailoring each letter to a specific type of potential donor with specific likely motivations for giving. Think of a typical college's annual fund drive. The text of the letter you receive soliciting a donation varies depending on whether you are a recent graduate, an active alumnae, a lapsed donor, a parent, and even perhaps whether you spent most of your college years in the field house or the chemistry lab.

tool of
the trade
Grouping potential customers into segments is as much an art as a science. Here are three common ways to "segment" a market:

Segmentation Method	Definition	Example (Illustrative Only)
Demographic	Based on identifiable factors, such as age, sex, family size, income, education, etc.	YMCA segments: young professionals, midlife men, mothers working in the home, youth, seniors, etc.
Behavioral	Based on actual behavior, particularly use of a relevant service or product	YMCA segments (based on gym use): daily workout, class attendee, occasional workout, twice a year, etc.
Lifestyle	Based primarily on activities, interests, and opinions	YMCA segments: body-conscious yuppie, male-bonding basketball player, doctor's orders exerciser, family fitness outings, etc.

The segmentation method you choose depends on what information is relevant for the customer decision that *you* want to influence and on what information you can obtain. For example, a human services or-

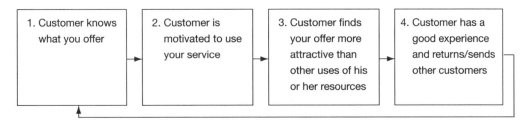

EXHIBIT 8.1 Participation decision process.

ganization might find that the gender of homeless people tends to influence their desire to stay in a shelter, so gender should be included in a shelter customer segmentation; however, the organization may discover that gender is irrelevant to attracting customers to its soup kitchen. Instead, the best way to group these customers may be in terms of self-image and length of time living on the streets—if people who share these characteristics tend to think in similar ways about soup kitchen offerings.

So why is segmentation valuable? As seen in Exhibit 8.1, at least four things need to happen for a customer to make a decision to participate in a program or make a purchase.

Segmentation provides a useful way for you to ensure that you meet each of these four conditions in the best way for each customer group. For example, you may need a sophisticated strategy to get your message out to one segment and may be able to do very cost-effective promotions to reach another segment. Based on a strong understanding of the specific behavior of one of its segments, very low-income youth, Spiral Arts, a Portland, Maine community arts group, created an "art-mobile." Knowing that this target segment is likely to be "hanging out" on the street, two artists show up at the street corner with a van, cover it with easels and canvases, and start to paint. Within a few minutes of the first curious kids coming close to inspect what's going on, a whole group of youths are painting with no hesitation because they're on their own turf.

Understanding and distinguishing among different potential types of customers can be extremely valuable for startup organizations. Smart social entrepreneurs can determine a particular kind of customer they will be able to serve most effectively and can concentrate their initial efforts on creating something of value to this group. Once these entrepreneurs have demonstrated the success of their approach or service with one type of customer, they have the credibility to obtain the resources to serve additional customer segments.

Unfortunately, treating customer segments differently can be costly. Marketing experts suggest segmenting your customer base only if the following conditions exist:

1. You can identify and measure segments that are clearly different from each other.
2. The segments are sufficiently large to be worth the investment in treating them differently.
3. You can actually communicate different messages or services to each segment.
4. The segments are likely to respond differently to your messages or services.

Market research and consulting firms use multiple information sources and statistical techniques to carefully define segments. Organizations with fewer resources can still generate significant insights by trying an entrepreneurial tactic for identifying different customer segments in their market.

1. Gather all of the data you have on potential customers and their behavior, such as referral sources, demographic information, surveys, mailing lists, days when you serve the most customers, number of services used or items purchased per customer, responses to outreach campaigns, promotions, or anything that might hold a clue about your customers. Include potential customers who did not take advantage of your services.
2. Look for natural groupings within each characteristic or behavior. For example, what type(s) of customers sign up for your different programs? What day of the week and time of day are your busiest— who tends to come then? What kinds of customers ranked "quality" as most important on a survey? What do your strongest supporters among your customers or your biggest accounts have in common?
3. Solicit information from the employees who are closest to your customers, the social workers, the receptionist, the store clerks, the volunteers from the phone-a-thon, etc.—a group session works best. Ask them to describe the kind of customer(s) who meets the following criteria:
   ✔ Uses all or buys most of the services you offer.
   ✔ Takes advantage of your most successful programs or buys your highest-profit-margin items.
   ✔ Signs up for a program then never shows up or looks but doesn't buy.

    ✔ Never comes to an open house or looks in the store window and doesn't come in.

    ✔ Uses only your lowest-fee services or looks first at the price.

    ✔ Refers friends to your organization or wants to know more about your social mission.

    Ask the group questions to create an image of the people they are describing. How do they recognize these people? When do they see them? What service or product do these people seem to value most? What motivates them to use our service? What reactions do they typically exhibit when they first hear about what we offer them? What other nonprofit services do they consume? Where would you go to look for them in their free time?

4. Classify your findings from steps 2 and 3 into between five and ten customer segments. Make sure that each group of characteristics makes sense together and that a customer would have more in common with others in its segment than it would with those in other segments.

5. Ask your employees if they can picture an example of each segment. Then, ask them to give each segment a descriptive name, such as "Nervous Mother," "Talk-a-lot Tourist," or "I-don't-want-to-be-here Youth."

6. Brainstorm how you could better reach and satisfy each segment. Combine any segments that you would respond to in a similar manner.

If you're launching a new enterprise, start with the customer segments you discover in your market research. At a minimum, start thinking about how different demographic breakdowns might respond differently to what you hope to offer. Talk to organizations currently working in your field to understand more revealing segmentations—you can even try asking them some of the aforementioned questions.

VALUING SOCIAL ENTERPRISE CUSTOMERS

Most organizations, including for-profit companies, spend their early days just trying to get up and running. They then tend to frantically try to attract their first customers. In these early days, any customer is a good one; however, as an organization becomes more savvy, it recognizes that it serves some types of customers more successfully than it serves others. For example, one nonprofit may find that it really makes a difference in the lives of the WCA's "have nots" but has very little success with the "will nots." With this type of customer understanding, a nonprofit can decide how to maximize its ability to accomplish its mission—a decision that will likely be as unique as the nonprofit itself.

If you are just starting out, now is the time to assess the type of customer you can serve most effectively and to focus your organization around serving that segment. Once you succeed, you can always grow to serve more segments!

When for-profit businesses decide what customer segments to target, they tend to focus on the bottom-line profitability of each customer or customer segment, sometimes even estimating profits over the total "lifetime" of each customer. The larger the total dollar profit, the more valuable the customer is to their organization. Social entrepreneurs often create a different kind of "bottom-line." They use their social objectives as the measure of success. Instead of calculating the average financial gain or loss from each customer segment, social entrepreneurs want to know the social outcome(s) they accomplish relative to the funds they expend on each customer group.

Why should a social enterprise founded explicitly to help those most in need—*not* those with the most money—bother to determine its "most valuable" customer segments? A most valuable customer analysis does not necessarily lead a mission-driven organization to either pursue or avoid a certain type of customer. It should lead, however, to the organization examining the range of opportunities it has to make a positive social impact. Here are several questions to consider when evaluating customers:

1. Given our finite pool of resources, what are the pros and cons of focusing on the types of customers we seem to serve most effectively?
2. If we want to serve more of these clients, how do we attract and serve them in the best way possible?
3. What makes us good at serving these type of clients, and how can we apply that learning to drive better social outcomes in our other segments as well?
4. What makes our cost to serve certain types of customers so high relative to their social outcomes? With that knowledge, what can we do to decrease those costs without lessening our effectiveness?

For companies, calculating the profitability of each customer segment usually translates into big profit improvements. Often, a mere 20 percent of a business' customers generate 80 percent of its profits. A large percentage of customers tend to be moderately profitable to break even (see Exhibit 8.2).

Shockingly, most companies unwittingly aggressively market and sell to customers who are money losers, customers who cost the company much more than they bring in, even when that profit is calculated over

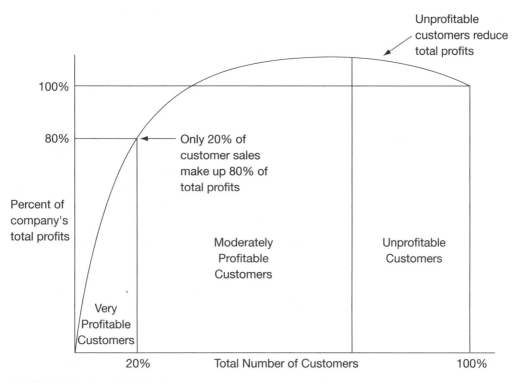

EXHIBIT 8.2 The 80-20 effect.

the long-term. Companies are becoming more skillful at identifying and pursuing customers who fit the "top-20" profile and at not investing to meet the needs of customers they are unlikely to serve profitably.

reality check   Ashbury Images, a San Francisco screen printer founded to employ individuals in transition from homelessness, recently analyzed its sales by customer type. Ashbury found that its oldest and most traditional screen printing customers, small nonprofits, were actually its least profitable segment. This social-purpose enterprise now expects much higher future profits from having reoriented its businesses to serve larger corporate clients. The corporate segment not only offers better margins and more predictable scheduling, but these customers also place the highest premium on Ashbury's strengths, a high-quality product and a social mission.

How do nonprofits respond when they learn that some of their target customer groups appear to be more "expensive" to serve than others? Several tools have emerged in the last few years to help organizations make the hard choices about how to devote their finite resources.

Among others, Jed Emerson of the Roberts Enterprise Development Fund and Fay Twersky of BTW Consultants have advocated incorporating a "degree of difficulty" factor in measuring social impact. They suggest that adjusting "success measures" for the difficulty and risk of working with a given customer group or a specific mission creates a more accurate picture of the results per dollar spent. This technique also recognizes those who take on the most challenging work because these adjustments mean the most difficult work has the highest potential "return on investment" when it is successful.[3]

Various authors have used matrixes like Exhibit 8.3 to help organizations think through the relationships between "Mission" and "Money" (e.g., the economic implications of serving a specific customer segment or running a specific program). Academics R. E. Gruber and M. Mohr first suggested that nonprofits consider the different activities that make up their "portfolio" when they determine their strategy.[4] Professor Sharon Oster uses a similar product portfolio map to help organizations determine the right balance among their activities, as does the National Center for Social Entrepreneurs.

tool of the trade   Mapping your activities, programs, or customer segments can give you a good idea of what your organization can "afford to do" and a mechanism for evaluating potential strategies. For example, most organizations continue to support any activities in the top right-hand corner of the product portfolio map, ones that contribute highly both to the mission and to economic viability. At the other extreme, activities or customer segments with little social impact and a low or negative contribution to the organization's economic viability (bottom left) are good candidates for either a redesign (in the entrepreneurial spirit!), being shut down, or being transferred to an organization that can do them better. Knowing the size of activities (illustrated by the diameter of the

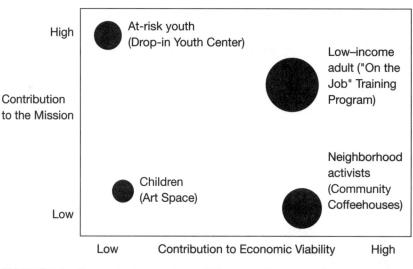

EXHIBIT 8.3   Example product portfolio map: Community nonprofit. (Size of spot represents program budget.)

spot on the map) that are of high social value but very costly to the organization (upper left) can lead to either an emphasis on controlling costs, while not compromising program quality, or on raising funds elsewhere in the organization that can subsidize these activities. Social entrepreneurs should be wary of customer segments that contribute significantly to the organization's viability but not much to the organization's mission (bottom right). The resources associated with these segments can be attractive but run the risk of dragging the organization's focus too far from its social mission.[5]

tool of the trade So, how do you calculate the "contribution to economic viability" axis of the matrix? You can calculate the profit of a customer segment by estimating the total revenues generated by all sales to the segment, then by subtracting the total cost of making those sales. Total costs include not only the direct costs of providing the product or service but also all costs of marketing to the segment and all overhead costs allocated to the segment based on use or necessity. For example, the total cost of serving a hypothetical "youth segment" at the YMCA might include not only youth staff, but also the following costs:

✔ The cost of developing a structured youth curriculum

✔ The cost of developing posters and marketing collateral to distribute in the schools

✔ The marketing director's time spent in meetings with school principals

✔ The administrative time spent processing registrations and permission slips

✔ An additional lifeguard

✔ Ten hours a week of locker room attendant time

By tracking and accurately allocating costs, this YMCA may find that it costs $50 per month to double the average amount of physical exercise done by 9- to 12-year-olds and $200 per week to do the same for 15- to 16-year-olds.

action step Do you know who your customers are? Who you want them to be? Take a moment to jot down several customer types that spring to your mind. Write a short paragraph describing each type, including where they're located, how they use your product, what other related products they use, what kind of radio station the primary decision maker probably listens to, and so forth. Use lots of adjectives. Share your profiles with others in your organization to see what they can add and to get everyone intrigued about starting a more rigorous process of customer segmentation.

Finally, choose the customer or customer segment you suspect is most "cost effective" in terms of social outcome per dollar or hour of time spent on them, the least "cost effective," and the one you assume is in the middle. Enlist your accountant's help in doing a "back of the envelope" calculation of total annual costs of serving that segment, including estimating overhead costs actually used (e.g., what costs would go away if you didn't have that customer or type of customer). Now add up the number of the social outcomes that you care about (i.e., meals served, certification examinations passed, childhood diseases prevented) by that dollar amount. Were you right about what segment you served for less? What will you do differently now that you have this information?

UNDERSTANDING YOUR CUSTOMERS' NEEDS AND WANTS

Unfortunately, knowing who your customers *are* is not enough. To grow, indeed even to survive, you must understand *why* they are your customers, what they like, and what would turn those who are not participating in your programs or buying your products into customers. With a little diligence and creativity, you can do just that.

RESEARCHING YOUR MARKET

For-profit companies spend billions of dollars every single year on customer research. Luckily for social entrepreneurs with limited resources, you *can* do insightful market research on a budget.

Effective market research provides the information that will help your organization make specific decisions. Alan Andreasen, author of both *Cheap but Good Marketing Research* and *Strategic Marketing for Nonprofits,* recommends "backward marketing research" to make sure your research efforts will be useful *before* you start spending any money. Here's a version of the process he suggests:

1. Determine what key decisions will be made using the results of your research.
2. Determine the information you would need to make the best decision.
3. Draft an example of the results of the research you're proposing and ask yourself or the decision makers if this type of information is what they need.
4. Figure out what analysis you'll need to do to get these results.[6]
5. Determine what questions you must ask to provide the information for this analysis.
6. Check whether these questions have already been answered by your organization or elsewhere.

7. Design your sample (based on the customer groups you want to learn about).

8. Do your research.

9. Analyze your data and communicate your findings.

10. Help your decision makers use the findings to guide them.[7]

Existing Information

Information that has already been gathered by third parties can be effective for answering questions such as "how big is the market for the program we are considering launching?" Local organizations such as the Chamber of Commerce, the Small Business Development Center, or your state economic development office often have good information about the local population. Trade associations, government agencies, and industry-specific journals can be great sources for insight into the kind of people who might attend programs like yours or use services like yours, how often, and what they can afford to pay. Several resources on the Internet can provide additional data on how to link this information to the general demographics of your area to understand your potential customers. For example, at least one company provides free neighborhood "lifestyle" descriptions and demographic information by zipcode and more detailed information by zip+4.[8]

Exhibit 8.4 shows sources you might consult and questions you could ask to research the market for a summer jobs program.

1. Will there be sufficient youth who want to work for the summer?
   - School System: How many juniors and seniors in target neighborhoods?
   - Dept. of Labor: How many under-18-year-olds worked last summer?
   - Local youth organization: Estimate of how many juniors and seniors looked but could not find a job last summer

2. Are enough employers likely to hire summer youth at the proposed wage?
   - Chamber of Commerce: How many businesses in target area with more than five employees?
   - Dept. of Labor: Average starting hourly wage and number of seasonal jobs
   - National pilot program: Average number of students hired per size of business under comparable economic conditions

3. Will there be sufficient economic benefit to the community to underwrite the summer jobs program?
   - Census bureau: % of families at given income levels in target neighborhoods
   - Youth advocacy group: Studies showing medium-term benefits of internship-like summer jobs in terms of being role models, office and interviewing skills, etc.

EXHIBIT 8.4 Example: Determining markets.

You can often also learn a lot from another source of existing information—your own organization. Although it might not look like "data," your organization's records may be revealing if you look at them systematically. For example, before acting on a suggestion to start providing in-house child care for residents of a program for formerly homeless mothers moving back into the workforce, you could analyze the child care situations of past and present residents. Job coaches' reports could reveal how many potential jobs residents were not able to accept because of child care constraints. Case managers' reports may provide the data needed to identify the primary child care providers used to date by residents and the solutions found by other women in comparable situations. The numbers may even suggest that partnering with an existing provider might offer the extra coverage needed.

Observation

core concept

Observation is an effective and usually inexpensive means of collecting new information about your market and how your customers or potential customers actually behave in their natural environment. Observing, counting, and measuring physical clues can provide social entrepreneurs with information that can become ammunition for social change. For example, counting how many full buses pass by a bus stop in a low-income neighborhood without stopping during rush hour could be a compelling rationale for increasing service. Or analyzing the amount of litter in specific downtown locations could lead to a campaign focused on encouraging shoppers to deposit their trash or urging high school students to use the school's recycling bins.[9]

When observing customers, you can heed the guiding rules of for-profit "new market researchers" as follows:

> "*Explore natural settings. Observe. Listen.* Really *listen. Put aside biases. Analyze.*"[10]

Not only is this sort of "new market research" inexpensive—anyone can be an observer—but there's also lots of room for creativity. For example, a nonprofit developing a "nonviolent games" curriculum could take a cue from the founders of Skyline Products, creators of children's toys. Having no kids of their own, Skyline's founders created play groups at local schools and parks. With the parent's permission (and while receiving payment for child care!), these entrepreneurs carefully observed the kids playing with new toys, asked them lots of questions, and used these insights to develop toys that would appeal to their target customers.[11] As a nonprofit service provider, you might take note of the first brochure customers pick up when they enter your waiting room or how different types of customers respond when they hear about prices or payment options. Similar to all market research, however, be careful not to extrapolate your findings too far. It's well worth your time to understand such basic principles of research as how to select the "sample" you observe to make sure it accurately represents the market you're trying to understand.[12]

Focus Groups

tool of the trade   By definition, social entrepreneurs look for innovative ways to meet society's needs. Focus groups are useful ways to get new ideas about your potential customers' needs and reactions to new services or marketing messages—straight from the source. A focus group consists of eight to ten members of your target market (try to include both current customers and potential customers who don't know you at all) who are guided by a facilitator to answer open-ended questions about a specific topic. Focus groups are a low-cost means of conducting face-to-face interviews, with the additional benefit of interactions that occur within the group. Relatively homogenous groups whose members share similar verbal skills, values, and experiences reduce the risk that some participants will feel intimidated and not voice their own opinions—often a particular concern for entrepreneurs in the social sector.

Volunteers of America, a large, national volunteer organization with 43 affiliates, recently conducted focus groups before deciding on a statement to describe itself in a major media campaign. The focus groups were a real eye-opener. The organization was surprised to find that the statement that had motivated its staff for years "didn't resonate with the public . . . we were [just] talking to ourselves."[13] In response to this finding, Volunteers of America restated its mission in terms to which the general public could relate.

Focus group participants are recruited from places you are likely to find individuals who represent your customer base. Depending on your mission, you may draw participants from a soup kitchen, a symphony hall lobby, or the local shopping center. Explain what you're doing and prepare to offer participants $30 to $50 for their time. Professional facilitators who can guide and subtly focus the group and can get all of the participants to contribute will get the best results, but you can also guide a session yourself—if you are convinced that you can be objective. Remember that it's just as important to know what customers don't like! The key is to set a specific goal for the focus group, such as understanding how to provide better customer service or how to promote a desirable behavior. Then ask questions such as the following:

- ✔ What appeals to you about the program I've just described?
- ✔ What aspects of this program turn you off?
- ✔ For whom do you think it's designed?

✔ How often would you attend this program? What if it had this additional feature? This one?

✔ What would convince you to try this program for one session?

Encourage participants to say more about comments that take you by surprise and be sure to videotape the session so that you capture all of the details and observe participants' nonverbal reactions.

Test Marketing

tool of the trade Once you have a concrete service or product you'd like to offer, make sure to do your test marketing, even if your funder already thinks the program's a great idea! *Test marketing* is essentially performing an experiment. Rather than asking your customers what they think they'd do, you give them the opportunity, record the results, and if you're entrepreneurial, you figure out why they did what they did. Celestial Seasonings, the U.S. leader in herbal tea, has put its teas through taste tests since its earliest days, when its entrepreneurial founder walked up to health food store shoppers with cups of different blends. The now $100 million company estimates that 250,000 people tested its products in 1998—that's one tester for every $400 in sales.[14]

You can test your service or product by taking prototypes to potential customers or to distributors that you can count on to be honest. For example, when the nonprofit Grupo de Trabajo Redes prepares health education brochures for low-income women in Peru, the editors take time to show drafts of the illustrations to women from their target audience. One-on-one discussions that reveal how a typical customer is likely to interpret their colorful drawings help ensure that the message of the text is effectively communicated, particularly to customers with limited literacy.

gem of wisdom Although testing can seem time consuming, Ava DeMarco, cofounder of Little Earth Productions, a company that makes fashion accessories from recycled rubber, license plates, and the like, explains why they believe market information is essential. "If you design a product, introduce it and it fails, you've lost time and money on that product—time and money you could have spent on something else [including your social mission!] so there's a double loss. The sooner you can do your market research, the sooner you'll guarantee yourself you've got your ladder leaned up against the right wall."[15]

Organizations with nonprofit origins may be surprised to hear that the need to test products holds true even when products are donated. The San Francisco City Store, a social-purpose enterprise that sells unusual San Francisco memorabilia in stores that employ individuals in transition from homelessness, found out that even "free" products can be expensive. In its early days, the store stocked many unusual items donated because of its social mission. Management did not factor in the opportunity cost of not filling its shelves with other products that they had proof customers would actually buy. Needless to say, once proven products were featured, overall sales and profits went up, despite the higher cost of stocking these goods.

Surveys

tool of the trade The *survey* is another low-budget market research tool at social entrepreneurs' disposal. Indeed, mentioning your organization's social mission may be one way to convince customers to answer your questions, along with more traditional enticements such as coupons or free merchandise. Keep the survey short and easy to return, and you will get information that is a valuable start to understanding your customers, even when it's not statistically significant. For example, wholesaler Little Earth designed a short survey that fit on a small tag attached to its products. The survey asked customers for their names, addresses, salary ranges, whether they were students, why they bought the product, and what other products they tended to buy. The results confirmed many hypotheses and identified a brand-new group of buyers.[16]

National Public Radio conducts informal surveys of its listeners during each pledge drive. By specifically encouraging listeners to call in "if this is a program that you value," NPR enables members to "vote" for their favorite programs by calling in pledges during that timeslot.

The Internet is also rapidly increasing the speed and volume of available customer data. Because the Internet is interactive, customers can instantly tell you what they like. Whether you use a survey to ask or whether you just observe customers' preferences, you can use your "research" to tailor what you offer each online customer—whether you're promoting a healthy behavior, a new book, or graduates from your job-training program.

Regardless of the medium, however, asking "valid" questions—questions that do not bias the survey's findings—is no easy task. Your interviewers, your respondents, and especially the way you write your questionnaire can all distort your results to the point that they do more harm than good. If you can't enlist the help of an expert question writer (they do exist!), try to use questions that have already been tested by qualified researchers, and have your questionnaire both reviewed by harsh critics and tested by real people.[17]

red flag Market research is far from infallible. Our world would be very different, without the telephone, the Xerox machine, and much more, if valiant entrepreneurs had not persisted in pursuing ideas despite customers' initial lack of interest. As a social entrepreneur, you may very well come up with a service or product that your target customers don't yet know that they will come to value. "Pushing" an idea, rather than responding only to what your customers say they want or need, can make sense—if you truly know your customers.

GETTING TO KNOW YOUR CUSTOMER

If you can go beyond demographic facts and survey responses to under-stand the needs and attitudes of the customers you have targeted, you can learn how to make them glad they use your services. If you can make today's customers happy, they'll stay with you and will tell their friends. You'll know you're creating value, and you'll have the best chance of growing your customer base—and of doing more good.

 core concept "The value of any product or service is the result of its ability to meet a customer's priorities."[18] Nonprofit and for-profit organiza-tions alike often assume that they know what their customers need. In fact, you can only discover customers' priorities, spoken and unspoken, through careful listening.

Jack Welch, CEO of General Electric (GE) led this corporate giant in the customer-focused thinking that made it one of the most profitable com-panies in the 1990s. Welch pioneered the technique of CEO marketing. Rather than trying to sell a product, Welch and his executives sat down with the CEOs of their customers to understand the forces that influ-enced the profitability of their customers' businesses. Using that cus-tomer perspective, GE developed solutions that increased the profitabil-ity of its customers. In the words of the President of a GE customer with more than $1 billion in sales:

> *"My plant guys love [GE]. They're used to dealing with product pushers. With GE, they're dealing with a group of people who have taken the time to learn their problems, and to help solve them. When it comes to decid-ing who's going to get our plastics business, it's not even close."*[19]

From CEO to plant engineer, GE also makes sure to talk to the *multiple* individuals who influence a purchase decision. Similar careful listening provides clues to the multiple individuals that may have an interest in your service. For example, a nonprofit manufacturer of custom-designed adaptive equipment for children, The Kids' Project, realized that al-though physical therapists were strong advocates for their equipment, they also needed to educate mainstream teachers and principals, the de-cision makers with control over the classroom and the budget.

City Lore, a nonprofit folklore and urban culture center in New York City, describes the customer priorities that underlay its Culture Catalog for teachers:

> *"We need to begin with the premise that folk arts does not sell. We have learned that lesson over and over again. No teacher who will get this cat-alog is teaching folk arts or has folk arts at the top of a list of priorities. We need to bring OUR vision to THEIR needs. Their needs are not: 'How can I teach my children about folk arts in the city or in rural Nevada?' In-*

stead, their needs are something like: 'How can I bring the Civil War to life for my students? How can I put together a unit on Latin America that speaks to my Dominican students?' . . . Organizing the catalog around questions like these will give it a far greater chance of success."[20]

City Lore's customer understanding has not changed its mission, but it has enabled City Lore to present this mission in the form of a customer solution. The folk arts catalog preserves 100 percent of City Lore's core belief that "grassroots culture and local learning are crucial to building a creative, viable society"—yet actually gets these materials into the classroom.

In the world of the social entrepreneur, it's not unusual to find a situation in which your core customers seem to want something directly opposed to the mission of your organization. Don't translate "getting to know your customers" into "give the customers what they want." Instead, use customer understanding to help you identify the "sweet spots," those areas where what benefits your customers *also* directly advances your organization's mission.

core concept Understanding what is important to your customers can inform your strategy without dictating it.

INTERVIEW

JOHN DURAND, MINNESOTA DIVERSIFIED INDUSTRIES

John DuRand founded Minnesota Diversified Industries (MDI) in the 1960s to create jobs with long-term career opportunities and good benefits for the developmentally disabled. From an idea initially "capitalized" with $100, DuRand grew MDI into a $60 million a year manufacturing and assembly company that today employs and offers great benefits to more than 1,000 people with a range of barriers to employment. MDI sells to corporate customers like 3M and Toro through one division. Its other division is the exclusive supplier of heavy-duty plastic mail crates for the demanding U.S. Post Office.

We asked John DuRand how MDI used its understanding of its customers to start up an organization that has had tremendous social impact.

QUESTION: How did you find your first customer?

DURAND: I started calling numbers I found in the Yellow Pages. Then I went to look at the buildings of the company to make sure it would be large enough to be a good customer. Next I visited the plant. I talked my way into a meeting with the plant managers and asked, "Do you have any

(continued)

problems?" I didn't tell them what *we* did. Instead, I let the potential customers talk about what *they* needed. It turned out they needed something we could do quite well. Once we were done with that job, I asked the same question, "What other problems do you have?" The plant manager was frustrated with some high-labor stitching requirements. I said, "We're good at that" and we figured out very quickly and successfully how to do stitching.

QUESTION: How do you create the strong customer relationships to which you often allude?

DURAND: I don't talk about me. I want to talk about you, the customer. That's how we figure out how I can help you. Occasionally, MDI has fallen into the trap of focusing on ourselves too much. For example, some of our customers asked us if we could warehouse some product. MDI refused because we had decided on a policy of entering only high-labor-content businesses. Later I realized that we had been wrong. We're in business to serve our customers. Therefore, if our customers want warehousing for their product, our business should automatically be eager to provide that warehouse.

gem of wisdom

QUESTION: Who are your most valuable customers?

DURAND: I select my customers carefully. I probably spend more time qualifying customers than pursuing them! After even a small contract, we can usually rule out the customers who are buying only on price. We chose to have very deep relations with just a few customers. We feel it's no more risky than tying your business to producing only one or two products.

Early on in the process, we talk to customers about issues with their previous supplier. What couldn't their past supplier provide? What changes are they expecting in their industry? What changes could we help them anticipate, such as better materials, speedier delivery, etc.? The goal is to communicate that we're serious about wanting to be part of their solution. If I can't have that conversation after having done good work for them, I don't want the company as a client. We continue meeting with clients throughout our relationship, usually with a mixed team of plant managers, production managers, engineers, quality assurance, etc. We not only ask them what we're doing well and where we can improve, but also talk about what they anticipate for the future. We often meet with our suppliers and bring their ideas back to the client. For example, we'll find out about a new machine that would substantially reduce the client's unit costs. We might offer to buy that machine in return for our customer signing a two-year contract.

QUESTION: How do you price?

DURAND: We price for next year; that is, we look at the total cost for the customer to work with us over time. If there's an investment we can make that will increase our productivity or lower the unit cost, we'll do our homework, then ask them to partner with us. We frequently lower our unit prices in the second or third year when we see our own costs go down.

A "getting to know you" strategy doesn't just work when you have a few big customers, like GE or MDI. You can apply these same tactics to learn more about segments of individual participants. Whether it takes the form of public recognition for a large charitable donation, mastering a marketable skill, or the perfect gift for Father's Day, customers are looking for solutions to their needs. You can understand those needs through casual conversation as well as direct questions. Do you hear comments such as "I'm in such a hurry" or "My daughter would love this!"? Are your customers dressed as if they're coming from work? Do they have kids in tow? Do they seem to enjoy their time in your location? These tidbits are all clues to your customers' lifestyles and potential needs. Make a habit of jotting them down and looking for patterns. Test your hypotheses in regular conversations with customers, and you will start to develop a constantly evolving picture of your customer segments.

action step Make an appointment today with three of either your largest or most frequent customers. If you work with many individuals, the next time a regular customer comes in, offer to take him or her out for coffee to briefly get an opinion on how to increase customer satisfaction. Don't try to promote anything during this interaction. Instead, do your homework about the customer and come armed with open-ended questions focusing on them and their family, business, etc. And make sure to include the questions to which you're afraid to hear the answers because they'll be your best guide to continuing to please your customers in the future.[21]

LEARNING FROM YOUR COMPETITORS?

Competitive analysis? We're a nonprofit! We don't have competitors! The authors of *High Performance Nonprofit Organizations* disagree, arguing that "Nonprofits are in fact engaged in various forms of competition. They compete for funding, but also for staff, volunteers, and sometimes even clients."[22] Think about it as learning from the "best practices" of others.

Competition keeps the marketplace of capitalism in check and for-profit companies constantly on their toes, making sure they deliver the best value at the lowest cost. Because they know their customers can vote with their participation and/or resources, social entrepreneurs must also observe the competition to get insights into what customers value.

First, identify your direct competitors. Who is offering a similar opportunity to the customers you target? For example, for a nonprofit organization hoping to partner with corporations for cause-related marketing, "competitors" would include other nonprofits with different missions but the same goal of corporate partnership. In the era of many "Welfare to Work" programs, nonprofits have found themselves competing with one another and with private companies for government-qualified job-training candidates. The local animal shelter may not face any competition for receiving stray cats and dogs, but it could easily find its fundraising campaign competing for local funding dollars with nonprofits ranging from the local Boys & Girls Club to national organizations for the prevention of cruelty to animals.

tool of the trade
To make sure you are gleaning customer insight from those who are competing for your customers' attention or dollars, be able to answer the following kinds of questions, and revise your answers at least every six months:

✔ *What types of services/products do my competitors offer that I do not?* Vice versa?

✔ What additional services or conveniences does the competition provide?

✔ How are our competitors' programs structured?

✔ What level of customer service do my competitors achieve?

✔ *What sales and marketing tactics are my competitors employing?* (e.g., guaranteed job after training, referrals from case workers)

✔ *What prices do my competitors charge?* Who pays that price? (e.g., participants, government contracts)

✔ *What else do my competitors require of their customers?* (e.g., mandatory attendance, tests, early morning work schedules)

practical tip
What is often the cheapest source for an entrepreneur to obtain competitive information? "Visiting" the competition! Stop by competitors' offices or showrooms. Ask a hard-to-answer customer service question. Buy a product and try it out. Ask for information on a program. Get a quote for a project. Place an order. Notice every detail about your experience as a customer: atmosphere, product quality, signs, professionalism, prices, customer service, efficiency, convenience, and so forth. If you can't visit your competitors yourself, send a volunteer.

To truly learn from other organizations, you'll also need to take a long look in the mirror. Immediately after visiting a competitor, make yourself walk through the same process at your organization. What is different? Where can you improve or modify what you do? Remember the details.

Tom Stemberg, the CEO of Staples, the office-supply superstore chain, is a competitive shopping disciple. Every week, Stemberg still visits at least one of his competitor's stores nationwide and at least one of his own stores. He claims that such observation is critical to his company's growth and that he has "never visited a store where I didn't learn something."[23]

Social entrepreneurs serving customers without a "retail front" can gather their competitive information in other circumspect ways. Collecting brochures, handouts, and annual reports from your colleagues and competitors enables you to keep track of others' themes and positioning, as well as their program and fundraising outcomes. Websites also provide an often informative yet anonymous glimpse into organizations. And don't underestimate the value of a good chat with a customer, employee, or volunteer who has first-hand experience with a similar organization. After explaining what you're hoping to learn from these questions (how to improve your ability to serve your mission, right?), you can ask these individuals what they especially liked or didn't like, what was different from their experience with your group, and so on.

Now think beyond your immediate competitors. Read the magazines about your industry. Go to trade shows and association meetings. What can you learn from organizations in other parts of the state or the country? What other organizations are filling similar needs for your customers? If you are a nonprofit developer of educational software, what can you learn from the most successful videogame producers? Internet sites for kids? Educational cable programs? The world is full of examples of ideas to replicate (and to avoid!).

By their nature, social entrepreneurs are constantly on the lookout for new ideas, no matter what the source. You can even look at what your customer types like in completely different industries. For example, when the Boston Ballet wanted to learn how to change its public image, it looked not only at the San Francisco Ballet but also at The Boston Museum of Science, which had recently improved its public image, and at Au Bon Pain, a locally headquartered chain of bakeries with a reputation for good customer service.

action step Visit three direct competitors during the next three weeks—physically or through brochures and conversations with participants. Gather at least three new ideas from each visit. If your organization compares favorably on all aspects, use the visits to observe what seems to matter most to the other organizations' customers and make a commitment to focus on improving that aspect of your own organization. Within the following three weeks, visit three organizations that serve your customer segments but in different industries or markets. At each one, challenge yourself to find three lessons you can apply to your organization.

CREATING A WINNING VALUE PROPOSITION

LEVERAGING YOUR COMPETITIVE ADVANTAGE

 core concept Competitive advantage is an overused term but an incredibly powerful concept. Simply stated, a competitive advantage is a resource or characteristic that gives your service, program, or product a cost, quality, or other benefit relative to others competing in the same market. In all likelihood, these competitive advantages will vary by customer segment.

Entrepreneurs are known for creating their competitive advantages by identifying customer needs that are not being met by others and responding to those needs with their own innovations. For example, Celestial Seasonings is constantly searching for opportunities based on what their competitors have *not* done.

> *"It's extremely important that you identify and understand your competition's equity. If you don't do that, you're not clearly differentiating yourself in the marketplace. Find out what needs are not being met by your competition. We talk to Lipton users, for example, and say 'Okay, you like Lipton because it's cheap and you can find it everywhere, but how is it not meeting your needs? What would you like to see Lipton doing that they are not doing?"—Michael Karrasch, Senior Manager of Consumer and Marketing Research, Celestial Seasonings*[24]

The Initiative for a Competitive Inner City (ICIC), led by competitive strategy guru Professor Michael Porter, wanted to encourage businesses to move into urban areas suffering from unemployment and poverty. It began by investigating how such a move could benefit businesses. The ICIC found that inner cities offered four primary competitive advantages:

- ✔ "A strategic location at the core of major urban areas, highways, and communication nodes with potential logistical advantages
- ✔ An underutilized workforce with high retention amid a tight overall national labor market
- ✔ An underserved local market with substantial purchasing power that can support many more retail and service businesses than it now has
- ✔ Opportunities for companies to link up with and provide outsourcing for competitive clusters (for example, health care and tourism) in the regional economy"[25]

For Gateway Security, the company ranked number 66 on *Inc.* magazine's Inner City 100, the founder's link to the inner city was his competitive advantage. When large corporations were looking for security services in crime-ridden Newark, New Jersey, Louis Dell'Ermo got the job precisely because he was a lifelong resident and veteran of the local police force. Over the years, Dell'Ermo has built on that competitive advantage with strategies such as hiring graduates of local security-training programs who, as he says, "Can tell by the noise of the traffic what's happening. They know what to expect."[26]

As a nonprofit entering new markets, you are likely to find that the characteristics that have enabled your core programs to prosper are different from the advantages you need in these new markets.

red flag   In fact, some of your traditional competitive advantages may actually turn out to be liabilities in your new endeavors.

"We discovered that our brand name was so strong and so strongly associated with helping the disadvantaged that potential customers of our staffing services businesses assumed we would not send qualified workers. We changed the staffing business' name to Community Employment Services."—Jane Kenneally, Director of Development and Community Relations, Goodwill Industries of Northern New England

As an entrepreneur fighting to get your voice heard over the general din of marketing messages, it makes sense to focus your marketing on communicating your competitive advantages. Once you know why you are a different and better choice than the alternatives, make sure that your target customers hear that as well.

tool of the trade   Before you launch any marketing efforts, take this "test" developed by Jay Levison, the author of *Guerrilla Marketing Excellence,* to make sure that you've really hit on a competitive advantage— you might even consider asking these questions of your frontline staff or, in a different format, asking a sample of customers:

✔ "Will my target market perceive this as an advantage?

✔ Is this advantage really different from what competitors offer?

✔ Will customers honestly benefit from this advantage?

✔ Will potential customers believe my statement about the advantage?

✔ Does this advantage motivate customers to buy or to take the desired action right now or very soon?"

If you answered "no" to any of these questions, go back to your customer and competitor research and your assessment of your own organization to find, or create, a stronger advantage to promote.[27]

DESIGNING YOUR VALUE PROPOSITION

core concept   Simply put, a *value proposition* is "the value of what you get relative to what you give in exchange for it." Although your marketing highlights the most compelling reason for customers to be interested in your program or product, you are still offering a total package. Many factors besides the service or product affect the customer (e.g., interactions with staff, convenience, a follow-up phone call, referrals to other services). The combination of quality, delivery, interaction with your employees before, during, and after participating in your program, the features and price of the product or service, the relative ease of volunteering, the requirements for completing a program, and so forth, all compose your "value proposition."

Think about how you decide where to buy groceries on a given day. You might consider a supermarket's selection of foods, the quality of its vegetables, and its prices, but you might also make your decision on the basis of the store's hours, its location, the ease of parking, how crowded the store is likely to be, or whether you will also be able to pick up a prescription in the same store. Alternatively, you may simply go to the neighborhood grocery you patronize as a matter of principle. A community food-bank customer might make a similar set of decisions based on his or her priorities. Designing a value proposition means disaggregating the

CASE STUDY

WORKING ASSETS LONG DISTANCE

Working Assets Long Distance uses a carefully crafted value proposition to successfully compete against companies many times its size. Working Assets matches the rates and calling plans of the major long-distance companies, but instead of spending billions of dollars on mass-market advertising, the company distinguishes itself by helping its customers "build a better world." Working Assets tries to incorporate and communicate this value in everything it does. The company donates 1 percent of its revenues to progressive nonprofits nominated by its customers. Working Assets also makes it easy for its customers to donate to these types of groups by allowing them to "round up" their bill each month—any money paid over the amount due goes to charities. The company features key social issues in each monthly bill and offers its customers free calls to Washington to support these issues. Working Assets also keeps its customers informed by promoting a short list of "thought-provoking" books on the back of its bills and by including progressive syndicated columnists on its Website. The company does joint promotions with like-minded socially responsible companies such as Ben & Jerry's Ice Cream. All Working Assets billing statements are sent out on 100 percent post-consumer recycled paper. Even its calling card is made of recycled plastic! The result of this internally consistent "socially responsible" value proposition is that Working Assets customers are among the most loyal in the industry. Working Assets saves a bundle by not having to re-recruit former customers back from competitors, has extremely low bad debt, and grows primarily through word-of-mouth and great public relations. And from 1986 through 1998, a relatively small phone company has given more than $16 million to progressive nonprofits.

individual factors that are likely to contribute to a customer's decision to participate in what you offer.

action step How do you create a winning value proposition? Start by going back to what you've learned about your target customer segment. Ask yourself not only what services or products they like but also what else is important to them. Do they value friendly human interaction? Are they consumed by the need to feel efficient? Do they like having technical advice before making a decision? Are they only comfortable speaking in a language other than English? Will they involve their children or spouses in major decisions? Try describing the "ideal package" from their viewpoint. What are the one or two changes to your value proposition that would be most important to your customers. How can you get there?

You can also identify customer priorities that are unspoken, maybe even hidden to the customers themselves, by thinking through the total *economics* of their worlds. Instead of focusing on your organization's service or product, imagine that you are the head of a household in each of your top five segments (or president of your five largest customers) and answer the following questions:

- ✔ What are my goals for my family (or my business)?
- ✔ What things worry me?
- ✔ How could this organization help me meet my goals? What is this organization doing that keeps me from meeting those goals?[28]

core concept The dollar cost of participating in your program or using your service is only a small portion of your customer's investment. A customer may also have to take off time from work, pay for child care, prepare for the program, pay for transportation, and maybe even wait around for your services. In return, using your service promises to produce tangible and/or intangible benefits for your customer. A customer's total economic equation is this sum of dollars, time, hassle factor, and related costs, balanced by the "value" of benefits received.[29]

Two entrepreneurial social-purpose enterprises in Maine, Alpha One and Faithworks, successfully use their understanding of their customers' economics to accomplish their social missions.

action step How close are you to becoming your targeted customers' first choice for meeting their needs? Take your best guess at ranking your customers' priorities, including total economic cost, whether or not you have the market research to back you up (but do repeat this exercise when you've got some more precise customer data!). Now give your organization a score from 1 to 10 on meeting each of these priorities. As objectively as you can, score your competitors—direct and indirect—on how they meet each priority. A winning profile looks like this example below, in which your company outperforms its competitors by the largest margin on the highest priority items.

CASE STUDY

ALPHA ONE

Alpha One's mission is to "be a leading enterprise providing the community with information, services, and products that create opportunities for people with disabilities to live independently." Since well before the Americans with Disabilities Act, Alpha One has been convincing decision makers to ensure that new public buildings are designed to be accessible to all. Their most compelling argument? Comparisons between concrete examples of the costly renovations and/or lawsuits caused by lack of accessibility and the costs of incorporating these objectives from the earliest planning stages. Over time, Alpha One became known for its expertise and began offering information and assistance to builders. Today the organization's access consultation and barrier-free design services employ architects who are experts in their field and charge for their services.

The business card of Faithworks founder Paul Rubin summarizes his organization's goal, "Providing a productive workforce for the packaging industry and employment opportunities for all." Rubin has figured out how his biggest asset, a pool of more than 1,000 workers who can be mobilized on a few hours' notice to handle more than 500,000 pieces a day that must be inserted, sealed, stuffed, packaged, or otherwise prepared to be sent to the consumer, can be his customers' biggest asset as well. Faithworks' customers tend to be companies that have a tight deadline for a large project with manual labor requirements that they couldn't possibly meet with their own workers. Because it employs individuals with barriers that have prevented them from obtaining work in typical structured environments, is very flexible, and pays on the basis of performance, Faithworks can quickly fill its more than 150-person shop with eager workers. Faithworks' quick turnaround and high quality often saves its customers thousands of dollars. In turn, Rubin's ability to meet his customers' economic priorities has translated into the equivalent of more than 80 full-time jobs for individuals living on the edge.

Customer	My Score	Competitor 1 Score	Competitor 2 Score	Competitor 3 Score	Me Relative to Best Competitor[30]
Priority #1	10	8	6	7	+2
Priority #2	8	7	6	5	+1
Priority #3	7	7	7	6	+1
Priority #4	7	8	6	4	−1

How can you change your value proposition to make sure you have the winning profile?

Meeting Market-driven Demand
with Mission-driven Supply

What do you do when your social mission stands in the way of what your target customers want? Typical dilemmas include the following scenarios:

✔ A wood furniture maker that employs the developmentally disabled realizes that its current employees can't make enough volume in the short turnaround time required to get profitable large orders, yet the organization can neither find new developmentally disabled candidates with the right skills nor run a second shift.

✔ Volunteers make top-quality custom-designed adaptive equipment, but do it on their schedule, not the customers' timing.

✔ When homeless individuals in an art-therapy program get the chance to have their work sold, the participants' creations become more and more commercial and less and less therapeutic.

A few real-life solutions are as follows:

✔ *Make sure you're focusing on the customer segments that are the best fit for your organization.* After diversifying into several higher-end, multistep wood products, The Nezinscot Guild—a Maine wood product manufacturer with a developmentally disabled workforce—looked carefully at its core strengths. They decided to target only customers who wanted the more basic products that employees could produce most efficiently.

✔ *Check your assumptions about how you pursue your social mission.* Initially, nonprofit Juma Ventures assumed that to fulfill its mission it had to employ exclusively at-risk youth in its San Francisco Ben & Jerry's Ice Cream franchises. Over time, however, Juma's managers found they could employ more at-risk youth in total if they also hired a few more seasoned employees who would help the business grow.

✔ Creative Work Systems began as a manufacturing facility exclusively employing the developmentally disabled. Today only 50 percent of their furniture-manufacturing workforce comes from that population. Creative Work Systems discovered that having a mix of workers improved its profitability at the same time as it furthered its mission of integrating the disabled into the community.

✔ *Proactively offer a different type of value to your customer.* The Kids' Project, a program of Easter Seals in Maine, relies on volunteers to make the customized adaptive equipment it offers to schools, physical therapists, and families. They make sure that each customer understands that The Kids' Project can't guarantee delivery dates, and they also make sure that each customer knows that their low prices depend on volunteer labor.

✔ *Think through the mission implications of your business design during the planning stages.* Before launching its greeting card line, Portland Maine community arts organization Spiral Arts asked store owners and graphic designers to select images from its arts programs that would likely sell well. Once customers began buying cards with images designed during its normal programs, Spiral Arts was comfortable that featuring its students' work would not compromise the integrity of its classes, and the organization started encouraging participants to submit their favorite works specifically with greeting cards in mind.

PRICING TO MAXIMIZE SOCIAL IMPACT

Price is what customers are willing to give up—in the form of freedom, money, or anything they value—in exchange for something else. Price is just one of the many factors that go into a customer's decision to participate in your program or use your services. Nonetheless, for entrepreneurs who are willing to shake things up, pricing can be a valuable tool to accomplish a social mission. We'll take a look at some of the more common options for setting prices, how you can use different pricing strategies to meet your organization's objectives, and how you can take advantage of customers' price sensitivity. Although pricing takes many forms, this section addresses monetary payment. Please see the case study about Social Marketing on page 238 for a brief discussion of other forms of "prices."

YOUR PRICING OPTIONS

To Charge or Not To Charge?31

In contrast with for-profit entrepreneurs, social entrepreneurs often face situations in which there are compelling reasons not to charge the customer anything at all. Before you simply set a price that covers your costs, think about the following circumstances. Most of us would agree that it doesn't make sense to charge drivers who "use" a stop sign to guide their driving.

Customers who obey a stop sign also benefit society as a whole because they reduce traffic accidents. This rationale for not charging users is known as a "positive externality." Rather than discouraging drivers from using the guidance of stop signs by asking them to pay for this privilege, communities choose to encourage unlimited use of stop signs by not charging. Similarly, eliminating tolls for carpoolers and fees for local shuttle buses makes sense because of the positive externalities they provide.

Other factors may also influence your pricing decision. For instance, you'll notice that few churches require even a minimum donation for attending their services, presumably on ideological grounds. Sometimes it doesn't make economic sense to charge a customer: the costs of collecting the amount charged would be larger than the total fees collected. At many small parks, for example, station rangers collect user fees in the summertime but allow visitors free access to the park during the rest of the year because the total number of visitors is so low that it's literally "not worth the time."

On the other hand, as heart-wrenching as it might be, there are also excellent mission-driven reasons why social entrepreneurs should charge their customers. In the first case, charging a fee requires customers to allocate their dollars, time, or other resources among different options and by so doing demonstrate the programs or services they value. By agreeing to pay for a service (even a small amount of the total cost), customers indicate that the service is worth at least that much to them. Services that are underutilized when they have a price tag suggests that the intended customers don't (or can't) value the service at that price. Customers' responses to prices can translate into useful guides for social entrepreneurs who are trying to allocate their scarce resources to best serve these customers.

Asking customers to pay a price for using a program or service also tends to reduce their consumption. For example, when towns introduce a "per-garbage-can" collection fee, they often see residents reduce their "trash" and increase the amount of waste they recycle. Of course, charging a fee can also accomplish ideological objectives, such as generating additional commitment from a customer who is literally "more invested" in a program outcome.

Rationales for Not Charging the Customer	Rationales for Charging the Customer [32]
Public good	Program resource allocation
Positive externalities	Understanding minimum value to the customer
Ideological goals	Reducing consumption
Costs of collection	Ideological goals

Who to Charge?

Someone has to pay the costs of your service, and it turns out that *who* pays the bills does matter. As in many families, those who pay the bills tend to make the rules, or at least they wield significant influence. Think about how you can align your sources of funding to your mission. For example, the first Board President of Seattle's Hugo House, "a literary arts center dedicated to serving the community," restrained herself from using her ample personal financial resources to solve the startup's growing pains. Rather, she encouraged the arts center to make connections and generate funding throughout the community. As a result, two years later Hugo House had a very diverse funding base, including 30 percent earned income, and a close "customer relationship" with a much more diverse group in the community.[33]

Asking beneficiaries to pay, in monetary or other terms, can be a form of treating them with respect. Contributing in visible ways gives beneficiaries a voice in the organization, the voice of the customer. For instance, Habitat for Humanity's requirement that low-income families contribute "sweat equity"—that they pay for their future dwelling with hours worked on their own and others' homes—makes the home-buying process more a transaction than a donation. And Habitat never has a shortage of families eager to work their way into a home.

Your pricing strategy must also take competitive realities into consideration. Someone or some combination of people does have to pay. Many years ago, Bennington College made a philosophical decision not to be beholden to large donors. As a result, the college now does not have the option of subsidizing tuition with endowment funds and has found itself at a competitive disadvantage when recruiting students.

Calculating a Price

The most common, although not necessarily the best, formula for pricing a good or service is "cost plus." Cost plus means calculating the organization's cost to produce or procure one unit (for example, one hour of counseling) and marking that cost up by a given percent. For example, if an art museum gift store purchases an item from its supplier for $5, it will likely mark up this cost 100 percent and charge the consumer $10. There is an inherent assumption that this markup will at least cover all of the organization's overhead costs, such as rent, salespeople, advertising, and the like.

Pricing to "break even" is a slightly more complex endeavor. An organization calculates how many units it must sell at a given price to pay for both the costs of each unit sold and the organization's fixed costs. Setting this price means making assumptions about the likely volume that will be sold at a given price.

core concept   Instead of focusing internally on a company's costs, pricing based on *economic value to the customer* (EVC) focuses on the maximum price a customer is likely to pay for a specific item or service purchased for a specific purpose. This customer perception may be based primarily on tangible economic value (e.g., "I will save $400 in one year on heating bills if I install new $300 windows") or may be intangible (e.g., "I'll spend up to $100 on a pair of pants if they make me look and feel great"). As you may have guessed, EVC is likely to vary widely among heterogeneous customers, so it is usually used in conjunction with the segmented pricing strategies we discuss later in this section.

Unlike their for-profit counterparts, whose existence is predicated on maximizing profits, nonprofits often struggle with the concept of charging more than the bare minimum for a product or service. At the non-profit-owned San Francisco City Store, young employees questioned the ethics of a nonprofit charging "too much" for certain products. These at-risk youth understood the need to mark up products in order to cover all of the business' costs, but they were uncomfortable about charging more than the local drugstore's price for a roll of film simply because of the store's tourist destination location. Likewise, these employees were often surprised to find that customers would pay two or three times what they estimated an item was "worth" based on their own incomes and priorities.

Of course, customers' willingness to pay is often directly influenced by the price of alternative services or products that can meet the same need. *Competition-based pricing* means pricing in relation to the "going rate" in the industry. Pricing at or very near competitors' prices is almost obligatory in a commodity-like business in which a small price difference is likely to have a large impact on the customer decision. Organizations bidding for contracts by submitting sealed bids engage in another form of competition-based pricing. They attempt to price their work just under the price of the other competitors while still covering their costs and making the largest possible profit.

All organizations whose customers have a choice, including all social entrepreneurs, must be aware of the prices of their competitors, direct and indirect. Choosing a consistent level of prices relative to what competitors are charging (e.g., match, at a premium, always the lowest) is a key strategic decision.

Forms of Payment

Thinking entrepreneurially about how you structure your fees, no matter how high or low they are, can give more customers access to your service and can potentially strengthen your organization.

✔ *Payment over Time.* A dental clinic in a low-income neighborhood might make orthodontic work available to parents for whom paying a single $2,000 bill would be impossible by simply offering an installment plan. Creative timing options exist for fundraising "customers" as well. For example, the Stanford Business School Alumni Association cleverly assumes that recent graduates are "feeling poor" and are likely to increase their earning power over time, so it offers a five-year pledge with the lowest donation in year 1 and the highest in year 5.

✔ *Loans.* As car manufacturers and real estate agents have clearly recognized, average customers think about affordability in terms of their monthly income. Social entrepreneurs may be able to create a world of opportunities by offering loans or layaways for nontraditional items. For instance, microenterprise lenders have successfully built on the fact that very small business owners can and do consistently meet the required monthly payments on loans for business investments that would have been out of their range as one-time purchases.

✔ *Single Unit versus Package Deal.* Consider giving consumers the option of purchasing just an individual item, rather than a package. For example, many arts presenters have recognized that few 30- to 50-year-olds will commit to a series of concerts far in advance and have responded by also making "series" seats available as a single-ticket purchase at a higher price per performance.

✔ *Package Deal versus Single Unit.* Payment structures can also be used to benefit an organization. Offering good deals on concerts sold as a complete series can help increase attendance and advance ticket sales, not to mention improve the presenter's cash flow.

✔ *Money-Back Guarantee.* Thomas College, a small business college in Maine, recently created headlines by introducing a "money-back guarantee" for its Bachelor of Arts program. Thomas believes that reducing potential students' risk removes a big initial hurdle for students who might not otherwise be in school. At the same time, the policy gives the school additional incentives to ensure that it's actually helping its students meet their career goals.

TAILORING YOUR PRICING TO YOUR OBJECTIVES

Step 1: What are your strategic objectives?

Step 2: What pricing strategy will best accomplish your objectives?

Like every other element of your marketing strategy, your prices should be carefully calculated to bring about a desired response, whether you're running a Fortune 500 company or an entrepreneurial nonprofit. Let's look at possible outcomes of a few pricing strategies.

Price to Maximize Revenues at the Lowest Possible Price that Covers Your Unit Costs

For-profit rationales: The laws of supply and demand say that as price goes down, demand goes up. You'll sell more widgets if you sell them at a lower price, and you will gain a larger share of your market. Producing or selling a high volume of widgets may bring down your total cost per widget, meaning that you may actually make a higher profit by selling at a lower price.

Social entrepreneur rationales: Lower prices mean that your products or services are accessible to more people in the community, regardless of their economic means.

One of the primary goals of The Good Shepherd Food Bank is to lower its prices. For Good Shepherd, a consolidator of donated and low-cost food for food banks across the state of Maine, the lower the per-pound maintenance fee it charges, the more the food banks can provide to families in need.

The fact that lower prices lead to a higher volume of sales (i.e., more work) also makes this a tempting strategy for supported employment businesses—the more work, the more jobs—as long as the work enables the organization to fully cover its costs, including paying a "fair wage" to its employees.

Because Faithworks often takes on unique projects, it sometimes estimates a price that is higher than their actual cost plus a markup turns out to be. In these instances, Faithworks routinely passes on that saving to its customers. The organization believes that the best way to keep the maximum number of its employees working is to develop an honest relationship that keeps customers coming back repeatedly.

Price To Maximize Profit from Those Who Are Able To Pay and Charge Each Type of Customer the Price at Which You Receive the Most Total Profit

✔ Choose a single price for the entire market based on the combination of price and resulting sales volume that will generate greatest total profits.

✔ Give discounts to groups of identifiable customers who are likely to be willing or able to pay less than other groups of customers. For example, offer a student or senior citizen discount or a sliding scale for fee based on family income.

The sliding-scale fee that Planned Parenthood charges for health services is directly tied to patients' self-declared income. Those who identify themselves as not being able to pay the entire bill are charged less than those whose income exceeds a certain level. This segment-based pricing ties directly to Planned Parenthood's belief in the "fundamental right of each individual to manage his or her fertility regardless of the individual's income."[34]

✔ Use price promotions that appeal only to price-sensitive customers because they require some type of effort. For example, offer a rebate, coupons, hold short sales, offer to match competitor's prices, and so on.

✔ Give discounts based on customers' usage of your product. The customers who use the most of your product are likely to be most concerned about its cost. At the same time, they tend to cost you the least because of the size of their orders. Treat them right.

For-profit rationales: A business should extract maximum dollars from customers over the lifetime of the relationship.

Social entrepreneur rationales: Charge a higher price to those customers who are willing to pay more so you can subsidize customers in need. Check your product portfolio map to make sure you're keeping a viable balance of programs to achieve this goal.

Alpha One also operates Wheelchairs Unlimited, retail stores that sell adaptive equipment that enables the disabled to live more independently. Wheelchairs Unlimited may sell custom equipment to Medicaid recipients even when management knows it won't break even on those transactions. Founder Steven Tremblay believes that using profits from higher-margin clients to subsidize equipment for those without financial means is simply "part of the organization's mission."

red flag Price can be simply calculated by Cost + Operating Expenses + Profit = Price. If you've gotten this far into the book, you're not likely to think that you should just substitute "zero" in profits' place in this equation just because you're a nonprofit. Remember that for their first five to seven years, most small businesses plow all of their profits (and more) right back into building their business. A reasonable amount of profit will not only help you subsidize your social goals, but it may also help you build an organization that will be there over the long haul.

Price To Encourage Customers To Try a New Product or Service at Zero or Low Initial Cost

For-profit rationales: Once customers try a great product, they will come back for more at the same or higher price.

Social entrepreneur rationales: Make it easy to change behavior. In 1984, the nonprofit Populations Services, Inc. (PSI) introduced condoms into Bangladesh to help reduce the country's population growth. PSI successfully priced condoms at the same price as other "little luxuries," such as one cigarette, a cup of tea, and the like.

red flag Make sure your price is greater than the cost of collection, unless you are prepared to make an even larger subsidy.

Price To Increase Perceived Value by Setting a Higher Than Necessary Price

For-profit rationales: Maximize profit by capitalizing on the "snob appeal" of a product.

Social entrepreneur rationales: Increase the perceived value of a service or product that furthers a social mission. PSI also introduced birth control pills into Bangladesh at a low price, thinking this would increase demand. In fact, the organization soon realized that it needed to raise its prices to the level of other brands on the market—a price many times PSI's break-even cost—in order to give potential users confidence in the product.

A select $1,000 per plate fundraising dinner may generate much more interest and net profit than a lower entry price, but larger event.

Price To Generate Commitment From Your Customers by Setting a Price High Enough that Customers Are Motivated To Take Full Advantage of Your Service or Product

Resources is a private job-training program for immigrants in New York City. Among the organization's distinctive features is that the participants themselves, not the government or local charities, must pay for a part of their training. The immigrants pay $400 per semester, either in advance or from their salaries once they are working—and about 98 percent of the program's graduates are now employed.[35]

Price to Test the Value of Your Offering by Setting a Price That Customers Will Pay if They Attach a Minimum Value to Your Product or Service

Medical clinics often charge a minimum co-payment, in part to encourage customers to use only the services they need.

action step Jot down your current pricing strategy. Is it consistent with your overall strategic objectives? Look through the previous list of common strategies. Is there a pricing strategy that can better support your core mission?

USING PRICE SENSITIVITY TO YOUR ADVANTAGE

core concept *Price sensitivity* describes how dramatically a group of customers will react to a price change. High price sensitivity means that even a small increase in price will cause customers to buy much less of a given item and, similarly, that a small price decrease will prompt a noticeable increase in purchases. When there is low price sensitivity, customers change their buying habits relatively little in response to prices moving up or down, unless the price changes are dramatic.

Price sensitivity can vary by product, by product category, by total price range, by type of store, by service level required, by geography, by time of year, and so on, as well as by customer segment. A social entrepreneur can apply an understanding of price sensitivity to provide more service at a higher price that is still perceived as "good value" by the customer. Alternatively, for example, by taking advantage of price sensitivity, a social entrepreneur may be able to reduce the individual fee for a class, yet still cover the fixed cost of the class because the lower fee attracts more students.

red flag   Nonprofit staff members who are used to providing free services or serving low-income populations are likely to assume that customers are more consistently very price sensitive than proves to be the case. For example, Senior Spectrum, a nonprofit Maine Area Agency on Aging, recently launched a for-profit business that provides services to help seniors live more independently. Some Senior Spectrum staff who made the switch to the for-profit business initially felt uncomfortable charging for their services. These staffers projected their own assumptions that customers would not want to pay for the assistance they were providing, even though their *customers,* many of whom were contracting for services on behalf of elderly family members, valued the service highly and felt the price was absolutely fair.

The following kinds of factors lead to *decreased* price sensitivity:

✔ Perception that the product or service is unique

✔ Small relative cost in total product or service purchase

✔ Perception of good price/quality ratio

The following kinds of factors lead to *increased* price sensitivity:

✔ Awareness of easily available alternatives or substitutes

✔ Ease of using directly competing products

✔ Large total expenditure for the customer

The best way to determine price sensitivity is to experiment. Staying aware of the potential backlash of perceived injustices, try changing your prices on different services. Track your participation rates at the new price, and compare them with your rates at the old price (make sure it's over a comparable period). Whenever possible, watch your customers. Do they inquire about the price of a service, only to say "no thank you" when they learn how much it costs? Do they see a low price and sign up for two classes when they would normally commit to only one? Also check for competitors' responses to your changes and factor their moves into your own strategy.

You are likely to find that you've been charging customers less than the optimum price for some types of items and the converse, that you would generate more interest (or sell more of your socially desirable service) if you lowered the price for other services or items. Keep experimenting over time. Even if your customers' tastes and priorities aren't changing (and they usually are), your competitive environment is.

You can also develop pricing techniques to enable customers who are very price sensitive to pay less for the same product than customers from low price sensitivity segments. Go back to the Pricing to Maximize Profit examples to review ethical techniques for making this distinction.

 Conduct at least one price sensitivity experiment. Lower the price of one of your best-selling services or products by 10 percent. Make sure the markdown is clearly visible and watch the results. Observe what happens when you move it back up again. What if you increase the price by 5 percent? Which price best meets your organization's ultimate goal?

PROMOTING YOUR PRODUCT, SERVICE, AND MISSION

Marketing takes many forms. Relationships are the most quiet, but perhaps the most effective form of marketing. Most social entrepreneurs are also justifiably proud of their reputations. Building a strong brand can reinforce those reputations. And many social entrepreneurs have a "shouldn't be a secret" weapon, their social mission—if they choose to use it. We'll look at each of these forms of marketing individually.

MARKETING BY BUILDING RELATIONSHIPS

Management scholar Peter Drucker once said, "The purpose of business is not to make a sale, but to make and keep a customer."[36] Marketing by building customer relationships makes sense for social entrepreneurs because it is effective, can be done at *very low cost,* and draws on the people skills that often reside in nonprofit leaders. Social entrepreneurs can benefit from thinking strategically about customer relationships, customer referrals, and key valuable intermediaries with whom to create relationships.

One challenge for social entrepreneurs is to channel their strong relationships in the community to their greatest advantage. Carrie Portis, Director of Enterprise Development at Rubicon Programs, gives a great example: "At Rubicon Bakery, when people [would-be volunteers] ask how they can help grow our bakery, we tell them to buy our cakes, tell their friends to buy our cakes, and thank the grocery store for stocking our cakes. At first they laugh, then they get it and hopefully they go out and make a purchase."[37] Rubicon knows that relationships can create customers.

Your continued investment in understanding your customers' needs and exceeding their expectations is the best source of repeat business. When we asked Rick Surpin, the founder of Cooperative Home Care Associates, what marketing techniques he used to grow his home health care business from a startup created to employ women moving off welfare to a profitable $7 million business, his answer was simple.

gem of wisdom

"I don't know anything about marketing," he said. "I just built good re-lationships with clinics and with government agencies, one by one."[38]

A recent survey of 900 sales and marketing professionals con-firmed that entrepreneurs should focus their energy on those who al-ready know and support them. These experts ranked "referrals" as the most effective technique for attracting new customers. The survey's au-thors, the Nierenberg Group, concluded that "the shortest path to new customers comes from reviewing existing contacts and asking them who might give the warmest reception."[39]

Relationships can also play an important role for social enterprises trying to reach small individual customers. You may simply need to iden-tify the right intermediary. The owner of Hereford House Restaurant (#70 on *Inc.* magazine's 1999 Inner City 100) illustrated this technique when he turned around a dying steakhouse in the middle of a very tough part of Kansas City. He "cozied up to concierges at downtown hotels, coaxing them to stop by his restaurant by handing out gift certificates. And to en-sure that cabbies would steer newcomers his way, he occasionally threw 'cabbie soirees' with free finger food."[40] Similarly, the nonprofit San Fran-cisco City Store developed a good relationship with the San Francisco Tour Guide Guild when it realized that the Guild's members could liter-ally lead tourists to their stores.

Advocacy group Alpha One figured out that architects would be strategic allies in its fight to ensure that all public buildings were acces-sible. Although building owners must approve the costs associated with accessibility, architects have a powerful voice—and the trust of these de-cision makers. Alpha One has actively cultivated those relationships and educated architects about the social and economic benefits of designing buildings for maximum accessibility.

Social Marketing

As we talk about marketing tactics, it's important to acknowledge that some social entrepreneurs face special challenges. Social change often requires participants to alter their behaviors for the "good of society" at a high personal cost. For example, low-income farmers in Colombia are unlikely to switch from cultivating coca plants to growing crops that do not earn them enough to feed their families, even if they sympathize with the goal of reducing cocaine addiction. Convincing individuals to partic-ipate in a social program when their personal costs of participation seem to outweigh their personal benefits is a much more difficult task than convincing customers to make purchases that are arguably in their own best interest.

Professors V. Kasturi Rangan, Sohel Karim, and Sheryl Sandberg argue that the best way to approach social marketing is to first systematically analyze the desired behavior change from the target participant's perspective. Social entrepreneurs should plan their marketing on the basis of two factors: (1) the desired participants' costs, whether financial, psychological (such as giving up smoking), or in terms of time, and (2) the tangible and intangible benefits that these participants will enjoy as a result of making the proposed change. The most effective marketing approaches vary according to the combination of these costs and benefits. Exhibit 8.5 can help you determine the key marketing tactics to apply in a given situation by mapping the participants' cost and benefits.[41]

BUILDING A BRAND

core concept

According to a recent ranking, McDonald's is the #1 brand in the world, "the quintessential international brand with consistent brand values, industry dominance, and a living personality."[42] *Brands* are valuable because they directly influence customers' decisions. They provide buyers with shortcuts in processing all of the information involved in choosing a product, service, or action. In the words of Norio Ohga, Chairman of Sony, "Our biggest asset is four

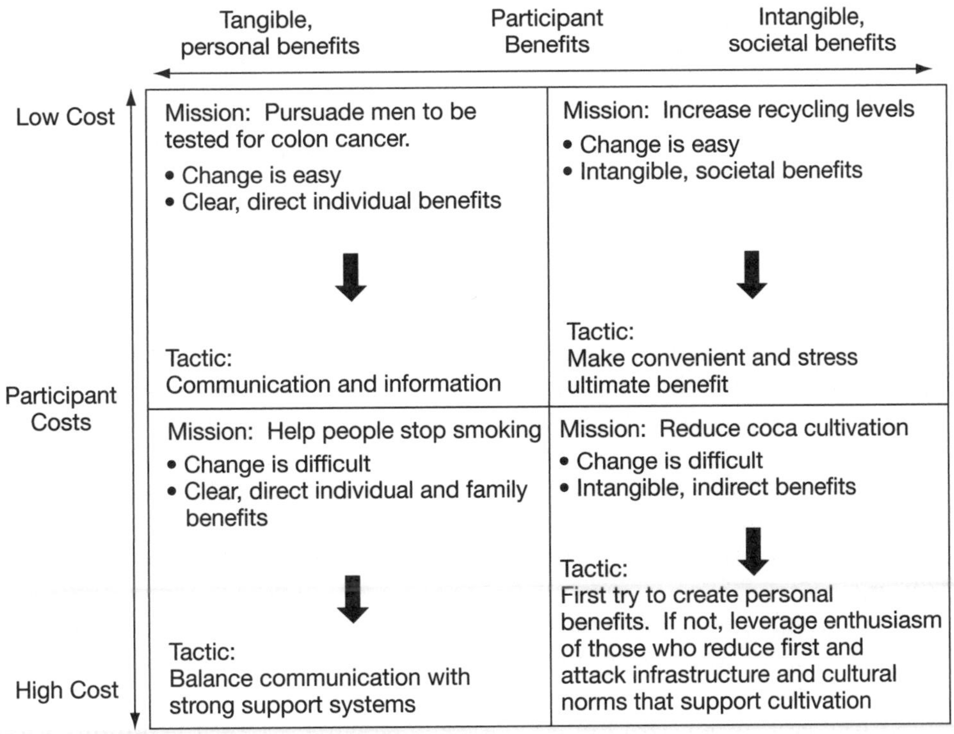

EXHIBIT 8.5 Marketing plan analysis.

letters: SONY. It's not so much our buildings or our engineers or our factories, but our name . . . we must preserve and build our reputation, because that determines the value of the company in the 21st century."[43] Brands can be very powerful for startup organizations as well. Two brands that did not exist in 1990, Amazon.com and eBay, are now so strong that their names instantly evoke Internet commerce and stock market success.

core concept   Social entrepreneurs working in the nonprofit sector may have an advantage when it comes to building a brand. According to a former Procter & Gamble marketing executive, "Most nonprofit institutions are a brand already. The question is whether they are defining, articulating, and managing it to their advantage."[44] Today, many nonprofits are paying attention to their brands and trying to create holistic approaches to building loyalty with donors, clients, and the public through their group's reputation and image. Nonprofits are hoping to use their brands for increased fundraising pull, merchandising, for-profit alliances, even, they say, to increase their voice in public policy. Steven Abbot, spokesperson for Volunteers of America, describes branding as a defensive tactic: "If you don't brand yourself, focus your message, integrate your message delivery, and use every means at your disposal to get your message out there, you are going to be lost in this message bombardment."[45]

The Boston Museum of Science has incorporated a brand remake into its traditional marketing materials. Both a new slogan, "It's Alive," and a new logo conveying a sense of movement were created to reinforce the museum's goal to be seen as constantly changing (i.e., worth frequent visits). But the Boston Museum's logo and slogan are also doing double duty. For the first time, they are helping sell merchandise in the museum's store. Why this pairing of a museum-quality brand and gift shop merchandise? Says the museum's retail sales manager, "we recognize the real need to perpetuate ourselves commercially."[46]

red flag   More than their for-profit counterparts, social entrepreneurs run a risk when they market their brand too aggressively or stray from their core mission. Going after the spotlight, funding dollars, or donor loyalty can distract from your organization's programs. And if the public thinks that your marketing is more fluff than substance or that you sound like you're selling soft drinks, instead of promoting a good cause, you can quickly alienate donors, volunteers, and the wider community.

Branding campaigns also have their limits. No amount of marketing is a panacea for a weak or disorganized organization. In the words of the vice-chairman of the Boston Museum of Science, "Branding requires a truthful statement about what an organization has to offer. You don't just make up an image and pray."[48]

The Soho Rep Brand

The Soho Repertory Theater in New York recently tried its hand at improving its brand identity. Guided by Board member Cynthia Round, Soho Rep analyzed what consumers thought of the theater. Not only did Soho research what its customers thought about its avant garde plays, but it also asked them what they thought of the theater's logo, its seating capacity, and its niche in the arts world. Soho liked the fact that its audience expected it to be "innovative" and "experimental" and decided to build this expectation into a true competitive advantage through its brand.

Soho's branding plan includes much more than creating an image. In Round's words, "the delivery of a consistent personal experience of using the service" was the goal. The theater's artistic director, Daniel Aukin, put this concept in more concrete terms: "When an audience member or prospective member interacts with the theater—whether they're seeing a show, waiting in the lobby, seeing a poster on the street, or receiving a postcard or letter—there is a consistency and vision beyond those interactions."

Informed by its customer research, Soho Rep is implementing its brand strategy in big ways and in small details. The theater's advertising now clearly reflects its avant-garde image, and so do Aukin's business cards. Soon even the color of the theater lobby's painted walls will subtly do the same.

And Aukin, who came in with the skeptical attitude that a branding strategy "sounded like something you would do if you were trying to sell potato chips" has found the process nothing short of "incredibly useful."[47]

tool of the trade So, how do you strengthen your brand, albeit carefully? Scott Bedbury, the force behind both the Nike "Just Do It" branding campaign and the Starbucks brand identifies eight brand-building principles:

✔ A great brand is in it for the long haul.

✔ A great brand can be anything (think Intel, as well as Starbucks and Nike).

✔ A great brand knows itself (ask the consumers to find out what they believe).

✔ A great brand invents or reinvents an entire product category (Disney, Apple).

✔ A great brand taps into emotion (like the emotion of a close basketball game).

✔ A great brand is a story that's never completely told (The Levi's story, The HP Way).

✔ A great brand has design consistency (Ralph Lauren, Nike).

✔ A great brand is relevant (not just trying to be cool).[49]

As Bedbury states, building a brand is a "long haul," and it can mean investing scarce resources. Before you make that commitment, ask yourself whether your organization falls into one of these common situations in which investing significantly in your brand makes sense:

✔ *Do we need to build our identity relatively quickly because we're moving into new markets where we're not known?* The Habitat for Humanity brand helps small volunteer groups around the world to recruit volunteers and donors by communicating a recognized set of values and approach to low-income home ownership, eliminating the need for each local affiliate to slowly develop credibility over time.

✔ *Is perceived quality a very important value to our customers and does quality vary significantly among providers?* The nonprofit Visiting Nurses Associations, better known as the VNAs, have continued to prosper in an era of increased health care provider competition in part because of the strength of their name and tradition of caring and quality that harken back to the founding nurses' early house calls to the sick in poor communities.

✔ *Do we have little chance for direct interaction with a large segment of our customers?* UNICEF has almost no direct contact with the average American consumer, yet it sells millions of dollars of cards and gifts each year. UNICEF counts on its brand to convey its explicit focus on helping children, to evoke the image of "what just a dollar can buy," and to engender a sense of international goodwill.

So what can resource-strapped entrepreneurs do to strengthen their brand without breaking the bank? Think creatively and draw on their organizations' assets. Here are a few examples:

Think visibility: City Year gave President Clinton a sweatshirt and a watch with its logo—and in return got its name on national TV and radio in a context that communicated the importance of its work and respect for the organization.

Build on what you do well: Through their cookie sales, the Girl Scouts reach far beyond the young girls and parents who are the organization's core customers. Recognizing that each box of cookies will be handled and perhaps read several times by consumers, the Girl Scouts have turned the cookie packages themselves into effective vehicles for communicating the new ways that their organization is preparing young women for the future—mountain biking, computer classes, and building self-confidence.

Design a product that reinforces your brand and mission: The National Headache Foundation's newsletter, HeadLines, demonstrates the organization's commitment to improving the quality of life for migraine sufferers by devoting several pages to detailed answers to members' specific migraine questions. At the same time, HeadLines reinforces its credibility as a cutting-edge information source by enlisting different specialists to answer each question, reporting on the latest advances in migraine treatment (actually listing the dates of the latest academic studies), and sticking its neck out to recommend specific drugs.

red flag   Social entrepreneurs can borrow many low-cost marketing tactics from their for-profit colleagues.[50] Just as branding and marketing campaigns can reinforce a reputation, however, they can also bring it down. Cash-poor entrepreneurs often face the "do-it-yourself" temptation. Although you can use many guerilla marketing techniques to effectively implement the principles in this chapter, beware of shortchanging your marketing materials and making a lasting bad impression.[51]

action step   Go back and think about your most valuable customers. In general, what kind of reputation do they value? What brands attract them? Now, imagine what they would say if they were asked to describe your brand. Could they? Conduct your own focus group or enlist the help of a marketing professional to actually ask your customers how they perceive you. Armed with that knowledge, decide how you can build on or change that perception with two or three concrete steps.

Cause-related Marketing

Cause-related marketing can be a very effective way for social entrepreneurs to leverage the financial and creative resources of more established organizations. Cause-related marketing often takes the form of linking two brands in the customers' eyes or "co-branding."

Got Milk?—The California Milk Producers linked up with the Girl Scouts to create a high-impact billboard ad that conveyed the altogether wholesome appeal associated with a cute Brownie, Girl Scout cookies, and milk.

Charge Against Hunger—Over several years, American Express donated $.03 to Share Our Strength's (SOS) hunger relief efforts every time an American Express card was used during the holiday season. Together with other corporate partners, American Express gave more than $16 million to SOS, while increasing its own transaction volume, its cardholder satisfaction, and the number of merchants accepting its card.[52]

Adopt-a-Pet—A local Humane Society gets free advertisements for one or two pets available for adoption every week in a local newspaper. The paper scores points for supporting the community and undoubtedly pleases a few readers with the cute animal photos and profiles. The featured animals often find a home, and the issue of proper pet care gets good visibility.

Marketing professor Alan Andreasen encourages nonprofits to think of themselves as bona fide "partners" in these marketing pair-ups. He suggests three steps: (1) Evaluate your organization to understand what value you could offer a potential partner; (2) Identify and approach the potential partners that could most benefit from what your organization offers; and (3) Actively help create and monitor the partnership. Here are the questions he recommends you answer to understand what your organization could offer a potential corporate partner:

- ✔ What is our image?
- ✔ Do we have strong brand recognition?
- ✔ Is our cause especially attractive to certain companies and industries?
- ✔ Is our core audience particularly appealing to some corporations?
- ✔ Do we promote a cause that the public considers especially urgent?
- ✔ Do we have clout with certain groups of people?
- ✔ Are we local, national, or international?
- ✔ Do we have a charismatic or well-known leader?
- ✔ Is our organization experienced and stable?[53]

MISSION-DRIVEN PUBLIC RELATIONS

Social entrepreneurs have an enviable advantage when it comes to generating publicity, the lowest direct cost form of marketing. Most media folks *like* to tell human interest stories about people doing "good things," particularly when the approach is original. The first step in public relations is to assess how publicizing your social mission is likely to work in favor of your organization . . . or against it. Then you can put the basic tools of public relations to work.

If you're a social-purpose enterprise offering a product or service not directly tied to your mission, you'll need to check your market research to make sure that your target customers are likely to feel motivated by the social mission of your organization. Unfortunately, for many people, the word *nonprofit* conjures up associations such as "inferior quality" or "unprofessional." Potential customers who view your product or service as "charity" are unlikely to let themselves perceive the value in your value proposition. John DuRand of MDI explains: "In my experience, the business world does not trust nonprofits. They assume that if an organization doesn't have monetary incentives driving its quality or timeliness, it just won't do a good job." DuRand avoids this issue by not mentioning MDI's social mission in his sales pitches. The management of San Francisco's CVE, a social-purpose commercial janitorial service, take a more proactive approach. "Sometimes we will wait until we've been cleaning a building very successfully for six months before we really highlight our mission to the customer. At that point, the fact that our employees are recovering from mental illness is more likely to be seen as a plus. In fact, we think that conversation helps break down some of the stigma attached to mental illness. However, earlier the same information might have been seen as a potential weakness," says John Brauer, CVE's Executive Director.[54]

Alternatively, your social mission may be a powerful selling point. Ask yourself how many Girl Scout cookies are purchased every year at a premium price. The Girl Scouts have completely incorporated their mission into their marketing. East End Kids Katering, a provider of low-cost nutritious meals for low-income child care programs in Portland, Maine, has found its mission to be a major factor in attracting the initial customers for a new catering business. Screen printer Ashbury Images markets its social mission strategically, to different degrees to different customer segments.

Publicizing a social mission with the goal of generating sales for a market-driven activity often raises ethical questions, as can "poster child" forms of fundraising in some organizations. The leadership of social enterprises must set a clear policy with examples of what is and what is not acceptable for this type of promotion. When formulating your policy, make sure you ask questions such as the following:

- ✔ *What is the right thing to do from the point of view of our beneficiaries?* (Do not forget to get *their* input because it may not be what you expect.)
- ✔ What do we expect from beneficiaries in terms of stories, interviews, photos, and so forth?
- ✔ Would a public relations opportunity truly advance our social cause?
- ✔ How will our traditional supporters react?

Revisit the issue of promoting your social mission periodically as your enterprise evolves. After many years, Creative Work Systems, a nonprofit organization with three supported employment wood-manufacturing businesses, decided to include on its tags: "Saco Bay Provisioners is a nonprofit Maine company producing quality products for the discerning customer. Your purchase of products supports people with physical, mental and acquired disabilities." Susan Percy, Executive Director, explains that a fear of "exploiting" their beneficiaries made the decision difficult, but that the organization believed that the value of promoting their work in terms of a high-quality Maine product made the tag's social "hook" acceptable.

Once you've decided if and how you'd like to communicate your social mission to the public, put the traditional tools of public relations to work; it's by far one of the best ways to stretch your marketing dollars.[55] Start by recognizing that you've probably got the basis for something that most reporters want—a good story. Next, help the media turn your story into "news" with a positive spin. Like any company, you can send out press releases promoting your "new" programs or products, giving lots of specifics about what makes them newsworthy. As a social entrepreneur, you're probably even better positioned than most companies to host an event that the public should hear about. Don't forget that politicians love to publicly support good causes at such events and that where politicians go, the media follows. If your social endeavor is underpinned by research or if you think the outcomes of your work are something to crow about, try preparing intriguing information in an easy format for the local newspaper or television station to use. Or use a classic nonprofit asset, the volunteer. Suggest profiling a superstar volunteer or warn a junior reporter that 50 employees from a local company will be painting your homeless shelter on Saturday morning with a great photo opportunity (talk about reciprocal goodwill!). Here are a few tips to make sure your great story makes it to your customers' eyes and ears:

- ✔ Target your efforts to the magazines, newspapers, television, or radio programs that are most likely to be seen by your customers.

- ✔ Get familiar with these publications and shows. What kinds of stories do they include? Are they analytical? Lots of human interest? Do they have monthly new product features?

- ✔ Ask how you can help the journalist. Talk briefly with the editors. Ask for writers' guidelines and other information to help you prepare your press release appropriately.

- ✔ Start to network and build relationships with the media. Tap into relationships already cultivated by Board members and other stakeholders in your organization.

- ✔ Remember that you don't buy public relations. Be flexible and work with journalists even if they don't want to put your organization on the front page—every little mention helps awareness.

- ✔ Make it easy on the journalist. Pull together a one-page fact sheet. Facilitate access to anyone in your organization. Suggest great photo opportunities.

- ✔ Focus on what you're trying to market and structure easy ways for the story to include these specific benefits. Depending on your goals, you may highlight the benefits of your social programs or focus on the biggest selling points of the craft items whose sales support your mission.[56]

action
step   Answer the following questions:

✔ How would promoting our social mission affect our most valuable customer segments?

✔ What is our organization's social mission public relations policy? Has it been revisited in the last three years? If not, revisit this policy.

Now think about the last year. What "news" did you not publicize that would have had good public relations value? Think of this year. What is the key message you would like to communicate? Go through your calendar to identify three potential news items that would showcase that key message. Lay out an action plan for getting at least one of those stories placed where your most valuable customer segment will see it.

SUMMARY

Social entrepreneurs have energy, conviction, creativity, compassion, drive—you name it, you've got it. A conscious customer focus can channel *all* of these resources in a single direction, creating an incredibly powerful force for social good. Here are keys to finding and maintaining that focus:

✔ *Identify your customers.* Separate your customers into distinct groups that you can picture, reach, and, above all, understand. Figure out what type of customers you serve most effectively, ask yourself why, and use that knowledge to serve your "best" customers exceptionally well and to improve your service for others.

✔ *Research—don't assume you know what customers value.* Dig into information sources. Observe. Most important, ask your customers! Listen attentively to their answers and get to know the people who make up your market . . . and who will determine your success.

✔ *Meet your customers' priorities.* Once you've grasped what your customers value, make sure you provide it in big and little ways. Constantly be on the lookout for better ways to delight your customers.

✔ *Market your competitive advantage.* Identify how you can serve your customers more effectively than anyone else can. Make sure potential customers know just how well you could meet their needs.

✔ *Use price to help accomplish your goals.* Select the pricing tactics and price levels that support your overall strategy.

✔ *Create a strong brand image.* Define, communicate, and manage your organization's name and reputation. Ensure that your customers' experience is consistent with the image you strive to convey.

✔ *Market your mission.* Decide how and when publicizing your social mission will further your goals. Employ public relations tactics to translate your mission into free marketing.

Endnotes

1. J. Gregory Dees, "A Customer by Any Other Name," *Who Cares Magazine,* 1998.
2. Adapted from speech by Maxene Johnston, "Tackling Social Ills with Business Skills," in Philip Kotler and Alan Andreasen (eds.), *Strategic Marketing for Nonprofit Organizations* (Englewood Cliffs, New Jersey: Prentice Hall, 1991), pp. 58–59.
3. Jed Emerson, "Social Return on Investment: Exploring Aspects of Value Creation in the Non-Profit Sector" chapter in upcoming publication by the Roberts Enterprise Development Fund (San Francisco: REDF, 2000).
4. R.E. Gruber and M. Mohr, "Strategic Management for Multiprogram Nonprofit Organizations," *California Management Review,* Spring 1982. v. 24.
5. Sharon Oster, *Strategic Management for Nonprofit Organizations* (NY: Oxford University Press, 1995), p. 93.
6. Alan Andreasen, *Cheap but Good Marketing Research* (Dow Jones-Irwin, Homewood, IL, 1988) describes several options and "how to do" basic market research in layman's terms. It is very useful to have such a guide in hand if you're looking to do this research inhouse; we think it's often a viable option.
7. Alan Andreasen, *Cheap but Good Marketing Research* (Dow Jones-Irwin, 1988), p. 65.
8. CACI has developed a segmentation of U.S. households into 62 neighborhood types called ACORNS. Look for their Website and free neighborhood profiles at www.demographics.caci.com.
9. Alan Andreasen, *Cheap but Good Marketing Research,* p. 87.
10. Joshua Macht, "The New Market Research," *Inc.,* July 1998, p. 86.
11. Joshua Macht, "The New Market Research," p. 86.
12. See Andreasen's *Cheap but Good Marketing Research* or other introductory guides for valid do-it-yourself market research.
13. Thomas Billitteri, " 'Branding': A Hot Trend for Charities," *The Chronicle of Philanthropy,* May 20, 1999, online version.
14. Jessica Hale, "The Secret Ingredient," *Business Start-Ups Online,* December 1997, online version.
15. Carla Goodman, "Can You Get There From Here?" *Entrepreneur Magazine,* online version, "Tips Archive."
16. Carla Goodman, "Can You Get There From Here?"
17. Alan Andreasen, *Cheap but Good Marketing Research,* p. 186.
18. Adrian Slywotzy and David Morrison, *The Profit Zone* (New York: Random House, 1997), p. 23.
19. Adrian Slywotzy and David Morrison, *The Profit Zone,* p. 82.
20. Amanda Dargan and Steve Zeitlin, "The Culture Catalog," in *Lessons Learned: Case Studies by the National Endowment for the Arts Publications* (http://arts.endow.gov/pub/Lessons/Casestudies/CityLore.html).
21. Adrian Slywotzy and David Morrison, *The Profit Zone,* p. 22.
22. Christine Letts, William Ryan, and Allen Grossman, *High Performance Nonprofit Organizations* (New York: John Wiley & Sons, 1998), p. 98. Letts, Ryan, and Grossman's work builds on Ellen Greenberg's earlier discussions of "Competing for Scarce Resources" (*Journal of Business Strategy,* 1982) and Sharon Oster's treatment of competition in Chapters 3 and 4 of *Strategic Management of Nonprofit Organizations* (Oxford, 1995).

23. Tom Stemberg with Stephanie Gruner, "Spies Like Us," *Inc.* magazine, August 1998, p. 45.
24. Jessica Hale, "The Secret Ingredient," *Business Start-Ups Online,* December 1997, online version.
25. Michael Porter and Anne Habiby, "Understanding the Economic Potential of the Inner Cities," *Inc.* magazine, May 1999, p. 49.
26. Emily Barker, "The Old Neighborhood," *Inc.* magazine, May 1999, p. 65.
27. Jay Conrad Levinson, *Guerilla Marketing Excellence* (Boston: Houghton Mifflin, 1993), p. 116.
28. Adrian Slywotzy and David Morrison, *The Profit Zone,* p. 293.
29. Adrian Slywotzy and David Morrison, *The Profit Zone,* p. 26.
30. Adrian Slywotzy and David Morrison, *The Profit Zone,* p. 99.
31. This entire discussion of the value of pricing for a nonprofit draws on the discussion in Sharon Oster, *Strategic Management for Nonprofit Organizations* (Oxford University Press, 1995), p. 98–102.
32. Adapted from Sharon Oster, *Strategic Management for Nonprofit Organizations* (Oxford University Press, 1995), p. 101.
33. Laura Hirschfield, "Richard Hugo House: A Study in Social Entrepreneurship," in *Lessons Learned: Case Studies by the National Endowment for the Arts Publications* (http://arts.endow.gov/pub/Lessons/Casestudies/Hugo.html).
34. Excerpt from Planned Parenthood's "Mission Statement" at www.plannedparenthood.org/about.
35. Barbara Elliot, "A Job Tree Grows in Brooklyn" on Center for Renewal's website, January 1997 (http://centerforrenewal.org).
36. Jonathan Levine, "Customer, Sell Thyself," *Fast Company,* No. 3, p. 148.
37. Carrie Portis and Kristin Majeska, "Managing Key Relationships with the Rest of the World: Lessons Learned (the Hard Way) by Social Purpose Enterprises" in *Social Purpose Enterprises and Venture Philanthropy in the New Millennium: Practitioner Perspectives* (Volume 1) (Roberts Enterprise Development Fund, San Francisco, 2000), p. 73.
38. Interview with Rick Surpin, founder of Cooperative Home Care Associates.
39. Cheryl McManus, "Customer Bait," *Inc.* magazine, July 1999, p. 93.
40. Joshua Macht, "The Inner City 100: Creative Instincts," *Inc.* magazine, May 1999, p. 73.
41. V. Kasturi Rangan, Sohel Karim, and Sheryl Sandberg, "Do Better at Doing Good," in *Harvard Business Review on Nonprofits,* pp. 167–190. Modified diagram pp. 174–175 (Harvard Business School Press, 1999), also available for $5.50 as a reprint from the May-June 1996 *Harvard Business Review.*
42. "The World's Greatest Brands," *Fast Company,* August 1997, online.
43. Mercer Management Consulting, "Managing Brands as Strategic Assets," *A Mercer Commentary,* 1997, p. 1.
44. Thomas Billitteri, "'Branding': A Hot Trend for Charities," *The Chronicle of Philanthropy,* May 29, 1999, online.
45. Thomas Billitteri, "'Branding': A Hot Trend for Charities."
46. Thomas Billitteri, "'Branding': A Hot Trend for Charities."
47. Thomas Billitteri, "'Branding': A Hot Trend for Charities."
48. Thomas Billitteri, "'Branding': A Hot Trend for Charities."
49. Alan Webber, "What Great Brands Do," *Fast Company,* August 1997, p. 96.
50. The *Guerilla Marketing* series by Jay Conrad Levinson provides particularly useful practical advice and "how-to" suggestions. Also refer to *Inc.* magazine's *301 Do-It-Yourself Marketing Ideas: From America's Most Innovative Small Companies.*
51. See the *Guerilla Marketing* small business series written by Jay Conrad Levinson (Boston: Houghton Mifflin).

52. Alan Andreasen, "Profits for Nonprofits: Finding a Partner," in *Harvard Business Review on Nonprofits* (Harvard Business School Press, 1999), pp. 117–118, also available for $5.50 as a Nov.-Dec. 1996 *Harvard Business Review* reprint.
53. Andreasen, pp. 126–130.
54. FND Carrie Portis and Kristin Majeska, p. 67.
55. Many resources aimed at small businesses, like the Levinson *Guerilla Marketing* series, are applicable to this aspect of your marketing.
56. Includes some tips from Gene Koprowski, "Smart Companies Use Public Relations Tactics to Get Good Ink," in Dallas Murphy, *The Fast Forward MBA in Marketing* (New York: John Wiley & Sons, 1997), p. 132–135.

Chapter 9

FINANCIAL MANAGEMENT

Tom McLaughlin, Manager, Management Consulting Services,
BDO Seidman, LLP

IN THIS CHAPTER

The only five financial reports you'll ever need
The basics of financial management
Keeping track of it all (cost accounting)
The price of success (isn't terribly high)

You don't start the climb up Mt. Everest with just energy and enthusiasm. You need to know that you can trust your colleagues, your equipment, your supplies, your plans, and your support network. In short, you have to be able to trust your systems. It's the same way with social enterprise. Okay, maybe the Mt. Everest thing is overdoing it, but you get the idea.

Financial demands are implicit in virtually all of the components of social enterprise. They are particularly important in innovation, resourcefulness, and accountability. Innovation is nearly impossible when finances are in chaos. What may look like innovation in the face of financial crises is really just clever reactionary management. Resourceful managers know how to recognize and use their financial strengths to their advantage.

Traditional ideas about accountability play out a bit differently for social entrepreneurs because accountability in traditional nonprofit funding is almost always associated with accountability to external funders or regulators. In traditional nonprofit funding, external funders often predefine the need as well. Government agencies do that all the time when they issue Requests for Proposals for specific programs. By contrast, social entrepreneurs rarely get proof of the need and the funding for it tied up in the same tidy package, so internal financial accountability is critical. Financial systems must be in place, financial information flow and budget management practices must be sound, and there must be a heightened sense of mutual accountability to make it all work smoothly. All of these factors have operational implications that we will consider later.

Effective social entrepreneurs know their financial resources without being unduly constrained by them, so a lot of the work in the financial area of social enterprise consists of knowing what you can take for granted in your own organization. Your financial management system already has to be working well, or else you need to first spend your time making it better.

tool of the trade   In all of the examples in this chapter, we refer to the Federal IRS Form 990, the nonprofit corporate equivalent of the IRS Form 1040 that we all put in the mail on April 15. (By the way, nonprofit corporations have it easier than us individuals. The 990 isn't due until the fifteenth day of the fifth month after the end of the fiscal year.) When we quote a ratio or make a point, we'll often include the exact number of the relevant line from the 990.

THE ONLY FIVE FINANCIAL REPORTS YOU'LL EVER NEED

Controlling a nonprofit's finances is only possible if you have the right information at the right time. Who gets these reports and when they get them is as important as what they are because different people need different types of information about their respective areas of responsibility.

Here are the five reports:

- ✔ *Balance sheet ("Statement of Financial Position").* This is the window into the nonprofit's financial health. It lays out lots of good, cumulative information about the assets and liabilities of the organization and is the source for many of the components of the financial ratios described later in this chapter.

- ✔ *Profit and loss statement (Statement of Activities).* On an agency basis, this statement should show the extent of the organization's profitability. Individual program statements of profit and loss do the same thing and should go to every manager whose program produces receivables.

- ✔ *Aged receivables.* Especially for nonprofits engaged in fee-for-service work or social enterprises that receive some of their revenue on a credit basis, this report is invaluable. It should show the age of agencywide unpaid bills in 30-day increments for each major revenue category. As in the previous report, program managers should get their own targeted version of this report.

✔ *Cash-flow projection.* It's much easier to plan for a cash-flow disaster than to be surprised by one. Someone familiar with your nonprofit's operations should be putting together a cash-flow projection stretching out one year in advance, or at the very least every quarter.

✔ *Utilization report.* This will vary in every setting. It should specify information about the quantity of services provided and other critical data as needed. As a bonus, these kinds of reports also help spot trends and opportunities.

The following grid helps show key points about financial report distribution. Take it as a guide, not a prescription.

Report	Who Should Get it	When
Balance Sheet	CEO, Board	Monthly, but should be available on demand
Profit and Loss	Corporate: CEO, Board Program-based: individual program managers	Monthly, but should be available on demand
Aged Receivables	Corporate: CEO, Board Program-based: individual program managers	Monthly, but should be available on demand
Cash-Flow Projection	CEO	At least quarterly
Utilization	Corporate: CEO, Board Program-based: individual program managers	Monthly, but should be available on demand

EXHIBIT 9.1   Key points on financial report distribution.

THE BASICS OF FINANCIAL MANAGEMENT

Here's the simplest, quickest, most revealing test of your financial statements that you can do without a calculator. Find the balance sheet, which on the 990 starts with line 45. Run your finger down the list of end-of-year assets from lines 45 through 58. Let it stop on the single largest number in that range. *Whoever controls that asset controls the organization.*

Think about it. If the single largest asset is cash, whoever controls cash flow has a lot to say about the agency. If it's a large endowment held as a portfolio of stocks (line 54), whoever controls that portfolio sits firmly in the driver's seat. If the largest single number is in accounts receivable—the money owed to the agency for services already delivered—then whoever owes that money essentially controls the organization.

What does this mean for social entrepreneurs? It's straightforward: get the support of whomever controls the largest asset before embarking on a social entrepreneurial journey. Better still, *be that person.*

In general, you should already know whether your organization manages its finances well. Are financial reports available when you need them? Do they give you valuable information? Can your financial management people use your systems to produce special reports? Are your yearly financial audits surprise-free? If you answered "yes" to all of these questions, the chances are that you have adequate financial systems in place.

A CASH SYSTEM OF ACCOUNTING? OR ACCRUAL?

From the grocery store bagger, you get a choice—paper or plastic. Not so for nonprofit financial management systems. Accounting systems are maintained on a cash basis or on an accrual basis. Using the accrual method should be automatic. In cash systems, money is not considered to have been received until it exists in cash, and expenses aren't real until the checks that paid them have cleared. This distorts both incoming and outgoing resources. Accrual systems provide far more accountability and accurate reporting by documenting such things as revenues that are owed but have not yet been received (accounts receivable) and expenses that are owed but haven't yet been paid (accounts payable). Paper or plastic may be a tough choice, but accrual versus cash for nonprofits is easy.

FINANCIAL RATIOS

In addition to these quick tests for busy people and/or math phobics, you can calculate various financial ratios to analyze your financial statement more deeply. Generally, these ratios produce information about three categories of financial health: liquidity, capital structure, and profitability.

The following ratios use column B (End of year) from the 990 balance sheet for all balance sheet calculations unless indicated otherwise.

Liquidity

core concept

Liquidity measures the ability of an organization to take actions in the short term via cash or liquid assets. Mostly these actions are routine ones such as paying bills and covering payrolls, but they can also include major organizational life events like buying a vehicle or a piece of property. Cash is king (or queen, if your organization is a matriarchy) in a nonprofit. With it, you can do practically anything. Without it, you stagger.

Some important indicators of liquidity are as follows:

Current ratio

RATIO: Current Ratio

CATEGORY: Liquidity

FORMULA: $\dfrac{\text{Current Assets}}{\text{Current Liabilities}}$

FORM 990 FORMULA: $\dfrac{\text{sum of lines (45 to 54)}}{\text{sum of lines (60 to 63)}}$

SAMPLE RATIO: $\dfrac{(29{,}000 + 139{,}800 + 12{,}000 + 10{,}000)}{132{,}000} = 1.45$

What Is It

The current ratio is probably the most widely recognized measure of liquidity. This simple calculation—made easier since most audited financial statements have subtotals for both current assets and current liabilities—matches the short-term assets of an organization with the liabilities that it expects to face during the same period.

The power of this ratio lies in its simplicity. "Current" for most industries is defined as one year so, in effect, it selects a 365-day timeframe and asks, "During this period of time, how do the resources that can be converted to cash compare with the liabilities that we know will be coming due during the same period?"

What It Should Be

The conventional wisdom is that this ratio should be at least 2:1, that is, for every dollar of liabilities coming due there should be at least two dollars of assets available to pay them. Generally speaking, the higher the ratio the better—to a point. An excessively high current ratio can actually be a problem (and a sign of management timidity or inattentiveness) if it means that unneeded assets are being allowed to build up in short-term forms instead of being invested for longer term results.

The nature of the nonprofit agency's need for cash is critical to a sensible interpretation of this ratio. Nonprofits with substantial amounts of complicated billing procedures need to have a stronger ability to meet short-term fluctuations in liabilities than those that get half of their revenues in cash at the door.

What It Is Not

This is actually a rather crude measure. Lumping a large number of asset categories into "current" masks the lack of meaningful liquidity that characterizes some of them. Inventories, for instance, do not typically get turned into cash easily—nor should the ongoing agency want to convert them because they are presumably essential to continuing service delivery.

Fortunately, the inventory consideration is irrelevant for many nonprofits, and so the current ratio is as useful as anything one might need.

For groups needing a more fine-tuned measure of liquidity where inventory is an issue, try the acid test:

$$\frac{\text{Cash + Marketable securities + Receivables}}{\text{Current liabilities}}$$

Working capital—you may have heard that phrase before—is simply current assets *minus* current liabilities.

Days' cash

RATIO: Days' Cash

CATEGORY: Liquidity

FORMULA: $\dfrac{\text{Cash and Equivalents} \times 365}{\text{Operating expenses} - \text{Depreciation}}$

FORM 990 FORMULA: $\dfrac{(45 + 46) \times 365}{(17 - 42)}$

SAMPLE RATIO: $\dfrac{(29,000) \times 365}{(1,019,400 - 26,000)} = 10 \; days$

What It Is

Deprived of food, the human body proves surprisingly resilient. It slows its pace, shifts its focus, changes its systems. When the nourishment resumes, it readily returns to its former rhythms. The same is true for the nonprofit organization and its supply of cash. Deprived of cash, the entity adjusts its systems and compensates. This is a natural phenomenon, at least in a management sense, so the important question is, How long can it continue if the cash somehow gets completely shut off? The days' cash ratio gives that answer.

Think of days' cash as the number of days of average size cash disbursements the organization can withstand without any cash income. If a nonprofit spends $10,000 per day on average over a year and it has $200,000 of cash and cash equivalents on hand, it has 20 days' cash.

What It Should Be

To some extent, higher is better. However, by itself, the number doesn't tell us much, since it is pretty unlikely that incoming cash will be completely shut off for an extended period of time. What makes the number so useful is that it can be a good benchmark. In fact, the days' cash ratio is helpful mostly in the context of comparative analysis.

What this means is that industry norms are essential to full usage of days' cash calculations. While some clear-cut inferences can be drawn from the ratio in a vacuum, the deepest insights come from careful comparison with similar organizations. If nothing else, calculating this average helps focus management on how close to the bone their cash flow is running. Cash balances can be an eye opener, especially in a larger organization, but this number will cut through all of the fantasies and tell you exactly where you stand.

Days' receivables

RATIO: Days' Receivables

CATEGORY: Liquidity

FORMULA: $\dfrac{\text{Accounts receivable} \times 365}{\text{Operating revenue}}$

FORM 990 FORMULA: $\dfrac{47c \times 365}{(1d + 2 + 3)}^{*}$

SAMPLE RATIO: $\dfrac{139{,}800 \times 365}{(974{,}700 + 37{,}700)} = 50 \text{ days}$

---

*The idea here is to use only revenue sources that typically generate receivables. Lines 1 and 2 on Form 990 also include grants, which typically are not considered receivable in the same way as invoices; however, "government grants" is a bit of an old-fashioned phrase that often means "government contracts," so it is usually safer to include line 1c. This part of the formula requires judgment.

What It Is

This is a multipurpose ratio if ever there was one. In one number, this measure not only says some very significant things about the size and nature of the bills owed to the organization at any one time, but it also offers insight into the effectiveness of financial management systems as well as management philosophy.

To get the days' receivables, take the total amount of accounts receivable and divide it by the average amount of billings generated each of the 365 days of the year.

What It Should Be

Lower is better. Time is definitely money, and the less time it takes to collect one's bills, the more cash one is likely to have on hand. In turn, that means more cash to be turned into another productive form of asset—such as investments—rather than being tied up in non–revenue-producing receivables.

Days' receivables can offer a terrific window into management styles. A bloated number can mean bloated and inefficient billing systems (which probably implies some combination of poor personnel preparation and supervision, weak administrative systems, inadequate computer technology, or inattentive management). On the other hand, there's some fine irony here. A ratio at or lower than the industry standard in an otherwise lackluster set of ratios can actually mean not efficient management but a desperate, hand-to-mouth, beg-the-clients-we've-got-a-payroll-to-meet-tomorrow style of management.

practical tip   A tip. Ballooning accounts receivable represent one of the best areas for a new manager to make fast progress in halting a financial slide. Most agencies have little or no idea how long it takes them to collect their bills, and many don't understand how necessary it is to care. Or rather, they don't sense how important it is to keep receivables under control. Sometimes all it takes to improve the situation is to begin tracking the days in receivables (also called the collection period) and to set a lower target for the chief financial officer to hit.

What It Is Not
As presented, the days' receivables doesn't reveal anything about the quality of the bills. For that, one needs: (1) access to the internal records, and (2) knowledge of the industry. To some extent, one can count on the organization's auditors to insist that receivables that will never be collected get thrown out of the total count, but if the auditors don't understand the industry—or if management is determined to finesse them—the total amount of accounts receivable will be inflated.

Analyzing your agency's liquidity is a worthwhile undertaking, but what can you do about it if the results aren't to your liking—or if you simply need cash to undertake a social enterprise? Here are some suggestions:

✔ *Make a profit.* This year's excess of revenues over expenses can be used for next year's investments.

✔ *Collect the amounts owed to you faster (reduce accounts receivable).* Tighten up your billing systems and policies. Try to get cash up front; check for possible bad credit risks before delivering services; computerize your billing system. An inexpensive method is to calculate your days in receivables and tell the business manager he or she will get evaluated favorably if that ratio improves by 20 percent this year.

✔ *Stretch your payables.* Some nonprofits automatically pay their bills as soon as they receive them even if the vendor doesn't expect payment for several more weeks. Use the invoice scheduling feature on your accounting software to slow down the cash outflow. Just make sure you don't exceed your vendors' payment terms, or this will be a self-defeating strategy. Alternatively, try to negotiate longer payment terms without any charges.

✔ *Reduce your inventory.* If you must regularly maintain a substantial amount of goods in order to provide your services (such as a vocational workshop program), try to shrink it. Same goes for any equipment you may use. Note: relatively few nonprofits need substantial inventory or production equipment, so this may not be viable.

✔ *Negotiate better financing.* Any time you borrow money, the interest payments add up quickly. See if you can reduce the interest charges by aggressively shopping the loan, or simply by asking to renegotiate. Better still, borrow large amounts of money via traditional capital markets ("the bond market"). If your agency is too small to issue its own bonds (90 percent of all nonprofits are too small), check around to see if your statewide association or some other group can assemble a pooled bond issue in which multiple smaller non-profits participate in a single bond issue to drive down rates.

✔ *Get it donated.* Okay, so it doesn't happen very often that a friendly local foundation is willing to drop a few hundred thousand dollars into your agency and let it sit there for five years to cushion your social enterprises. But maybe you can find some in-kind services that can be donated, or possibly a piece of equipment, a building, or something similar. The ability to offer donors a tax deduction is an advantage that only nonprofit public charities have, so you might as well try to use it.

MAKE OR BUY?

It's the classic business question. Do you provide your own services and products, or do you acquire them from others? The question takes on special importance for social entrepreneurs because they usually must favor flexible options, payment plans that save cash, and staged commitments of resources.

Capital Structure

core concept The next most important financial health category is *capital structure*. Why is capital structure so important to a nonprofit? All organizations need capital to acquire assets such as equipment and buildings, and simply in order to provide a solid foundation for the agency. Nonprofits, however, cannot simply sell shares to raise capital since—by definition—they cannot be "owned" by individuals. The only alternative short of finding a foundation willing to drop a few hundred thousand dollars into your organization and let it sit there for a few years is to generate it yourself out of either profits or loans. Many funding sources want to limit nonprofits profitability, and banks will always cap the amount they're willing to lend, so nonprofits have relatively few options for building an adequate capital structure. Following are some ways to measure the adequacy of your capital structure:

Cash Flow to Total Debt

RATIO: Cash Flow to Total Debt

CATEGORY: Capital

FORMULA: $\dfrac{\text{Net income + Depreciation}}{\text{Total liabilities}}$

FORM 990 FORMULA: $\dfrac{18 + 42a}{66B}$

SAMPLE RATIO: $\dfrac{34,000 + 26,000}{132,000} = 0.45$

What It Is

Having liabilities means being obligated to pay them off. One of the quickest tests to use to understand something about the nonprofit's capital structure is the contrast between profit and depreciation as sources of cash and total liabilities. This ratio puts a slightly different twist on the idea of internally generated cash. What it asks is how much free cash is available each year to satisfy the liabilities on record. As will be seen in later chapters, profit creates cash for the nonprofit. Since depreciation is an expense that is not paid for in cash, it too leaves cash in the organization. Together, these two sources of cash are measured against the total liabilities of the organization.

What It Should Be

Higher is better. This is one ratio where most nonprofits will not score high because their net incomes are usually relatively low. Still, profit and depreciation are inescapable sources of cash regardless of tax status, so the ratio is a fair indicator of capital structure.

Debt to Fund Balance (Net Assets)

RATIO: Debt to Fund Balance (Net Assets)

CATEGORY: Capital

FORMULA: $\dfrac{\text{Long-term liabilities}}{\text{Net assets}}$

FORM 990 FORMULA: $\dfrac{64a + b}{74}$

SAMPLE RATIO: $\dfrac{0}{77,800} = \text{NA}$

Note: To get a more precise number, add the end of the year's net assets to the prior year's net assets and divide by 2. This gives a more accurate picture of the average net assets.

What It Is

Straight from the for-profit world (where fund balance or net assets means equity), this ratio says something about the amount of long-term indebtedness an agency carries in order to do its business. Long-term debt means money loaned for any purpose with a payback period longer than one year, so the debt/fund balance ratio stacks an organization's total indebtedness against its accumulated net worth, or fund balance. Another way to think about it is that it pits borrowed funds against "owned" funds. If an organization is highly leveraged—meaning that it has borrowed lots of money—you'll see it here.

What It Should Be

This one is important for itself. Lower numbers indicate low debt loads. Since the number is expressed as a percentage, it's easy to compare it with other nonprofits' debt/fund balance ratios. Industry ratios help put the answer in perspective, but the heart of the question is simply how high the number goes.

Perhaps not surprisingly, the best results here are well under 1.00. Accumulated wealth is not as desirable in a nonprofit setting as it is in a proprietary one, yet it's still nice to know that the total amount borrowed is less than the corporation's "net worth."

Again, some careful interpretation is necessary. Many nonprofits operate in fields where little capital investment is required, so the debt/fund balance ratio should be low and even irrelevant. Sometimes the board is debt-shy and refuses to authorize any long-term debt if they can possibly avoid it. Other groups must invest heavily in equipment and usually have to borrow to do it, so the issue for them is more like the nature of the debt and how one nonprofit's debt load compares to its peers.

The other consideration here is what happens to this ratio over time. Look for the relationship between this ratio and the strategic direction of the organization. If conditions warrant expansion, expect the number to increase, probably for several years. If debt is declining or gets restructured, you'll also see some change. Remember that a significant change in *either* direction in debt load will translate into a significant increase or decrease in the dollars paid out of operations for interest.

Incidentally, you can reverse this ratio and get an equally useful number showing how many times the fund balance covers the long-term debt level.

Total Margin

RATIO: Total Margin

CATEGORY: Profitability

FORMULA: $\dfrac{\text{Revenue} - \text{Expenses}}{\text{Revenue}}$

FORM 990 FORMULA: $\dfrac{18}{12}$

SAMPLE RATIO: $\dfrac{34,000}{1,053,400} = 3.2\%$

A FEW OTHER THINGS TO LOOK AT IN THE AUDITED FINANCIAL STATEMENT

Check your opinion letter, which is the signed letter from your auditing firm that can be found just under the cover of your financial statements. Does it say that your financial statements were "audited"? If it says that they were "reviewed," you can't rely on the information as fully as necessary. In a later paragraph, it should also say something to the effect that "management's financial statements present fairly" the condition of the agency. If there is doubt expressed about the organization's ability to "continue as a going concern," regard this statement as the equivalent of a ringing fire alarm.

✔ Calculate the elapsed time between the last day of your fiscal year (usually stated in the first paragraph of the opinion letter) and the date of the letter itself. The date of the letter is the last significant day that the audit team spent on site and therefore is considered to be essentially the end of the audit. If there is more than about 90 to 120 days between these two dates, one of two things may be true: (1) either the audit team forgot to show up on schedule (unlikely, since they get paid to do these things), or (2) your agency was not prepared to be audited on schedule. Find out which one it was.

✔ Read the notes at the end of the financial statement. If any of the following things apply, it's worth some more exploration.

—Related party transactions (for example, a professional services contract between the agency and the executive director's spouse). Not inherently wrong or even unethical, just worth investigating.

—A statement of long-term debt where the numbers in future years *increase.* This means increasing indebtedness; if this is known and there's a plan in place to deal with it, fine. If not, it's another warning sign.

—A maxed-out line of credit—means the agency desperately needs cash. Not a good time to be thinking entrepreneurial thoughts.

—Unresolved lawsuits.

Profitability

core concept

Finally, we get to *profitability,* or "the bottom line," as breathless media types like to call it. While the average seventh grader knows the formula for the total margin—total revenue minus total expenses divided by total revenue—nonprofits have another profitability formula they can use: profit from operations.

The operations profit margin considers that nonprofits derive revenue from other sources besides those services strictly provided in return for money. The proceeds from fundraising and from unearned sources such as interest or rents are classic examples of this type of nonoperating revenue.

More than a few nonprofits lose money on their operations and make it up by fundraising. This is a classic pattern, and there's nothing inherently wrong with it. But an agency interested in social entrepreneurial activities that consistently loses money on its operations and makes it up through fundraising has a potential weakness because it depends on the largess of third parties to be profitable. Perhaps more important, there may be a subtle organizational ethic that accepts program losses as unavoidable. This could be dangerous in an entrepreneurial context.

Total Margin ("Profit")

RATIO: Total Margin
CATEGORY: Profitability

FORMULA: $\dfrac{\text{Revenue} - \text{Expenses}}{\text{Revenue}}$

FORM 990 FORMULA: $\dfrac{18}{12}$

SAMPLE RATIO: $\dfrac{34,000}{1,053,400} = 3.2\%$

What It Is
This is the bottom line, the one editorial writers point to with gusto, the one that tough, no-nonsense managers of all stripes supposedly focus on single-mindedly. It's what is left over after subtracting all the expenses from all the revenue, then dividing that number by all the revenue. It's the fundamental profitability indicator, and the IRS requires you to show half the math just by filling out the Form 990 anyway.

What It Should Be
Higher is better, up to a point. While most nonprofit managers now recognize the necessity of at least trying to turn a profit each year, that accomplishment is merely a condition of nonprofit business, not the purpose of it.

The logical question is, "How much profit is enough?" The answer is, "What do you need it for?" Since most types of nonprofit corporations can't sell stock and since most foundations are not keen on the idea of contributing working capital (to put it mildly), profit is one of the few ways that the organizations can generate cash for investment, innovation, or capitalization. Generally speaking, the more stable and unchanging the organization, the less there is a need for profit. Nonprofits planning expansion, new ventures, or just trying to build a more reliable future will need higher total margins. Specific industry standards, if available, will give excellent guidance on exactly how much profitability similar groups enjoy.

Operating Margin
RATIO: Operating Margin

CATEGORY: Profitability

FORMULA: $\dfrac{\text{Operating revenue} - \text{Operating expense}}{\text{Operating revenue}}$

FORM 990 FORMULA: $\dfrac{(1d + 2 + 3) - (13 + 14)}{(1d + 2 + 3)}$

SAMPLE RATIO: $\dfrac{(974,700 + 37,700) - (785,100 + 130,800)}{(974,700 + 37,700)} = 9.5\%$

What It Is
Push to the next level of analysis by calculating the operating margin. As useful as it is, the total margin can disguise some critical things going on

in the organization. For instance, one organization experienced a giant deficit one year. Fortunately for them, that was the same year that some recently departed soul left them a more than giant bequest. One more than giant bequest minus one giant deficit equals one small profit. For one year, at least. But such good fortune masked a problem with their underlying economics that the operating ratio would have revealed.

What this ratio asks is that we compare all the revenue derived from operations against all the expenses associated with those operations. This means eliminating any revenue gained from fundraising as well as dividends, extraordinary income, and so on. To be fair, it also means eliminating identifiable expenses associated with that fund-raising. Sometimes this subtlety is not possible because data the outsider gets often does not separate out fund-raising expenses reliably (although the Form 990 does). This will tell us the true profit, minus all of that fund-raising noise.

What It Should Be

There's a funny thing about this ratio; old-timers, especially those serving on boards, often feel proud of a high level of fund-raising (i.e., a negative operating margin). And, indeed, doing a substantial amount of fund-raising is something to be proud about. But it means that the agency is extremely dependent on its contributors. Looked at another way, whoever contributes the operating revenue is unwilling or unable to pay full freight. The continued existence of the services is at the mercy of the tastes—and means—of those third-party contributors.

The answer to this dilemma only sounds evasive: The operating margin should be exactly where the organization wants it to be. Either the corporation willingly relies on fund-raising to supplement a chronically negative operating margin, or it uses fund-raising to pay for the difference between merely good programs and great ones. It's an individual choice—no one size fits all—but it should be a conscious, deliberate choice.

Portfolio Management

One of the quiet realities of nonprofits is that they do what for-profit financial types call portfolio management. If you think of a nonprofit's group of programs and services like a portfolio of stocks and bonds, it is easy to imagine that some programs and services will be profitable while others may be sure money losers. This is to be expected. The difference between for-profits and nonprofits is that the latter can expect to keep providing the money-losing services—*if* doing so is necessary for the community or helpful to the agency in other ways. The trick is to balance the money losers with an equivalent weight in profitable programs.

For further thoughts on this nonprofit "portfolio" approach, see Sharon Oster (*Strategic Management for Nonprofit Organizations,* Oxford Press, 1995) or Robert Gruber and Mary Mohr's article "Strategic Management for Multiprogram Nonprofit Organizations" in the spring 1982 *California Management Review.*

WHAT ABOUT STARTUPS?

All of these comments apply to ongoing entities, usually entrepreneurial programs within established agencies (for-profit types call this "intrapreneuring"). But what about social enterprises that are starting from the very beginning? For them, financial ratios aren't going to mean much until they have been established for a while. Startups by definition won't have any benchmarks available to them, but they can still use ratio analysis. The first step is to make financial projections for the first three years, and the next step is to apply the ratios to understand the financial underpinnings of your strategy. True, financial projections are almost certain to change, but the discipline of putting into numbers a specific three-year financial plan can be helpful in identifying strengths and weaknesses of your model, and to help you begin thinking about the various scenarios that may unfold.

To Profit or Not To Profit, and How Much?

The term *nonprofit* is most unfortunate in one way because it seems to imply that these types of organizations cannot make a profit. In reality, nonprofits must make a profit the same way that every other economic entity needs to make a profit. It's just that nonprofits can't pay out any of that profit in the form of dividends to shareholders (because they can't have shareholders).

Some people believe that nonprofits "shouldn't" make a profit. Their reasoning is that a single dollar of profit means that the organization could have provided another dollar's worth of service. While laudable in intent, this attitude is very shortsighted. Nonprofits need the extra cushion of a profit for growth, reinvestment in tangible assets, improvements in cash flow, and for many other operational needs large and small.

How much profit is enough? This is the key question, and unfortunately it has to be answered with an unsatisfying *it depends*. A fast-growing organization needs to be as profitable as possible to help fund the growth; so does a nonprofit that has borrowed a significant amount of money. Entrepreneurial nonprofits should be as profitable as possible to help lessen their dependence on outside sources. But a nonprofit that feels it has reached a comfortable size, has little or no debt, and has a good niche for its services doesn't need very much profitability at all. In the end, the answer to this question is a highly individualized judgment call.

Using Financial Ratios To Benchmark Your Organization

Financial ratios are powerful in and of themselves, but using them as benchmarks will help amplify and clarify their message. There are two types of benchmarks: internal ratios, especially over a period of years, and external benchmarks. An internal benchmarking program identifies a set of meaningful ratios for a nonprofit and then tracks them over time. By getting familiar with their meaning and regularly compiling and analyzing your nonprofit's profile, you can easily see the effects of seemingly unrelated decisions and the outcomes of financial policies.

The second and even more powerful approach is to gather the same information about many other organizations and compare them to your own. Of course, getting that information may not be easy. Some cities and states maintain public databases based on financial reports filed by nonprofits that provide them with services. If that's not possible, check with associations, accounting firms, and other industry advisors to see if they keep such information.

KEEPING TRACK OF IT ALL (COST ACCOUNTING)

Once you have the enterprise up and running, you'll need a system for keeping track of costs associated with it. There are two characteristics of costs associated with running entrepreneurial activities. First, it's critical to know the cost of your efforts to help decide whether to expand, contract, or end the program altogether. The second characteristic is that it's an extremely difficult thing to do, and few organizations can do it satisfactorily.

Here's a subtle reason why cost accounting is so important. Many readers interested in social enterprise have a lot of experience with traditional government-funded programs. In these arrangements, the government actually does a lot of the work for the nonprofit. Specifically, it demands cost reports, which it uses to do things like set rates and conduct research for related programs. But this effectively means that the nonprofit doesn't have to think about things like pricing and profitability, and it doesn't get into the habit of building systems to respond to market conditions because it only needs to please its government funder.

When the open market is the ultimate determinant, as in social enterprise, the nonprofit's cost management muscles may be flabby. Often it will think only about cost tracking and management as though it were just another program on which it must report rather than one that must be actively managed.

Why won't existing accounting systems produce adequate reports? In practice, good accounting systems should be capable of producing many usable reports, but these are about financial matters. What entrepreneurs need—and what they probably understand intuitively—is information about *economics*. It isn't enough to know what it cost the food service program to operate last month; what's important is knowing why catering 200-person banquets is less profitable than 12-person dinner parties.

The solution to the dilemma depends on a variety of factors. In some cases, it may be practical to build a cost accounting system, and there may very well be tools available to do that. Any type of production environment, for example, may be able to use one of the many manufacturing job costing and tracking software packages on the market today. In other cases, it may not be practical to do anything more than improvise a system based on accounting information and whatever else is available. The key is to be aware of the need and to take steps even before starting the enterprise to ensure the availability of usable cost information.

LOSING THE HIDDEN GOVERNMENT SUBSIDY: STABILITY

Traditional nonprofit management usually relies on heavy government funding, and why not? Who else in our society has the incentive to put large amounts of money toward devalued populations such as youthful delinquents or disabled people? The nonprofit service providers who work in these areas get obvious benefits each time they deposit a government payment for their services, but they also get something far less obvious: revenue stability. Social entrepreneurs often have no such stability, and in fact must prepare themselves for what could be the most volatile swings in revenue (and expenses and capital investments) of any programs they manage. Nothing wrong with that—it's part of the charm of social enterprise. Be prepared for it by testing out various financial scenarios, doing traditional break-even analysis, and gaining a full understanding of what the enterprise means for the rest of your organization.

THE PRICE OF SUCCESS (ISN'T TERRIBLY HIGH)

No good deed goes unpunished, so if your organization finds that its social enterprise is wildly successful, you'll need to think about a topic that otherwise doesn't get much air time in nonprofit management—taxes— Unrelated Business Income Tax, or UBIT to be specific.

When this happens, the first thing to do is to stop hyperventilating. You're already in thin air and it's not good for you. These are *taxes* we're talking about, not matters of life and death. They are the product of other human beings, they have their own special logic, and they're not nearly as intimidating as some people might want you to believe.

THE UBIT STORY

In the ordinary course of things, Uncle Sam and his various nieces and nephews in state and city governments claims the absolute right to tax the profits that corporations make (notice that we said "profits," not "revenue"—a time-honored American tradition to tax the dollars that land on the table after expenses, not the dollars that go into the machine in the first place). In the case of nonprofit organizations, especially public charities, which are supposed to be organized to serve the public, our good Uncle voluntarily gives up that right to tax profits. This is why nonprofits are also known as tax-exempt organizations.

There is one catch. In return for giving up the right to tax profits, Uncle Sam asks that nonprofits operate within their intended missions. (To make things easy, we're going to speak about nonprofits as being equivalent to public charities, although that's not precisely true—lots of nonprofits are not public charities—but for our purposes the difference is immaterial.) If the nonprofit ever operates outside of its mission and makes a profit doing so, it may have to pay what is called Unrelated Business Income Tax.

core concept What is an *unrelated business?* That is the heart of the question. According to the IRS (and they're the boss when it comes to these kinds of definitions), it is a regularly carried on activity unrelated to the charitable mission that produces income from the sale of goods or services. Note that we've only talked about income, not profits. Taxes aim at profits, but we haven't gotten there yet.

Let's suppose that a major university law school decided to hold a really big yard sale to help raise a few million dollars. Are the profits from the yard sale subject to UBIT? No, because yard sales are not traditional commercial activities carried on to produce income.

Now let's suppose that that same law school figured out that it would be a lot easier to raise a few million dollars if they owned a pasta factory and simply funneled the profits into the school. Is this arrangement subject to UBIT? As it turns out, this is the actual case that caused Congress and the IRS to establish the concept of UBIT. New York University Law School for a time actually owned the C. F. Mueller Company, a major maker of pasta, and the lack of clarity in the law at the time prompted the UBIT provisions that we know today. This story is all true, except that this all happened so long ago that they called it macaroni, not pasta.

Here's a list of business activities that would be considered related or unrelated to select nonprofits:

What's Related
- ✔ Student tuitions
- ✔ CDs made by the symphony
- ✔ Trade show revenues
- ✔ Products made by handicapped clients

What's Unrelated
- ✔ Fair market rent from tenants that don't expressly serve the landlord's mission
- ✔ Most mailing list rentals
- ✔ Sale of advertising

Tom McLaughlin Knows Profit When He Sees It

First, a bias. Taxes don't scare me. I don't like them, of course—who does?—but I can live with them. It helps that, one way or another, taxes help support most of my clients. So I've made a kind of peace with them. I'll take every break legally available to me, but in the end if there's genuine corporate profit left over, I'll take my lumps on it. Just apply the rules fairly and universally.

Many years ago I ran a trade association's insurance program. We offered all kinds of insurance to our nonprofit corporation members. Through a combination of one very smart move (made by my predecessor, I'll admit) and a very nasty national insurance crisis, we were the only source for nonprofits in our state to get insurance coverage. Naturally, we insisted that any organization taking advantage of our insurance program be a member of the association. So we took in lots of dues. Plus, our insurance company reimbursed us for the expenses associated with running the program.

For two or three years, we were in Fat City. Our functional profit margin on the program could be politely described as obscene. The members and their money rolled in, we all looked like heroes, and we were able to do lots of things that we couldn't otherwise have done for our members.

The point is, we were making so much money on this program that our lawyers and accountants started getting that little frown they tend to get when they smell profit in a nonprofit. They showed us how to take every break legally available to us—and still we had lots of leftover profit. They were extremely worried, but we dealt with the problem in what was apparently an innovative way—*we paid the tax*. Simple. The IRS was happy, the lawyers and accountants were puzzled but relieved, and we still had lots of money left over to pay for our good work. More important, the world didn't end.

Okay, we know you're wondering. Yes, eventually the bubble burst and we went back to being a mildly profitable insurance program, but that's a story for another day.

HOW MUCH IS THE TAX?

The basic formula for determining any corporate tax is the same: revenues less IRS-approved ("qualified") expenses equals taxable profit. There is always the possibility of argument over the precise definitions of each of these terms, of course, but that may get worked out in each situation. The tax rates on UBIT are based on the amount of net income reported and are the same as the tax rates on net income of for-profit corporations. The first $1,000 is exempted, then the tax rates increase in increments as the amount of profits increase.

Get Qualified Advice

Most nonprofits, and even many nonprofits running social enterprises, will never need to be bothered with UBIT matters. Startup situations usually lose money anyway, and even profitable ongoing social enterprises may not make more than a small profit at best. Nevertheless, the best strategy is to secure a qualified advisor ahead of time. Even if you never get much beyond the base camp, it's a wise idea to know the terrain.

SUMMARY

Every organization, whether it's a commercial or a social enterprise, needs to have accurate and timely financial information to help decision makers direct the allocation of resources. If information is inaccurate or late, not only may clients lose out, but the organization itself may soon find itself in jeopardy. In this chapter, we reviewed the five most important financial reports for social enterprises, and we learned about the basics of financial management. We considered the importance of cost accounting, and we took a close look at a tax that strikes fear in the heart of nonprofits everywhere—Unrelated Business Income Tax, or UBIT.

Ready for the journey? Okay, let's break camp. On to the summit!

Key points to remember are as follows:

✔ Effective social entrepreneurs know their financial resources without being unduly constrained by them.

✔ To be effective, a social enterprise demands thorough accountability.

✔ Keep a close eye on your liquidity, capital structure, and profitability.

✔ Have an ongoing system of internal financial reports.

✔ Get qualified advice.

✔ Don't be afraid of UBIT.

Chapter 10

PLANNING FOR THE SOCIAL ENTERPRISE

Jeanne Rooney, Vice President and Director UMB Bank
Nonprofit Financial & Advisory Services

IN THIS CHAPTER

Business planning: Why?

Business planning: How?

Business planning: Whatever the purpose, no matter what the scope, it works

Business plan for the social enterprise: The document

Comparing a social enterprise plan with a traditional business plan

All types of organizations, both nonprofit and for-profit, in all stages of development, from startup to growth to maturity, can benefit from the discipline of business planning. Social entrepreneurs can benefit from developing a business plan whether they are starting up a new nonprofit or growing an existing nonprofit. A business plan can be valuable to social entrepreneurs who want to explore the possibility of starting up a for-profit, which will be related to and support an existing nonprofit.

To complement the existing literature on business plans, throughout this chapter the term *business planning* will be used to refer to all of these reasons for planning. *Business* and *business plan* are equally relevant to the nonprofit and the for-profit, whether starting up or seeking growth. To bridge the language of the nonprofit and for-profit sectors, the terms *social enterprise* and *social enterprise plan* are occasionally used instead.

BUSINESS PLANNING: WHY?

The conventional wisdom today is that anyone starting a new venture—or moving an existing organization into a major, new direction—should draft a business plan first. Why? The business plan, and perhaps even more important, the *process* of developing the business plan, can be powerful tools for creating clarity in direction, real knowledge about the organization and its marketplace, strong commitment by all of the stakeholders, and energy for action.

Business plans are the direct link from an organization's strategic plan to all other types of planning. An effective business plan provides an operational framework that ensures that decisions about customers, products and services, and human and financial resources are correlated with the strategic vision and mission. A good business plan invites—and even inspires—a cornucopia of public interest and investment in the organization.

This chapter is intended to invite—and even inspire—you to learn about business planning, to understand how it can be readily adapted to a social enterprise, and to incorporate this powerful tool into the repertoire of your organization. So, let's get started!

THE VALUE OF COMPLETING A BUSINESS PLAN

As defined in Chapter 1, "Social entrepreneurs recognize and relentlessly pursue opportunities without being limited by resources currently in hand, and are guided by an explicit mission to create and sustain social value." If social entrepreneurs are doing this, how do they explain it to someone else?

Social entrepreneurs do not allow their own initial resource endowments to limit options. In the absence of sufficient financial or other resources, entrepreneurs mobilize the resources of others to achieve their entrepreneurial objectives. How are they going to convince the "others" that they should invest resources in the social enterprise?

Chapter 1 also describes being a change agent as one of the roles of social entrepreneurs. The description includes: "Exhibiting a heightened sense of accountability to the constituencies served and for the outcomes created. Taking steps to ensure that the social enterprise is creating value. Seeking to provide real social improvements for customers and communities, as well as an attractive social and/or financial return to investors."

Business planning, both the process and the resulting documents, can be incredibly powerful and positive tools for change agents. A business plan is not just one forecast about one program, one function, or one resource. Instead, it is a blend of the expectations about multiple factors into one plan framing the future. The frame is built with key stakeholders, moving toward the shared vision, making daily decisions, and measuring success. The plan is a prompt for identifying, evaluating, and acting on opportunities.

Through business planning, social entrepreneurs can better understand the connection between the end and the means.[1] They can start to close the gap between where the social enterprise is and where they want it to be. The targeted readers of the social enterprise plan can be inspired to take the requested action.

There are many reasons for completing a business plan, including the following:

✔ *Attracting investment.* The social enterprise can easily find itself competing with other nonprofits and perhaps even with commercial enterprises for scarce financial and human resources, and customers. Most investors aren't in the habit of giving money away to anyone who just asks; they expect thoughtful and well-presented business plans. Investors in social enterprises are increasingly adopting this same philosophy, and they are more and more receptive to—and sometimes demanding—business plans. If social entrepreneurs plan to set up a for-profit company, a business plan is essential to expanding the range of options for acquiring capital, including traditional sources such as banks.

✔ *Identifying risks.* A conversation about uncertainty and risk might seem theoretical, even philosophical, but if risks are ignored in the startup, development, or growth phases of a social enterprise, they rapidly become very real. See Chapter 6, "Understanding Risk," for a discussion of the imperative to identify and reduce risk. When considering a move into any type of unfamiliar territory, social entrepreneurs should not rely simply on their gut instincts. The business planning process is an excellent tool for minimizing risk. Through the use of narrative, assumptions, and financial forecasts, the impact of various risks can be determined and documented. As long as the nature and potential impact of the risks are anticipated, they won't take social entrepreneurs and stakeholders by surprise.

✔ *Measuring outcomes.* Nonprofits and their investors are radically and rapidly shifting toward outcomes-based, rather than needs-based, approaches to funding. Effective business planning includes not only insights about customer needs and the benefits provided by the product or service, but also forecasts of the results of successfully meeting those needs. Businesses rely heavily on financial forecasts, and so too should the social enterprise. Other important forecasts include market position, customer satisfaction, and market share. Because the social enterprise has "double bottom lines"—social *and* financial—its business plan should include forecasts of outcome evaluations and other measurements of social value. See the section later in this chapter entitled "Comparing a Social Enterprise Plan with a Traditional Business Plan" for additional ways in which business planning can include the development of social results and social value added.

✔ *Using a business approach.* In conjunction with the outcomes-based approach to funding, the nonprofit sector is sometimes embracing, sometimes tolerating, openness to experimentation with market-based approaches and businesslike methods. The business planning process envelops many business and market subjects, issues, and questions, so it is a good way to experiment with and to continue to develop new perspectives. Many investors, customers, Board members, and volunteers are businesspeople; the planning process can be particularly beneficial if it includes these major stakeholders and uses language that bridges the perspectives of the business and nonprofit worlds.

✔ *Showcasing the management team.* Business planning—both the document and the process—is a demonstration of entrepreneurs' ability and potential to achieve their missions. Social entrepreneurs showcase their skills by clearly identifying the issues; leading the stakeholders through the requisite research, thinking, and decision making; and laying out substantial plans.

✔ *Building alliances.* Both nonprofits *and* businesses have discovered that collaborations are often the only way to leverage resources to tackle complex markets and issues. Increasingly, investors in social enterprises are seeking evidence of collaboration to ensure maximum utilization of their investments. Business planning is an excellent way to get all of the parties involved to focus on the collaboration itself and to reduce misunderstandings and enhance the accountability of each.

✔ *Checking thinking.* Planning within the framework of the widely accepted business planning model ensures that the critical questions have been considered—and answered, if necessary. Social entrepreneurs know that the necessary subjects have been addressed, the logic seems sound, and the plan appears feasible. Business planning helps social entrepreneurs avoid the continuation of "what we've always done," and the easy and dangerous "let's just add 10 percent to this year's plan." A good plan can be a touchstone for social entrepreneurs, to keep them from drifting too far afield into unrelated or unproductive activities.

✔ *Checking feasibility.* Preparing a business plan forces the testing of market viability and financial stability of the product or service and, indeed, the entire social enterprise. A business plan ensures that the product and service plans are correlated with the strategic

REJECTING ONE IDEA: FINDING THE NEXT

Bonnie Bellehumeur is the President and CEO of Second Harvest of Wisconsin, a food bank. When Bonnie entered the Denali Fellows, she was sure that her business plan was going to be about starting a grocery in the central city, providing lower prices, higher quality, and greater selection than what was currently available. She started her market research and found that the major grocers had discovered that they could do the same thing and make a profit. Bonnie said, "I couldn't compete with them. I was devastated. Timing is everything. I should have started the grocery years ago when I first thought of it." The Denali Fellows challenged Bonnie to identify another opportunity to assess. She took a new look at one of Second Harvest's small programs and realized that it had the potential to serve new types of customers in the nationwide marketplace. Bonnie reported that the discipline of doing market research and getting feedback from the planning team "gave me the encouragement to think big, then even bigger and to see that it might be doable."

plan and integrated with the financial plan. It is a way to confirm the adequacy of the management, human resources, and marketing plans supporting the product or service development and delivery.

BUSINESS PLANNING: HOW?

There is a right way and a wrong way to approach the business planning process. In this section, we'll find out how to create the right kind of business plan in the right way, and how to stay motivated throughout the process.

THE RESISTANCE TO STARTING A BUSINESS PLAN

Most entrepreneurs are so excited about their product or service that they are convinced the marketplace will feel the same. Most social entrepreneurs are so passionate about their mission and so concerned about the needs of their customers that they are completely focused on getting their program to as many customers as possible. So why take the time to plan?

Even without planning, individuals have successful careers, entrepreneurs find a market for their products and services, and social entrepreneurs serve community needs. Could these individuals have reached even higher goals if they had planned? Are they ignoring the even greater accomplishments of the entrepreneurs who did effective planning? Perhaps.

In 1997, the Small Business Administration published a study of businesses that met criteria for longevity, viability, and growth. Eighty percent of those successful small businesses reported that they had prepared a business plan. So, given this overwhelming evidence that creating a business plan can help lead to a successful enterprise, why do people resist planning?

In some cases, entrepreneurs might *know* that planning is important, but *feeling* like actually undertaking a planning effort might be elusive to them. Action-oriented social entrepreneurs might have a natural resistance to anything that sounds like it could be bureaucratic. Because planning implies potential change, the reluctance to do planning might be a form of resistance to change. This type of resistance can be felt by social entrepreneurs, staff and/or Board members. The resistance to starting might be the result of previous bad experiences with the planning process. Such a person might think the following regarding planning:

1. It was a waste of time. The future is never what you expect. Things change so rapidly that any planning is outdated before it's completed.

2. We hired some consultant to come in and write the plan, then we never used it.

3. We spent a lot of time writing a plan, then it sat on the shelf in a three-ring binder.

4. It was too complex, too difficult, and too time-consuming.

5. Lots of successful businesses don't do planning, so why should we?

All of these unsuccessful experiences can—and do—happen in real organizations. Business planning is similar to any other organizational process in that it might not be understood or implemented properly, or it might be approached with low expectations that doom it to failure. The same thing, for example, can happen with client intake, volunteer management, and grant writing. If an organization's leadership team is not committed, its staff is not well-trained, and the expected results are not clearly defined, then any process can be ineffective.

So, how can this negative thinking be avoided?

1. *Plan no farther ahead than the next three to five years.* Longer-term plans are more speculative and subject to change, and therefore less useful to most organizations.

2. *Involve stakeholders in developing the business plan.* This includes an organization's executive director, staff, Board of Directors, and

representatives of customers, volunteers, and the community. A consultant can be engaged to guide the stakeholders through the process, but a knowledgeable consultant will not do the business plan *for,* but rather *with* the stakeholders.

3. *Integrate business planning into the mainstream of operations.* If planning is set up as a parallel process that never intersects with the program development or budgeting processes, then chances are the plan won't be used once it's completed.

4. *Use the plan.* If the members of an organization put a lot of time and effort into the business planning process, they will be much more energized and agreeable to future planning efforts when the plan is actually used by an organization rather than simply filed away.

The simple fact is that business planning is not as hard as it looks. It's like starting, building, and maintaining a personal fitness program. A lot of information is available on what to do and even how to do it, and plenty of computer programs and Websites are available to help walk you through the process. Check out the appendix for a listing of some of the best business planning resources on the Internet.

GETTING STARTED ON A BUSINESS PLAN

Okay. You understand the value and the challenges of business planning—now what should you do? Remember that the results you're looking for in

action step

the business planning process come from actually *doing* the business plan, not just *thinking* about doing it.[2] Here's a step-by-step approach:

1. *Make the commitment.* You have to want to do it.

2. *Review previous planning efforts.* Remind yourself of the resulting accomplishments. Identify the resistance you previously encountered in getting started, following through to completion, and/or following up with implementation. Anticipate the current resistance, and address it directly.

3. *Make sure that it is* your *business plan.* You must be involved, perhaps even leading the entire process. You have to understand the questions, reflect on the answers, and be relatively certain about the decisions that result.

4. *Develop a "plan to plan."* Incorporate intensity, frequency, and duration of your and your stakeholders' involvement in the process. You must make space for planning. Structure and celebrate early success. See the following section for ideas on how to break business planning into more manageable pieces.

CASE STUDY

FOUR BUSINESS PLANS IN SEVEN YEARS: THE VALUE OF COMPLETING A BUSINESS PLAN

Sandra Sanders is a believer in business plans. She has been involved in preparing four of them in the last seven years! For example, the Women's Employment Network (WEN) is a Kansas City nonprofit that provides resources to low- to moderate-income women seeking employment. A Board member encouraged Sandra, at that time WEN's Program Director, to investigate the global growth of microenterprise and see how WEN could support it in Kansas City. In 1993, Sandra attended the FastTrac Entrepreneurial Training and Development Course, offered by the Kauffman Center for Entrepreneurial Leadership at the Ewing Marion Kauffman Foundation. Her plan focused on the feasibility. Sandra said, "It was of great value to the WEN board in making their decision. They were able to assess the financial risks and decided that they didn't want to take them."

Nonetheless, during the FastTrac course, others became aware of the microenterprise concept, and potential investors stepped forward. A separate nonprofit, the First Step Fund, was set up.

In the meantime, Sandra became the Resource Development and Planning Manager for the Francis Child Development Institute at Penn Valley Community College, one of the Metropolitan Community Colleges in Kansas City. The Institute's major investors, the Francis Families Foundation and the Metropolitan Community Colleges, were poised to make significant investments; however, they wanted to "see the plan." Using Sandra's experience with the First Step Fund and the guidance of a consultant, the Institute prepared a business plan that captured the status of the Institute, the opportunities for growth, and the limitations of its current resources, especially its facilities.

Soon thereafter, the investors made multimillion-dollar investments in a new facility and long-range commitments to the Institute's operations. Carole Ellison, the Institute's recently retired Executive Director, and Sandra *know* that the business plan was the key to the investors' understanding of what the Institute is all about and the resources needed to secure the Institute's position. Sandra observed: "Many nonprofits had been doing strategic planning, which can seem fuzzy. Business planning is more hands-on, more direct. You really have to think. You are forced to ask why you are doing something. There is more clarity about making a decision to pursue funding."

5. *Learn about business planning and get support.* Arrange for outside support. Social entrepreneurs should not, and probably cannot, do an effective business plan alone, so the next step is to talk with the key stakeholders so that they understand the value and the challenges of business planning. With the commitment and involvement of this key group, you will be enthusiastic about getting started and finishing. Contact nonprofits in your community whom you respect and who have effective planning skills, or a Board member, staff member, or volunteer. Ask them to share their process and their documents with you.

6. *Survive interruptions.* Do not let feeling guilty because of interruptions keep you from restarting the planning process. Chances are, during the interruption, you learned something relevant to your plan.

The preceding sections of this chapter describe many of the incentives for business planning. Astute social entrepreneurs recognize that significant effects often have significant causes. In this setting, a worthwhile business plan is usually the result of a worthwhile process for developing it.

The flexibility in the purpose and scope of business planning allows the following actions to occur:

✔ *Entrepreneurs and their teams do not have to wait until everything is planned before they act.* They can be doing as they are planning. They do not "stop everything" to plan. They do not need to spend months planning "something." They know that it doesn't have to be perfect before they can act. During the process, they notice immediately actionable research, contacts, and improvements.

✔ *Indeed, the plan itself never has to be considered "done" in order for business planning to have a significant impact on the social enterprise and its stakeholders.* The process can trigger positive and high energy among the parties involved. And the energy can quickly start rippling throughout the enterprise.

✔ The emphasis should be on making the business planning process work for the organization, not on adhering to a cumbersome procedure or burdensome detail.[3]

What is "good" business planning? The answer highly depends on the needs of the social enterprise. In addition to the "Value of Completing" described in a preceding section, good business planning probably should generate the following activities:

✔ Opening and enhancing multidirectional communication among the stakeholders—all of the parties critical to the success of the social enterprise.

✔ *Asking challenging questions.* Learning the answers. Knowing more about the social enterprise and its marketplace.

✔ *Tying together market feedback and financial projections* so those opportunities that are feasible—and those that are not—are identified.

✔ *Giving the stakeholders clarity* about how the social enterprise can move rapidly toward its social mission.

✔ *Developing a framework for interpreting new information.* Social entrepreneurs and their teams recognize when new information and changes impact their business plan. The new information might remind them of a question that was initially marked as "not applicable," and should now be considered.

Business planning should be one of the skills of social entrepreneurs. They should gather the resources they need to "Just Do It" and gain the personal experience.

Entrepreneurial Energy

The Kauffman Center for Entrepreneurial Leadership at the Ewing Marion Kauffman Foundation sponsors the national dissemination of the Fast-Trac Entrepreneurial Training and Development Program. FastTrac II is an 11-week course during which the entrepreneurs of existing small businesses learn how to prepare their first business plans.

One of the courses is located at the Kauffman Foundation in Kansas City, Missouri. Fifty entrepreneurs fill the training room, arranged in small groups of ten. Each group has a business counselor—who is either an entrepreneur or an expert in small business—and there are two instructors. Guest entrepreneurs and experts are invited to visit the class, and on any given night, close to 60 entrepreneurs and their advocates are gathered together. The room literally rocks with entrepreneurial energy!

The students come early to network with each other and to meet with their counselors. The place seems to explode at the quick dinner breaks, during which everyone eagerly shares their ongoing, real-time stories. Often, students report that they didn't complete their homework because they took what they learned in the last class and implemented it in their business the next day! The students stay late, often to the point that the staff gives up and leaves them in the care of the security guard. Many of the entrepreneurs start doing business with each other, have reunions for months, if not years, and even merge their businesses.

Although the stated goal of the course is to prepare a business plan, realistically, only a good first draft can be completed within the 11 weeks.

Nonetheless, the testimonials and the subsequent successes of the alumni strongly indicate that the value of the course was immeasurable. For example, in interviews with the media, the alumni repeatedly volunteer that the FastTrac course was a turning point in working toward their missions.

What happened? At the end of the class, the students didn't have fancy documents, but they did just experience a challenging, dynamic, and invigorating process—one that they could continue within their businesses—the business planning process.

Suggestions for Getting Started

"Stop approaching ventures as 'if we are doing good, it will work.' Look to business and how they make decisions. Start to borrow the best, but keep the heart of your work. If you don't adopt the best business practices, that's OK, but be sure to know why not. Get a really good consultant. Develop an ongoing relationship with them. They provide a reality check. They will ask you questions that even a foundation might not think to ask."—Sandra Sanders, Resource Development and Planning Manager, the Francis Child Development Institute at Penn Valley Community College, one of the Metropolitan Community Colleges

"I did my business plan mostly myself. Someone else can do it for you, but you won't understand it, or be able to explain it to investors. I do recommend coaches. If you keep quiet about what you are doing, then it won't progress. Talk to as many people as you can. They will give you affirmations and corrections. The plan will be better. The Denali Initiative was wonderful. Jeffry Timmons' *New Venture Creation* has real-life examples of business plans. When I saw them, I thought, 'I can do that!' A wonderful Board member walked me through all of the financial section."—Bonnie Bellehumeur is the President and CEO of Second Harvest of Wisconsin, a food bank in Milwaukee

Writing a business plan "would have been lonely" if I hadn't had my advisory panel. "It was an energizing process. One of our Board members is a former successful greenhouse entrepreneur and a current Ph.D. in horticulture at Kansas State University. He helped me with all types of market research and Department of Agriculture statistics. The Kansas City area floral buyers for a grocery and a hardware national chain store were on my panel. Don Wise, our former Executive Director, who built the current greenhouse, helped me. I didn't even know the questions to ask about finances. One of the Denali Initiative faculty showed me that while the financial analyses were the most difficult, they were also the most helpful part of the business plan."—Dennis Vanderpool, Executive Director, Associated Youth Services in Kansas City, Kansas

BUSINESS PLANNING: WHATEVER THE PURPOSE, NO MATTER WHAT THE SCOPE, IT WORKS

Business planning works—it's just that simple. But, to create a winning business plan, we have to first learn more about the process. In the sections that follow, we'll do just that.

BUSINESS PLANNING: WHEN?

The Massachusetts Institute of Technology's Enterprise Forum encourages and assists fast-growth businesses. In a highly respected related book, the authors state: "Every organization should have a business plan to guide its operations and ensure its viability and growth."[4] "We are convinced that individual businesses always differ enough that to attempt to fit them all into a common cookie-cutter format is ridiculous and risks glossing over important individual issues and giving undue emphasis to minor subjects. Nevertheless, in identifying the principles which we believe guide the investment process, we have sought to be specific."[5]

By considering the guiding principles of business planning, avoiding a "fill-in-the-blanks" approach, and repeatedly practicing effective planning, entrepreneurs have learned that the business plan approach covers a wide range of business situations, including the following:

- ✔ Startup for-profits and nonprofits
- ✔ Existing for-profits and nonprofits seeking growth and/or additional financing, whether equity, debt, or grants
- ✔ Existing nonprofit starting up another nonprofit or a for-profit, as either a stand-alone legal entity or as a subsidiary of the existing nonprofit
- ✔ National nonprofit: Starting a new or growing an existing chapter
- ✔ Any stage of the nonprofit's or for-profit's life cycle of development, growth, and maturation
- ✔ Any point along the social enterprise spectrum described in Chapter 1, "Social Entrepreneurship," whether purely philanthropic, completely commercial, or somewhere in between in generating revenues and offering products/services
- ✔ Whether breaking even or generating net income to invest in the social mission
- ✔ New activities within existing for-profits and nonprofits, for example, new products, services or programs, new targeted market segments (customer groups), or a new facility

✔ Department-by-department within a large organization

✔ An alliance among any number and combination of for-profits and nonprofits

Regardless of the purpose or scope, all of these situations must address the following items: management and organization, the market, customers and competitors, the product or service, development and delivery, finances, growth, and exit strategy.

This flexibility allows entrepreneurs to get started on planning by trying it with a small part of the organization. Instead of preparing a business plan for the entire organization, entrepreneurs can practice the business planning process on one existing program, service, or product that they want to grow or a new one that they would like to add.

Business planning: For whom?

For any of these situations, there is also a range of readers and users of the business plan. Although the most common reader of the plan is the potential investor, a surprising number of plans are prepared for other reasons, such as the following groups:

✔ Existing investors and funders

✔ Existing/potential major vendors, customers, partners, and agents

✔ Internal use, by the staff, Board, and volunteers

Often, a basic business plan is customized for various readers. For example, a foundation might be interested in general information about a social enterprise, but it might be specifically interested in financing a specific program. A bank might want to know about the synergies between a for-profit company and its nonprofit parent, but it might be specifically interested in the viability of the for-profit as a stand-alone business.

A business plan can easily be customized to the level of sophistication, level of detail, and type of format that the readers and users find most useful. Although all of this flexibility is attractive, social entrepreneurs must remember that for any specific business plan, the purpose and scope must be clearly stated.

Business planning: How often?

Once is not enough. Many entrepreneurs are rightfully proud of having completed a business plan, especially one that they really use, but the luster is tarnished when they explain that it was done 10 years ago, and they haven't done another one since. Although the purpose and scope of the original business plan might no longer be relevant, the need for current business planning continues. Organizations change, and business plans have to change along with them.

Although entrepreneurs should be "using" their business plans daily, they do not need to update the business plan document itself every time they get new information or make new assumptions. An annual review is about the right frequency. Entrepreneurs should compare what has actually happened with what the business plan predicted would happen. And as needed by the Board, management team, and investors, they can prepare a report explaining both planned accomplishments and unplanned developments. Social entrepreneurs should use this comparison as an opportunity to learn more about the organization, to change assumptions, and to modify future planning.

BUSINESS PLANNING: HOW MUCH?

Despite the high value of a business plan, do remember that it is a *plan*. If circumstances change so that the assumptions and plans are no longer valid, then do not feel obligated to carry on with them. Instead, use the new information as an opportunity to discuss the changes needed with stakeholders and to update the business plan and the related action plans.

 Social entrepreneurs should accept and even embrace the fact that things do change, but now they have a framework within which to adapt to the change. They can adjust to market feedback and adapt ideas as they go along.

The overriding goal should be to maintain good planning skills. This depends on acquiring the skills, then generalizing them. Entrepreneurs should push the edges of the way they currently use planning. Any variation in what they do now makes their planning skills more flexible and adaptable to future changes.[6]

BUSINESS PLAN FOR THE SOCIAL ENTERPRISE: THE DOCUMENT

What is a "good" business plan? It has the following qualities:

- ✔ A working document that becomes dog-eared, not dusty.
- ✔ *A document that captures the entire social enterprise, or every important aspect of a new service, or the synergies of a collaboration.* It breaks a large and complex organization into manageable pieces that people can get their arms around.

Growth

In 1998, Dennis Vanderpool became the Executive Director of Associated Youth Services (AYS), which now operates a 5,000-square-foot greenhouse and can boast of several graduates employed with local commercial greenhouses. Dennis launched AYS's second business planning cycle five years after the first. At first Dennis thought that he was just looking for ways to refine the greenhouse model. Then he started focusing on the fact that while the greenhouse was a great learning experience for the youth, there were not enough greenhouse jobs in the community for the graduates. And the size of the greenhouse was limiting the ability to financially support it, let alone anything else in AYS.

Dennis said that the business planning helped him "think bigger, stretch the limits of possibilities, think more creatively, and think about those things that nonprofits don't even imagine are possible." For example, "changing the culture from 'scrimping' along and doing with less than adequate to risk managing something new and big, generating profits, and upgrading resources." Significant growth has been planned to address the two major concerns described above. Stay tuned.

✔ *A set of complementary objectives.* The plan focuses on a few major, quantifiable opportunities rather than many less significant projects.

✔ Integrated words and numbers, thinking and talking.

A good plan should be one of the tools of social entrepreneurs. They should gather the resources they need to "Just Do It."

Business planning resources

Businesses have been preparing business plans for decades. As a result, many good resources are available to you, but to put together a winning plan, you do not have to read dozens of books on how to do it.

This does not mean, however, that you can simply complete a generic fill-in-the-blanks business plan template, or that you can engage an outside business plan consultant to write a standard one for you. Instead, you should complete the following tasks:

action step

✔ Buy a well-written book that includes the many difficult questions you must answer about each business plan subject.

✔ Use well-developed software that requires you to make market and financial assumptions and offers you the opportunity to develop multiple scenarios, or "what-ifs."

✔ Engage a knowledgeable consultant who guides you and your key stakeholders through a rigorous business planning process, and encourages you to write your own business plan.

This chapter cannot begin to cover the smorgasbord of all the subjects, issues, questions, research, and forecasts that should be considered for inclusion in a business plan. Social entrepreneurs should get a good book and good advice and start through the suggested points.

A business won't find every suggested point relevant, nor will a social enterprise; however, the lists of subjects are not to be taken lightly. The guidance and lists are meant to prompt readers to consider if this is a subject or a question that they have overlooked or don't know about. The readers should take the time to see if the subject could be interpreted or adapted to their social enterprises. For example:

✔ *Many business plan books are oriented toward products, including manufacturing, assembly, and logistical issues different from those faced by a business providing a service.* But when the book asks about product development, the service provider should not dismiss the question. How will the service be developed? For example, what expertise is needed to research the customers' needs, infuse knowledge into the new programs, develop materials, and train those who provide the services? Are pilot tests, test markets, and a controlled rollout needed? What is the timeline for the service development?

✔ *Most of the books include a section for "exit strategy."* This might be one of the paradoxes of entrepreneurship—planning the development and growth of a business while wondering how it might "end." Of course, for a high-growth, high-tech business that is seeking venture capital and the near-term possibility of "going public," the exit strategy is of immediate concern. For other entrepreneurs who foresee long-range involvement in the business, exit might better relate to risk assessment. For example, what if adequate financing is not available, or if revenues do not meet minimal requirements? Although the organization might not be shut down, should a specific service or a type of customer be abandoned?

✔ With the purpose and the scope of the business plan in mind, social entrepreneurs come up with a workable list of information, decisions, and plans that should be included in the business plan.

The traditional business plan

The following is a list of the generally accepted subjects that should be included in the business plan. It is *not* an all-inclusive example of the points that should be considered for inclusion in each section.[7] Be sure

tool of the trade

to refer to other, more complete business planning resources before you start.

1. Executive summary
   - Write it so that it could stand alone.
2. Description of the business
   - What is the nature of the business? What does it do and for whom?
   - Describe the opportunities that are the reasons for writing the business plan.[8]
   - What industry is this business in? What is the maturity of the industry? What role in the industry does this business play?
   - What are the products and services provided and why are they needed?
   - What is the business' stage of development? What is the stage of development for each major product or service?
   - If the plan is for other than an entire business, describe the fit of the smaller part into the larger structure.
   - Provide a summary of the strategic plan.
   - Provide a history of the business to the extent that it is relevant to the future.
3. Management and organization
   - What relevant expertise does each member of management bring to the business? Who does what, why, and how?
   - Outline the compensation packages.
   - How does the organization grow with the business?
   - Describe the management information systems.
   - What relevant expertise does each member of the Board of Directors bring to the business?
   - What are the significant liability, legal, insurance, and tax issues? How are they handled?
4. Market
   - Customers
     - —Describe the customers who could be served, then the targeted market segments, both current and desired.

—Define the needs and wants of the customers.
- Describe the features of the product or service and their benefits to the targeted customers.
- Competitors
  —Who are the competitors? What are their products and services? What markets do they serve? What are their revenues, shares of the market, and gross profit margins?
  —What are the competitors doing that makes them successful?
  —What is the nature of future competition?
- Market position: current and desired
  —What is unique about this business? What makes the products and services different?
  —What is the size of the market within which the business is operating? What share of the market could be secured?
- Pricing
  —What is a unit of sale? What pricing method is used to set its value to the market?
  —Are prices different across market segments?
  —How does the price compare with the competition?
- Marketing and sales: current methods and plans
  —Include public relations and advertising.
  —What expertise (internal and external) is needed for these functions?
  —Does the business depend on repeat customers or continuous new customers?
  —How to market "the message?"
- Support all of the above with market research and analysis that makes the data relevant to this business; in other words, perform fact-based decision making.

5. Product and service
   - For each product/service, what are the processes, resources (i.e., human, technical, capital, and financial), and costs involved from the research to the receipt by the final customer?
     —Development and testing
     —Manufacturing and assembly
     —Delivery
   - How are product performance, quality of service, and customer satisfaction measured? What have been the results? What are the planned changes?

- Describe intellectual property issues, both as a holder and a user of such rights.

6. Assumptions (These are critical and are too often overlooked or underprepared.)
   - The basis for estimating all of the significant numbers in the financial and other sections must be clear, substantial, and documented. For example, the number of product or service will be sold and the basis for this estimate; the unit price along with its supporting rationale, and so forth.
   - These assumptions are critical to readers in their assessment of the validity of the plan, and thus their subsequent investment (financial or other) in the business.
   - They are valuable to entrepreneurs in preparing various scenarios and in later remembering the assumptions when actual results are compared to the plan.

7. Uncertainty and risks
   - Describe the causes of uncertainty and risks; for example, economic, technological, and seasonal factors; legal and regulatory issues; supply, distribution, and financial considerations. Describe the action needed to minimize their impact.
   - What is the impact of uncertainty and risks on the assumptions used in forecasting? As appropriate, prepare several scenarios, especially financial. There is not one "the future," and neither the best-case nor worst-case scenarios are likely.
   - Identify milestones—points at which the viability of the business, product, or service are assessed so that adjustments can be made to minimize risk.

8. Growth and exit
   - Define growth as any combination of revenues, net income, number of customers served, number of units sold, variety of products and services, market share, improvements in customer service and quality of products and services, bricks-and-mortar, and virtual locations, etc.
   - What is the basis for believing that growth is possible?
   - How will the growth be achieved? Over what period?

9. Financial
   - The traditional financial statements projected for the timeframe of the business plan.
     —Always: Income statement, balance sheet, cash-flow analysis
     —Usually: Financing structure; for example, schedule and terms of debt and equity

—Often: Income statement for each major product and service line, break-even analysis for each

—As appropriate: Startup costs for a new business, new product or service, or entry into a new market; capital expenditures

- Key financial information, such as gross profit margin on each major product and service, rate of return on investments, revenue per employee, etc. How do they compare to industry standards?
- Include narrative as well as statements.

10. "Rules-of thumb"

- The business plan should cover at least three years. In this way, startup, development, and/or growth can be captured.
- A formal plan covering the entire business and prepared for external parties is usually about 50 pages, including the financial section, but not counting any appendices. Many business plans are never presented to external parties. And certainly, *all* of the materials that support the development of a business plan are rarely presented to external parties, except in the case of venture capitalists who actually become actively involved in managing the business.
- The business plan should be both optimistic and realistic.[9]

Because most entrepreneurs find the financial section the most daunting, the following are a few more guidelines that may help you get through it in one piece:

✔ Generally, the financial section of the business plan is not as detailed as an organization's annual budgets, which are based on specific estimates about customers and specific plans of work for known human resources. When it is prepared, the business plan is based on assumptions about the future. Later, as the annual budget is prepared, more is known about the immediate future.

✔ Generally, business plans are presented to external parties as part of a request for financial resources. This includes startup costs, financing to maintain operations until revenue covers expenses, and financing to support growth.

Can a "back-of-the-envelope" approach to a business plan be effective? Of course, there are stories about entrepreneurs who write their revenue projections and capital requirements on a cocktail napkin and the onlooking venture capitalists commit the financing on the spot—and many of these stories are in fact true. But there are no stories about the many napkins that are thrown into the trash.

Yet, a cautionary "yes" can be given to this question. As noted in the previous section, "Resistance to Starting," many entrepreneurs prepare business plans in a random way. For example, they know that they *must* have:

- A *strong* management team
- A product or service that is *demonstrably* wanted by the market
- A financial plan that is *complete* and *realistic*

The entrepreneur who is "in a rush" would be well-advised to grab a good business planning book, corral the management team, and block out sufficient time for a working session. Review the questions in the previous sections and at least verbally debate them and confirm that they have been covered, or that they are truly not applicable—for now.

COMPARING A SOCIAL ENTERPRISE PLAN WITH A TRADITIONAL BUSINESS PLAN

As you may have noticed, most business planning books and other resources are oriented toward for-profit companies (that's why we wrote this book!). But even then, not every point in a suggested business plan outline is relevant to every for-profit organization. Social entrepreneurs leading for-profit companies will find these books helpful, but leaders of nonprofits should also use the points as prompts for the issues relevant to their enterprises. They should simply consider the purpose of the questions and ask if they could be adapted to their organization.

The following outline loosely tracks the one presented in the previous section, and it describes *some* of the ways in which the definitions and interpretations might be different for the nonprofit and the for-profit with

tool of the trade a social mission. These differences should be acknowledged and addressed in the social enterprise plan.

1. Description of the business
   - The tension between the social mission and the need for financial empowerment. As explained by Peter Konrad and Alys Novak: "Nonprofits are not just judged on bottom-line profit, but on their efficiency and effectiveness in meeting their charitable goals. Nevertheless, if they fail to meet their bottom-line fiscal objectives, they will also generally fail to meet their charitable objectives as well."[10]

2. Management and organization
   - In surveys, investors in for-profit companies state that the strength of the management and organization drives their

decision to invest. They have learned that an average product or service in the hands of a talented management team is more likely to be profitable than a great product or service offered by a poorly managed organization.

- Within the nonprofit community, there is a growing recognition that financing the organizational capacity and effectiveness of the nonprofit should have the same importance as supporting innovative programs. While preparing a social enterprise plan, the stakeholders should assess the management and organization, forecast the costs of improving capacity and effectiveness, cast it in the light of growth, and seek investors who are willing to invest in the structure critical to the long-range success of the programming.

- Showcase the training, development, and other opportunities being offered to employees and volunteers.

3. Market

- An effective social enterprise plan shifts the focus from a program-driven perspective to a market-driven one. Sometimes this really does mean: ask the customer what he needs and give it to him. More often, the market input is subtler. One way to think about this challenge is that while the social enterprise should meet the needs of its customers, many of its customers do not know what their needs are, and most of them do not know what services would satisfy their needs. By building knowledge about its customers and applying its expertise, the social enterprise will identify the services that improve and/or add value to the customer's life. The social enterprise will offer services that capitalize on its competitive advantages.

- Every enterprise, social or commercial, has many types of customers. Probably the most difficult situation is when the one who buys the product or service is not the one that uses it. This arrangement is common in the nonprofit sector. The user of the service pays nothing or less than the full cost. The one who pays the balance is the government, a foundation, an individual, or some other third party.

- Third-party payment creates complex challenges for the nonprofit. For example, if a for-profit company identifies a product wanted by customers, now, the company can secure the financing, now, to build the product and get it to the market, now. Usually a nonprofit identifies an immediate need of a user customer, but because the financing of the third-party payer customer cannot be rapidly accessed, there is a delay in being responsive to the market. In addition, the value of the product to the third party is often different from the nonprofit's costs, so multiple-payer customers must be tapped for the revenue needed. A way to think about these third parties is as customers and/or investors. This can be empowering to the social entrepreneur because it shifts the perspective away from feeling that the third party is receiving "nothing" in return for the funding.

- Respond to market-driven demand with mission-driven supply. Promote the product, service, *and* mission. Market the social mission!

- Collaborations extend the reach of the nonprofit to leverage the resources of the community to work toward the social mission. These collaborations should be showcased in the management, marketing, and/or financial sections of the social enterprise plan.

- The marketing plan should support the resource development effort, which in turn should be integrated with the financial plan.

4. Financial

- The financial plan is a way for social entrepreneurs to forecast the resources they need to create/sustain social value, and a way to show how these resources will be used, thus giving investors assurances that the value of the investment will be maximized.

- Nonprofits can and should produce a net profit—a surplus of revenues over expenses—that can be reinvested to continue striving toward the mission. In this way, nonprofits can generate their own capital for capacity, research and development, growth, and more.

- Commercial entrepreneurs ask for money all of the time. That's one of the major reasons they prepare business plans—to demonstrate the financial investment needed to get a product or service to the customer. Social entrepreneurs should not hesitate to show a need for money. They should try not to be constrained by the amounts and sources of funding currently in hand. They should realistically forecast and clearly present the investments and/or revenue streams needed from external resources to reach the desired market position.

- According to Peter Brinckerhoff, financial empowerment "means that you have the money to pursue your mission with flexibility and high-quality service . . . beyond mere stability. (Nonprofits) are financially positioned to take prudent risk on behalf of the people whom they serve, they have resources to apply now, this week, this month to meet service needs that arise in their community, they have diverse income sources."[11]

- Investors in commercial enterprises expect a return, generally financial. If the definition of investor is expanded to include the third-party payer customer described previously, then what is the nature of the return on their investment? Indeed, foundations and others increasingly are asking this question.

As in Chapter 1, "Social enterprises have a social objective achieved through a social method. The primary objective of a social enterprise is to improve social conditions in a way that goes beyond financial benefits created for the organization's customers, employees, managers, or investors. The social enterprise relies on the goodwill of at least some of its key stakeholders." Thus, the return on a social investment could include any of the following outcomes:

- Estimating the financial return on investment. It might show a profit, break even, or a loss, but it should be calculated and be one of, although not *the,* driving factor for decision making.
- Demonstrating a measurable impact through outcomes evaluations, customer satisfaction, and other assessments.
- Achieving financial empowerment as defined earlier.
- Demonstrating integrity, capacity, and accountability in the prudent use of resources, including human, financial, technological, and capital.
- Having impact not only through direct service but also outreach, influence, and leadership in the community. In this way, the investments of the current funders are leveraged beyond the absolute dollars by influencing others to be involved in and make a commitment to the social vision and mission.
- The reward of volunteerism and contribution to aesthetic life and personal growth.[12]
- Social entrepreneurs should work with their accountants to properly present the following in the plan.

    —Value given to contributions of resources, including volunteer human resources and in-kind capital and expenses. Both the IRS and accounting standards address how these values should be determined. An estimate of the fair market value of any significant donations should be included in the social enterprise plan because they are resources to the nonprofit that don't require a cash outlay to secure.

—Capital campaigns and endowments

—The full cost to develop, start up, offer, and deliver services, whether or not any one user or payer is willing to cover it.

SUMMARY

Say what you like about the business planning process, but the simple fact is that organizations that make plans for their future—and then follow through with them—are much better able to meet challenges than those organizations that do not make plans for their future. In this chapter, we explored the answer to the question: "Why business planning?" and then we learned exactly how to do it. We considered different aspects of the business planning process—such as for whom, when, and how much planning to do—and we looked at the characteristics of a good business plan. Finally, we discovered how a social enterprise plan differs from a traditional business plan.

Key points to remember are as follows:

✔ All types of organizations, both nonprofit and for-profit, can benefit from the business planning process.

✔ Business plans are the direct link from an organization's strategic plan to all other types of planning within an organization.

✔ Business plans help close the gap between where the organization is today and where it should be in the future.

✔ Plan no farther ahead than the next three to five years.

✔ Always involve stakeholders in the business planning process.

✔ Plan to plan!

✔ Business planning works!

Endnotes

1. *The Best of Inc. Guide to Business Strategy* (Englewood Cliffs, NJ: Prentice Hall Press, 1988), p. 53.
2. David W. Virtue, Ph.D., Adapted from the "Start Out Training" series, Behavior in Fitness and Big Miles Training, 1997.
3. Inc., p. 13.
4. Stanley R. Rich and David E. Gumpert, *Business Plans that Win $$$: Lessons from the MIT Enterprise Forum* (New York: Harper & Row, 1985), p. 3.
5. Rich and Gumpert, p. xi.
6. Virtue.
7. Some of the points are adapted from the following: Rhonda M. Abrams, *The Successful Business Plan: Secrets and Strategies* (Grants Pass, OR: The Oasis Press, 1993); Terrence P. McGarty, *Business Plans That Win Venture Capital* (New York: John Wiley & Sons, 1989); Rich and Gumpert.

8. Frederic M. Alper and Jeffry A. Timmons, "Business Plan Guide for Non-Profits," based on the "Business Plan Outline" in *New Venture Creation,* by Jeffry A. Timmons (1999), and prepared for the exclusive use in the Denali Initiative program.
9. Alpers and Timmons.
10. Peter Konrad and Alys Novak, *Financial Management for Nonprofits: Keys to Success,* (Denver, CO: Entrepreneurial Education Foundation, 1996).
11. Peter C. Brinckerhoff, *Financial Empowerment: More Money for More Mission* (Dillon, CO: Alpine Guild, Inc., 1996), p. 1 and 17.
12. Bruce Sievers, "If Pigs Had Wings," *Grantmakers in the Arts,* Autumn 1997.

APPENDIX A

SOCIAL ENTREPRENEURS' BRIEF GUIDE TO THE LAW

Bruce Hopkins, JD, LLM, Polsinelli, Shalton & White

As social entrepreneurs relentlessly pursue new opportunities, they are at risk of colliding with legal issues. This appendix has been created to provide a guide to the basic legal rules that are most likely to affect social entrepreneurs. It is not a complete guide to the relevant law, nor is it intended to replace a consultation with a lawyer. Rather, it is a starting point. It should alert social entrepreneurs to key legal requirements and help them frame questions for a lawyer when they need legal advice.

I would like to thank my colleagues Jeffery E. Fine, Virginia C. Gross, and Thomas J. Schenkelberg for their contributing to this Appendix. For more comprehensive treatment of these and other legal issues, see Bruce Hopkins's book *Starting and Managing a Nonprofit Organization: A Legal Guide* (New York: John Wiley & Sons, 2001).

The questions addressed in this appendix include the following:

1. What do I need to know before I start a new nonprofit organization?
2. How will new earned-income operations affect my tax status?
3. When does it make sense to create a for-profit affiliate or separate joint venture?
4. How can I protect my intellectual property?
5. What are the legal issues I need to know about using the Internet?

WHAT DO I NEED TO KNOW BEFORE CREATING A NEW NONPROFIT?

A nonprofit organization is an organization, typically a corporation, that is organized and operated for a purpose that is beneficial to the public, or at least a community. It cannot distribute its net earnings to individuals who control it, such as its offices or directors. The main distinction between a nonprofit organization and a for-profit organization is that the latter is carried on to eventually distribute its earnings (profits) to its owners and investors.

That is not to say that a nonprofit organization cannot earn a profit. It can, but it cannot merely distribute profits to private persons. Instead, any profit derived by a nonprofit organization must be used for its purposes which may include compensation.

Additionally, a nonprofit organization typically is not owned by private persons. A nonprofit organization may have members, but most state statutes do not allow a nonprofit organization to issue stock or other evidence of ownership. If a nonprofit organization has members, its members generally take the actions comparable to those the shareholders of a for-profit corporation would take (for example, electing the Board members and voting on major corporate events, such as merger or dissolution). If a nonprofit organization does not have members, the Board of Directors alone will decide these matters.

A nonprofit organization may be established as a corporation, a trust, or an unincorporated association. A corporation is the most common form of a nonprofit organization and provides the most liability protection for its founders.

MEANING OF "TAX EXEMPTION"

Generally, how an entity is organized under state law determines whether it is a nonprofit organization. Whether an organization is tax-exempt (i.e., exempt from federal income tax) is determined by federal law, namely the Internal Revenue Code ("Code"). Not all nonprofit organizations are tax-exempt, but an organization almost always must be a nonprofit entity to be tax-exempt.

The Code sets forth many different categories of tax-exempt organizations. For example, charitable, educational, and religious organizations are generally designated in Section 501(c)(3) of the Code, whereas trade, business, and professional associations are described in Section 501(c)(6) of the Code (as "business leagues").

BASIC FEDERAL TAX REQUIREMENTS
FOR TAX-EXEMPT STATUS

To be a tax-exempt organization for federal tax purposes, an organization must satisfy two tests: an organizational test and an operational test. The first test requires that the nonprofit entity be organized for one or more specific tax-exempt purposes. This test can be met by having the nonprofit's organizational documents state its purposes in conformance with its tax exemption, and that upon dissolution or liquidation its assets be distributed to a qualified organization. If the organization is a corporation, language meeting these requirements must be found in its articles of incorporation.

The organization must also be operated in conformance with one or more tax-exempt purposes. This operational test assesses not only whether the activities conform to an organization's tax-exempt status but also whether the organization is engaged in impermissible activities, such as excessive lobbying.

A nonprofit organization's net earnings cannot inure to the benefit of private shareholders or individuals. This prohibition against the inurement of an organization's earnings to a private shareholder or individual is commonly referred to as "private inurement." A private shareholder or individual refers to a person having a personal and private interest in the activities of the tax-exempt organization. This type of person is referred to as an "insider," who essentially is in a position to exercise a significant amount of control over the affairs of the organization.

Additionally, a nonprofit organization cannot confer a private, rather than a public, benefit. Unlike private inurement, this private benefit analysis considers the scope of the class to be served by an organization's otherwise exempt activities, rather than direct transfers of income or provision of services unrelated to the exempt purpose.

The prohibition against private benefit is not limited to situations in which benefits accrue to an organization's insiders. An organization's conferral of private benefits on disinterested persons (i.e., persons who are not private shareholders or individuals having a personal and private interest in the nonprofit) may cause it to confer a private benefit.

The IRS is authorized to impose monetary penalties on unfair transactions between certain tax-exempt organizations and members of its management team and others with influence over decisions of the organization. These penalties are called the "intermediate sanctions." The intermediate sanction rules apply to Section 501(c)(3) public charities and Section 501(c)(4) social welfare organizations. Unlike the private inurement provisions, the intermediate sanctions impose excise taxes on the persons benefiting from the transaction, rather than revoking the organization's tax-exempt status. The IRS may impose both individual taxes and revocation of exempt status in situations warranting such penalties.

These unfair transactions for purposes of the intermediate sanctions are called "excess benefit transactions." The definition of this term is based on the contract law concept of consideration, which requires, for a contract to be valid, that the parties to it receive approximately equal benefits from the transaction. Thus, an excess benefit transaction essentially is one in which one party in a transaction receives undue or excess benefits in relation to those received by the other party.

PROHIBITION AGAINST LOBBYING

By statute, no "substantial part" of the activities of a charitable organization can be "carrying on propaganda, or otherwise attempting to influence legislation." If a substantial part of an organization's activities are attempts to influence legislation, the organization is an "action" organization and cannot qualify as a charitable entity. Whether or not a substantial part of an organization's activities are considered lobbying is a factual determination.

The Federal tax law provides for an election by which a charitable organization is allowed to spend a certain amount of its funds, based on a formula, on lobbying activities. A charitable organization that plans to engage in more than a minimal amount of lobbying may wish to consider making this election.

In other instances, taxes may be imposed in lieu of or in addition to revocation of tax exemption. Unlike a charitable organization, a social welfare organization has no such lobbying limits and may be an action organization. Business leagues similarly do not have limits on their lobbying activities.

POLITICAL CAMPAIGN ACTIVITIES

Charitable organizations are prohibited from participating or intervening in any political campaign on behalf of or in opposition to a political candidate. Taxes may be imposed in lieu of or in addition to revocation of tax exemption. Social welfare organizations and business leagues may engage in some political campaign activity but may be subject to tax on such activities. Usually these entities conduct their campaign activities in related political action committees.

OBTAINING RECOGNITION OF TAX-EXEMPT STATUS

Nonprofits desiring recognition as Section 501(c)(3) organizations are generally required to apply for recognition of this status with the IRS. Section 501(c)(3) organizations include both public charities and private foundations.

A public charity is an organization that is tax-exempt under Code Section 501(c)(3) and is classified by the IRS as a charitable entity other than a private foundation. Public charities generally derive their funding or support primarily from the general public in carrying out their social, educational, religious, or other charitable activities serving the common welfare. These charities also include "supporting organizations." Public charities are eligible for maximum income tax–deductible contributions from the public and are not subject to the same rules and restrictions as are private foundations.

A private foundation is a charitable organization that is funded by a single source (such as an individual, family, or corporation) and has a grant-making program managed by its own trustees or directors. It was established to maintain or aid social, educational, religious, or other charitable activities serving the common welfare, as conducted by other organizations.

A Section 501(c)(3) organization must complete and file an IRS Form 1023 with the IRS. The form requires the organization to fully describe its activities and operations, as well as its financial history and projections. If a nonprofit applies for recognition of Section 501(c)(3) status within 27 months of its formation, the IRS's recognition of Section 501(c)(3) status begins on the date of the formation of the organization.

Nonprofits other than Section 501(c)(3) organizations (such as social welfare organizations) are not required to apply for recognition of tax-exempt status with the IRS. Even so, such a nonprofit would be well-advised to apply with the IRS to receive assurance that the IRS agrees with its own position that it is tax-exempt. A nonprofit takes this step by filing a Form 1024 with the IRS.

REPORTING REQUIREMENTS

A tax-exempt organization with more than $25,000 per year in gross receipts generally must file an annual information return (usually, Form 990) with the IRS. Organizations normally receiving $25,000 per year or less in gross receipts are exempt from this filing requirement. If an organization has unrelated business income, it must also file a tax return (Form 990-T).

Private foundations also file annual information returns (Form 990-PF) with the IRS and are required to file a copy with the attorney general for the states in which they were formed and are operating.

SOLICITATION REGISTRATION

Organizations engaged in solicitation (fund-raising) within a state should investigate the state's charitable solicitation requirements. Most states

have some form of charitable solicitation act. These registration requirements vary widely from state to state.

A "solicitation" is typically defined as any contact (by telephone, mail,
or otherwise) with a state's residents. Many states exempt certain
501(c)(3) organizations from registration but require other nonprofit organizations to register. Additionally, most states require professional
fundraisers and solicitors to register.

For more detail on the creation of a new nonprofit organization, refer to
Anthony Mancuso's *How to Form a Nonprofit Corporation in all 50 States,*
ed. 4, (Berkeley, CA: Nolo Press, 1997) or Bruce Hopkins's *Starting and
Managing a Nonprofit Organization: A Legal Guide* (New York: John Wiley
& Sons, 2001).

How Will New Earned-Income Operations Affect My Tax Status?

Many tax-exempt organizations engage in activities either independently
or with outside individuals or entities that do not further the organization's
exempt purposes. These activities are known as unrelated business income ("UBI") activities. UBI is found if the activity is a trade or business, it
is regularly carried on, and it is unrelated to the exempt purposes of the
organization.

The IRS can generally establish that an activity is a "trade or business."
Therefore, the issues usually are whether the activity is regularly carried
on and is unrelated to the exempt function of the organization in question. An example would be an exempt hospital's operation of a hot dog
stand at a carnival. If the activity is planned for and conducted within a
few weeks, it likely would not be considered UBI because although the activity is unrelated to operating a hospital, it is not regularly carried on.
An example of an unrelated activity that is regularly carried on would be
the operation of a grocery store 12 months a year by an exempt hospital.
Such an activity would be considered both unrelated to the exempt function of the organization and would be considered regularly carried on. A
more difficult case where UBI is found may be the operation of a phar-
macy by the hospital, which sells products to both patients and nonpatients. Sales to the patients of the exempt hospital are not taxed under
the convenience doctrine, but sales to the nonpatients would be considered UBI.

There are many exceptions to the finding of UBI, including (1) trade or
business carried on by volunteers; (2) convenience exceptions; (3) exceptions for donated property; (4) qualified public entertainment activities; (5) trade shows; (6) certain hospital services; (7) certain bingo and

other games of chance; (8) certain distributions of low-cost articles; and (9) certain exchanges in rentals of mailing lists among certain charities. Under these exceptions, tax is not imposed even if the three elements of UBI discussed earlier are established.

Although the exempt organization must report and pay tax on its UBI activities, the UBI activities will not jeopardize the exempt status of the organization if the activities do not rise to such a significant level that the activities become the primary activities of the organization. Unfortunately, there is no objective percentage of gross revenues or time spent that constitutes an impermissible level of UBI resulting in the loss of exempt status. Therefore, tax-exempt organizations should proceed cautiously to avoid a challenge by the IRS.

WHEN DOES IT MAKE SENSE TO CREATE A FOR-PROFIT AFFILIATE OR A SEPARATE JOINT VENTURE?

When UBI reaches significant levels, exempt organizations other than private foundations should consider the use of a for-profit subsidiary corporation in which to operate the UBI activities. The UBI activities would be transferred to the subsidiary, while the exempt parent organization would continue its exempt function activities. If the entities are separately operated, the UBI activities of the subsidiary will not be attributed to the exempt parent and, therefore, the parent's exempt status would not be jeopardized even if the subsidiary's activities are significant.

In addition to ownership in wholly owned corporate subsidiaries, exempt organizations other than private foundations often engage in activities with unrelated individuals and entities called *joint ventures.* Such activities are carefully scrutinized by the IRS to ensure that the activities further the exempt purposes of the organization and do not provide prohibited private inurement or private benefit to the private persons involved. Joint ventures are typically operated in entities that enjoy flow-through partnership tax treatment, such as limited partnerships, general partnerships, and limited liability companies. If the activity operated in the joint venture vehicle furthers the exempt purposes of the exempt partner, any income that flows through to the exempt tax-partner is treated as related function income not subject to tax. If the joint venture, on the other hand, is not found to further the exempt function of the organization, the income would flow through to the exempt organization as UBI. If the UBI is not significant relative to the exempt function activities of the organization as a whole, the flow through UBI, while taxable, should not jeopardize the exempt status of the organization.

The other planning challenge involving joint ventures is avoiding private inurement and private benefit. Transactions structured with both flow-through entities and C corporations may not provide undue private inurement or private benefit to the for-profit joint venturors. The IRS carefully scrutinizes joint ventures to ensure that these proscriptions are not violated.

How Can I Protect My Intellectual Property?

The U.S. legal system provides rights and protections for owners of property that results from the "fruits of mental labor." Such property is referred to as "intellectual property." Rights and protections of owners of intellectual property are based on patent, trademark, copyright, and state trade secret laws, affording protection to profit-motivated, as well as nonprofit, entrepreneurs. In general, (1) patents protect inventions of tangible things; (2) copyrights protect various forms of written and artistic expression; (3) trademarks/service marks protect a name or symbol that identifies the source of goods or services; and (4) trade secrets protect know-how that provides a competitive advantage.

Copyrights

A copyright is a statutory property right that grants to authors, artists, composers, photographers, or other creative parties exclusive rights in their creations (i.e., books, graphics, sculptural works, music, paintings, computer programs) for a limited duration. A copyright arises upon fixation of a work in a tangible medium of expression and endures for the life of the author plus 70 years. A copyright applies to both published and unpublished works. Registration of a copyright with the Copyright Office in Washington D.C. is not required for the existence of a copyright or for the use of the copyright symbol (© 1999 John Doe); however, registration is a prerequisite to a lawsuit for copyright infringement and to the recovery of statutory damages and attorneys' fees. Copyrights are registered in the Copyright Office in the Library of Congress.

The U.S. copyright laws have historically favored the creative party who actually develops the work product. One exception arises in the employer-employee relationship. Works that are created by employees within the scope of their employment are owned by employers under the "work made for hire" doctrine. On the other hand, works created by independent contractors or freelancers are owned by the creators of such works, even though the commissioning party has actually paid for such work product, unless (1) the creative parties assign or relinquish their rights in the work by a written instrument, or (2) the commissioning parties contribute separately copyrightable subject matter, in which case the work may be jointly owned. Museums, charities, and societies that hire advertising agencies, artists, or designers to create copyrightable subject matter, such as greeting card designs, ad campaigns, or other graphic works, should require such parties to assign their copyright interests in the work product to the nonprofit entity as part of the engagement or commissioning process.

TRADEMARKS

A trademark is either a word, phrase, symbol or design, or combination of words, phrases, symbols or designs, that identifies and distinguishes the source of the goods or services of one party from those of others. A service mark is the equivalent of a trademark except that it identifies and distinguishes the source of a service rather than a product. The purpose of a trademark or service mark is to identify the origin of goods or services and not simply to describe the underlying goods or services. Trade identity rights are valuable for nonprofit entities as well as for-profit entities. In general, a mark for goods is affixed to the product or on its packaging, whereas a service mark appears in advertising for the services. Trademark rights arise from either (1) actual use of the mark, or (2) the filing of a proper application to register a mark in the U.S. Patent and Trademark Office. The holder of an unregistered mark may use the symbol "TM" to denote its claim of rights in a trademark, or "sm" to signify its claim of rights in a service mark. Only the holders of a federally registered mark may use the registration symbol (®) in connection with their use of trademarks or service marks, however. Unlike patents or copyrights, trademark rights can last indefinitely if the owner continues to use the mark to identify its goods or services. The initial term of a federal trademark registration is 10 years, with 10-year renewal terms. Between the fifth and sixth year after the date of initial registration, an affidavit must be filed, setting forth certain information to keep the registration alive. Failure to file this affidavit results in cancellation of the registration.

While rights in a mark are established by use and adoption, maintaining or protecting rights in a mark depends partly on whether the mark is distinctive, suggestive, descriptive, or generic. Distinctive marks are the strongest marks, often because the words are coined, arbitrary, or fanciful. EXXON® is a coined phrase used by an oil company and is considered a strong, inherently distinctive mark. OLD CROW® for whiskey is an example of an arbitrary mark because, although the words may be common, when used with the goods in question the mark neither suggests nor describes any ingredient or characteristic of the product. STRONGHOLD® for nails is a suggestive mark because the word suggests the nature of the products without actually describing them. TENDER VITTLES as applied to cat food draws attention to the ingredients, quality, or nature of the product and is therefore descriptive. Generic words are synonymous with the name of the product, such as "facial tissue" or "butter."

Generic terms are always, and descriptive marks are usually, denied trademark protection. Descriptive words may be afforded protection upon proof of "secondary meaning"—an ambiguous phrase that indicates that the mark has acquired source-indicating significance and distinctiveness, even though it is descriptive. Suggestive marks are stronger than descriptive marks, although the classification of marks as either suggestive or descriptive is often blurry. Distinctive marks are regarded as the strongest source identifiers.

Trademark infringement requires proof of "likelihood of confusion" in the relevant marketplace, which does not necessarily require actual confusion. Actual confusion, however, is often the best evidence of likelihood of confusion. Marks can infringe based on similarity of appearance, sound, or connotation. Although actual competition is not required, the likelihood of confusion increases when the goods sold under similar marks are competing or closely related. Trademark holders may enforce their rights in goods or services that represent a natural line extension of their brands. Infringement is often proven by consumer surveys and the testimony of marketing experts. Infringement cases involving nonprofits often position a national charity, such as the YMCA, against a dissident local chapter, which has fallen out of favor with the national organization but still uses the national organization's marks without authorization. The local chapter is usually held liable for creating a false association and misappropriation of the trademark holder's trade identity, as well as for diluting the value of the marks.

PATENTS

A patent for an invention is a grant of a property right by the U.S. Patent and Trademark Office that grants to its owner (or heirs or assigns) a legally enforceable right to exclude others from practicing the invention described and claimed in the patent. The term of a patent is 20 years from the date on which the application for the patent was filed in the United States, subject to the payment of maintenance fees. Like other forms of property, the rights symbolized by a patent can be inherited, sold, rented, mortgaged, and even taxed.

Congress has specified that a patent will be granted if the inventor files a timely application that adequately describes a new, useful, and unobvious invention of proper subject matter. To be timely, an application must be filed *within one year* of any act that reduces the invention to practice.

Patents are usually granted to individual inventors, who typically assign their patents to their employers. If the inventors discovered the topic of the invention during the course of their employment, but fail to assign the patent to their employers, the employers may be deemed to have acquired a "shop right," entitling the employers to use the patent internally as part of their business operations, without owing a royalty to the inventors. Many employers require their employees to assign any developments or patentable discoveries to the employer to avoid any ownership controversies.

A patent doesn't necessarily have to cover a machine or a new gadget—many items can be patented, including business methods, carpet designs, clothing accessories and designs, computer software, fabrics and fabric designs, food inventions, jewelry, plants, and much more.

TRADE SECRETS

Trade secrets embody all forms and types of financial, business, scientific, technical, economic, or engineering information, including patterns, plans, compilations, program devices, formulas, designs, prototypes, methods, techniques, processes, procedures, programs, or codes, whether tangible or intangible, and whether or how stored, compiled, or memorialized physically, electronically, graphically, photographically, or in writing if (1) the owner has taken reasonable measures to keep such information secret; and (2) the information derives independent economic value, actual or potential, from not being generally known to, and not being readily ascertainable through proper means by, the public. Trade secrets are usually protected from misappropriation or unauthorized disclosure by specific state statutes or agreements by and between employers and employees or independent contractors restricting use of such trade secrets.

Trade secrets for nonprofit organizations might include confidential lists of donors and fundraising techniques, long-range strategic plans, acquisition strategies, and much more.

LICENSING

Licensing is the grant of the right to another party to use of an idea, trademark, patent, or copyright in exchange of bargained-for consideration. The licensor retains the rights to the idea, trademark, patent, or copyright. Assigning is selling the rights to the idea, trademark, patent, or copyright outright.

A licensing agreement usually provides the owner of intellectual property with royalties based on fixed or variable rates. The licensor must reserve the right to control or inspect the licensee's activities with respect to the nature and quality of the goods or services marketed or sold, or the idea, mark, or copyright may be deemed abandoned or forfeited. Licensing arrangements have been utilized by nonprofit entities to reinforce the affinity relationship between the organization, its members, and certain providers of goods or services. For example, many charities (such as the Sierra Club) offer affinity credit cards whereby a portion of the funds charged is donated to the charity. Under existing IRS interpretations, a passive royalty from the card issuer is regarded as tax-exempt income, but the provision of any ancillary services by the charity may result in the characterization of the royalty proceeds as unrelated taxable business income.

UNFAIR COMPETITION

Unfair competition consists of acts or practices, in the course of trade or business, that are contrary to honest practices, including, in particular: (1) acts that may cause confusion with the products or services, or the industrial or commercial activities, of an enterprise; (2) false allegations that may disparage or discredit the products or services, or the industrial or commercial activities, of an enterprise; (3) indications or allegations that may mislead the public, in particular as to the manufacturing process of a product or as to the quality, quantity, or other characteristics of products or services; (4) acts in respect of unlawful acquisition, disclosure, or use of trade secrets; and (5) acts causing dilution or other damage to the distinctive power of another's mark or taking unfair advantage of the goodwill or reputation of another's enterprise. Unfair competition is sometimes referred to as "Business Torts." Although the Lanham Act, the federal trademark statute, has broadened into a federal law of unfair competition, various state laws also address unfair competition. Unfair competition claims are not limited to commercial enterprises. On the contrary, nonprofit businesses are vulnerable to unfair and deceptive trade practices, especially unscrupulous fundraisers who try to confuse the public by adopting names or marks that are confusingly similar to well-known, respected charities.

WHAT ARE THE LEGAL ISSUES I NEED TO KNOW ABOUT BEFORE USING THE INTERNET?

We live in a digital age, whether or not one wants to admit it. The proliferation of the Internet signifies a revolution in the way of doing business. Even those who do not know how to "double click" cannot deny the growing emergence of e-commerce as the wave of the future. The Internet at the end of the 1990s was the historical equivalent of television in the 1940s—a powerful medium that will someday affect virtually all persons within its path. The Internet and e-commerce present wonderful new marketing opportunities and horizons for profit-motivated, as well as nonprofit, entrepreneurs. Consumers have overcome their initial fears of privacy and security issues and are now accumulating millions of dollars of goods and services regularly through the Internet.

INTERNET/E-COMMERCE

The Internet is a global telecommunications network, connecting computer networks and users. The Internet permits immediate, global communication and transmission. Part of the excitement (as well as the challenge) of effectively using the Internet is acknowledging that persons around the world may access content and information that is posted. In fact, international boundaries and local jurisdiction dissolve, to some extent, in cyberspace. The interplay between enforcement of local, state laws over Internet transmissions and disputes will be one of the hotly contested legal issues at the start of the 21st century. For example, many entrepreneurs attempt to increase Website visits by sponsoring sweepstakes or contests. Unfortunately, overeager entrepreneurs sometimes fail to recognize that individuals residing in remote, far-off countries can access the sweepstakes just as readily as residents of the United States. State laws, as well as the laws of many foreign countries, regulate games of chance, and the unwary entrepreneur may have violated laws in many jurisdictions governing lotteries or gambling.

WEBSITE USE AND MANAGEMENT

In order to maintain a presence on the Internet, a business or enterprise must first establish a Website. A Website is an electronic location on the World Wide Web that may contain text, graphics, visual images, or sound. The site is accessed by a unique uniform resource locator (URL) or domain name, which is the equivalent of a telephone number or address for the site. Domain names are applied for and issued by domain name registration services, such as Network Solutions, Inc. (Internic), which, for some time, held an exclusive right to allocate domain names. Now, 29 organizations have the right to allocate top-level domain names, ending in the now-common .com, .net, .org, .edu, .gov, and other domain name strings will soon be available. While the .org suffix was initially reserved for charities, the distinction between .com, .net, and .org has blurred to the degree that .org is no longer synonymous with a charitable venture.

The single-most important aspect of Website management is to take appropriate precautions to ensure that the developer of the Website, usually an independent contractor, assigns and relinquishes ownership in and to the site and its hypertext markup language (html) to the commissioning party. As noted elsewhere, in the absence of such written assignment, the Website developer could claim ownership of the Website and its content. The Website's owner should consider using disclaimers or a statement of terms and conditions governing access to the Website, alerting the user to any rules or regulations governing use of the site and/or its content. It is becoming common for such disclaimers and policy statements to require the user to click on an "I Accept" icon, to create an evidentiary record of consent, before being permitted to access the site any further. The user should also be warned that transmissions across the Internet are not secure, and that there should be no expectation of privacy in any information transmitted (or even in the user's access to the site).

red flag   The Website owner should be cautious about using "links"—connections from one site to the site of another party. Linking can create liability if the user is deceived or confused about the origin of a site or association between the owners of two sites. A link could also be construed as an endorsement of another party's goods or services.

APPENDIX B

FOR FURTHER READING

Chapter 1: Social Entrepreneurship

Peter C. Brinkerhoff, *Social Entrepreneurship*. (New York: John Wiley & Sons, 2000).

William D. Bygrave, *The Portable MBA in Entrepreneurship,* ed. 2 (New York: John Wiley & Sons, 1997).

J. Gregory Dees, "Enterprising Nonprofits," *Harvard Business Review,* January-February 1998.

EntreWorld website for more information on social entrepreneurship, and for updates to this book; www.entreworld.com

Christine W. Letts, William P. Ryan, and Allen Grossman, *High Performance Nonprofit Organizations* (New York: John Wiley & Sons, 1999).

Heather McLeod, "The New Social Entrepreneurs," *Who Cares,* April 1997; Roberts Enterprise Development Fund website; www.redf.org

Chapter 2: Defining Your Mission

Peter F. Drucker, *The Drucker Foundation Self-Assessment Tool: Participant Workbook* (San Francisco: Jossey-Bass, 1998).

Peter F. Drucker, *Innovation and Entrepreneurship* (New York: Harper-Business, 1985).

Frances Hesselbein, *Excellence in Nonprofit Leadership,* video program (San Francisco: Jossey-Bass, 1998).

Frances Hesselbein and Paul M. Cohen, editors, *Leader to Leader* (San Francisco: Jossey-Bass, 1999).

Richard Pascale and Anne Miller, "Acting Your Way into a New Way of Thinking," *Leader to Leader,* No. 9, Summer 1998.

Gary J. Stern, *The Drucker Foundation Self-Assessment Tool: Process Guide* (San Francisco: Jossey-Bass, 1998).

Chapter 3: Recognizing and Assessing New Opportunities

Peter C. Brinckerhoff, *Mission-Based Management: Leading Your Not for Profit into the 21st Century* (New York: John Wiley & Sons, 1998).

William D. Bygrave, *The Portable MBA in Entrepreneurship,* ed. 2 (New York: John Wiley & Sons, 1997).

R.E. Gruber and M. Mohr, "Strategic Management for Multiprogram Nonprofit Organizations," *California Management Review,* Spring 1982, p. 15–22.

Peter Schwartz, *The Art of the Long View: Planning for the Future in an Uncertain World* (New York: Doubleday, 1996).

Herbert A Simon, "What We Know About the Creative Process," paper, Carnegie-Mellon University.

Howard H. Stevenson, Michael J. Roberts, and H. Irving Grousbeck, *New Business Ventures and the Entrepreneur,* ed. 4, (Burr Ridge, IL: Richard D. Irwin, 1994).

Jim Taylor, Watts Wacker, and Howard Means, *The 500-Year Delta: What Happens After What Comes Next* (New York: Harperbusiness, 1998).

Jeffry A. Timmons, *New Venture Creation: Entrepreneurship in the 21st Century,* ed. 5 (Burr Ridge, IL: Richard D. Irwin, 1998).

Jeffry A. Timmons, *New Business Opportunities: Getting to the Right Place at the Right Time* (Amherst, NH: Brick House Publishing Co., 1990).

Measuring Program Outcomes: A Practical Approach, United Way manual.

Karl Vesper, *New Venture Mechanics* (Englewood Cliffs, NJ: Prentice Hall, 1992).

Chapter 4: Mobilizing Resources

Amar Bhide, *The Origin and Evolution of New Businesses* (New York: Oxford University Press, 2000).

Amar Bhide and Howard H. Stevenson, "Attracting Stakeholders," Harvard Business School, note #389-139.

J. Gregory Dees, "Enterprising Nonprofits," *Harvard Business Review,* Jan.-Feb. 1998.

Malcolm Gladwell, *The Tipping Point: How Little Things Can Make a Big Difference* (Boston: Little Brown & Company, 2000).

Kay Sprinkel Grace, *Beyond Fund Raising: New Strategies for Nonprofit Innovation and Investment* (New York: John Wiley & Sons, 1997).

Regina Herzlinger, " Effective Oversight: A Guide for Nonprofit Directors," *Harvard Business Review,* July-August 1994.

Dick Levin, *Buy Low, Sell High, Collect Early & Pay Late* (Englewood Cliffs, NJ: Prentice-Hall, 1983).

Rita Gunther McGrath and Ian MacMillan, "Discovery-Driven Planning", *Harvard Business Review*, July-Aug. 1995.

Robert D. Putnam, *Bowling Alone: The Collapse and Revival of American Community* (New York: Simon & Schuster, 2000).

Bob Reiss with Jeffrey L. Cruikshank, *Low Risk, High Reward: Starting and Growing Your Business with Minimal Risk* (New York: Free Press, 2000).

Jennifer A. Starr and Ian C. MacMillan, "Resource Cooptation via Social Contracting: Resource Acquisition Strategies for New Ventures," *Strategic Management Journal,* vol. 11, 1990.

Chapter 5: The Accountable Social Entrepreneur

Adam Brandenberger and Barry Nalebuff, *Co-opetition: A Win/Win Mindset that Redefines Competition and Cooperation in the Marketplace,* (New York: Doubleday, 1996).

Marc J. Epstein and Bill Birchard, *Counting What Counts: Turning Corporate Accountability to Competitive Advantage* (Cambridge, MA: Perseus Publishing, 1999).

Harvard Business Review on Nonprofits (Boston: Harvard Business School Press, 1999).

R. Edward Freeman, *Strategic Management: A Stakeholder Approach* (New York: HarperInformation, 1986).

Regina E. Herzlinger, "Can Public Trust in Nonprofits and Government be Restored?" *Harvard Business Review,* March-April 1996.

Regina E. Herzlinger, "Effective Oversight: A Guide for Nonprofit Directors," *Harvard Business Review,* July-August 1994.

Laura L. Nash, *Good Intentions Aside: A Manager's Guide to Resolving Ethical Problems* (Boston: Harvard Business School Press, 1993).

Oliver Williamson, *The Economic Institutions of Capitalism* (New York: Free Press, 1985).

Chapter 6: Understanding Risk, The Social Entrepreneur, and Risk Management

Max H. Bazerman, *Judgment in Managerial Decision Making,* ed. 4 (New York: John Wiley & Sons, 1997).

William D. Bygrave, *The Portable MBA in Entrepreneurship,* ed. 2 (New York: John Wiley & Sons, 1997).

Hugh Courtney, Jane Kirkland, and Patrick Viguerie, "Strategy Under Uncertainty," *Harvard Business Review,* November-December 1997.

Ron S. Dembo and Andrew Freeman, *Seeing Tomorrow: Rewriting the Rules of Risk* (New York: John Wiley & Sons, 1998).

Robert F. Haebert and Albert N. Link, *The Entrepreneur: Mainstream Views and Radical Critiques* (Westport, CT: Praeger Publishers, 1982).

John S. Hammond, Ralph L. Keeney, and Howard Raiffa, *Smart Choices: A Practical Guide to Making Better Decisions* (Boston: Harvard Business School Press, 1998).

Harvard Business Review on Managing Uncertainty (Boston: Harvard Business School Press, 1999).

Robert D. Hisrich and Michael P. Peters, *Entrepreneurship: Starting, Developing, and Managing a New Enterprise,* ed. 3 (Burr Ridge, IL: Richard D. Irwin Publishers, 1994).

Robert D. Hisrich and Candida Brush, *The Woman Entrepreneur: Starting, Financing, and Managing a Successful New Business* (Lexington, MA: Lexington Books, 1990).

Jim Schell, *The Entrepreneur Magazine Small Business Answer Book: Solutions to the 101 Most Common Business Problems* (New York: John Wiley & Sons, 1996).

William A. Sahlman, Howard H. Stevenson, Michael J. Roberts, and Amar Bhide, *The Entrepreneurial Venture* (Boston: Harvard Business School Press, 1999).

Richard W. Snowden, *The Complete Guide to Buying a Business* (New York: AMACOM Publishing, 1994).

Chapter 7: Mastering the Art of Innovation

David Bornstein, *The Price of a Dream: The Story of the Grameen Bank and the Idea that is Helping the Poor to Change Their Lives* (New York: Simon & Schuster, 1996).

Clayton M. Christensen, *The Innovator's Dilemma* (Cambridge, MA: Harvard Business School Press, 1997).

Donald K. Clifford and Richard E. Cavanagh, *The Winning Performance* (New York: Bantam Books, 1985).

Grameen Bank; www.grameen.com

Alice Howard and Joan Magretta, "Surviving Success: An Interview with the Nature Conservancy's John Sawhill," *Harvard Business Review,* Sep.-Oct. 1995.

Paul C. Light, *Sustaining Innovation: Creating Nonprofit and Government Organizations that Innovate Naturally,* (San Francisco: Jossey-Bass, 1998).

Geoffrey Moore, *Crossing the Chasm* (New York: Harper, 1991).

The Nature Conservancy; www.tnc.org

Thomas Peters and Robert H. Waterman, *In Search of Excellence: Lessons from America's Best-Run Companies* (New York: Harper & Row, 1982).

John C. Sawhill, "Mission Impossible? Measuring Success in Nonprofit Organizations," paper, 1999.

Michael L. Tushman and Charles A. O'Reilly III, *Winning through Innovation: A Practical Guide to Leading Organizational Change and Renewal* (Boston: Harvard Business School Press, 1997).

Muhammad Yunus, *Banker to the Poor: Micro-Lending and the Battle against World Poverty* (New York: Public Affairs, a member of the Perseus Books Group, 1999).

Chapter 8: Understanding and Attracting Your Customers

James C. Anderson and James A. Narus, "Business Marketing: Understand What Customers Value," *Harvard Business Review,* November-December 1998.

Alan Andreasen, "Cost-Conscious Marketing Research," *Harvard Business Review,* July-August 1983.

Emily Barker, "The Inner City 100: Creative Branding," *Inc.* magazine, May 1999.

Thomas Billitteri, " 'Branding': A Hot Trend for Charities," *the Chronicle of Philanthropy,* May 29, 1999; www.philanthropy.com, registration required

Jim Collins and Bill Lazier, *Beyond Entrepreneurship: Turning Your Business into an Enduring Great Company* (Englewood Cliffs, NJ: Prentice Hall Press, 1995).

Barbara J. Elliot, "A Job Tree Grows in Brooklyn," Center for Renewal, January 1997; www.centerforrenewal.org

R.E. Gruber and M. Mohr, "Strategic Management for Multiprogram Nonprofit Organizations," *California Management Review,* Spring 1982, p. 15–22.

Jessica Hale, "The Secret Ingredient," *Business Start-Ups Online,* December 1997; www.entrepreneur.com

Harvard Business Review on Nonprofits (Cambridge, MA: Harvard Business School Press, 1999).

Gene Koprowski, "Smart Companies Use Public Relations Tactics to Get Good Ink," in Dallas Murphy, *The Fast Forward MBA in Marketing.*

Rebecca K. Leet, *Marketing for Mission* (Washington, DC: National Center for Nonprofit Boards, 1998).

Christine W. Letts, William P. Ryan, and Allen S. Grossman, *High Performance Nonprofit Organizations: Managing Upstream for Greater Impact* (New York: John Wiley & Sons, 1998).

Jay Conrad Levinson, *Guerilla Marketing Excellence: The 50 Golden Rules for Small-Business Success* (Boston: Guerilla Marketing Series, Houghton Mifflin Company, 1993).

Joshua Macht, "The Inner City 100," *Inc.* magazine, May 1999.

Joshua Macht, "The New Market Research," *Inc.,* July 1998.

Mercer Management Consulting, "Managing Brands as Strategic Assets": A Mercer Commentary, 1997; www.mercermc.com

Sharon M. Oster, *Strategic Management for Nonprofit Organizations: Theory and Cases* (New York, London: Oxford University Press, 1995).

Larry T. Patterson and Charles D. McCullough, "A Market Study Methodology for Small Business," *Journal of Small Business Management,* July 1980, p. 30.

Michael Porter and Anne Habiby, "Understanding the Economic Potential of the Inner Cities," *Inc.* magazine, May 1999.

V. Kasturi Rangan, Sohel Karim, and Sheryl K. Sandberg, "Do Better at Doing Good," *Harvard Business Review,* May-June 1996.

Adrian Slywotzy and David Morrison, *The Profit Zone: How Strategic Business Design Will Lead You to Tomorrow's Profits* (New York: John Wiley and Sons, 1998).

Tom Stemberg with Stephanie Gruner, "Spies Like Us," *Inc.* magazine, June 1998.

Alan Webber, "The World's Greatest Brands," *Fast Company,* August 1997; www.fastcompany.com

Chapter 9: Financial Management

Robert N. Anthony, *Essentials of Accounting (sixth edition),* (Reading, MA: Addison-Wesley Publishing Company, 1997).

Jody Blazek, *Tax Planning and Compliance for Tax-Exempt Organizations,* (New York: John Wiley and Sons, 1993).

Peter C. Brinckerhoff, *Mission-Based Management,* (New York: John Wiley and Sons, 1994).

Peter C. Brinckerhoff, *Financial Empowerment,* (New York: John Wiley and Sons, 1996).

Malvern J. Gross, Jr, William Warshauer, Jr., Richard F. Larkin, *Financial and Accounting Guide for Not-for-Profit Organization (fourth edition),* (New York: John Wiley and Sons, 1991).

Thomas A. McLaughlin, *Streetsmart Financial Basics for Nonprofit Managers,* (New York: John Wiley and Sons, 1995).

Thomas A. McLaughlin, *Trade Secrets for Nonprofit Managers,* (New York: John Wiley and Sons, 2001).

Web sites

FASB
http://www.rutgers.edu/Accounting/raw/fasb/

Summary of FASB 116
http://www.1800net.com/nprc/fasb116.html

Summary of FASB 117
http://www.1800net.com/nprc/fasb117.html

IRS Form 990
http://www.irs.ustreas.gov/prod/forms_pubs/forms.html

Other useful web sites

www.guidestar.org

www.wiley.com

www.nptimes.com

www.redf.org

INDEX